LEARNED HELPLESSNESS

LEARNED HELPLESSNESS

A Theory for the Age of Personal Control

Christopher Peterson
Steven F. Maier
Martin E. P. Seligman

New York   Oxford
OXFORD UNIVERSITY PRESS

Oxford University Press

Oxford   New York   Toronto
Delhi   Bombay   Calcutta   Madras   Karachi
Kuala Lumpur   Singapore   Hong Kong   Tokyo
Nairobi   Dar es Salaam   Cape Town
Melbourne   Auckland   Madrid

and associated companies in
Berlin   Ibadan

Library of Congress Cataloging-in-Publication Data
Peterson, Christopher
Learned helplessness : a theory for the age of personal control /
Christopher Peterson, Steven F. Maier, Martin E. P. Seligman.
p. cm. Includes bibliographical references and indexes.
ISBN 0-19-504466-5
ISBN 0-19-504467-3 (PBK)
1. Helplessness (Psychology)   2. Locus of control.   3. Psychology,
pathological.   I. Maier, Steven F.   II. Seligman, Martin, E. P.
III. Title.
BF575.H4P48 1993
155.2'32-dc20   92-21473

9 8 7 6 5

Printed in the United States of America
on acid-free paper

To Richard L. Solomon
guide, mentor, and skeptic

Preface

When experience with uncontrollable events leads to the expectation that future events will elude control, disruptions in motivation, emotion, and learning may occur. This phenomenon has been called *learned helplessness*. First described in the 1960s, learned helplessness has given rise to several lines of basic and applied research. In this book, we tell the story of learned helplessness, from its beginning to the present.

This is a personal account. Steven F. Maier and Martin E. P. Seligman were there at the very start, graduate students at the University of Pennsylvania, working in the animal learning laboratory where learned helplessness was originally observed. Christopher Peterson joined the journey later, studying first with Maier at the University of Colorado and then with Seligman at the University of Pennsylvania. From our perspectives as participants, we detail how work on learned helplessness has unfolded and why it has been both popular and controversial. We try to say what is known about learned helplessness and what is not. We place learned helplessness in the larger context of a society that exalts individuality and personal control.

Research is far from a solitary endeavor, and we wish to acknowledge the many contributions made by others to our studies and thus to this book. Over the years, much of our research has been supported by grants from the National Institute of Mental Health, the National Institute on Aging, the National Science Foundation, the Office of Naval Research, and the MacArthur Foundation.

Writing is similarly made possible by the help of others. Lisa M.

Bossio helped blend our three voices into one, and we thank her for the consistency she created. Frank Fincham provided thoughtful comments and suggestions on a draft of the entire manuscript. It has been a pleasure to work with everyone at Oxford University Press; Joan Bossert has been especially supportive and helpful in her role as our editor.

Ann Arbor, Michigan   C. P.
Boulder, Colorado   S. F. M.
Philadelphia, Pennsylvania   M. E. P. S.
August 1992

Contents

LEARNED HELPLESSNESS

1

Introduction

Over the last thirty years, we have witnessed a vast change in how the social sciences explain our behavior. As students, we were taught that people were pushed and pulled by their inner and outer environments. The details of this pushing and pulling became the preferred explanation of our actions. We learned such explanations as:

Organisms persist in their responses, if these are reinforced by the occurrence of positive events or the cessation of negative ones.

Organisms display their habits when their biological drives are high and will repeat responses that have been followed by the reduction of biological needs.

Under appropriate releasing conditions, organisms display fixed action patterns.

Adult behavior is driven by unresolved sexual and aggressive conflicts from childhood.

When organisms are frustrated, aggression results.

The scholar will recognize these brief explanations as paraphrased versions of the positions popularized by Skinner, Hull, Tinbergen, Freud, and Dollard and Miller—all major theorists of motivation from the previous generation. Some of the time, we see some truth in these theoretical statements. People may act because they are driven from within or rewarded from without. The rest of the time, however, they undoubtedly choose their own courses of action.

Scientific explanation is a matter of strategic focusing and ignoring. From 1920 to 1965, psychological theory often focused on the

3

external determinants of our actions (hence the word "response") and ignored individual initiation. The favorite concept of this previous generation of motivational theorists was "stimulus," which is derived from a Latin word meaning "cattle prod."

Explanations that focus on the individual as a source of action have since become popular. Here are the sorts of explanations the students of today learn:

When an individual expects that nothing she does matters, she will
    become helpless and thus fail to initiate any action.
Successful action flows from a sense of self-efficacy.
Individuals generate and monitor their own actions, reinforce themselves, and correct their unsuccessful actions.
Individuals decide among goals and choose the most highly preferred.

These explanations represent a dramatic shift in the way that our actions are conceived. One of the catalysts for this change, and the subject of this book, was the work on personal control and its flip side, what we call *helplessness*.

THE PHENOMENA OF HELPLESSNESS AND PERSONAL CONTROL

Consider the following vignettes, which capture the range of topics that we cover in subsequent chapters. All of them have some pertinence to personal control and helplessness.

Passivity in the Laboratory Rat

Suppose that a white rat is placed in a steel chamber. A mildly painful electric shock is conveyed through the floor. The rat scrambles about frantically. Five seconds later, the shock is turned off. One minute later, the shock goes on again, and the rat again is frantic. In rapid succession, it rears up, climbs the walls, tears at the floor, and freezes. This pattern of shock coming on and going off regardless of what the rat does is repeated eighty times. By the end of the session, the rat huddles in the corner, and each time the shock comes on, the rat takes it, motionless.

This experience of uncontrollable shock changes the rat. When it is later placed in a shuttlebox, in which merely running to the other side will turn off the shock, the rat will move very little, making no particular attempt to seek any relief. Furthermore, its biological defenses no longer work. If the rat had malignant tumor cells in its body before it became helpless, the tumor cells may now grow wildly. And its very biology may be radically altered. Its T lymphocytes may not reproduce themselves at a normal rate, and its natural killer cells may no longer kill invaders as actively.

Unipolar Depression

This has been an awful month for Laura. Two things have happened that make her feel that the future is hopeless. First, she got a "C" on her Abnormal Psychology midterm, and if that wasn't bad enough, she then heard that her steady boyfriend all through high school became engaged to someone else.

Since then, she has felt very sad. She cries herself to sleep. She thinks there is nothing she can do now to get into a psychology graduate program. She expects never to find love. She feels untalented and unattractive and believes that these faults will be the source of endless failure and disappointment. In the morning, it is a struggle just to get out of bed and start the day. More days than not this month, she has just stayed in bed. She burst into tears over dinner the other night and fled from the table. She isn't hungry anyway and has lost ten pounds in two weeks. Laura thinks she would probably be better off dead. She has had a vivid fantasy about swallowing the whole bottle of her roommate's sleeping pills.

Reaction to Defeat in the National Basketball Association

A look at the sports pages in 1982 and 1983 showed the Boston Celtics to be towers of optimism. When they lost, the team members pointed to such causes as "the ball just wouldn't drop" and "that heave really hurt us." Notice that these causes implicate factors other than the players themselves. These causes are specific to a particular game, and they remain in the past. The New Jersey Nets, on the other hand, sounded like depressives after they lost. They invoked such causes as "we just aren't functioning right" and "we aren't getting it done." The Nets explained their failures by blaming themselves. Their statements implicated general as opposed to local causes, enduring causes rather than transient ones.

In the next season, the Celtics' optimism and the Nets' pessimism may have had consequences for both teams. In games after a loss, the Celtics did much better than they were expected to do. They beat the "point spread" (which handicaps teams for such factors as past record, home court advantage, and injuries) fully 69 percent of the time. The Nets fell apart in the games following their losses; they beat the point spread only 38 percent of the time after defeats.

Mortality in a Nursing Home

On its two floors, the Arden House Nursing Home had about 100 patients in residence. Their average age was eighty. Two psychologists, Judy Rodin and Ellen Langer, decided to introduce some additional good things to this particular nursing home: movies and decorative plants. At a meeting on the first floor, the director told the patients,

> I was surprised to learn that many of you don't realize the influence you have over your lives here. It's your life and you can make of it whatever you want. You made the decisions before you came here, and you should be making them now. I want to take this opportunity to give each of you a present from Arden House. [Plants are passed around, and each patient chooses one.] The plants are yours to keep and take care of as you like. One last thing; I wanted to tell you that we're showing a movie two nights next week, Thursday and Friday. You should decide which night you'd like to go.

On the second floor, the patients were given the same things, under crucially different circumstances. Here's what the director told them:

> I was surprised to learn that many of you don't know about the things that are available to you. We feel that it's our responsibility to make this a home of which you can be proud, and we want to do all we can to help you. I want to take this opportunity to give each of you a present from Arden House. [Each patient is handed a plant by a nurse.] The plants are yours to keep. The nurses will water and care for them for you. One last thing; I wanted to tell you we're showing a movie next Thursday and Friday. We'll tell you later on which day you're scheduled to see it.

The patients on the first floor had control over these new events in their lives, whereas those on the second floor, who were given the same things, had no such control. The residents on the first floor became more active, had higher morale, and were less depressed. Eighteen months later, they were also more likely to still be alive.

Betty Jo: An Abused Woman

Shortly after their teenage marriage, Betty Jo and her husband Paul fell into the habit of going to the corner bar every Saturday night. This was their entire social life. Both of them would drink heavily, and when they got back to their dingy one-room apartment, Paul would beat Betty Jo.

He would punch her in the face and stomach, accusing her of flirting with other men. As time went on, Paul became more and more brutal, and Betty Jo spent most of the week nursing her bruises. She tried to talk to her friends, but no one would take her seriously. She thought about leaving Paul, but she didn't know where to go. When Saturday night came around, Betty Jo would do her best to appear docile, stupid, and suggestible, but this only seemed to egg Paul on. One week he threatened to beat her with the butt of a pistol he had bought.

Last Saturday night, three years after the beatings began, she was really afraid for her life. Paul began to beat her about the mouth with his pistol, knocking two of her teeth out. When Betty Jo screamed in protest, her husband dared her to do something about it. She wrested the pistol from him and fired two shots into his brain.

Selling Insurance Policies

Caroline and Ben were both hired at the same time by the Buffalo branch of the Metropolitan Life Insurance Company. Both passed the aptitude battery with flying colors and went through a costly and lengthy training period.

In her first year, Caroline set a new branch record for the number of policies sold. Like all insurance agents, she had her share of rejections. But she kept coming back. When a prospect told her that he didn't want insurance, she believed that he was in a bad mood and would change his mind if he heard the right argument. When she heard an unchangeable "No," she went right on to the next prospect, believing that the previous prospect was an isolated bad apple. When Caroline sold a policy, she attributed it to her persuasive powers and persistence.

Ben, in contrast, has been miserable since his first day on the job. Whenever he was rejected, he believed it was because he had no talent and was unlikable. He would then dawdle for a whole day before making a new contact. When he made a sale, Ben thought that the customer must have been feeling flush that day. He wanted to quit but didn't know where he could get another job.

THE THEORY OF LEARNED HELPLESSNESS

According to some theorists, all of these vignettes capture what is meant by learned helplessness. The theory behind this phenomenon is straightforward. It consists of three essential components: contingency, cognition, and behavior, which we now discuss in turn.

Contingency refers to the objective relationship between the person's action and the outcomes that he then experiences. The most important contingency here is uncontrollability: a random relationship between an individual's actions and outcomes. The opposite contingency, controllability, obviously occurs when the individual's actions reliably produce outcomes.

Cognition refers to the way in which the person perceives, explains, and extrapolates the contingency. This process consists of several steps. First, the person must apprehend the contingency. His perception of it may be accurate, or he may see it as something it was not. So, for example, a controllable event may be perceived as uncontrollable, or vice versa. Next, the person explains what he has perceived. A failure might be explained as being caused by hard luck or stupidity. Third and finally, the person uses his perception and explanation to form an expectation about the future. If he experiences a failure that he believes was caused by his own stupidity, then he will expect to fail again when he finds himself in situations requiring intelligence.

Behavior refers to the observable consequences of (non)contingency and the person's cognitions about it. Most typically, helplessness studies measure someone's passivity versus activity in a situation different from the one in which uncontrollability was first encountered. Does the individual give up and fail to initiate any actions that might allow her to control this situation? In addition, helplessness theory claims that other consequences may follow as well from the individual's expectation of future helplessness: cognitive retardation, low self-esteem, sadness, loss of aggression, immune changes, and physical illness.

THREE USES OF "LEARNED HELPLESSNESS"

One immediate result of the three-part theory just outlined is that learned helplessness has been used in three ways: to refer to noncontingency, to the expectation of helplessness, and to passive behavior. This has led to the claim that the theory is ambiguous. But it is important to keep in mind that a pure case of learned helplessness must have all three components: noncontingency between the person's actions and outcomes, the expectation that the outcome will not be contingent in the future, and passive behavior.

We believe that learned helplessness has been overused and applied promiscuously to situations that do not bear a convincing resemblance to pure cases. What one often finds are cases that have only one or two components, not all three. These are incomplete cases. One of the main tasks of this book will be to separate incomplete cases from complete ones, and both from those that misuse the concept entirely.

Let us return to the six examples that started this chapter and see which of them are complete cases of learned helplessness.

1. Passivity in the laboratory rat involves directly manipulating the contingency and observing its subsequent maladaptive behavior. Cognition is inferred from a series of experiments on immunization, therapy, and cognitive retardation that we detail in Chapter 2. This is therefore a "complete" case.

2. In unipolar depression, we see the passivity (Laura had trouble getting out of bed and getting started in the morning) and the cognitions (she believes she will not get into graduate school, will never find love, and so on). We do not know if noncontingency is the precipitating factor here. In order to establish noncontingency, we would have to find out if Laura tried in vain many different ways to keep her boyfriend and to do well on her midterm. But if, for example, we found that she pushed him away, this would not be a case of learned helplessness. This stands as an incomplete case, which becomes either a complete case or a misuse of the theory, depending on further information about noncontingency.

3. The reaction of the New Jersey Nets to defeat is also an incomplete case. One aspect of cognition, their explanatory style, is measured. Passivity is inferred from their poor performance in games following defeats. Contingency is not measured but rather is inferred from the prior defeat.

4. The nursing home study is a complete case. The researchers manipulated contingency by making available movies and flowers either irrespective of what the residents did or as a consequence of their choice. Cognition is measured, as well as such outcomes as passivity, poor morale, and death.

5. The vignette about Betty Jo—the abused woman—is a highly

incomplete case and quite typical of applications that overuse the theory of learned helplessness. Here part of the outcome is observed: Betty Jo fails to leave her husband despite repeated beatings. We infer passivity on her part. But she might have stayed as an active choice because there were other payoffs involved. We just don't know. Cognitions are not measured. And we don't know about contingency. Was she beaten irrespective of what she did, or were there actions she took that set off the beatings? Passivity is ostensibly a part of the picture, but for it to be illuminated by the concept of learned helplessness, it is additionally necessary to find helpless cognitions and noncontingent beatings.

6. Finally, the insurance case is also incomplete. The cognitions are present, and passivity versus activity is present, too. But we don't know if the rejections came about regardless of what Ben did, or if they were controlled by his actions. Did he insult his prospects? Did he have bad breath?

Throughout this book we look at a rich variety of experiments, field studies, and case histories. We try to be careful in evaluating whether each is a complete or incomplete case and what an incomplete case would need to become complete. We also try to identify applications that have little to do with learned helplessness beyond a surface similarity.

LEARNED HELPLESSNESS: INWARD, DOWNWARD, AND OUTWARD

Our ambition for this book is to move learned helplessness in three general directions: inward, downward, and outward.

By inward we mean the unraveling of the basic processes involved in the phenomenon. Thus, we encounter learned helplessness in learning theory, the story of which is found in Chapter 2. Moreover, we see the collision of learned helplessness with social psychology, and in particular attribution theory. This collision began when researchers tried to duplicate animal experiments on helplessness with human subjects, but these workers soon found the phenomenon among people to be much more complex. We tell this story in Chapters 4 and 5.

By downward we mean the biological processes that underlie learned helplessness. Chapter 3 explains the relationship of the contingency, cognition, and behavioral aspects of helplessness to neurotransmitters, hormones, and the immune system.

Finally, by outward we mean the application of learned helplessness to the understanding of human suffering and growth. Chapter 6 examines it as a model of depression, and Chapter 7 discusses a set of speculations about the role of helplessness in a variety of social problems. In Chapter 8, we address the role that learned helplessness might play in physical health and illness.

WHY LEARNED HELPLESSNESS HAS BEEN CONTROVERSIAL

Since its beginnings in the mid-1960s, learned helplessness has been a center of debate. We believe that there have been several sources of controversy. Most generally, as already pointed out, the concept has been overused. Sometimes we have been guilty of this ourselves, using our learned helplessness hammer to treat everything we encounter as if it were a nail. We suggest that learned helplessness remains a useful idea, and excesses in some applications should not detract from the benefits of others.

Another source of controversy has been the conflict between cognitive and behaviorist views of learning. The initial observations of learned helplessness were of dogs who had received inescapable shocks while strapped down in a harness (Overmier & Seligman, 1967). Afterward these dogs appeared passive and failed to escape from further shocks in a shuttlebox. To explain this,[1] we hypothesized that the harnessed dogs had learned that the administered shock was independent of their responses and expected shocks to be similarly uncontrollable in the shuttlebox (Maier, Seligman, & Solomon, 1969; Seligman, Maier, & Solomon, 1971).

The controversy arises because traditional learning theory seems to imply that it is impossible for a dog to be helpless. To learn that the administered shock is independent of responding, the dog must appreciate that the probability of shock occurring is the same when a response is made as when it is not; as typically phrased, learning theory does not allow these processes to occur. It allows the animal to learn when a response follows an outcome (acquisition) and when it does not (extinction). But it does not allow animals to learn when an outcome occurs in the absence of a response, nor does it allow an animal to put this piece of information together with information about acquisition and extinction contingencies.

Learning theory is not about knowledge; it is about responses. We claim that animals become passive as a consequence of learning that responding is futile. Learning theory claims that animals only learn responses.

Behaviorism flourished partly through strict adherence to a method: objective measurement. Its predecessors, structuralism and functionalism, were mired in subjective reports. In contrast, Pavlov and Thorndike made the associationism of the British empiricists objective. (It must be remembered that British associationism stressed associations between ideas.) The dog displayed its association by a countable number of drips of saliva, the cat by a plottable curve of lever presses. This methodological concern soon crept into the metaphysics of behaviorism and resulted in a forty-year confusion between epistemology and ontology. The response, which was measurable, became what was learned, and the association, which was an inference, was dismissed, first as unimportant and then as nonexistent.

Learning theorists argued that if the animals had given up and ceased responding, the data must necessarily be false. Helpless animals must have been engaged in some learned motor response that competed with jumping in the shuttlebox. For years, we tested these different accounts of the helplessness phenomenon.

Another source of controversy surrounding learned helplessness has stemmed from a long-standing debate within the social sciences between those who simplify phenomena in their attempt to understand them versus those who complicate them. "Complophiles" focus on the richness and complexity of human behaviors and despair when faced with attempts to reduce them to a few simple laws. "Simplophiles" strategically ignore this richness and try to explain as much as they can about human behavior with the fewest possible principles. We are card-carrying simplophiles in a field dominated by complophiles.

Learned helplessness has tried to explain a variety of very complex phenomena—unipolar depression, sudden death, victimization, among others—with very few principles. In our efforts to explain animal helplessness, the principles that we proposed—expectations and learning of noncontingency—were more complex than those used by S-R (stimulus-response) learning theorists, and so we were once thought of as complophiles. But in trying to explain failures of human adaptation using a theory of helplessness, we in effect became simplophiles.

Nowhere is this dispute more clear than in the field of depression. We have spent much of the last fifteen years looking for similarities among people suffering different degrees of depression: college students, demoralized women on welfare, prisoners, and unipolar depressed patients. We have argued that the simple process of learning helplessness and giving up may be common to many depressions and that learned helplessness in the animal and human laboratory may provide a model of them.

Yet here is what Isaac Marks (1977), a noted British clinical researcher, has said about this endeavor:

> In contrast, present behavioral approaches are not specially promising for the management of depression. One idea which has been mooted about is that the state known as "learned helplessness" in animals and in man constitutes a paradigm for clinical depression. However, it has not so far been shown that learned helplessness is associated with anything more than mild mood change without the concomitants of serious clinical depression such as guilt, nihilism, suicidal ideas, anorexia, and insomnia lasting at least several weeks.

Martin Seligman (1977) replied,

> You seem to think that any *model* of depression in the laboratory must somehow produce suicide, crying, weight loss, guilt and nihilism. I think that this is a demand that does not bear scientific scrutiny. Model airplanes do not need to make transatlantic flights; they only need to embody the essence of flying in an airplane. A laboratory model of anxiety need not produce screaming, defecation, and panic attacks—it need only isolate the essential properties of anxiety.

The work on learned helplessness started well within the mainstream of a discipline—animal learning. But because our interest has been the pursuit of a phenomenon, and not adherence to what a particular discipline defines as its domain, we have wandered far afield, as this book documents. We discuss topics in abnormal psychology, cognitive psychology, social psychology, and behavioral medicine. We also touch on history and political science.

WHY LEARNED HELPLESSNESS HAS BEEN POPULAR

With all this basis for controversy, why, you might ask, has learned helplessness been as popular as it has? Some of the reasons are obvious: (a) replicable and easy-to-use research tools: laboratory helplessness in animals, laboratory helplessness in people, and the Attributional Style Questionnaire; (b) grounding in basic psychology: learning theory, neuropsychology, and attribution theory; and (c) possible application to a variety of human troubles—depression, cancer, poor school achievement, crowding, abused women, among others—in an era that yearns for "relevance" from academic psychology.

But there is another reason that is not at all obvious, which cuts so deep that we have used it as the subtitle for this book. We began this chapter by referring to a sea change in what counted as an explanation in social science: from people being pushed and pulled by their environment to people choosing outcomes and controlling their environment. Before 1960, it was not fashionable to explain our behavior as something we initiate and direct. By 1990, however, such explanations abounded. How and why did this change come about?

Sociologists of science attempt to identify the forces that legitimize various explanations. For example, Francis Bacon (1561–1626) proposed the shocking notion that science need not be confined to observation alone but that human beings could actually control nature. The idea of the experiment embodies the idea that people might actively manipulate nature, not just passively predict its inevitable course, as Western science prior to Bacon had always been content to do. What forces legitimized Bacon's ideas and allowed them to become popular?

One possibility is the Black Death and the ensuing social mobility throughout Europe. Because the plague killed so many members of European society, jobs and positions opened to people who had seen no upward social mobility for almost a thousand years. The rock of feudal society proved itself to be a river. If society could move, if one's social position could be bettered by one's actions, perhaps nature itself could be controlled. It is interesting to note that Bacon's father rose dramatically in social position to be lord keeper of the seal under Queen Elizabeth, after the family had been serfs for hundreds of years.

Let's jump forward to the 1960s and speculate as to what happened in the United States to legitimize personal control as an explanation of human action. We suggest several related events that capture the forces that conspired to highlight the role and function of personal control or its absence.

The Rhinestone Refrigerator. The assembly line brought a wide range of goods to an enormous market at low prices. But every Frigidaire was white, and every Model T was black. When computer technology was applied to the assembly line in the 1960s, machine intelligence could be cheaply used to customize consumer goods. It became almost as cheap—and just as profitable—to paint each refrigerator white as to encrust every fiftieth one with rhinestones. There was now a huge, untapped market for individual, idiosyncratic choice. Jeans are now no longer uniformly Levis but come in hundreds of varieties and dozens of colors and in scores of "designer" variations. As advertising began to exalt individual choice, perhaps it became a new reality for social science to explain and to use as an explanation of other phenomena.

The Kennedy-King-Kennedy Assassinations. The United States has witnessed an erosion of belief in the efficacy of its institutions. It is commonplace to talk of the loss of our faith in the church, the death of God, and the decline of the family. In addition, our belief in government as a benevolent and effective source of control has eroded. The futility of our government's massive exercise of force in Vietnam and its failure in bettering the lives of the poor have surely contributed to this erosion as well.

Even more crucial in this decline may have been the series of political assassinations in the 1960s. Many young people just coming into political awareness invested their faith in the future in such charismatic leaders as John Kennedy, Martin Luther King, and Robert Kennedy. All were gunned down. Their young followers, we believe, turned from the belief that larger movements could control the future and make it better to the hope that they, as individuals, could at least control their own lives. These same people are now middle-aged, and many of them have shaped modern social science.

Along these lines, the Vietnam War may have taught individuals a similar lesson: larger social forces exist that are oblivious to the wants and wishes of individual people; it is better to turn one's attention to matters of personal control. We may have seen the newest version of this in the bifurcated reaction of Americans to the Persian Gulf War: confusion about the war itself but unconditional support for the soldiers who participated in it.

Undreamed-of General Prosperity. The United States is a Croesus-rich country. We will not enter into debate about the haves and the have-nots in our society or about the illusory nature of wealth. Suffice it to say that more people have much more buying power now than at any time or place in history. And wealth means something different today than it did in centuries past. Consider the wealthy medieval prince. Most of what he owned was inalienable. He could no more sell his land and buy something else than he could sell his name. Today, wealth means choice, an incredible, bewildering array of choices—more records, more clothes, more education, more autos, more concerts and books, more knowledge available to buy than ever before. And who chooses? The individual.

Perhaps it is not just fashions of explanation that have changed.

Perhaps the very facts of life are now different for those of us in the here and now. Is there now actually more personal control, which is distributed over more individuals than ever before? We think so. The upshot of this is that social and economic change in the second half of the twentieth century may have legitimized and even helped to create the notion of personal control. With this change it became more viable to explain human action as centered in the initiative of individuals and less viable to explain it in terms of the pushes and pulls of the environment. Notions like learned helplessness, self-efficacy, and locus of control were spawned by Rhinestone Refrigerators, political assassinations, and general affluence.

We end this chapter on a somber note. What is the future of notions like personal control? We believe that it may be limited. An overriding belief in one's own control presents two problems: it brings increased depression in its wake, and it makes meaning in one's life difficult to find.

NOTES

1. Let us be explicit about the use of pronouns here. "We" three were not all involved in every study and theoretical pronouncement mentioned here—far from it. Learned helplessness has been the work of numerous individuals. We use "we" simply to make the text flow smoothly.

2

Learned Helplessness in Animals

Our work on learned helplessness grew out of the study of animal learning. Indeed, the learned helplessness phenomenon was accidentally encountered in the mid-1960s during our attempts to test predictions of two-process learning theory. Because we (Steven Maier and Martin Seligman) were students of learning theories, the development of our explanatory principles was both constrained by and at the same time a reaction against these theories. Moreover, the controversy that surrounded learned helplessness research from roughly 1967 to 1975 concerned not so much the nature of the phenomenon and its limits but rather the clash between the explanation that we had offered and the tenets of traditional theories. In this chapter, we trace the development of learned helplessness in animals and evaluate its current status.

THE FIRST LEARNED HELPLESSNESS EXPERIMENTS

We entered graduate school in 1964. These were the days of *S-R theory:* the attempt to explain all behavior—animal and human—by considering only *stimuli* present at the moment or shortly before the moment of behavior and the *responses* and reinforcements that occurred in the presence of these stimuli in the past. Behavior was explained by reference to physical stimuli in the present, not by purposes and events in the future.

In the 1950s, much of the research and theorizing in this tradition tried to show that seemingly purposive behavioral acts could be reduced to an S-R analysis. By the 1960s, *avoidance learning* in animals—because it looked so purposeful—had become the focus of this effort. An animal such as a dog or rat sits quietly on one side of a shuttlebox. A light comes on signaling that the animal's feet will be shocked in ten seconds unless it jumps a hurdle and crosses to the other side of the shuttlebox. The animal rather casually gets up and jumps to the other side of the box. The theoretically "naive" observer would say that the light told the animal that the shock was coming and that the animal then jumped the hurdle to avoid the shock.

S-R theorists did not accept this simple explanation, largely because of their (mistaken) belief that it explained a present event (jumping the hurdle) by reference to a future cause (the avoidance of the shock). In point of fact, the cause here is obviously the animal's expectation about the relationship between jumping and shock avoidance, and this expectation is contemporaneous with the response. But neither animals nor people were permitted expectations because the S-R approach required explanatory entities to be directly observable. "Expectations," of course, are mentalistic and cannot be seen. S-R theorists did not so much deny the existence of expectations as hold them inappropriate as explanations.

Some "appropriate" process that did the theoretical job of expectations had to be found. *Two-process theory* fit the bill (Mowrer, 1947, 1960; Rescorla & Solomon, 1967).Let us explain. First, an animal's fear becomes conditioned to the light in the avoidance situation because it is paired with shock during early trials, before the animal has learned the avoidance response. Second, in the standard avoidance procedure, the animal's jumping not only prevents the impending shock but also turns off the light. This reduces the fear that has been classically conditioned to the light. According to two-process theory, the animal does not jump to avoid shock; that is just a happy coincidence. Rather, it jumps because it is reinforced by the termination of the fear-arousing light. The animal is therefore not motivated by shock avoidance (in the future) but by escape from the light (in the present). Here we have no purposive action, just classical conditioning (the first process) combined with instrumental reinforcement (the second process).

Radical behaviorists argued against two-process theory. Rather than invoking emotions such as fear, they believed that the animal's avoidance could be explained solely in terms of its instrumental component; jumping is reinforced, and the light simply acquires "stimulus control" over jumping.

Here is where we entered the fray. We were at the University of

Pennsylvania, studying with Richard Solomon in the Department of Psychology. Prior to our arrival, Solomon and his students thought of a way to test between two-process theory and the radical behaviorist alternative. In the paradigm just described, pair the light with the shock *before* the animal (a dog in this case) learned to jump in the shuttlebox, while it is still strapped down in a harness. This way, the light could hardly acquire stimulus control over jumping. Then after this phase, train the dog to avoid some other signal, say a tone, in the shuttlebox. If fear of the signal motivated jumping to the light, and if fear had been conditioned to the light, then turning on the light should cause the dog to jump, even though it had never experienced the light in the shuttlebox.

Just this experiment was attempted by two students in Solomon's laboratory: Russell Leaf and Bruce Overmier. The experiment did not work as planned (Overmier & Leaf, 1965). Dogs who had received pairings of light and shock in the harness simply would *not* learn to jump when they got to the shuttlebox. This was considered by many in our lab as merely an annoyance that got in the way of testing two-process theory. After all, the experiment could be done at least as adequately by reversing the phases—doing the avoidance training first, then pairing the light and shock while the dog is in the harness, and finally testing the light in the shuttlebox. The light still cannot gain stimulus control over jumping unless one assumes the animal is making miniature or mental jumps over a hurdle while strapped in a harness.

One scientist's artifact can be another's phenomenon. In the late fall of 1964, Bruce Overmier showed us a "helpless" dog in the shuttlebox, passively accepting shock and not jumping the hurdle to turn it off. He asked us if we wanted to collaborate with him to unravel the puzzle it represented. We found the phenomenon to be dramatic and worthy of attention in its own right.

If the dog failed to jump when the light came on, it was shocked. This shock could itself be discontinued if the dog jumped. If the dog did not jump, the shock was turned off after 60 seconds. These dogs did not learn to jump the hurdle to turn off the shocks and would continue to "take" the full 60 seconds of shock on trial after trial. Interestingly, the animals would occasionally leap over the hurdle. But on the next trial, they would revert to taking the shock. It was as if they did not profit from their exposure to the relationship between their jumping over the barrier and the termination of shock. Intrigued by these results, we decided to pursue an explanation for this laboratory annoyance.

LEARNED HELPLESSNESS THEORY

The classical conditioning phase of the Overmier and Leaf (1965) experiments involved administering 10-second tones to a dog followed by 0.5-second shocks to its feet. This produced later failure to learn to escape and avoid in the shuttlebox. Of course, because this was classical conditioning, the dogs were unable to alter the sequence of events or the events themselves. Our first experiments investigated just which aspects of this classical conditioning procedure were critical. Were the tones necessary? Did the shocks have to be brief? And so on. These studies revealed that the essential feature was that the dog be given a sufficient number of shocks that it could do nothing to prevent or terminate. The occurrence of the tones and the duration of the shocks were not essential. Indeed, the delivery of eighty 5-second inescapable and unavoidable shocks became the standard procedure used to produce and study later failure to learn in the shuttlebox.

Why does exposure to inescapable shock produce a dog who does not learn a very simple shuttlebox task later on? We proposed an answer (Maier, Seligman, & Solomon, 1969; Seligman & Maier, 1967; Seligman, Maier, & Solomon, 1971). When shock is inescapable, the dog learns that it is unable to exert *control* over the shock by means of any of its voluntary behaviors. It expects this to be the case in the future, and this expectation of uncontrollability causes it to fail to learn in the future. We further suggested that the expectancy reduces the dog's incentive to attempt to escape, thereby producing a deficit in its response initiation. And it also interferes with the actual learning of response–shock termination relationships, thereby producing a cognitive deficit.

Here is the theory of learned helplessness in unvarnished form. It has three components: (1) critical environmental conditions; (2) translation of these conditions into an animal's expectations; and (3) alteration of the animal's psychological processes by these expectations. We now explicate this theory more fully and attempt to give you some idea of why it proved so controversial.

Control, Contingency, and Contiguity

Although it may seem obvious that animals can learn the degree to which their behavior exerts control over important environmental events, the traditional S-R approach did not allow for this. For S-R theorists, animals learned only motor responses. The strength of such learning was presumably determined by the frequency or probability with which reinforcement follows. One conditional probability, the probability of reinforcement given the occurrence of some response, governs all instrumental learning: P(Rft/R).

To learn that an animal's behavior does *not* control some outcome means that the animal must learn two conditional probabilities and the relationship between them. It must learn what happens when it does respond—P(Rft/R)—as well as what happens when it doesn't respond—P(Rft/No R); it must also appreciate that the outcome is the same either way: P(Rft/R) = P(Rft/No R).

We argued that the traditional S-R approach inadequately characterized the sensitivity of animals to the possible relationship between act and outcome. The S-R approach acknowledged sensitivity only to the temporal conjunction of the response and the reinforcer. However, animals are actually sensitive to all possible variations and combinations of P(Rft/R) and P(Rft/No R), as shown in Figure 2-1. Said another way, animals are sensitive to the *contingency* between the response and the reinforcer: the dependency or correlation between the two. Whenever the two probabilities are unequal, there is a dependency between the response and the reinforcer. Here the animal has some control over the reinforcer in the sense that it can make its occurrence more versus less likely by making or withholding the response, as the case may be. In rough terms, the greater the difference between the two probabilities, the greater the degree of control. When the two probabilities are equal for some response, the reinforcer is not dependent on that response. Thus, it follows that the animal cannot exert any control over the reinforcer, regardless of what it does or does not do.

The difference between traditional S-R theory and our proposal is deeper than it might seem. S-R theory stresses only temporal *contiguity* between the response and the reinforcer, viewing the animal as trapped by momentary co-occurrences of events. If a response is followed by a reinforcer, it is strengthened even if there is no "real" relationship between them. And events that occur in the absence of a particular response have no bearing on learning. In contrast, learned helplessness theory proposes that the animal is able to detect cause-effect relationships, separating momentary noncausal relationships from more enduring "true" ones.

To see this difference more clearly, think of a dog in a learned helplessness experiment receiving a series of inescapable shocks.

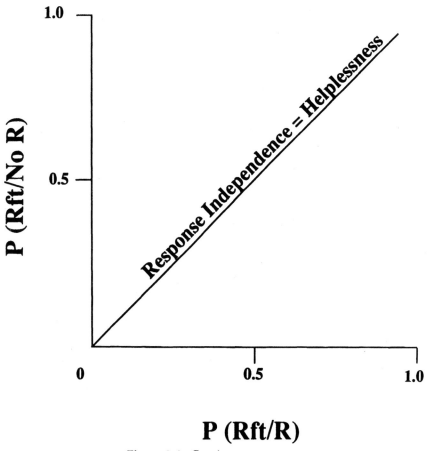

Figure 2-1. Contingency space.

On a given trial, it makes some response (e.g., barking) just before the shock goes off. The contiguity position would expect this happenstance to make barking more likely to occur on the next trial of shock. Each such accidental contiguity should further strengthen barking as a response to shock. The fact that shock also ends without any barking is irrelevant. All that matters is that each conjunction of barking and shock termination strengthens the connection between the two. If this happens a sufficient number of times, the dog will bark in reaction to the shock. Learned helplessness holds that the dog will compare the likelihood of the shock going off when it barks versus when it does not. And barking should *not* take place as a response to shock.

Representation, Expectation, and Perception

We also argued that the animal transforms objective environmental evidence about the degree of contingency or control into a cognitive representation. Although we were initially vague about this process (see the discussion by Alloy & Seligman, 1979), it must involve at least two steps. First, the animal must somehow perceive the present contingency. Our theory does not specify the molecular processing steps that allow this to happen. Second, the animal must somehow form an expectation about future contingency or lack thereof.

It is the animal's expectation that we claimed to be the critical mediating cognitive event in learned helplessness and thus responsible for the observed deficits. The step from perception to expectation allows factors such as beliefs, knowledge, already existing expectations, and causal attributions to come into play. Said another way, many processes can intervene to influence the resulting expectation.

Psychological Processes

Finally, we argued that the animal's expectation that an aversive event is uncontrollable should lead to alterations in at least three psychological processes. We now review these processes, which are directly responsible for the behavioral changes that we observed.

Incentive Motivation. Learning that responding and outcomes are independent and expecting that noncontingency to hold in the future require further processes to produce the animal's subsequent failure to learn tasks, such as escaping from a shuttlebox. Rather, the cognition of uncontrollability affects two types of processes involved in the animal's acquisition of instrumental tasks, one motivational and the other cognitive. The motivation to respond is often said to involve two components—drive and incentive (e.g., Bolles, 1967). *Drive* refers to biologically determined urges such as hunger and thirst, whereas *incentive* refers to the anticipation of some future reinforcement. Incentive theories of motivation claim that much (Spence, 1956) or all (Mowrer, 1960) of the motivation to respond in an active manner is determined by incentive. If the animal's motivation to respond is determined by the anticipated reinforcement for doing so, then the expectation of a noncontingent relationship between response and reinforcement should undermine it. If the animal does not expect its responses to increase the probability of reinforcement, then why try?

Cognition.   In addition, as already discussed, we proposed that exposing an animal to uncontrollable shock also results in a cognitive deficit, an interference with what the animal actually learns when exposed to the relationships between its own behavior and shock. In this situation, there is an alteration in the manner in which the animal processes information concerning the learning task, rather than just a diminution in its response initiation or movement. When inescapably shocked animals are given a subsequent learning task that involves escape, they do occasionally respond appropriately and turn off the shock. But they differ from normal animals in what they learn about these episodes and what they come to expect about the future.

Animals previously exposed to inescapable shock may not register the contiguity between their response (jumping the hurdle, for example) and the cessation of shock. This could happen in a variety of ways. For example, learning that some particular external cue such as a light or a tone is "irrelevant" in predicting the occurrence of a reinforcing event such as food or shock reduces the "associability" of the cue (Mackintosh, 1975).

Associability here means the ability of the cue to be later associated with the reinforcing event when there is a predictive relationship between them. Exposing an animal to a random relationship between a cue and a reinforcer interferes with it developing an association between them if they are subsequently made contingent. Although a number of mechanisms have been proposed for this reduced associability, one possibility is that the animal is not attentive to the external cue. Another possibility is that the animal may cease paying attention to internal cues. In any case, this perceptual bias requires, first, the perception of noncontingency between act and outcome during inescapable shock and, second, the expectation that this will later be true in a different learning situation.

Animals previously exposed to uncontrollable shock may accurately register the co-occurrence of their behavior with the termination of shock but then not expect the relationship to hold in the future. They have an expectational tendency rather than a perceptual block. In other words, they might not "attribute the cause" of shock termination to their response and so have no expectation that voluntary responses will work on future trials (see Testa, 1975, for a discussion of the perception of causality by animals).

Consider a rat given a series of inescapable shocks. On any given trial, it may well have engaged in some specific behavior immediately before the shock terminated. It might have lifted its right front paw. On the next trial, the rat might try this response in order to terminate the shock, only to find that it has no effect. On this trial, some other response might accidentally precede the termination of shock, but this too will prove ineffective on a later trial. In short, the rat is exposed to a number of occasions on which any response that happens to coincide with relief has no real relation to shock termination. Why should the rat later attribute significance to a perceived co-occurrence of jumping the hurdle and shock cessation?

In sum, we hypothesized that the animal's perception and expectation of noncontingency interfere with both its perception of response-reinforcer relations on a given trial and its expectation that responses will be followed by reinforcers on subsequent trials. Another way of saying this is that the animal's individual trial perception and its overall contingency perception are both impaired.

Emotion. Finally, we proposed that the experience of uncontrollability leads to emotional changes. More specifically, we suggested that learning that one has no control over aversive events leads to anxiety that is then followed by depression if the experience continues (Maier & Seligman, 1976). Learned helplessness has been suggested as a model for depression, and we review in detail the evidence bearing on this claim in Chapter 6.

Initial Supporting Evidence

As you might expect, our statement of learned helplessness theory was followed by a series of experiments designed to test its essential assertions. The core of the theory is that the impact of inescapable shock does not depend on the shock itself but rather on its uncontrollability. When the animal learns that it has no control and expects this to be true in the future, it undergoes motivational and cognitive changes that are responsible for its failure to learn to escape.

The straightforward test of this hypothesis is to compare the effects of controllable and uncontrollable shock. Clearly, controllable shock should not lead to the learning of noncontingency and thus should not lead to later learning deficits in different situations. Even though controllable shock is aversive and painful, it should *not* produce learned helplessness.

To conduct this experiment most appropriately, the researcher must arrange exactly equal exposure to shock in those animals that do and do not have control. Otherwise, any subsequent behavioral difference can be attributed to the difference in shock rather than to the control dimension. To meet this requirement, we introduced the *triadic design.* One group of animals is exposed to a series of escapable shocks, each of which can be terminated by some response such as pushing a lever or turning a wheel. A second group receives a series of inescapable shocks that are yoked to those delivered to the first group. That is, each member of this second group is paired with a member of the "escape" group and given the identical series of shocks. Each shock begins and ends identically for both animals, with the duration of course determined by when the escape animal responds. A third group of animals receives no shock at all, which allows the researcher to assess the effects of shock per se.

Well over a hundred studies using this design have now been conducted. The almost invariant outcome is that only uncontrollable shock produces helplessness effects. Controllable shock, even though it is physically identical, does not have these consequences. Controllability—not shock per se—is the critical determinant.

However, learned helplessness theory does not say that controllability alone is critical. It also points to the perception of noncontingency and the expectancy of future uncontrollability. If we can interfere with these processes, we should influence the occurrence of learned helplessness effects even if noncontingency is objectively present. Therefore, we reasoned that if an animal initially had control over an aversive event, this ought to interfere with its subsequent learning of noncontingency when it encounters inescapable shock. At the same time, an initial experience like this might also reduce the animal's tendency to expect future noncontingency even if it did learn that the subsequent inescapable shocks were uncontrollable. We found that when an animal was initially exposed to escapable shock, learned helplessness effects were completely eliminated (Seligman & Maier, 1967). Later on, we discuss such "immunization" effects more thoroughly.

If the animal's expectation of uncontrollability is really critical, then altering it by introducing controllability should eliminate learned helplessness even after it has been fully developed. Thus, we gave a group of dogs inescapable shocks and tested them repeatedly for escape learning in a shuttlebox (Seligman, Maier, & Geer, 1968). After their failure to escape had become chronic, we removed the hurdle and dragged the dogs back and forth across the shuttlebox during escape trials. When each dog was dragged across the center of the box, the shock terminated. After thirty to fifty such draggings, the dogs began to respond on their own. Then we replaced the hurdle, and the dogs continued to escape.

This "therapy" does not depend on exposing the subject to controllability with the same escape response used for testing. Even if the helpless animal is exposed to a totally different response that controls aversive events, this experience still eliminates the learned helplessness effect. For example, an inescapably shocked rat can learn to escape in a shuttlebox if it is first trained to escape shock by turning a small wheel with its paws. It is the animal's expectation and not its response that proves critical (Williams & Maier, 1977).

Learned helplessness theory is not restricted to dogs and rats, electric shock, and shuttlebox escape/avoidance learning. It is intended to apply to a range of species, to reinforcers other than shock, and to a variety of learning tasks. This sort of generality was quickly established (see Maier & Seligman, 1976, for a review). Escape deficits following inescapable shock have been demonstrated in cats, goldfish, gerbils, guinea pigs, mice, rats, and people (see Chapter 4). And in addition to shuttlebox escape, bar pressing, pole climbing, wheel turning, treadling, and swimming have been used to demonstrate learned helplessness effects.

The most obvious question is whether there is something peculiar about inescapable shock, or whether other inescapable aversive events would also lead to a failure to learn an escape response. There has not been much research on this topic, because it is not easy to find aversive events whose controllability can be manipulated as readily as shock. However, exposing animals to water that cannot be escaped does produce a later failure to learn to escape, whereas exposing them to "escapable" water does not (Altenor, Kay, & Richter, 1977).

The learned helplessness position further suggests that learned helplessness will ensue even if the uncontrollable event is positive or neutral. Animals exposed to positive events independently of their behavior should learn that these are uncontrollable and should subsequently be slow to learn that they have been made contingent on their behavior. Indeed, "appetitive" learned helplessness has been reported by a number of investigators (e.g., Engberg, Hansen, Welker, & Thomas, 1973; Welker, 1976). Moreover, even exposing an animal to noncontingent "neutral" sensory events such as lights or tones interferes with its subsequent acquisition of responses to control them. And rats and other animals frequently learn responses whose only consequence is to initiate or terminate events in their environment, and this tendency is undermined by initial exposure to these events without being able to control them (Glow & Winefield, 1982).

Up to this point, we have seen that noncontingent exposure to an event interferes with an animal's ability to later learn to control that event. But is the interference specific to the particular event in question? To test this aspect of the generality of learned helplessness, Altenor, Kay, and Richter (1977) exposed rats to either shock or water, each of which was either controllable or uncontrollable. Thus there were four groups of rats, and half of the animals in each group were then tested for water escape and the other half for shock escape. Uncontrollable shock interfered with both types of escape learning. So too did uncontrollable water. In other words, learned helplessness effects are general across the type of aversive event.

Along these lines, inescapable shock has even been shown to interfere with an animal learning to escape an aversive state induced by a psychological process rather than a noxious stimulus. Rosellini and Seligman (1975) first gave rats either escapable, yoked inescapable, or no shock. The rats were then trained to run down a runway to obtain food in a goalbox. The rats then received an extinction procedure: that is, they continued to be run in the runway, but there was no longer food in the goalbox. Extinction has been shown to be a frustrating and aversive experience, and rats will learn to perform responses to escape from places where this has occurred. Rosellini and Seligman gave their rats an opportunity to escape from the frustrating goalbox cues, and the rats that had experienced inescapable shock did not learn to escape.

Such generalization even extends across appetitive and aversive categories. Animals exposed to inescapable shock are later poor at learning instrumental responses to procure food (Rosellini, 1978), and noncontingent food can interfere with learning to escape from shock (Goodkin, 1976)! Transfer, then, is quite broad and extends well beyond the actual noncontingent event that the animal experiences.

THE CONTROVERSY

After we published the learned helplessness hypothesis, others quickly responded with a variety of alternative explanations for why animals exposed to inescapable shock later failed to learn to escape. Two different types of explanations were offered—behavioral and neurochemical. In this chapter, we consider the behavioral alternatives in detail. The neurochemical alternatives are the focus of Chapter 3, where we discuss the biology of helplessness. Here we briefly describe both alternative explanations, then speculate on the reasons for the intense controversy that followed, and finally consider some of the evidence that bears on the controversy, particularly as it entails behavioral alternatives. Space will not permit an exhaustive discussion. The interested reader should consult Alloy and Seligman (1979), Maier (1989b), Maier and Jackson (1979), and Maier and Seligman (1976).

Incompatible Motor Response Theories

All of the behavioral alternatives had the same form, specifying three steps:

1. The subject acquires a motor response during exposure to the inescapable shocks.
2. The presence of shock in the test situation mediates the animal's transfer of this motor response to the test situation.
3. This motor response is incompatible with the required escape response (e.g., jumping the hurdle) in the sense that it and the escape response cannot be performed simultaneously.

By this view, the subject fails to learn the escape response because it engages in another behavior that prevents it from performing the escape response. There is no deficit in its motivation or information processing, only a performance deficit. According to these hypotheses, the inescapably shocked subject is perfectly well motivated and capable of learning to escape, but it simply does not emit the proper motor response with the same probability as other animals.

The various incompatible motor response theories differ among themselves in terms of the mechanism by which the animal acquires the alleged incompatible response. For example, Bracewell and Black (1974) argued that it hurts the animal more to move while it is being shocked than to hold still. Consequently, the animals exposed to inescapable shock learn to hold still instead of jump the hurdle, press the lever, or whatever.

Alternatively, Glazer and Weiss (1976) asserted that the inescapable shocks in learned helplessness experiments are typically 5 or 6 seconds long and that the motor activity elicited by shock subsides in 3 or 4 seconds. Therefore, reduced activity on the part of the animal ends up followed by shock termination and is thereby superstitiously reinforced. Again, the animal's lack of activity keeps it from escaping. Related proposals have been made by Anisman and Waller (1973) and Levis (1976).

For these hypotheses, the bottom line is that animals who have received escapable versus inescapable shock do not differ in motivation or cognition, only with regard to the particular motor response they have learned to cope with the shock: one is compatible with the subsequently required escape response, whereas the other is not.

Neurochemical Theories

A number of investigators have maintained that inescapable shock is a severe stressor and depletes the animal's neurotransmitters necessary for movement. The inescapably shocked animal subsequently performs poorly in escape learning tasks because it is literally unable to perform the escape response. Weiss and his associates (e.g., Weiss, Glazer, & Pohorecky, 1976) focused on norepinephrine as the depleted substance, whereas Anisman (1975) argued for both noradrenergic and cholinergic involvement. Even though these proposals reside at a different level of analysis than the incompatible motor response alternatives, they similarly argue that inescapable shock interferes with later escape learning because it affects an animal's motor processes. Again, inescapably shocked animals are seen as cognitively unchanged by the experience.

Why the Controversy?

Once these alternative explanations were offered, the literature was soon filled with papers attacking *these* positions as well. Why this unusual amount of disagreement concerning how best to explain a seemingly simple phenomenon? As we noted in Chapter 1, controversy was fanned because the learned helplessness hypothesis exemplified a new way to explain behavior. It contained a number of assumptions at odds with those of traditional S-R theories of learning. The intense disagreements concerning the explanation of the behavioral effects of inescapable shock can be seen as part of a larger debate: S-R versus cognitive accounts. The alternative explanations of the learned helplessness effect assumed only S-R mechanisms. The incompatible motor response theories, for example, assumed only the reinforcement of motor responses, transfer of those responses produced by common stimuli, and the mechanical incompatibility of different motor patterns. And the neurochemical theories made no assumptions about learning at all.

Let us take a closer look at exactly how the learned helplessness hypothesis departed from traditional S-R views. Appreciate, though, that cognitive and S-R views are not mutually exclusive at all points and thus not always easy to separate. Nevertheless, learned helplessness theory does seem to be at odds with four assumptions often made by S-R theories.

1. *Contiguity.* At the time that we first proposed helplessness theory, most learning theorists assumed that the temporal contiguity between events is the critical factor responsible for learning. Some viewed contiguity as necessary but not sufficient (e.g., Hull, 1943), and some viewed it as necessary and sufficient (e.g., Guthrie, 1935; Skinner, 1938). Regardless, they believed it to be of paramount importance. As we have already discussed, the helplessness hypothesis is phrased in terms of contingency and not contiguity.

2. *Automatic strengthening and simplicity of the associative process.* The strengthening effect of contiguity was viewed as direct, inevitable, and independent of the animal's cognitive activities. Conjunctions of stimuli and responses were thought to strengthen their connection automatically. The learned helplessness hypothesis argues that learning cannot be viewed as a product of simple coincidences. Rather, it holds that the animal compares the probability of reinforcement in the presence versus absence of responses. The temporal conjunction of an animal's response and the ensuing reinforcer is not seen as sufficient to strengthen a connection. Instead, the animal analyzes the causal structure of its environment. The learned helplessness hypothesis further argues that what an animal learns from conjunctions between stimuli and its responses depends on its prior representations of such relations and on the expectations it has formed.

3. *Responses.* Traditional S-R theorists proposed that what is learned from an encounter with a classical conditioning or instrumental training procedure is best characterized as a response (e.g., lever

Table 2-1. S-R Theory versus Learned Helplessness Theory.

	S-R Theory	Helplessness Theory
Critical factor in learning	Contiguity	Contingency
Associative process	Automatic	Dependent on cognition
What is learned?	Responses	Expectation
Transfer of learning	Narrow	Broad

pressing, shuttling, salivating) rather than as a representation of the environment and its contingencies. When learning is transferred between situations, this presumably reflects a mechanical interaction between the responses involved in the situations. So if an animal's experience in one situation facilitates learning in another, then the response learned in the first is compatible with that required in the second and augments it. And if interference occurs, then it is because the responses are incompatible, with the first somehow subtracting from the second.

In contrast, we argued that animals learn expectations. Specifically, response-independent shock leads them to represent and expect an independent relationship. This cognitive state—as opposed to a superstitiously reinforced motor response—interferes with later escape learning. It seemed to us that S-R theory confused what was learned with how that learning was measured.

4. *Breadth of transfer.* Most S-R theorists assumed that what is learned about a given stimulus or response remains specific to that stimulus or response. If there is any transfer of learning to new situations, it comes about by stimulus generalization along dimensions of physical similarity. In the absence of such physical similarity, there is no transfer. However, for us the animal's expectation generalized to a variety of other situations, whether or not they were physically similar.

In sum, the learned helplessness theory departs in several ways from traditional S-R notions about the essence of learning. These differences are summarized in Table 2-1.

We now turn to a more detailed consideration of the nature of the phenomenon itself and the evidence pertinent to its explanation. But first, we comment on terminology. Initially, the learned helplessness hypothesis was stated in S-R terms: responses, reinforcers, and their relationships. However, over the years, we gradually abandoned this terminology as our impatience with the entire S-R enterprise grew. In using the term "response" to describe behavior, one implies that an animal is necessarily driven by environmental events. Motivation here resides outside the animal; after all, a response has to be a response *to* something, and S-R theory required that something to be directly observable—an external stimulus. Similarly, in using the term "reinforcer" for events such as shock termination or the presentation of food, one assumes that these events necessarily influence behavior in a particular way—by strengthening connections. As we abandoned this framework, we began to substitute terms like "acts" for responses and terms like "relief," "positive outcome," or just "outcome" for reinforcer.

CONTIGUITY VERSUS CONTINGENCY

As we have already discussed, traditional S-R learning theories held that the temporal conjuction of a response and a reinforcer automatically strengthens that response. In contrast, learned helplessness theory argued that animals regulate their instrumental behavior by comparing $P(Rft/R)$ with $P(Rft/No\ R)$. The greater the difference between these conditional probabilities, the more frequently the animal will actively emit or inhibit the response in question, depending on whether the difference is positive or negative. Here we will attempt to evaluate the recent success or failure of these two positions.

Contiguity

The typical instrumental learning situation in which reinforcers are dependent on an animal's responding cannot distinguish between the operation of contiguity and contingency. Response dependency establishes *both* contiguity and contingency between act and outcome. To distinguish contiguity and contingency, one must conduct experiments that deliver outcomes independently of an animal's responses. Here there is no contingency, only accidental contiguity. Indeed, the major support for contiguity in instrumental learning came from Skinner's (1948) well-known "superstition" experiment and the conceptual framework to which it led. Skinner exposed pigeons to food reinforcement delivered independently of their behavior. Even though there was no experimenter-arranged contingency between the pigeon's behavior and food delivery, each pigeon developed an idiosyncratic response pattern, such as pecking at a particular spot on the wall. These response patterns became quite stable and were emitted by the pigeon at high rates for session after session.

Why should this happen when there is no "real" relationship between the delivery of food and the responses that had been acquired? Skinner hypothesized that, on some occasions, the food accidentally followed some behavior on the pigeon's part. Contiguity between that response and reinforcement strengthened the response, so that it now occurred more frequently. This in turn increased the chances that food would again follow that response closely when it occurred. According to Skinner, the pigeon does not compare what happens when it does and does not respond; it is simply trapped in a positive feedback loop that is driven by contiguity.

A variety of subsequent response-stereotyping studies seemed to further support the superstition notion. In these experiments, reinforcement is delivered independently of the animal's specific responses, so long as some general type of response was made. The typical result is that the animal's behavior became stereotyped in that it came to perform only a limited range of the allowable behaviors. For example, Antonitis (1951) required rats to insert their noses in a horizontal slot in a wall to get some food. The rats could put their noses anywhere along the slot and receive food, but they came to respond to the very center of the slot. This sort of stereotyped development has often been explained by reinforcer contiguity as in Skinner's superstition experiment.

However, there are strong reasons to question the claim that these sorts of results occur because of contiguous reinforcers. The superstitious reinforcement argument assumes that there actually is some accidental contiguity between the response that becomes established and the reinforcer. But this is not what occurs. Staddon and Simmelhag (1974) directly observed the behavior of pigeons during the delivery of periodic response-independent food. Just as did Skinner, they found that stereotyped response patterns developed, even though there was no contingency between these responses and food. However, while these responses were developing, they were *not* contiguous with food. Contiguity can hardly be offered as an explanation for the observed change in the animal's behavior because there was no contiguity.

Further arguing against the contiguity explanation resulted in Staddon and Simmelhag's discovery that the stereotyped behaviors that did emerge frequently appeared well in advance of food. Indeed, they often occurred at a point in time maximally distant from the following food presentation.

It might be possible to blunt the Staddon and Simmelhag observation by suggesting that perhaps pigeons are not good at discriminating the delay between their behavior and outcomes. But this is not so. Nussear and Lattal (1983) trained pigeons to peck at the center key among three when it was lit. The center key darkened under two different conditions. Sometimes it darkened immediately after a peck. And sometimes it darkened after a certain amount of time had gone by since the last peck. When the center key darkened, the two side keys were illuminated, and it was the pigeon's job to peck one of these if the center key had gone off with no delay and the other if there had been a delay. The pigeons were able to make this discrimination even when the delay was as short as 0.2 second, the smallest one examined in this study!

That the "superstitious" response is not contiguous with the reinforcer, coupled with the fact that the pigeon is very good at discriminating even very small response-outcome delays, makes the reinforcer-contiguity explanation of the superstition experiment very unlikely. More recent work indicates that the response-eliciting properties of reinforcers, response bias, and the arousal induced by reinforcers are really responsible for the development of "superstitious" responses (Killeen, 1978, 1981).

But what can we make of the response-stereotyping experiments? Here there is accidental contiguity between the response that becomes stereotyped and the reinforcer. In the Antonitis (1951) experiment, for example, the rat did obtain food immediately after inserting its nose into the slot, and so there is accidental contiguity between food and responding to a particular location. The response-stereotyping experiments seem to better support the principle of contiguity than does the superstition experiment.

But Davis and Platt (1983) noted that response-stereotyping experiments typically do not assess whether the various response values are functionally equivalent. There might be many reasons other than contiguity why the animal comes to focus on a response of a given value. The particular testing apparatus might constrain the animal's responses, for example, or particular responses might be more susceptible to reinforcement than others. Antonitis explained his results by suggesting that the location of the food tray in his apparatus—directly opposite the center of the food slot—was probably responsible for the stereotyping of responses near the center of the slot.

Davis and Platt (1983) went on to conduct a series of response-stereotyping experiments in which they first established the functional equivalence of the different response values. A vertical joystick that could be displaced in any direction was suspended from the ceiling of a chamber. Rats were given food reward for moving the joystick. In an initial series of experiments, the rats were given food only if they displaced the joystick in a particular direction, and all directions proved to be equivalent in their reinforceability.

The critical question was what would happen if the rats were given food regardless of the direction in which they moved the joystick. Would stereotyping to a particular position occur? If contiguity is sufficient to produce response acquisition, the animal's distribution of response directions should narrow as training progresses and contiguity operates. Oscillations might occur, but the response distributions should in general diverge from randomness as contiguity exerts its effects. This did *not* happen; that is, stereotyping did *not* occur.

The phenomena thought to provide support for contiguity do not do so upon more careful analysis. But are there data that directly contradict the predictions of contiguity? A number of investigators have provided such data by conducting experiments with the following strategy. First, train animals to perform some response in order to obtain reward. Use schedules of reinforcement such as variable-interval schedules so that the animal responds at a steady rate and receives reward for only a small fraction of the responses it made. Then, after the response has been well acquired, continue to reinforce the response on the usual schedule but *add* response-independent reinforcers to the situation. Does the addition of the response-independent reinforcers increase or decrease the rate at which the operant response is produced?

The additional reinforcers do not reduce the number of conjunctions of the response and the reinforcer, so contiguity would not predict a response rate decrease. Indeed, by a contiguity view, the added reinforcers should increase the number of response-reinforcer pairings because some of them will by accident follow the operant response very closely. However, the independently delivered reinforcers end up decreasing the rate at which the response occurs (Rachlin & Baum, 1972; Zeiler, 1977).

Contingency

The contingency view has two obvious requirements.[1] First, animals must be able to discriminate the occurrence of reinforcing events that are dependent on their behavior from those that are independent. If they cannot do so, P(Rft/R) versus P(Rft/No R) cannot have any psychological impact. Second, changes in the degree of contingency must produce changes in the animal's behavior. The *relationship* between the two conditional probabilities should control its behavior.

In an important series of studies, Killeen (1978; Killeen & Smith, 1984) arranged for pigeons to indicate whether they could distinguish response-dependent outcomes from those that were response-independent. They were first trained to peck a lit response key. Each peck darkened the key with a probability of .05. That is, 1 of 20 pecks was followed by the outcome of key darkening, but the pigeon had no way to predict which peck would do so.

At the same time, a computer generated "pecks" at the same rate at which the pigeon had recently been pecking. These computer pecks were also followed by key darkening with a probability of .05. Thus, some key darkenings were dependent on the pigeon's peck, and some were independent because they were due to the computer's input. When the key darkened, two side keys were illuminated. The pigeons were then given food if they correctly reported whether it was their peck or the computer's peck that darkened the center key. The pigeon had to peck the left side key if its own behavior had produced darkening of the center key, and the right side key otherwise.

The pigeons were able to perform this task quite accurately and indicate whether or not their behavior had darkened the center key. However, it should be obvious that there must have been occasions on which the computer peck coincided with the pigeon's own pecks, because the computer pecks were unconstrained. If the two coincided exactly, it would be impossible for the pigeon to make a distinction. It is therefore possible to assess exactly how well the pigeon performs this task. How close can the response-independent change be to the pigeon's own peck and still allow the pigeon to indicate that the key darkening was independent of its own behavior? Killeen has estimated the just noticeable difference (jnd) as roughly 1/20 of a second!

The heart of the contingency notion is that behavior should vary with *both* P(Rft/R) and P(Rft/No R). A response should be acquired only if P(Rft/R) is not equal to P(Rft/No R), and it should become stronger as the difference in the probabilities increases. Said another way, for any given P(Rft/R), the response should weaken as the P(Rft/No R) approaches the value of P(Rft/R). This prediction is clearly at odds with the contiguity notion, because it posits variations in learning with contiguity held constant.

Unfortunately, it is not easy to test this prediction. The appropriate experiment requires one to manipulate the value of P(Rft/No R), but how is it possible to calculate this probability and arrange for it to occur? It is simple to arrange any specified P(Rft/R), because instances of R can be easily observed. If one wants a .33 probability, one delivers a reinforcer one-third of the time following a response by an animal. But how can one arrange for P(Rft/No R) to be .33? To do this would require identification of every No R so that one-third of them could be followed by the reinforcer. If R does not occur for some designated period of time, how does one count how many No Rs have occurred in this period of time?[2]

Hammond (1980) provided one clever solution to this dilemma. He developed what might be called a probabilistic reinforcement schedule. The schedule determined whether or not a reinforcer would be delivered every *t* seconds, depending on whether one or more Rs had occurred during that period of time. For example, rats were put in a situation in which the P(Rft/R) was held constant at .12 for each 1 second. The response was lever pressing and the reinforcer was water. This means that a determination was made as to whether a lever press had occurred in the last second, and if so, water was delivered with a probability of .12. P(Rft/No R) could now be varied within the same time interval, namely 1 second. Every 1-second interval was examined to see if an R had occurred. If no lever press had occurred during that interval, then that was taken as a single instance of No R. Each 1-second interval could be examined for instances of R or No R.

It therefore was possible for Hammond to deliver the reinforcer with any probability he desired for No R. He found that lever pressing fell off as P(Rft/No R) increased from 0 to .12, as predicted by contingency theory. A parallel study by Tomie and Loukas (1983) using position in an open field as the response and brain stimulation as the reinforcer supported Hammond's conclusion. At an empirical level, the contingency between response and reinforcer does influence the animal's behavior.

Still, our contingency proposal is vague and unspecified in a number of ways. The very idea of contingency requires more defi-

Table 2-2. Contingency Matrix.

	Rft	No Rft
Response	*a*	*b*
No response	*c*	*d*

nition than we originally gave it. To understand the problem involved, appreciate that the animal does not directly encounter conditional probabilities in its environment. These probabilities are abstractions that can only be calculated from information that the animal actually does receive: its own actions, events in its environment, and the time between them. Responses, environmental events, and the conjunction of responses and events occur with certain frequencies, and probabilities are calculated from these frequencies.

There are four relevant frequencies that form a 2×2 contingency matrix as shown in Table 2-2. The four cells are the possible conjunctions of R versus No R and Rft versus No Rft. Cell *a* represents instances in which an animal's response is closely followed by a reinforcer; cell *b* represents cases in which its response is not closely followed by a reinforcer; cell *c* represents instances in which the nonoccurrence of response is followed by a reinforcer; and cell *d* represents instances in which a nonresponse is not followed by a reinforcer. We emphasize that the entries in this matrix represent the number of times these conjunctions occur. They are not probabilities but actual numerical occurrences.

Frequencies like these are the events that the animal actually experiences; they are the only information available for computing probabilities. For example, $P(Rft/R) = a/(a+b)$, and $P(Rft/No\ R) = c/(c+d)$. Without stating it explicitly, or even giving it much thought, we assumed that the animal somehow assesses contingency by computing such ratios and comparing their difference. It seemed so obvious that this was happening that we gave the matter no great attention. However, there are many ways to calculate contingency from such a 2×2 matrix, and the animal could be using any of these metrics (see Hammond & Paynter, 1983, for a discussion). For example, Gibbon, Berryman, and Thompson (1974) suggested that the animal computes something akin to the phi coefficient: $(a/[a+b] - c/[c+d])\ (a/[a+c] - b/[b+d])$.

We proposed a particular formula but were not aware of the other metrics that could be used to integrate contingency information. We had no good reason for choosing the one that we did. We simply wished to argue for the importance of contingency in general terms, and we suggested the metric that seemed most obvious. But the animal could be using any of a number of computations, and they embody different theories.

The obvious solution would be to manipulate some parameter (e.g., the frequencies in any of the cells of Table 2–2) and determine which metric best predicts the behavior that results from the manipulation. However, in order to conduct such experiments, one would need to calculate the degree of contingency for each of the metrics.

Unfortunately, this reveals another poorly specified aspect of our contingency theory. To perform such experiments, each of the cell frequencies of the table has to be unambiguously measured. However, the theory does not specify how close a reinforcer has to come to a response to count as a cell *a* entry. The same is true for the other cells. Clearly, the events representing the four cells of the contingency matrix must be classified in relation to some temporal unit, *t*, as we have discussed with regard to the Hammond (1980) experiment. Placement of an event in the table proceeds by examining every *t* interval and seeing whether it contains an R or No R, Rft or No Rft. This is not problematic.

But a daunting problem emerges because a given metric yields different contingency estimates depending on the value of *t*. We do not know what *t* should be. Indeed, the value of *t* is arbitrary, but then so too are the contingency estimates. One cannot even make ordinal predictions, because different metrics respond differently to variations in *t*.

Experiments in which the subject's behavior determines not whether reinforcers will occur but when they will occur highlight the problem of how to treat time in terms of contingency theory. In an instructive example, Thomas (1981) exposed rats to a schedule divided into consecutive 20-second segments. The rats were given food every 20 seconds regardless of whether they made a lever press response or not. If no lever press occurred by the end of a 20-second interval, the food was delivered at that point. However, the animal's first lever press in a 20-second interval was followed immediately by food. So the only consequence of pressing the lever was to move the food presentation for that interval from the 20-second point at the end of the interval to the point in time at which the rat pressed the lever. The animals learned to press the lever and continued to do so in almost every interval.

Note that in the above experiment the food was contiguous with the animal's lever press, but there was no obvious contingency (food was given whether or not the rat pressed). Because stable lever pressing resulted, it might seem that the experiment favors the contiguity principle. However, the contiguity that occurred in the Thomas experiment may not have been essential. In another experiment, Hineline (1970) devised a schedule in which an electric shock was delivered during every 20-second interval. If the rat pressed a lever, the shock occurred at the end of the 20-second interval. If the rat did not press, then the shock occurred at the 8-second point of the 20-second interval. The animal's response did not avoid shock; it merely delayed it. With this procedure, there is no obvious contiguity. If the rat presses the lever, there is no event that follows it immediately such as the presentation of food. But it still acquired the response. Wasserman and Neunaber (1986) conducted experiments similar to those of Thomas and Hineline but with human subjects, and the results were the same.

Is there a response-reinforcer contingency in these experiments? The answer depends on t. Consider the Thomas experiment. There is no contingency at all between lever pressing and food if t is assumed to be the cycle length of 20 seconds. Under this assumption, the probability of reinforcement is the same (1.0) whether or not a lever press occurs—food automatically appears in every 20-second cycle regardless of what the rat does. However, for some values of t, there is a positive contingency between lever pressing and reinforcement. This is not a satisfactory state of affairs.

Causality

The foregoing discussion suggests that the principle of contiguity provides a poor description of the factors determining the acquisition and performance of behavior. The contingency view is supported in a general way in that animals seem to integrate information about what happens after R and No R. However, the conditional probability analysis that we proposed encounters a number of difficulties.

Perhaps if we consider the concept of causality, it will help resolve the impasse. Keep in mind that principles of association and contiguity arose in the first place when philosophers attempted to specify the circumstances under which people infer a causal relationship between events. In *A Treatise of Human Nature*, David Hume (1739) proposed three principles that he believed gave people the impression of a cause-effect relation: (1) temporal precedence: causes must precede effects; (2) temporal and spatial contiguity: causes and effects must occur close together in time and space; and (3) constant conjunction: effects must regularly follow causes.

The notion of causality proves much more complex than it might initially seem. An event can have many different kinds of "causes" (proximate cause, material cause, ultimate cause, and so on). Further, causality does not inhere in physical events or objects. Rather, it is a label that we give to some orderly relationships between events but not to others. Hume held causation to be a psychological rather than a physical phenomenon. He saw it as a relationship between experiences. There are indeed many orderly relationships between physical events that we do not label as causal. For example, is the position of a planet at one point in time the cause of its moving to a different location? But sometimes we do ascribe causality to a relation, and that designation seems to have special properties (Michotte, 1963).

There is an intriguing similarity between the principles of causal inference and the laws of learning (Testa, 1975). Temporal precedence, spatial and temporal contiguity, and constant conjunction are all crucial for classical conditioning and instrumental learning to occur:

- The animal's response must precede the reinforcer for learning to occur.
- Learning is retarded if there is a time gap between the response and the reinforcer.
- Spatial contiguity between the response and the reinforcer facilitates learning (Boakes, 1977).
- The correlation between response and reinforcement is also critical (Hammond, 1980).

This similarity motivates our consideration of learning phenomena in the context of causality.

How does this bear on our discussion of learned helplessness? In 1967, we were trying to say that the dog learned that its behavior did not cause the shock to terminate. We conceptualized the animals we studied as searching for the causes of events, because knowing about causes helps them behave adaptively in future interactions with these events. We wished to allow animals to make the distinction between chance conjunctions and "'true" relations between events. We needed to develop a scheme that let an animal use information with regard to both sufficiency ("If I respond, what happens") and necessity ("If I don't respond, what happens").

We stated our position in terms of conditional probabilities, but this was arbitrary, we now realize. Our experimental procedure involved events going on and going off, either contingent on a response or not. So we framed our ideas in terms of the probabilities of events going on or off, given a response or no response. However, if in our initial experiments responses had been arranged to produce events sooner or later rather than turning them off or not, we would probably have represented our view as something other than P(Rft/R) and P(Rft/No R). Perhaps the problems with the details of the contingency notion have more to do with the translation into conditional probabilities than with the central concepts.

Consider in this regard the experiments in which responding does not change the overall probability of reinforcement but only moves the reinforcer to an earlier point in time. Wasserman and Neunaber (1986) explain their results by arguing that animals compare the relative delay of reinforcement that follows R and No R. Animals will perform R if it results in less delay than does No R because they prefer immediate to delayed reinforcers. This relative-delay principle can explain many of the findings that have been taken to support the conditional-probability statement of contingency theory.

Wasserman and Neunaber went on to argue for the primacy of delay and suggested that this might be intimately tied to the perception of causality. Perhaps to cause an event to occur means moving that event forward or backward in time. They further argued that their experiment and their analysis support contiguity theory and weighs against contingency views because in their formulation time is the critical variable. But contiguity theories do not merely assert that time is important. They view learning as the automatic strengthening of responses by rewards. They do not allow for a comparison process. Contingency theory, however, explicitly focuses on a comparison between what happens after R and No R, although the comparison is of probabilities of reinforcement. If we propose that the animal compares delays after R and No R, this is entirely in the spirit of contingency rather than contiguity theory.

A more general contingency view not tied to conditional probabilities seems consistent with the reinforcer advance and delay experiments. The subjects in the reinforcer advance and delay experiments have control over the time at which the reinforcer will occur but not over the probabilities. As we have noted, animals do not experience probabilities. Probabilities can be constructed from what they do experience, but there is no reason to believe that probabilities are primary.

But there is also no reason to think that time is primary. Consider the following sort of experiment. We allow the animal's response to change the intensity of a reinforcer. The probability that the reinforcer occurs and the exact time at which it occurs are unaffected by the subject's behavior. Is there any question that the animal will learn to perform the response under appropriate conditions? Indeed, Bersh and Alloy (1978) found that rats learn to press a lever to reduce the intensity of a later shock.

Our intent all along was to argue that animals analyze the consequences of their actions and learn the degree to which their actions have causal impact. Some philosophers have argued that causal efficacy means an interference with the flow of events (e.g., von Wright, 1974). This can occur with regard to event probabilities, delay, or intensity. A contingency analysis can be applied to dimensions other than event probability.

If the theory is broadened in this manner, then the experiments that seem to contradict contingency theory lose some of their force. The problems with how to treat time also diminish. It would not do any harm to our view to acknowledge that animals in learned helplessness experiments might not be computing probabilities but instead comparing the delay of shock termination following a response with the delay of shock termination in the absence of that response.

REPRESENTATION AND EXPECTATION

Learned helplessness theory claims that exposure to inescapable shock leads an animal to represent the noncontingency between its behavior and shock termination and to expect this noncontingency to hold in the future. This key assertion has been difficult to test because it is not easy to ask questions about what an animal thinks. All we can do is to investigate the behavioral consequences that presumably follow from such representations and expectations. Our argument has been that the representation and expectation of noncontingency between behavior and aversive events lead to deficits in response initiation and cognition. These, in turn, produce poor learning in escape tasks such as we observe in the shuttlebox. However, "inactivity" theories also account for poor escape learning, and so learning impairments in themselves cannot be taken as evidence for the representations and expectations we hypothesize.

This issue has been further confused by frequent misinterpretations of some of the evidence provided in support of the incompatible motor response theories. Three kinds of experiments have been conducted. The first kind demonstrates that inescapable—but not escapable—shock indeed reduces later activity by animals in the presence of shock (Anisman, deCatanzaro, & Remington, 1978; Jackson, Maier, & Rapaport, 1978). The second kind of experiment shows a strong correlation between whether an experimental treatment reduces an animal's unconditioned movement in reaction to shock and whether it interferes with its escape acquisition. For example, Crowell and Anderson (1981) manipulated inescapable shock intensity and duration and found a link between the effect of these different shock treatments on activity and escape learning. The third class of investigation demonstrates that manipulations that do not involve control can also interfere with an animal's escape learning. Anderson, Crowell, Cunningham, and Lupo (1978) found that teaching rats to escape shock by being immobile during shock led to poor shuttlebox escape acquisition.

However, the logic of these experiments may not allow an adequate test between incompatible motor response theories and learned helplessness theory. There is nothing in learned helplessness theory that denies that manipulations that lower an animal's activity might also reduce the speed of its responding in a shuttlebox. After all, learned helplessness is not a theory of shuttleboxes! Many factors influence how an animal responds in a shuttlebox, and learned helplessness theory does *not* suggest that they all entail control.

Part of the difficulty here is that the two perspectives—learned helplessness and incompatible motor responses—are neither mutually exclusive nor cumulatively exhaustive. An experiment that supports a prediction of incompatible response theory (e.g., the subject becomes less active) need not count against the learned helplessness account. There is an important asymmetry here. Incompatible motor response theories assert the reality of the processes to which they refer as well as deny the existence of the processes hypothesized by the learned helplessness account. On the other hand, learned helplessness theory only asserts the reality of the processes to which it refers; it does not deny that motor responses can be learned and even transferred to new situations. This asymmetry appears as well in human helplessness (Chapter 4) and depression research (Chapter 6).

These theories can be separated only by inquiring into the reality of the processes proposed in the learned helplessness hypothesis.

Response initiation and cognitive deficits are the visible reflections of the representational and expectational processes. However, response initiation and activity are so tightly related that this sort of deficit cannot be taken to support either view. The cognitive deficit most clearly distinguishes the theories. Learned helplessness argues for a cognitive change in addition to any activity or performance deficits that might also occur.

The Cognitive Deficit

Poor escape learning might appear to constitute a priori evidence for a cognitive deficit. However, the escape tasks that have been used confound any potential cognitive change with inactivity. An animal's poor escape performance in tasks such as shuttleboxes and lever pressing could result either from interference with the learning process or from reduced activity. To make matters worse, inescapably shocked subjects frequently fail to respond at all on a given trial with these tasks. This means that they are exposed to the escape contingency less frequently than are control subjects, making it difficult to conclude that differences in performance are caused by differential sensitivity to the escape contingency. Moreover, inescapably shocked subjects are often at a different level of performance than control subjects from the very outset of training.

How can an experiment demonstrate a cognitive deficit among helpless animals? The task must be one in which activity level and shock escape are either uncorrelated or negatively correlated. Second, inescapably shocked subjects and control subjects must receive equal exposure to the escape contingency. Third, all subjects must begin at the same level of escape performance. Although these requirements might seem quite stringent, several tasks actually do meet them.

Signaled Punishment.   Following the lead of Baker (1976), Jackson, Maier, and Rapaport (1978) examined the effects of inescapable shock on *signaled punishment.* Here animals (rats) were first trained to press a lever for food on a reinforcement schedule that generated a steady rate of responding. After the rats were well trained, they received either inescapable shock or no shock at all in a different apparatus. Twenty-four hours later, the rats were returned to the lever press chamber. Pressing the lever still produced food on the same schedule as before. However, now a 3-minute white noise signal appeared on the average of every 20 minutes. The food reinforcement schedule remained unchanged during the auditory stimulus, but two shocks were also programmed to occur during each of the 3-minute stimulus periods; these shocks were contingent on lever pressing. When a shock was ready to occur, it was delivered immediately following the next lever press. Thus, lever presses were punished during the white noise, and the rats could prevent the shocks by not pressing the lever.

In this experiment, learning the contingency between responding and shock resulted in the animal suppressing its response. Rats came to press the lever less often during the signal as they learned the relationship between responding and the occurrence of shock. The amount of motor activity and the degree of learning the relationship between response and shock were negatively correlated. Poor learning here was reflected in the animal's failure to suppress responding, to continue pressing the lever at a rapid rate. Moreover, all animals began at the same level of performance (no change in responding when the white noise comes on), and those animals failing to learn actually received more rather than less exposure to the contingency between lever pressing and the occurrence of shock. This experiment found that inescapable shock interferes with learning to suppress lever pressing when shock became contingent on this behavior. So we have an instance of poor learning reflected by more rather than less motor activity!

This experiment ostensibly demonstrates that inescapable shock interferes with an animal's learning of the relationship between its behavior and shock. However, the procedure also involved a contingency between the white noise stimulus and shock, and it is possible that the inescapably shocked subjects did not learn to suppress lever pressing during the auditory stimulus because of an interference with learning *this* stimulus-shock contingency, rather than the one between response and shock.

Jackson et al. examined this possibility by repeating the experiment with one critical exception. When a shock was programmed to occur during the white noise, it was delivered immediately rather than contingent on the next lever press. Thus, there was only a stimulus-shock contingency. Animals normally suppress their appetitively motivated responding as they learn the stimulus-shock contingency. Here inescapable shock did not interfere with learning. We can conclude that the signaled punishment results reflect a deficit in response-shock learning, and again the deficit is reflected by more rather than less responding.

Choice. Perhaps signaled punishment does not constitute an escape learning task; perhaps the cognitive deficit we hypothesize must be demonstrated with escape learning. We therefore sought an escape learning task in which activity and learning were not confounded. One possibility was a choice task in which shock is terminated by the animal choosing the correct response from a number of alternatives. Here escape learning is not assessed by response speed but rather by the accuracy of the subject's choices. High levels of activity need not produce accurate choices nor low levels poor ones, so long as enough activity is present for choices to occur. In any case, both response speed and accuracy can be measured and their correlation assessed.

Jackson, Alexander, and Maier (1980) developed a Y-maze escape task. The apparatus was small, and therefore not much movement was required for the rat to choose one of the arms. The three 22.5-centimeter arms of the maze were at a 120-degree angle to each other and connected to a small central section in the shape of an equilateral triangle. The rat only had to move 12 centimeters into an arm to register a response. The arms were all identical, and the maze was housed in a dark room to minimize any possibility of using cues outside the maze.

The animals spent the interval between trials in darkness. A trial began with shock to the grids and the onset of lights behind the end walls of the arms. The shock and lights terminated if the rat entered the arm to the left of where it was when the trial started. If the rat made a right turn, then a left turn was still required before the trial would terminate. If it turned right again, the rat was then required to move into the arm to the left of this arm, and so on. A trial ended only if the rat turned left, and so any number of incorrect choices were possible before a correct turn was made. Shock was automatically terminated if a correct turn was not made within 60 seconds. The rat was free to move about between trials, and its position at the beginning of the trial defined its starting point.

Rats first received either escapable shock, yoked inescapable shock, or no shock at all in an apparatus very different from the Y-maze. Twenty-four hours later, this was followed by 100 trials of escape training in the Y-maze. Of interest was the percentage of trials on which one or more errors (right turns) occurred across blocks of 10 trials. This measure represents the accuracy of the rat's responses rather than the speed with which they were made. All groups began by choosing the correct arm of the maze at a chance level. However, the performance of the groups quickly diverged. The nonshocked and escapably shocked animals soon eliminated errors and were making errors on only 10 percent of the trials by the end of the training session. In contrast, the inescapably shocked rats remained at random choice for 40 trials and were still beginning 30 percent of the trials with an incorrect choice by the end of training.

Failures to respond were not responsible for the difference between the inescapably shocked animals versus the others. There were virtually no failures to terminate a trial with a correct response. The inescapably shocked rats simply made more errors. These results reveal an interference with learning under conditions in which the animals are exposed to the correct contingency on every trial.

These suggest a true cognitive change. Moreover, this interference with choice learning seems to have some generality. Rosellini, DeCola, and Shapiro (1982) found that inescapable shock interferes with an animal's learning to choose between two responses in order to get food.

Nature of the Cognitive Deficit. What is the nature of this cognitive change? Many possibilities exist. For example, inescapably shocked subjects might have an attentional-perceptual deficit; they might not attend to cues correlated with their own responding and thus do not associate their response with shock. Alternatively, inescapably shocked animals might have an expectational deficit; they accurately register the events of a given trial but have a biased expectation so that they do not expect the contingency to hold on future trials.

A series of experiments conducted by Minor, Jackson, and Maier (1984) supports the attentional-perceptual possibility. We began by noting that the choice-accuracy deficit was difficult to obtain when the Y-maze was fully automated. In the original studies, Jackson et al. observed the rats in the Y-maze and depressed switches to record a rat's movement from arm to arm as it broke the photocell beam in each arm. This was done because the rat's tail would sometimes break a photocell beam even though the rat did not enter that arm. Of course, when this happened the observer did not register this photobeam break as a response. The photocell arrangement was eventually improved to be "tailproof," and a computer was added to conduct the whole experiment all by itself. Now that a human observer was no longer needed, the phenomenon disappeared!

With our fancy computer-run, fully automated, and personless procedure, inescapably shocked animals learned brilliantly and no longer chose poorly. At this point, we were confused and conducted an endless series of parametric variations (e.g., "maybe more shock is needed now"), all to no avail. Inescapably shocked animals simply loved to learn in our "properly run" Y-maze.

We finally reasoned that either the human observers (i.e., us) cheated in the initial experiments or that there was something critical about the human observer. What could be the role of the observer? Because he had to press a button to record the rat's breaking a photobeam, there must have been a small delay between a correct response and shock termination. But there is another possibility more subtle than delay. Remember that we had been careful to construct a maze with no external cues to differentiate the arms. We even kept the maze dark between trials. However, the observer could have functioned as a cue. He may have given off odors, made some noise, or whatever. He remained in a fixed position relative to the maze, behind one of the arms. Depending on the rat's position at the beginning of a trial, he was sometimes behind the rat's starting arm, sometimes behind the correct choice, and sometimes behind the incorrect choice. This means that the observer was an irrelevant cue.

Minor et al. began by investigating delay. The computer arranged for small delays in shock termination following the correct choice. The delays averaged 350 milliseconds, approximately human reaction time in this situation. Inescapably shocked subjects still learned. The delay was then eliminated, but a person was put in the room behind one arm of the maze. The experiment was still run by the computer, and the person did not intervene in any way. Inescapably shocked animals now had a learning deficit, but it was not as large as in the original experiments.

The next step was to combine the two factors: shock termination was slightly delayed, and a human stood in the room. Now a large deficit in choice escape learning occurred for animals previously exposed to inescapable shock. Subjects that had first received escapable shock or no shock at all were unaffected by the slight delay and presence of the person in the room; they learned well under all conditions. However, rats inescapably shocked 24 hours earlier were profoundly disrupted if there was a delay *and* a person in the room. They did not fail to respond and choose. They simply did not learn to choose correctly.

If the presence of a person interferes with the performance of inescapably shocked animals because he functions as an irrelevant cue, then other irrelevant stimuli, such as tones and lights, ought to have the same effect. In their next experiment, Minor et al. substituted a light for the person. A light behind one of the arms of the maze was lit at the beginning of each escape learning trial (an average delay of shock termination of 350 milliseconds was still in effect). The particular arm that was illuminated varied randomly from trial to trial and was unrelated to the animal's position. As before, escapably shocked and nonshocked rats were not affected by the light. However, inescapably shocked rats were impaired.

The role of the delay in shock termination is easy to explain. If an animal has registered the occurrence of a contingency between its behavior and shock termination on a given trial, there is no reason why a delay should affect whether the animal expects that this contingency will remain in effect on future trials. However, a delay would make the contingency on a given trial harder to notice and could magnify any effect that inescapable shock has on this "noticing" process.

How about the irrelevant cue? Maybe inescapable shock makes animals more distractible later, and the light operates as a distraction. However, remember that the normal Y-maze procedure without the cue included darkness between trials and that all three arms became illuminated at the beginning of each trial. Here even more light comes on than in the irrelevant cue condition, but the inescapably shocked animals still do not show any interference with their learning. Inescapable shock only interfered with learning when the light was a differential cue that could be used to guide behavior. Light cannot be used to guide behavior if all three arms are illuminated.

Our results support the idea that inescapable shock leads to an interference with the processing of the contingency information on a given trial rather than to a biasing of the expectational process. Moreover, an alteration in attention is indeed likely. The data are consistent with the following sort of argument. Exposure to inescapable shock leads the subject to learn that its own behavior is uncorrelated with shock termination. The subject expects that this will also be true in the Y-maze. This expectation has a number of consequences that include reduced salience of responses or of response-produced cues. Therefore, the subject is less likely to attend to these sorts of cues and associate them with shock termination.

Why then is there no interference with learning unless an external irrelevant cue is present? Why is a reduction in the salience of response-related cues not sufficient? Perhaps the reduced salience of these cues does not have much effect if the contingency is very obvious and if there is nothing else to which to attend. Other things being equal, a reduction in the animal's attention to internal behavior-related cues should increase its attention to external cues such as lights or odors. Inescapably shocked animals should show increased attention to such cues, and this should then interfere with their learning if these cues are present and irrelevant. However, if such cues are not present, a reduction in their attention to internal cues might have no impact.

This perspective suggests that the cognitive change produced by inescapable shock might not really be a deficit. It instead may lead animals to process trial information differently rather than less. That such subjects are biased toward attention to external rather than internal cues suggests that there are conditions under which inescapable shock improves learning. For example, what if the light cue in the Y-maze became a relevant cue rather than an irrelevant one? In other words, what if the light signaled which arm of the maze was correct? Our argument implies that inescapably shocked animals would now learn faster than controls!

This hypothesis has been examined by Lee and Maier (1988). Their experiments used an escape-from-water task shown in Figure 2-2. (Rats do not like to be in water even though they swim quite well. They are therefore motivated to find a way to escape from water.) The rat is placed at the start of a rectangular tank on each trial. The end of the tank (opposite the start) is divided into two compartments, with a piece of plastic placed in front of each compartment and coming down to water level. The rat is able to swim under either piece and enter the compartment to which it leads, but it cannot swim directly between the compartments. The rat has to swim out of the compartment in which it finds itself and around to the other side in order to go from one to the other.

Lee and Maier first determined whether inescapable shock would interfere with the rats being able to learn a left-right discrimination to escape the water. There was a platform that extended above the water in one of the compartments on each trial. If the rat entered the compartment with the platform, it could get out of the water by climbing onto it. The platform was either on the left side or the right side on each trial. A particular rat had to learn to go to the left or to the right. A black stimulus card was placed on one of the plastic pieces at the entrance to a compartment on each trial, and a white card was placed on the other piece. Whether the black or white card was on a particular side varied randomly from trial to trial. Left-right was the relevant cue for solving the problem, whereas

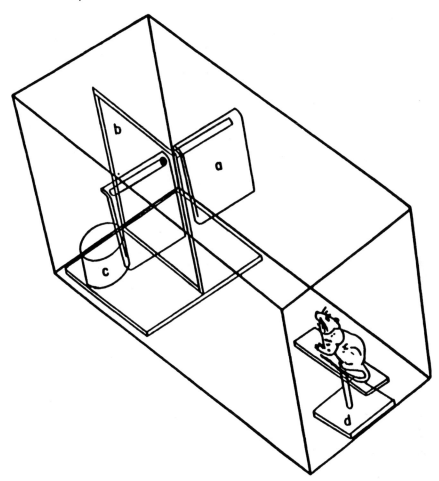

Figure 2-2. Water escape task. The rat starts each escape trial at the end of the tank *(d)*. It escapes by swimming to the platform *(c)*. It can enter either compartment by swimming under a plastic barrier *(a)*. Because the two compartments are divided from each other *(b)*, it cannot swim directly from one to the other.

black-white was irrelevant. A variety of cautions were taken to eliminate the possibility that the rat could use cues outside the maze to solve the problem. The result was that prior exposure to inescapable shock interfered with that animal being able to solve the problem. Inescapably shocked rats made many errors and learned slowly.

What happens if the problem is changed slightly? What if everything were kept the same except the rule the rat must use? What if the platform is not placed on either the left or the right side consistently but always placed above the compartment with either the black or the white stimulus in front of it? Not much is changed—the apparatus is still the same; the water is still the same temperature; the rat must still choose between two compartments. What has changed, however, is that the rat must attend to an external stimulus (black versus white) to solve the problem. We now find that inescapable shock no longer interferes with the animal being able to learn the water maze discrimination. Strikingly, it now improves learning over that observed in control animals!

Detection of Noncontingency

If inescapable shock really leads to the representation of noncontingency, it should facilitate the animal's later learning that events are noncontingent. Just this sort of finding was reported by Testa, Juraska, and Maier (1974). Rats were first given either escapable shock, inescapable shock, or no shock. Twenty-four hours later, all rats were given escape training in a shuttlebox using a procedure that leads to learning in all animals, whether or not they have experienced inescapable shock. All subjects were efficiently escaping by the end of the training trials. Now the shock was switched from being contingent on shuttling to being noncontingent; the shock simply stayed on for a fixed period of time on each trial regardless of the rat's behavior. Our assumption was that shuttling would diminish when the rat detected that the shock was no longer contingent on its responding. The inescapably shocked animals stopped shuttling much sooner than did the others.

In a similar experiment, Rosellini, DeCola, Plonsky, Warren, and Stilman (1984) trained rats to perform a response for food. The rats then received either escapable, inescapable, or no shock. They were later returned to the food task and given further training until the groups no longer differed in their rate of responding. Food presentations were then made noncontingent on behavior, simply provided at random intervals no matter what the rats did. Again, the inescapably shocked rats ceased to perform the learned response much more rapidly than did the other subjects.

Learned Mastery

If animals represent the degree of contingency between their behavior and outcomes, then prior exposure to *controllable* events might be expected to *facilitate* their subsequent learning. Learned mastery as well as learned helplessness ought to exist. Just as expectations about noncontingency should reduce incentive motivation and interfere with the perception of contingencies, expectations about future contingency should increase incentive motivation and augment the perception of contingencies. However, subjects given escapable shock rarely learn more rapidly than do the nonshocked controls.

Volpicelli, Ulm, Altenor, and Seligman (1983) reasoned that special conditions might be necessary to observe mastery effects. If passivity during shock reflects an expectation of lack of control over the shock, then animals previously trained to escape shock should continue to respond actively during inescapable shock longer than nonshocked animals. Animals gradually cease active responding when aversive events are uncontrollable, but this should be delayed in animals previously exposed to controllable events. So Volpicelli et al. exposed previously escapably shocked, inescapably shocked, and nonshocked rats to fixed-duration, 10-second, inescapable shocks in a shuttlebox. We simply measured how long the rats kept running back and forth across the shuttlebox. As predicted, the escapably shocked animals remained active much longer than did the originally nonshocked control animals.

But this result does not tell us whether escapable shock increases motivation to later attempt to escape, or facilitates the animal's tendency to detect response–shock termination relationships, or both. It does not isolate a motivational effect because escapably shocked subjects might be more sensitive to adventitious relationships between crossing the shuttlebox and shock termination. Volpicelli et al. tested this possibility by repeating the same experiment, except they tested with one continuous inescapable shock, and escapably shocked rats still remained more active. We went on to test for facilitated cognitive processing by using a difficult escape learning task. Escapable shock had no effect on the unconditioned tendency to perform this response, so any differences in learning could not be explained by activity or motivational factors. Escapably shocked animals still learned more rapidly than did nonshocked controls. The impact of experiencing contingency and noncontingency may therefore be symmetrical: noncontingency produces decreased motivation and difficulty seeing contingencies; contingency produces increased motivation and augmented contingency perception.

WHAT WE KNOW

How has learned helplessness theory fared since we proposed it in 1967? Quite well we would argue, given the usual half-life of any theory and given the minimal data on which we then proposed the theory. It is still alive in the 1990s, with numerous investigators using it to organize and guide their research, much of it in biological directions (Chapter 3). The central phenomena have been robust. The basic learned helplessness effect in animals has been replicated in at least twenty independent laboratories, the therapy and immunization effects in half a dozen. Occasional failures have been reported, but the conditions of this subsequent work were often quite different from those that we have established.

At a more theoretical level, the contingency between behavior and outcome controls behavior, and the pattern of learning alterations produced by inescapable shock can be explained only in cognitive terms. Finally, a wide part of the animal's behavioral repertoire is indeed undermined.

We have focused on the impact of the controllability on later learning because the theoretical dispute has centered on how best to explain the learning deficit produced by uncontrollable shock. But the effects of the controllability of aversive events are more profound. Incompatible motor response explanations expect the consequences of uncontrollable aversive events to be quite limited to later situations that contain a similar aversive event. Moreover, only outcomes produced by motor competition could be explained.

In contrast, learned helplessness theory expects a widespread impact of uncontrollability. The theory proposes that the uncontrollability of an aversive event adds to the fear-arousing properties of the event and leads to depression if the experience is prolonged or intense or becomes chronic. Obviously, one should then be able to observe either intense fear or depression after uncontrollable aversive events, depending on the duration of the exposure and the severity of the event. Because intense anxiety and depression affect a broad spectrum of behavior, all of these behaviors too should be influenced by controllability.

Inescapable shock indeed produces more fear in animals than does an exactly equivalent amount of escapable shock. Thus, a cue paired with shock produces more suppression of appetitive behavior if the shock is inescapable (Desiderato & Newman, 1971). Similarly, the environmental contexts in which inescapable shocks occur produce more fear-related behavior by an animal, such as crouching and defecating, than do contexts in which escapable shocks occur (Mineka, Cook, & Miller, 1984). Although it is more complicated to determine whether uncontrollable aversive events produce depression in animals, this also seems to be the case. We discuss the relevant research in Chapter 6.

WHAT WE DON'T KNOW

There are uncertainties with regard to each component of the theory. It is clear that variation in contingency leads to variation in behavior. However, the fact that the animal responds sensitively to contingency does not necessarily mean that it is extracting the degree of contingency and representing it cognitively. A more molecular model that does not refer to contingency at all might be able to account for behavioral sensitivity to contingency, just as the Rescorla-Wagner (1972) model explains contingency effects in classical conditioning with only contiguity mechanisms. Moreover, even if degree of contingency is psychologically real, a model is needed that specifies how contingency is computed from the data that the animal has available. It is not present in momentary sensory data but can only be abstracted from event relationships as they exist across time.

Similarly, the controllability of an event is critical in determining how an animal responds to it. But is it control per se, or some more molecular process that is responsible for these apparent effects? There are several possibilities that have been advanced in the literature. Both the predictability and the controllability of events influence their impact, so perhaps the effects of control might be mediated by prediction (Overmier, Patterson, & Wielkiewicz, 1979). Perhaps having control over an event inherently adds predictability concerning the event. In the case of escapability, the ability to escape allows the animal to predict when shock will terminate.

However, the logic of this argument is not clear. To predict an event means to have information about its onset or termination in advance of its actual occurrence. An escape response does not allow the prediction of when the next shock will occur. The assumption is that the escape response allows the animal to predict when the shock will go off, but does it really? The shock terminates immediately after the escape response, and so there is only a very brief period of time (perhaps 50 milliseconds using standard equipment) between the response and the event it is "predicting." Of course, the act of responding takes some amount of time, and so the response is initiated a short time before shock terminates, say a second or so. The animals with an escape response may be provided with information that shock will terminate before it actually does so, but only very shortly before the shock actually terminates. This is hardly what is meant by predictability. Indeed, the impact of predictability has only been demonstrated with relatively long stimuli.

For example, animals prefer predictable to unpredictable shock but do not do so if the signal is only 3 seconds long (Perkins, Seymann, Levis, & Spencer, 1966). Information about an impending event could hardly be useful a fraction of a second or a second before the event occurs. Moreover, when the animal has made an escape response, the durations of the shocks are highly variable from trial to trial, particularly early in training. It is hard to see in what sense the time of shock termination is more predictable for such a subject than for one who does not have an escape response but receives fixed-duration inescapable shocks of say 2 seconds.

Finally, predictability may be important because it allows an element of control. It is not at all clear, however, that control can be reduced to prediction. Nevertheless, there are many potential interactions between control and prediction, and they will not be easy to separate.

Despite our uncertainty about the logic contained in the predictability argument, it is clear that signaling the onset or the termination of inescapable shocks with an environmental stimulus, such as a tone or a light, can prevent inescapable shock from interfering with an animal's later escape learning (Jackson & Minor, 1988; Minor, Trauner, Lee, & Dess, 1990). That is, external stimuli paired with shock onset or shock cessation mimic the effects of control in that they prevent shock from interfering with later escape behavior. Perhaps escape is effective because the response provides internal stimuli that function as do the external stimuli provided in the above experiments. Some classical conditioning process might well be involved here, distinct from any predictability that the signal or response provides. This is an exciting area of research, and it will be some years before we know why control works.

The potential involvement of internal stimuli that signal shock cessation is related to the mediating role of fear and anxiety. Such stimuli might actually function as conditioned inhibitors of fear. Uncontrollable shock produces more fear than does controllable shock, and this intense fear rather than control per se may be responsible for some of the sequelae of uncontrollable aversive events (Minor & LoLordo, 1984). Anything that produces intense fear could produce some of these behavioral effects, whether it involves uncontrollability or not. The role of fear has not been resolved and is another area of current work (see Maier, 1990). We address this topic further in the next chapter.

In sum, uncertainties exist at several levels. First, the mechanism by which cognitive processing is altered is poorly understood. We presented evidence indicating that attention is altered, but the details of how this occurs are not yet known. Moreover, this does not imply that expectational biasing fails to occur. Second, it is not clear which of the behavioral consequences of uncontrollable aversive events are directly produced by the cognition of no control and which are produced by other consequences (motivational, motoric, emotional, or neurochemical). For example, is maternal behavior disrupted because of the cognition of no control or because inescapable shock has induced some other change?

There are two areas of particular ignorance. One concerns the limits of uncontrollable shock effects. Where do they stop? The other is related to a point we raised earlier. Are the behavioral changes that occur reducible to a single cause, or are the various behavioral changes produced by different processes induced by inescapable shock? If there are multiple causes, then what are they and how do they map into behavior?

NOTES

1. Parts of this section and the next on causality are based on Maier (1989b).
2. If this sounds obscure, think of a friend who has not called you on the phone for quite a while. How many times in a week has this happened?

3

The Biology of Learned Helplessness

The literature investigating the biology of learned helplessness is both large and confusing. There are numerous proposals, each pointing to a different neurotransmitter, or hormone, or brain structure, as the key player in mediating learned helplessness. Moreover, each proposal has a body of supporting evidence. Adding to the confusion is the fact that some of the neurochemical consequences of being exposed to uncontrollable aversive events have been offered as alternative explanations to learned helplessness theory. That is, they have been invoked to explain the "helplessness" effects that follow inescapable shock (Chapter 2).

We have several goals here. We examine learned helplessness in terms of the relevant biological literature. We provide a general view of what we know about the sensitivity of various biological systems to the controllability of stressors. We are honest about what remains unknown concerning the biology of learned helplessness. Because this work is ongoing on many fronts and quite complex, we hope to clarify some of the areas of confusion as well as point to promising hypotheses. Our overarching point, though, is that control proves a powerful psychological variable, with pervasive biological consequences.

Research interest has focused on the neural and neurochemical changes that are determined by stressor controllability/uncontrollability, and on whether these biological effects mediate the behavioral changes that result from uncontrollability. A considerable difficulty arises from the fact that the stressors studied are typically so potent that they alter the activity of almost every neurotransmitter in some particular brain region and some neurotransmitter in almost every brain region. Because stressors can have such widespread effects, almost any neurotransmitter is a potential mediator of the effects of uncontrollability. Not surprisingly, many have been studied, and researchers indeed find that virtually all neurotransmitters are altered in some way by the controllability versus uncontrollability of an imposed stressor.

Such discoveries have usually been followed by experiments showing that a pharmacological manipulation of the neurotransmitter or receptors for the neurotransmitter has an impact on learned helplessness. This is consistent with the notion that alterations in that neurotransmitter produce these effects.

For example, pharmacological agents that prevent the uncontrollable stressor (usually inescapable shock) from producing the neurotransmitter change typically preclude such learned helplessness effects as poor shuttlebox escape learning (see Chapter 2). Similarly, pharmacological agents that produce the neurotransmitter change typically lead to helplessness without any exposure to the uncontrollable stressor. These experiments may then be followed by the proposal that neurotransmitter X in region Y must be *the* mediator in producing learned helplessness.

However, things are not that simple, as we illustrate in this chapter. There appear to be several biological mediators of helplessness effects. Let us begin by looking at three different systems—norepinephrine, gamma-aminobutyric acid, and endogenous opiates—in relation to learned helplessness. In each case, we have convincing evidence that the system is importantly involved.

NOREPINEPHRINE

The earliest investigations of the neurochemistry of learned helplessness occurred in the early 1970s and focused on the catecholamine *norepinephrine* (called a catecholamine because it has a catechol nucleus and an amino group as part of its structure). There were many reasons why norepinephrine *(NE)* was chosen as the starting point. The scientific study of the nervous system began with the peripheral nervous system because it is much more accessible than the central nervous system. NE is the neurotransmitter at sympathetic nerve terminals, and so it was isolated and studied very early in the history of the neurosciences. When techniques to explore the central nervous system became available, it was only natural for researchers to ask if NE might be a neurotransmitter there as well. As a consequence, NE was one of the earliest known neurotransmitters in the central nervous system. The isolation of NE in the central nervous system was quickly followed by the development of fluorescent techniques to visualize NE-containing neurons, and thus we knew the distribution and organization of NE pathways before we knew those of most others.

The anatomy of NE pathways proves to be quite peculiar. NE-containing cell bodies are located almost exclusively in a group of nuclei in the pons and medulla of the brain. The largest and most compact of the nuclei is called the *locus coeruleus (LC)*, and its neurons contain almost 80 percent of all of the NE in the brain. However, this nucleus has only a very small number of neurons, about 1,500 cells in the rat. The reason why this small number of neurons can supply so much of the brain's NE is that the axon terminals of each cell distribute themselves over a very wide area.

The major output pathway of the LC is called the *dorsal NE bundle (DB)*, which runs through the midbrain and then fans out to innervate the whole neocortex, the cerebellar cortex, the hippocampus, and the amygdala. What this means is that a vast region of the brain receives NE from a very small number of cells in a single nucleus. These wildly bifurcating individual neurons release NE along the length of the fibers, not just at the terminals at the ends of the axon. So the activation of an NE neuron "sprinkles" NE over a wide region of tissue. Additionally, the neurons of the LC tend to fire in synchrony. Taken together, these anatomical and physiological facts suggest that this major NE pathway does not transmit detailed information but instead regulates some sort of general function. Arousal, mood, and the like are obvious possibilities.

In contrast to the LC, the other major NE pathways are less well defined. One of these is the *ventral NE bundle*. It originates in a number of smaller and less discrete nuclei, and its ascending axons terminate mainly in the hypothalamus. Most of these same nuclei also have descending pathways to the spinal cord, and these projections are importantly involved in the control of the autonomic nervous system.

Even before the organization of NE pathways in the brain was well understood, theorists hypothesized that NE was involved in the etiology of depression. Specifically, depression seems to entail some deficiency of NE in the central nervous system (Bunney & Davis, 1965; Schildkraut, 1965). The key evidence fueling such proposals entailed drug effects. Reserpine and tetrabenazine deplete NE, and they also produce depression. Conversely, drugs known to be effective antidepressants (the monoamine oxydase—MAO—inhibitor iproniazid and the tricyclic antidepressants) increase NE levels. In addition, a variety of studies have revealed that NE systems are activated when an animal or person is exposed to a stressor.

Evidence for Norepinephrine Involvement

All of the foregoing make NE an obvious choice as a potential mediator of learned helplessness effects. Let us take a look at the research that followed. In the first key study, Weiss, Stone, and Harrell (1970) showed that the NE content of the brain taken as a whole was reduced following a rat's exposure to inescapable shock but not to shock that could be avoided or escaped. They argued that this reduction in NE might be responsible for the poor escape learning of rats following their exposure to inescapable shock, and perhaps for other helplessness effects as well. Both escapable and inescapable shock may activate NE systems, but if the stressor is uncontrollable, the utilization of NE exceeds the capacity of NE neurons to synthesize new NE, thereby resulting in a net reduction in NE levels. This depletion persists for some period of time after the stressor has subsided, although NE levels eventually return to normal as utilization decreases and synthesis of new NE replaces what has been used. If the stressor is controllable, utilization remains at a level that can be matched by synthesis (see Anisman & Zacharko, 1986, for details). If normal NE levels are needed to maintain normal levels of motor output, then depleted NE should produce a motor deficit. The learned helplessness effect was thereby viewed as reflecting a motor deficit resulting from NE depletion.

There are several ways to directly test the hypothesis that reduced levels of NE are responsible for the learned helplessness effect observed among animals. The most obvious is to reduce NE by administering an appropriate drug to an animal rather than giving it inescapable shock, and then observing whether it shows deficits similar to those resulting from inescapable shock.

NE can be depleted in a number of ways. Some drugs (e.g., tetrabenazine and reserpine) directly deplete it in the nerve terminals, whereas others (e.g., FLA-63) prevent its synthesis in the first place. Depleting NE by either method causes rats to fail to learn to escape shock in shuttleboxes, just as we have seen for animals with prior exposure to inescapable shock (Anisman, Irwin, & Sklar, 1979).

Another obvious tactic is to use a drug that prevents inescapable shock from depleting NE. Does this intervention preclude helplessness effects such as failure to escape in a shuttlebox? The answer is yes. Agents that inhibit the enzyme responsible for breaking down NE (MAO inhibitors) prevent inescapable shock from depleting NE, and they also prevent rats from displaying the shuttlebox learning deficits that normally follow (Weiss, Glazer, & Pohorecky, 1976).

An alternative approach stems from considering what happens when NE levels are reduced. The presumed consequence is a reduced availability of NE at postsynaptic NE receptors, resulting in a reduced transmission at NE neurons. Whatever NE does when it is released from one cell to another (excitation or inhibition), there will be less of this activity at subsequent neurons. Thus, we should be able to overcome learned helplessness effects with pharmacological agents that activate these subsequent neurons, even if NE has been depleted by inescapable shock. By the same logic, we should be able to produce learned helplessness effects with pharmacological agents that block these subsequent neurons—that is, by preventing NE from activating them—even in the absence of any exposure to inescapable shock. Again, research produces precisely these results (e.g., Anisman, Suissa, & Sklar, 1980).

The research we have been describing measured NE in the rat's brain as a whole and administered drugs either systemically or into the cerebral ventricles. Drugs administered in these ways reach large segments of the brain. More recent research has attempted to isolate which regions of the brain and which NE systems might be of importance.

Jay Weiss and his colleagues have argued that changes in NE in the LC are crucial. When placed in water, rats previously exposed to inescapable but not to escapable shock cease swimming and become immobile sooner than do normal rats. This decrease in swimming is present for up to 48 hours after they have been exposed to inescapable shock, but not longer. Weiss et al. (1981) measured the duration of the NE changes produced by inescapable and escapable shock in a variety of separate brain regions. They found that only NE depletion in the LC had a time course that matched the swimming changes that the inescapable shock produced. Thus, NE was depleted in the LC for 48 hours, but not 72 hours after the termination of the shock.

Why? The LC contains the cell bodies of NE neurons, and these cell bodies themselves have receptors for NE. There are a number of different types of NE receptors, and these presynaptic receptors are of the alpha-2 class. If NE activates these "autoreceptors," it has the effect of inhibiting the activity of the neuron. Thus, NE released in the LC inhibits the activity of LC neurons. Recall that NE neurons release NE across their entire extent. When an LC NE neuron is activated, there is a negative feedback process that holds the activity in this pathway in check. If we continue this logic, a depletion of NE in the LC should *increase* the activity of NE neurons, because the source of the negative feedback has been reduced. This might lead to the release of excessive amounts of NE in the terminal fields of these neurons.

The next step in this line of research was to manipulate the LC directly. Weiss and his colleagues showed that *blocking* the depletion of NE in the LC of rats by directly infusing an MAO inhibitor prevented inescapable shock from producing immobility in the swim test. Moreover, they showed that *stimulating* alpha-2 receptors by the infusion of an appropriate drug overcame the immobility produced by inescapable shock. And finally, research shows that infusing a drug that blocks alpha-2 receptors again produces immobility (see Weiss & Goodman, 1985, for a summary).

Behavioral Implications

The data we have just reviewed suggest that NE is involved in mediating learned helplessness. What is the reason, then, for the debate surrounding the NE hypothesis? Part of it results from the view that neurochemical explanations are an alternative to the learned helplessness explanation of the helplessness effects (Chapter 2). NE has been the particular neurochemical usually cited in these arguments, and so the possible role of NE has been caught up in this more general controversy.

We think this has become a fruitless issue. The psychological processes involved in learned helplessness theory must be expressed in terms of the chemical and physiological processes of the brain. Evidence that there is a physiological mechanism for learned helplessness is hardly evidence for or against the viability of an explanation at a psychological level. Arguing about whether the learned helplessness effect is to be explained by reference to psychological or neurochemical processes is like arguing about whether what comes out of a shaker is salt or NaCl. The preferred level of description and explanation depends on the use to which one puts them. A complete understanding of any behavioral phenomenon requires that both psychological *and* physiological mechanisms be understood. That's a double bottom line, not psychology or physiology by itself.

Still, it is reasonable to ask whether NE systems mediate the sorts of psychological processes posited by learned helplessness theory. A second aspect of the NE debate emerges here. Proponents of a critical role for NE have argued that NE reduction results in motoric or movement deficits and that we should view helplessness effects as deficits in movement or response initiation, not in terms of altered cognition.

Whatever the role of NE in reducing motor activity or response initiation/maintenance, it might be useful to examine the other known functions of NE systems, particularly the LC-DB system. Indeed, various data indicate that this system is involved in the regulation of processes related to attention and vigilance (see Aston-Jones, 1985, for a review). Activation of the LC-DB system increases the signal-to-noise ratio of cells in the terminal regions of the DB (e.g., cortex, hippocampus) so that they can more selectively respond to "appropriate" input while filtering out irrelevancies. Animals with defects in this system are unable to inhibit their attention to irrelevant stimuli (e.g., Mason, 1980). Although there is controversy concerning these conclusions (e.g., Pisa & Fibiger, 1983), the LC-DB system does appear to play some role in attentional processes.

Along these same lines, remember that the learned helplessness effect involves a change in how the events that occur on a learning trial are processed, and that this change seems to involve a shift in attention so that animals differentially attend to external stimuli (Chapter 2). This suggests that NE might alter attentional processes, above and beyond any effects on response initiation and maintenance.

As we described in Chapter 2, inescapably shocked rats learn to escape in a Y-maze normally if external irrelevant cues are not present, but they learn only slowly if an irrelevant light cue is added to the situation. In contrast, escapably shocked and nonshocked rats are *not* disrupted by the irrelevant cue. They learn to ignore it, and they learn the Y-maze choice escape at their usual rate. These were the data that first suggested the attentional shift hypothesis. To begin to explore whether alterations in LC-DB activity might be involved in mediating this attentional effect, Minor, Pelleymounter, and Maier (1988) infused 6-hydroxydopamine—a neurotoxin that depletes NE—directly into the LC-DB of rats. The NE was depleted, and control animals were then given the Y-maze choice escape task, either with or without an irrelevant light cue. The control animals learned rapidly to choose the correct side to escape and were unaffected by whether or not an irrelevant cue was present. However, the group for which NE in the LC-DB had been depleted also learned rapidly when irrelevant cues were absent, but these animals were severely impaired when one was present. In fact, their performance did not improve at all over the 120 learning trials! What of the effects of the NE depletion on response speed? NE depletion had no effect whatsoever on the speed with which the animals responded.

GAMMA-AMINOBUTYRIC ACID

The case for the NE hypothesis is compelling. Will you be perplexed to discover that an equally compelling argument can be made for *gamma-aminobutyric acid (GABA)*? GABA is the major inhibitory neurotransmitter of the brain and is widely distributed throughout the nervous system. The brain contains more GABA than any other neurotransmitter. It binds to several different kinds of GABA receptors. These receptors produce inhibition when they are activated because they allow chloride to enter the neuron; chloride ions have a negative charge, and so the negativity of the inside of the cell membrane is increased even more than usual relative to the outside. This hyperpolarization of the neuron makes it more difficult for excitatory input to depolarize the cell, and therefore its firing is inhibited.

Evidence for Gamma-aminobutyric Acid Involvement

The first suggestion that GABA might play a role in learned helplessness was a series of studies conducted by Petty and Sherman (1981). In looking at slices of brain tissue taken from the hippocampus, they found that rats that had been exposed to inescapable but not escapable shock showed reduced levels of GABA. Furthermore, when GABA was injected into the hippocampus of rats, this reversed poor escape learning. And when a GABA-receptor antagonist was injected, this produced helplessness effects. Clearly, these findings support the idea that learned helplessness effects occur because inescapable shock somehow interferes with GABA function.

Recently, Drugan et al. (1989) provided even stronger support for this hypothesis by directly measuring the amount of chloride ion that travels into the neuron while it was being stimulated with a substance that activates GABA receptors. An animal previously exposed to inescapable shock showed a reduced amount of chloride in cortical neurons.

Another test of the GABA hypothesis is made possible by the fact that a number of other binding sites are associated with the GABA receptor–chloride channel complex. The most notable for our purposes here are benzodiazepine binding sites. *Benzodiazepines (BZs)* are minor tranquilizers such as Valium and Librium and are called BZs because of their chemical structure. These drugs exert an effect on GABA transmission by facilitating its binding to its receptor and thereby increasing the number of chloride channel openings induced by a given GABA concentration. So BZs do not influence the activity of GABAergic neurons in the absence of GABA but instead increase the amount of inhibition exerted by GABA that is present. BZs have a variety of effects on the brain and behavior. They reduce anxiety and fear, decrease seizure activity in the brain,[1] and relax muscles, all because they facilitate GABA action (Paul, Marangos, & Skolnick, 1981).

Given the facilitation of GABA produced by BZs, it is not surprising that if BZ is administered before a stressor, it reduces or prevents the usual effects of the stressor on GABA function (Biggio, 1983). If alterations in GABA are essential to producing learned helplessness effects, then BZ administration prior to inescapable shock should reduce or prevent learned helplessness. The administration of the BZs such as diazepam and chlordiazepoxide before inescapable shock does indeed prevent an animal's deficit in shuttlebox escape learning that normally occurs 24 hours after the shock experience (Drugan, Ryan, Minor, & Maier, 1984; Sherman, Allers, Petty, & Henn, 1979). Interestingly, if BZ is administered before the shuttlebox test rather than before inescapable shock, it does *not* eliminate or even reduce the learned helplessness effect. This suggests that the BZ/GABA system may be involved in initiating the processes responsible for learned helplessness effects as assessed by the animal's failure to escape from a shuttlebox, but it is not the system that mediates the animal's failure to perform at the time that it is tested. We return to this point later.

A final test of the role of GABA in learned helplessness is made possible by the curious fact that a class of compounds called *beta-carbolines* bind to the benzodiazepine site in such a way as to interfere with GABA action. Specifically, they make it more difficult for GABA to bind to its receptor and to open its chloride channels. This leads one to expect that beta-carbolines should have effects opposite to those of BZs: they should induce anxiety, facilitate seizure activity, and so on. Administration of beta-carbolines in animals leads to behaviors and physiological changes characteristic of fear and anxiety (Ninan et al., 1982). In humans, beta-carbolines lead to feelings of "uneasiness and impending doom" (Dorow, 1982).

Consistent with the notion that the processes involved in mediating learned helplessness involve interference with GABA transmission as an initiating event, the administration of the beta-carboline FG-7142 to rats produces a failure to learn to escape shock in a shuttlebox 24 hours later (Drugan, Maier, Skolnick, Paul, & Crawley, 1985). Again, we see the same deficit that is produced by exposing animals to inescapable shock. Moreover, the effect of FG-7142 proves to be mediated by BZ receptors because it is blocked by the simultaneous administration of a specific BZ-receptor antagonist (i.e., Ro15-1788). Finally, uncontrollable aversive events may impact on the entire complex by producing alterations at the BZ binding site. Exposure to inescapable shock alters the ability of the BZ receptor to bind this antagonist, which normally attaches itself to the receptor with very high affinity (Drugan et al., 1989).

Behavioral Implications

The following facts have been established:

- Substances that interfere with GABA transmission and produce anxiety can produce learned helplessness effects.
- Substances that facilitate GABA transmission and reduce anxiety can prevent learned helplessness effects when given before inescapable shock.
- Inescapable but not escapable shock reduces GABA function and alters BZ binding sites.

Taken together, these facts imply a relationship between anxiety and learned helplessness.

A number of questions thus arise. Does uncontrollable shock lead to more fear or anxiety (or both) than does controllable shock or stress? If so, does this state persist for some period of time following the termination of the stressor, and if so, for how long? If this sort of state is produced by uncontrollable stressors, does this occur because of some action at the BZ receptor? If a state of heightened fear or anxiety is produced, is this state responsible for other learned helplessness effects? We will consider each question in turn.

Fear and Anxiety.   Fear and anxiety are not easy to distinguish from each other. Fear generally refers to a complex of emotional, physiological, and behavioral reactions to signals of danger, be the signals innate or learned. Thus, fear is characterized by a sense of apprehension, physiological arousal (sympathetic nervous system and hypothalamus-pituitary-adrenal activation), and species-specific defensive behaviors, all in response to an explicit signal that danger is present. Anxiety involves many of the same emotional, physiological, and behavioral changes, but in circumstances in which a clearly definable stimulus for these reactions is not present. A typical definition is as follows.

> Anxiety is an emotion that signifies the presence of a danger that cannot be identified, or if identified, is not sufficiently threatening to justify the intensity of the emotion . . . Anxiety is different from fear. Fear signifies the presence of a *known* danger. The strength of fear is more or less proportionate to the degree of danger.   (Goodwin, 1986, p. 3)

Another way to look at this is to say that fear is driven by the environment. When the situation that elicited the fear no longer exists, the fear dissipates. Anxiety, however, is not so driven by stimulus input, and thus it can persist long after initiating events have ended.

Uncontrollable stressors produce more fear than do controllable ones. This was first suggested in a study by Mowrer and Viek (1954) in which rats given inescapable shock were more reluctant to eat when placed in the shock environment than were rats that had received escapable shock. These findings have been confirmed by Mineka, Cook, and Miller (1984). These researchers showed that rats exhibited greater levels of species-typical defensive behaviors in the presence of stimuli once associated with inescapable shock than did rats in the presence of stimuli once associated with equal amounts of escapable shock.

The rat's dominant behavioral reaction to either innate signals for danger (e.g., a cat) or learned signals (e.g., a tone indicating that a painful event such as electric shock is about to occur) is to freeze and become motionless. One can speculate that this reaction evolved because the absence of motion makes matters more difficult for a predator. At any rate, what is clear is that the degree of freezing varies in lockstep with factors arguably determining the amount of fear. Because it is so sensitive to variations in fear, freezing thus constitutes a good behavioral measure among rats (Fanselow & Bolles, 1979). Rats freeze more in an environment in which inescapable shocks occurred than in one in which equal amounts of escapable shock were delivered (Mineka et al., 1984).

These and other data make it clear that uncontrollable stressors produce more fear than do controllable stressors, but do they lead to an enduring state of anxiety? The experiments just described involved observing animals *in the situation* in which the stressor had occurred, and so the changes in their behavior were an immediate response to signals associated with the stressful event. If we return the subjects to this stressful environment at a later time, we would not resolve this issue. Any effects observed might simply reflect a conditioned response to the stimuli of the environment rather than a state that has persisted through time.

Here is an example that illustrates the point. Let's assume that you visit a city for the first time and are beaten and robbed on the subway. If you return a few years later and enter the subway, you are likely to become fearful, but this does not mean that the original event produced an emotional state that persisted for years. The emotional state undoubtedly dissipated after the original experience, only to be rearoused by the distinctive subway environment.

We have attempted to address this issue (Short & Maier, 1990). A number of behavioral measuring techniques have been used to assess anxiety in animals such as the rat. One that is particularly appropriate for our present purposes is the "social interaction" test developed by File and her colleagues (e.g., File, 1980). Here two rats unfamiliar with each other are placed together in an enclosed arena. The time they spend in active socializing is measured. These researchers have shown that both environmental and pharmacological manipulations known to reduce anxiety *increase* the time spent in active social interaction, whereas manipulations that increase anxiety *decrease* this kind of interaction. Moreover, agents that alter processes other than anxiety have little or no effect on the social interaction of such animals, thereby making this measure specific as well as sensitive. The major advantage for us is that this social interaction test does not involve shock or any other obviously aversive stimuli. Nor does it involve stimuli that have ever been associated with shock.

In the first experiment using this test to see if uncontrollable events produce an enduring state of anxiety, Short exposed rats to either escapable shock, yoked inescapable shock, or no shock at all. He then placed them in pairs in an enclosure 24 hours later. The enclosure was an open arena and bore no resemblance to the environment in which the shocks had been delivered. The shocks had occurred while the rats were in small Plexiglas restraining tubes. Bright illumination and a fairly loud masking noise were present. The enclosure was simply a large open wooden box, with dim illumination and no masking noise at all. Still, it is possible that the same odors might be present in both places. This matters because rats produce a distinctive "stress odor" when exposed to a stressor, and perhaps this might carry over to the second environment and serve as a conditioned stimulus. To minimize this possibility, the testing enclosure was in a different room from the one where the shocks had been administered. No shocks ever occurred in the testing room, and the enclosure was cleaned with an acetic acid solution after each test.

One potential difficulty with using the time spent in active social interaction as a measure is that animals freezing or remaining immobile cannot be simultaneously engaged in active interaction. Thus, it is typical practice to measure the amount of activity as well as the social interaction in the test enclosure and to correct the interaction measure for the amount of locomotion. Exposure to escapable shock had no effect on the time spent in social interaction as compared with nonshocked controls. However, those animals exposed to inescapable shock showed a reduced level of interaction. This effect was *not* minimized by correcting for the amount of locomotion.

If this behavioral change produced by the uncontrollable stressor represents a state of persistent anxiety, then perhaps it dissipates with time, eventually to vanish if testing is delayed long enough following the inescapable shock. In contrast, if the reduced social interaction represents a conditioned fear state, it should emerge even when testing is delayed for a long period of time. This is because conditioned fear is rearoused by stimuli present during the stressor even if long periods of time (e.g., months) intervene (Gleitman & Holmes, 1967). Short found that the decreased social interaction was present for up to two days after the inescapable shock occurred. After seven days elapsed, there were no signs of decreased social interaction.

The BZ Receptor. The foregoing research suggests that uncontrollable stressors do produce a state of heightened anxiety that persists for some period of time. Is this because of an action at the BZ receptor, and if so, what sort of action?

You may by now have wondered why the brain has receptors for minor tranquilizing drugs. Surely, evolution cannot have selected for a receptor for Valium. Much more plausible is the possibility that the brain contains its own endogenous substances (called *ligands*) that act on the BZ receptor. This is an active area of investigation, and researchers have suggested a number of possible candidates. We have already seen that there are artificial compounds, such as the BZs, that act at the BZ receptor to reduce anxiety *(agonists)* and others, such as the beta-carbolines, that increase anxiety *(inverse agonists)*. We can argue from considerations of adaptation for the likely existence of either endogenous anxiolytic (anxiety reducing) substances that are released in the brain in response to appropriate circumstances or endogenous anxiogenic (anxiety increasing) substances, or both. Interestingly, some have claimed that they have isolated an endogenous ligand in the brain for the BZ receptor that is anxiolytic (DeBlas & Sangameswaran, 1986), others have claimed to have isolated an endogenous ligand that is anxiogenic (Guidotti et al., 1983), whereas still others have argued for the existence of both types of endogenous ligands.

Several possibilities follow. Perhaps learning that one has no control over a stressor such as shock leads to the release of an endogenous anxiogenic substance that binds to the BZ receptor in a manner similar to that of the inverse agonists, thereby interfering with GABA function at some critical brain site(s) and thus causing anxiety. Or perhaps an opposite possibility is correct; maybe it is the existence of control that is key rather than its lack. Exposure to the aversive shock stimulus might produce anxiety, and learning that one has control might release an endogenous anxiolytic that binds to the BZ receptor in an agonist fashion to facilitate GABA function, thereby decreasing anxiety. Or perhaps both may occur.

Each of these possibilities—that control releases an anxiolytic and that lack of control releases an anxiogenic—makes the same prediction that the administration of a BZ before the shock experience should leave both groups with normal levels of anxiety when tested 24 hours later. Short and Maier (1990) found this to be the case. If the BZ diazepam is administered before the shock experience, both inescapably and escapably shocked animals engage in the same amount of social interaction as nonshocked controls.

The possibilities differ with regard to what they expect to happen if a BZ-receptor *antagonist* is administered before the shock exposure. A specific BZ-receptor antagonist (such as Ro15-1788) occupies the BZ receptor and prevents either agonists or inverse agonists from binding to the receptor but exerts very little in the way of intrinsic anxiolytic or anxiogenic activity itself. If lack of control releases an anxiogenic that is responsible for the observed effects on social interaction, then we should find that Ro15-1788 makes inescapably shocked animals behave as do their escapably shocked counterparts. It should reduce the increased anxiety in the inescapably shocked subjects because the anxiogenic cannot have an effect on the BZ receptors. It should have no effect on those that were escapably shocked. In contrast, if control releases an anxiolytic that is responsible for the controllability difference in social interaction, then Ro15-1788 should make escapably shocked animals behave as do those that were inescapably shocked. Not only should it increase the anxiety level in these animals that have control over the stressor, but it should have little effect on those animals that did not have control.

Short and Maier's results were clear. The administration of the BZ-receptor antagonist Ro15-1788 before the shock session altered the subsequent social interaction of only the inescapably shocked animals. Their level of anxiety was reduced to control levels, whereas that of the escapably shocked animals was not affected. This suggests that the lack of control activates an endogenous anxiogenic that acts at the BZ receptor.

These findings need not imply that control has no effects of its own on the BZ receptor. Other data suggest that control activates an endogenous anxiolytic, in addition to the lack of control activating an anxiogenic. For example, Drugan, McIntyre, Alpern, and Maier (1985) explored the impact of exposure to escapable and inescapable shock on the seizure activity produced by GABA-receptor antagonists. GABA antagonists lead to seizures, and these seizures are ameliorated by the anxiolytic BZ agonists and augmented by the anxiogenic BZ-receptor inverse agonists. As the above discussion suggests, exposure to inescapable shock increased the seizures produced by subsequent exposure to GABA antagonists. This mimics the effects of anxiogenics such as the beta-carbolines and supports the notion that inescapable shock releases endogenous anxiogenic inverse BZ agonists. However, escapable shock was not without its effect. Escapable shock actually protected the animals against the seizure-producing power of the GABA antagonists by reducing their seizures. Thus, escapable shock duplicated the effects of anxiolytic BZ agonists and suggests that control activates an endogenous anxiolytic. Perhaps both lack of control and the presence of control exert antagonistic effects on the BZ/GABA complex, thereby regulating anxiety in bidirectional fashion.

The Role of Fear and Anxiety in Learned Helplessness. From our preceding discussion, we conclude that:

- Uncontrollable stressors produce more fear than do equal amounts of controllable stressors.
- More fear is conditioned to cues that are present during the stressor experience if the stressor is uncontrollable.
- A state akin to anxiety persists for 48–72 hours after experience with the uncontrollable stressor.

Fear and anxiety can themselves produce many other behavioral changes. For example, fear motivates and organizes the occurrence of a whole series of defensive behaviors (Bolles & Fanselow, 1980) and can also alter cognitive processes such as attention (Eysenck, 1982).

Perhaps it is this intense fear/anxiety that is the proximate cause of such helplessness effects as poor escape learning and attentional shifts (see Chapter 2) rather than the processes proposed by learned helplessness theory. Stressor controllability or representations of controllability may not operate by directly altering incentive motivation and the direction of attention but by modulating fear. The fear then causes the behavioral symptoms we observe in animals. So, for example, poor shuttlebox escape learning might reflect the occurrence of high levels of fear-produced defensive behaviors, which obviously interferes with efficient learning. Williams and Lierle (1986) have proposed a similar hypothesis.

This is plausible. Animals that have experienced inescapable shock later engage in more fear-related behaviors when in shock situations than do animals that have experienced escapable shocks (Williams, 1987). However, the fact that these behaviors occur does not necessarily mean that they are the cause of the other outcomes, such as poor shuttlebox escape learning. Unfortunately, there are not that many ways to test this hypothesis. The most obvious strategy would be to employ conditions known to alter either fear/anxiety or the learned helplessness effect, and to determine whether the level of fear and the occurrence of the learned helplessness effect covary. If poor shuttlebox escape is a consequence of high levels of fear, then the two should go together. We should find that procedures that eliminate or reduce fear reduce or eliminate the learned helplessness effect, and that procedures that eliminate learned helplessness reduce or eliminate the heightened level of fear.

Maier (1990) used this strategy to explore the relationship between fear and learned helplessness. The goal was to measure the amount of fear and shuttlebox escape performance in the very same subjects. It has been argued that many behaviors reflect fear in a quantitative fashion. Disruptions in aggression, disruptions in "prod" burying, reductions in consummatory behavior, and freezing (the absence of all movement except that required for respiration) have all been seen as sensitive measures of fear. The only one of these that could be assessed during shuttlebox escape learning is freezing, and freezing has already been argued to be the single best measure (Fanselow & Lester, 1987). In any case, freezing does vary in a sensitive way with changes in parameters such as shock intensity, shock duration, and the number of shocks, all of which arguably modulate the level of experienced fear.

We should note that there are two different types of fear hypotheses. One involves a number of steps:

1. Uncontrollable stressors produce high levels of fear.
2. This leads to the conditioning of intense fear to stimuli present at the time of shock.
3. Stimuli similar to these stimuli (e.g., odors emanating from stressed animals) are present in the shuttlebox test situation.
4. These stimuli then elicit intense fear as a conditioned response.

The key idea here is that the experience of uncontrollable shock does not lead to an enduring change in the animal. Rather, it simply produces a great deal of fear at the time that it occurs. This fear becomes conditioned to cues present at the time.

The second fear hypothesis agrees that fear may become conditioned to cues. But it additionally proposes that the experience of uncontrollable shock may sensitize the physiological substrates that underlie fear/anxiety, and that this sensitization persists through time, gradually diminishing and dissipating. When the animal experiences shock during the shuttlebox test, the shock acts on a sensitized fear system in the case of the animal that has previously experienced uncontrollable stressors. Thus, enhanced levels of fear are produced. This sensitized state may be similar to anxiety.

The experiments, therefore, required the measurement of both types of fear. The shuttlebox environment would, of course, elicit conditioned fear. Various behaviors (including freezing) were therefore scored from the initial moment that the rat was placed into the shuttlebox. Care was taken to ensure that "stress odors" were always present. No experimental events were presented for the first 10 minutes of the session, and the rat's behavior was recorded. As for the second kind of fear, it would occur as the animals reacted to the shock in the shuttlebox. They were exposed to a small number of shock escape trials, and then further trials were postponed for 20 minutes while their behavior was again recorded. The session then progressed normally, and escape learning was measured.

What happened when animals were exposed to escapable shock, inescapable shock, or no shock and then tested 24 hours later as we have just described? There was only a small amount of freezing before the first shock, and there were no other behavioral signs of fear. However, the inescapably shocked animals froze more than did the others, indicating that a small amount of conditioned fear was transferred. The shock produced fear in all of the groups, but the fear was the greatest in the previously inescapably shocked rats, which remained almost completely frozen for the entire 20-minute observation period. Of course, these animals did not learn to escape the shock when the escape training trials took place after the observation period.

This initial experiment confirmed that fear and learned helplessness can be measured in the same subjects and that the two seem to go together. Additional experiments sought to determine whether they were indeed tied together or whether they might be *independent* consequences of uncontrollability. The most interesting of these experiments involved an examination of the effects of the BZ diazepam and the opiate-receptor antagonist naltrexone. Diazepam was examined because of its anxiolytic qualities, and naltrexone was examined because it prevents the escape learning deficit from occurring when it is given before shuttlebox testing (Whitehouse, Walker, Margules, & Bersh, 1983).

Here is an overview of this study. Rats were exposed to either uncontrollable shock or no shock at all and then tested 24 hours later, as we have already described. However, before the test they received an injection of either diazepam, naltrexone, or a control substance. Diazepam reduced the amount of freezing in inescapably shocked animals to the level of freezing observed in the non-shocked controls. This was true for freezing both before and after the shock was delivered. However, diazepam did not reduce the magnitude of the learned helplessness effect. The inescapably shocked animals still failed to learn to escape, even though diazepam had reduced their fear to that of the control animals. Naltrexone had no effect on freezing before the shock but increased it after

shock for the inescapably shocked rats. Naltrexone completely eliminated the learned helplessness effect; the inescapably shocked animals given this antagonist learned at a normal rate.

To recap, diazepam reduced fear during testing to control levels
but had no impact on the learned helplessness effect, whereas naltrexone increased fear following shock but eliminated the learned
helplessness effect. Some might object that testing fear at a different
point in the session might have yielded a different pattern, but this
was not the case (Maier, 1990). Others might argue that a different
measure of fear might produce a different pattern. Actually, other
measures of fear were tried, and the same results were found (Maier,
Ryan, Barksdale, & Kalin, 1988). These experiments together suggest that heightened fear during testing and the shuttlebox escape
learning deficit are not causally related. Both of them might be consequences of uncontrollability, but one certainly does not produce
the other.

What therefore can be said about the role of fear and anxiety in
learned helplessness? The evidence we reviewed at the beginning
of this section clearly suggests that the experience of intense fear
during the initial stressor exposure might be necessary to produce later
learned helplessness effects such as poor shuttlebox escape. Reducing the fear during the stressor with pharmacological agents that
act on the BZ/GABA system or by behavioral manipulations eliminates the shuttlebox escape learning deficit that occurs 24 hours later
(see Jackson & Minor, 1988). However, the level of fear during the
behavioral testing for learned helplessness is not important, and so
the behavioral effects such as poor shuttlebox learning are not produced by fear or behaviors produced by fear. Obviously, other behaviors may be a consequence of fear. For example, we have seen
that inescapably shocked animals freeze more than do escapably
shocked animals when tested later, and this differential outcome of
controllability is likely a consequence of fear at the time of the behavior. Here agents that reduce fear eliminate the behavioral difference. Some behaviors might be a consequence of conditioned fear
or of sensitized fear systems. We can distinguish these fear processes by allowing large amounts of time to lapse between shock
exposure and testing. Conditioned fear should persist; sensitized
fear should not (see Maier, 1990).

We can therefore derive the following scheme. Learning that one
has no control over a stressor intensifies fear and anxiety, possibly
by activating an anxiogenic endogenous ligand that acts at the BZ
receptor or some other site on the complex that contains the GABA

receptor. In addition, learning that one has control may reduce anxiety, possibly by activating an anxiolytic endogenous ligand that acts at the BZ receptor. These actions produce an alteration in the BZ/GABA complex that persists for some period of time and then diminishes. In the case of inescapably shocked animals, this can be described as a reduction in "GABAergic tone" (see Drugan & Holmes, 1991). This represents anxiety and a sensitized substrate for fear. In addition, fear is conditioned to the stimuli present during the shock exposure.

Some behaviors will be driven by conditioned fear and others by the sensitized-fear substrate. For example, the enhanced freezing in response to the shuttlebox environment produced by inescapable shock did not diminish if 72 hours were allowed to elapse between the inescapable shock and the shuttlebox testing. But the enhanced postshock freezing in the shuttlebox was completely eliminated (Maier, 1990). Recall that Short and Maier found that heightened anxiety persisted for only 48 hours after exposure to inescapable shock. Other behaviors will not be a consequence of fear or anxiety at all. Clearly, the BZ/GABA changes that uncontrollable stressors produce act on some other neurochemical system(s), which is then responsible for some behavioral changes such as poor shuttlebox escape. Fear and alterations in the BZ/GABA system might be important initiating events, but they might not always be direct causes.

Does this mean that all learned helplessness effects are at least traceable to the animal having once experienced intense fear or anxiety? In the last chapter, we argued that some consequences of uncontrollability are caused by cognitive changes such as attentional shifts that are the direct result of the animal learning that behavior and shock termination are independent, whereas other consequences result from motivational and emotional processes. Those behavioral changes directly produced by cognitive alterations need not depend on any initial experience of intense fear or anxiety. Recall that poor Y-maze choice learning represents such a behavioral change. It is noteworthy that the administration of a BZ before inescapable shock does not eliminate or even reduce the impact of the uncontrollable stressor on subsequent choice escape learning, nor does prior administration of an agent that produces intense anxiety (beta-carboline) lead to deficits in choice escape (Maier, 1992).

In sum, organisms learn about the characteristics of stressors to which they are exposed. This learning itself produces a set of cognitive changes that lead to a set of behavioral outcomes. This learning also impacts on those physiological systems that are involved in the mediation of fear and anxiety. They are altered in several ways, and the functioning of these systems then leads to a set of behavioral outcomes. Fear and anxiety processes in turn impact on other neurochemical systems and alter them, with these systems being responsible for yet other behavioral outcomes.

Relation to Noradrenergic Systems.   We have discussed the role of NE and GABA, and it is only natural to ask whether the two might be related. Anatomical considerations certainly suggest such a possibility. Of special relevance to our discussion is the fact that GABAergic neurons (neurons that synthesize and release GABA from their terminals) terminate on noradrenergic LC neurons and inhibit their firing (Cedarbaum & Aghajanian, 1978). Moreover, electrical stimulation of the LC produces behavioral symptoms of fear and anxiety in monkeys, and its destruction produces a placid and non-reactive state in animals such that they fail to respond with fear to danger signals (Redmond, 1987). Interestingly, the anxiety-arousing effect of beta-carboline is reduced by agents that inhibit NE LC activity (Crawley et al., 1985).

   The implication here is that a reduction in GABA function might produce anxiety because this decreases tonic or phasic inhibition (GABA is an inhibitory neurotransmitter) of NE LC neurons, thereby allowing greater increases in the activity of these neurons in response to excitatory input. Interfering with GABA might have the effects we described in the prior sections because this removes a "brake" on LC neurons. This neatly integrates the research implicating NE with the research implicating GABA. Moreover, there is good evidence that NE systems remain sensitized for some period of time after inescapable shock has been delivered. We saw the same effects with fear systems defined behaviorally. Anisman and Sklar (1979) found that the depletion in NE produced by inescapable shock recovers quickly. However, for some period of time, subsequent exposure to a small amount of shock insufficient to alter NE in control animals is able to redeplete NE in animals previously given inescapable shocks. Even though they are seemingly recovered, their NE systems remained supersensitive to subsequent stressors.

   Unfortunately for elegance, the NE cells in the LC are not the only likely locus of BZ/GABA action. Ascending serotonergic (5-HT) projections from the midbrain raphe nuclei are also involved in the anxiolytic effects of BZs and other compounds. These nuclei give rise to the 5-HT innervation of structures known to be intimately involved in the regulation of emotion. The dorsal raphe nucleus possesses receptors for GABA and BZs. If GABA or BZs are applied directly to the dorsal raphe, they reduce the release of 5-HT in the terminal fields of the ascending neurons (Soubrie, Blas, Ferron, & Glowinski, 1983). Moreover, we know that these projections are critical in producing some of the anxiolytic effects of the BZs (Soubrie, Thiebot, Jobert, & Hamon, 1981).

A case could be made for either the NE LC or the 5-HT raphe as a mediator of the anxiety that is produced by uncontrollable stressors. In an attempt to begin to study this issue, Short and Maier (1990) tested inescapably shocked and control rats for subsequent anxiety using the social interaction test as described earlier. Recall that the systemic administration of the BZ-receptor antagonist Ro15-1788 before the inescapable shock prevented the heightened anxiety that would normally be observed 24 hours later. Here we microinjected Ro15-1788 directly into either the LC or the dorsal raphe nucleus. Simplicity calls for an effect of diazepam when administered into the LC but not when injected into the dorsal raphe. Alas, the results were quite the opposite! Nature appears at odds with our human desires for parsimony. Clearly, much more work is needed before the anatomy of our effects is understood.

ENDOGENOUS OPIATES

Few discoveries in the last several decades have created as much excitement as finding out that the brain and spinal cord contain specific receptors for opiatelike molecules and endogenous substances that bind to and activate these receptors. It had long been suspected that the central nervous system had specific receptors for opiates (because opiates such as morphine are frequently only effective in one of their molecular conformations and because their effects can be reversed by specific antagonists such as naloxone). But it was not until 1974 that researchers provided the first convincing support for this hypothesis. This work initiated the search for the endogenous ligand for these receptors, and researchers in 1975 isolated two substances from the brain with actions similar to that of morphine (Hughes et al., 1975). They named these leu- and met-enkephalin (enkephalin meaning "in the head"). Other brain opioids were subsequently discovered, and the group as a whole has sometimes been called *endorphins* (*endo*genous mo*rphine*).

The discovery of opiate receptors and endogenous opiates raised obvious questions about their possible function. Pain was a natural area for investigation because opiates act as analgesics. It was already known that electrical stimulation of a number of discrete sites in the brain, mainly in and around the periaqueductal gray, produces a profound reduction in pain (Mayer, Wolfle, Akil, Carder, & Liebeskind, 1971), and it makes sense that these sites might contain opiate receptors and that their stimulation might release endorphins. This idea was soon supported by a variety of evidence. These sites do indeed contain opiate receptors and endorphins. Electrical stimulation analgesia is reversed by the administration of the opiate antagonist naloxone. There is also cross-tolerance[2] between electrical stimulation and opiate analgesia, a point to which we return shortly (e.g., Akil, Mayer, & Liebeskind, 1976).

This all led to the view that the brain contains an endogenous system that inhibits pain. There are a number of ways in which such a system could function. One way would be for its activation to "damp" the pain message in the brain once the message had arrived from the spinal cord, where the pain signal originates. Another way would be for the activation of the system in the brain to send messages down to the spinal cord, where the descending message initiates processes that inhibit the ascending transmission of the pain signal. A great deal of evidence has accumulated that indicates that endogenous pain-inhibition sites in the midbrain and medulla produce analgesia by sending messages down to the spinal cord, where the ascending transmission of the pain message is inhibited (see Basbaum & Fields, 1984, for a review). Moreover, opiate receptors and endogenous opiates play a critical role in pain modulation at the level of both the brain and the spinal cord.

The existence of endogenous pain-inhibition systems suggests that there are environmental circumstances that produce analgesia. It is unlikely that evolution selected for neural systems that could be activated only by the administration of an opiate such as morphine or by electrical stimulation from implanted electrodes. If there is pain-inhibition circuitry in the brain that involves endogenous opiates, something should be able to activate it.

There had been reports that exposure to stressors might activate analgesia systems (Hayes, Bennett, Newlon, & Mayer, 1978), and this led one of us (SFM) to investigate whether stressor controllability might be of importance here. There was a certain intuitive appeal in the idea that if one learned that a stressor was uncontrollable, then this learning would activate endogenous opiate systems. After all, if one *can* control an aversive event, then the best strategy for coping is by exerting the behavioral control one has available. However, when the event is uncontrollable and behavioral coping is not possible, it makes sense for one to conserve energy and withdraw from the situation as much as possible until such time as behavioral control becomes possible (see Engel & Schmale, 1972). It makes little sense to expend valuable energy resources attempting to control an event that is uncontrollable. Obviously, conservation and withdrawal in the face of a painful event are difficult. It would be much easier if the pain could be blunted. Moreover, opiates tend to be energy conserving in nature (Margules, 1979). They slow down one's digestion and respiration, close sphincters, and reduce the body's set point for temperature. Perhaps the analgesia produced by opiates is just a part of a larger reaction to conserve resources.

Exposure to uncontrollable stressors such as inescapable shock produced an analgesic state, and the analgesia was as potent as that produced by moderately large doses of morphine (Jackson, Maier, & Coon, 1979). For the reader unfamiliar with this literature, pain sensitivity/reactivity in animals such as the rat is typically measured with reflex tests such as the tail-flick to radiant heat. Here a small spot of radiant heat is focused on the animal's tail, which reflexively moves away. The tail is flicked at the moment when the heat on the tail builds to the point that it becomes painful. When animals are given analgesic drugs such as morphine, they flick their tails more slowly or not at all. The degree to which analgesic drugs inhibit the tail-flick to radiant heat correlates exactly with the analgesic potency of the drugs as assessed by human self-report.

Not only did exposure to inescapable shock produce an analgesic state, but the physiological substrate responsible for the analgesia also remained sensitized for 48 to 72 hours after the shock. During this period, a small amount of shock insufficient by itself to produce analgesia rapidly produced analgesia in animals previously exposed to inescapable shock. This effect is specific to inescapable shock. It is *not* produced by exposure to escapable or controllable shock. Finally, the inhibition of the tail-flick reflex produced by inescapable shock is a true analgesia, meaning that it is specific to *painful input* to the tail, not an inhibition of the reflex per se. The rats withdraw their tail in response to a nonpainful touch with a normal latency. Moreover, suppose we make a lesion in the pathway that descends from the midbrain and medulla to the spinal cord. This pathway carries the pain-inhibition message produced by morphine and electrical stimulation. Such a lesion abolishes the analgesia produced by inescapable shock (Watkins et al., 1984). Thus, we can conclude that pain transmission is inhibited by inescapable shock.

The demonstration of this analgesia led us to pose several ques-

tions. The first was whether the analgesia was really a learned helplessness effect, that is, sensitive to control. Recall from Chapter 2
that experiencing control over a stressor before exposure to uncontrollable stressors can immunize the subject against learned helplessness produced by the uncontrollable stressor. In addition, force-
able exposure to controlling the stressor after experiencing
uncontrollable stressors can eliminate learned helplessness altogether. We thus set out to determine whether these immunization
and therapy effects occur with regard to the analgesic consequences
of inescapable shock. Exposure to escapable shock before inescapable shock prevented the development of the analgesia in response
to inescapable shock, and exposure to escapable shock after inescapable shock eliminated it (Moye, Hyson, Grau, & Maier, 1983).
Exposure to inescapable shock before or after inescapable shock
merely increased the analgesia, so the immunization and therapy
depended on whether the shock was controllable. These experiments strongly support the notion that the analgesia produced by
inescapable shock is a learned helplessness effect, not just due to
stress. This is because the procedures that eliminated the analgesia
were themselves stressful. Controllable shock may well be less
stressful than uncontrollable shock, but it is still stressful (see Maier,
Ryan, Barksdale, & Kalin, 1988).

Complications soon emerged in this line of research. The first came
from demonstrations that other stressors also produced analgesia
but that the analgesia often did not seem to involve endogenous
opiates (e.g., Hayes, Bennett, Newlon, & Mayer, 1978). The analgesia apparently did not involve opiate mechanisms because the analgesia is not reversed by the opiate antagonists naloxone and naltrexone and is not cross-tolerant with morphine. This led to the
view that there were multiple endogenous pain-modulation systems, with some involving opiate mechanisms and some not (Watkins & Mayer, 1982).

The next step was to determine whether the analgesia produced
by inescapable shock was reversed by opiate antagonists and whether
it was cross-tolerant with morphine. What did we learn? The analgesia was completely blocked by naloxone and naltrexone and completely prevented by prior repeated exposures to morphine (cross-
tolerance).

This all led to the idea that learning that one has no control over
a stressor activates endogenous opiate systems, thereby activating
the brain's endogenous pain-inhibition systems. Moreover, this activation seems to leave the systems involved in a sensitized state

for some period of time. Perhaps opiate receptors become sensitized, or perhaps more opiates are released later on in response to shock.

There are a number of interesting ways to test this argument. If inescapable shock really does what it does vis-à-vis analgesia because it activates an endogenous opiate system, then it should be possible to produce the inescapable shock effects without using inescapable shock at all. The same effects should occur if the endogenous opiate system is activated in a more direct fashion. It is difficult to know what activates opiate systems, but one thing does for certain—opiates. So we should be able to mimic the effects of inescapable shock by simply administering morphine. Obviously, morphine will produce analgesia. However, recall that inescapable shock does not just produce analgesia. It also sensitizes analgesia systems so that a little bit of shock normally not enough to produce analgesia will do so, say 24 hours later. Our logic thus demands that a little bit of shock produces analgesia 24 hours after the administration of morphine (the direct analgesic effects of morphine only last an hour or two), and it indeed does (Grau, Hyson, Maier, Madden, & Barchas, 1981).

Are you still unconvinced? The rationale of the above experiment is that morphine and inescapable shock can substitute for each other. What blocks the analgesic effects of inescapable shock? A prior exposure to escapable or controllable shock. Thus, we are led to a rather strange prediction. Prior exposure to escapable but not inescapable shock should *block* the analgesic effect of morphine. Startlingly, this turns out to be the case (Grau et al., 1981). Moreover, we should be able to turn the rationale around. If uncontrollable stressors sensitize opiate systems, then animals recently exposed to inescapable but not to escapable shock should show exaggerated analgesic reactions and be supersensitive to morphine.[3] And this is what happens (Grau et al., 1981). Finally, we discovered that animals exposed to inescapable shock show exaggerated withdrawal reactions from morphine (Williams, Drugan, & Maier, 1984).

The convincing case for endogenous opiate involvement in the analgesia produced by uncontrollable stressors leads to the next complication. We have already noted that stressors often produce a "nonopiate" analgesia. What, then, determines which kind of analgesia occurs? Perhaps stressors that are uncontrollable and presented extensively enough to allow the animal to learn that the stressor is uncontrollable produce an opioid analgesia (for a review see Maier, 1986). And perhaps stressors that are controllable or not presented often enough to allow the animal to learn that they are uncontrollable produce nonopioid analgesia. Thus, for example, stressors that produce nonopioid analgesia do not lead to behavioral learned helplessness effects such as poor shuttlebox escape; stressors that produce opioid analgesia do lead to poor shuttlebox escape learning (Maier, Sherman, Lewis, Terman, & Liebeskind, 1983). It takes 80 to 100 inescapable shocks to produce learned helplessness effects, and it takes 80–100 inescapable shocks to produce opioid analgesia.

A final complication is worth noting. Although 5 to 60 inescapable shocks produce nonopioid analgesia, fewer shocks, such as 1 or 2, produce an opioid analgesia in that the analgesia is reversed by naltrexone and naloxone. Obviously, 1 or 2 inescapable shocks could not lead to the learning of uncontrollability. Watkins, Wiertelak, and Maier (1992) have explored this seeming contradiction and have resolved it. The naltrexone and naloxone studies had employed systemic injections of the drug. Here the drug gets to both brain and spinal cord opiate receptors. In our experiments, naltrexone was delivered directly to the brain or to the spinal cord. It reversed the analgesia after 1 or 2 shocks when administered to the spinal cord but had no effect on the analgesia when administered to the brain. In contrast, the analgesia after 80 and 100 shocks was reversed by naltrexone administered to the brain, as well as to the spinal cord. Thus, only the conditions that produce learned helplessness produce analgesia that involves brain opiate processes. What does this all mean?

The role of the nervous system in analgesia provides a hint. The opioid analgesia after 1 or 2 shocks and the nonopioid analgesia after 5 to 60 inescapable shocks are mediated at a relatively low level of the nervous system. They occur in undiminished form in decerebrate preparations (Watkins et al., 1984) and even in animals that are anesthetized, thereby precluding any cortical function. The analgesia here represents a reaction driven by the sensory input itself acting directly upon pain-inhibition circuitry at spinal and/or brainstem levels of the brain (Maier, 1989a). In contrast, the opioid hypoalgesia produced by 80 to 100 inescapable shocks is completely prevented by manipulations such as anesthesia (Maier, 1989a) and requires the operation of higher levels of the nervous system and "conscious processing" of the events. Here the analgesia is not produced by the sensory stimulation itself but by what the animal has learned about the events.

We can speculate that the analgesia that results from the aversive events themselves aids the animal in its attempts to behaviorally cope with or control the events in question. A reduction in the painfulness of aversive events might promote more efficient defensive behavior designed to deal with the situation at hand (see Fanselow, 1986). However, if the events cannot be controlled and the animal comes to appreciate that this is so, a different mechanism may be called into play. This analgesia may well be designed to be protective and to promote conservation of energy and withdrawal. The behavioral characteristics of the analgesias are consistent with these speculations. The analgesia that is produced by 1 to 60 inescapable shocks is relatively brief and dissipates quickly once the shocks are terminated. Moreover, the analgesia is easily disrupted by removing the animal from the dangerous situation. In contrast, the analgesia produced by 80 to 100 inescapable shocks lasts a long time once the shocks are terminated and is not disrupted by removing the subject from the shock situation. Once initiated, it lasts for a long time, is very potent, and is not easy to stop (Drugan, Moye, & Maier, 1982; Maier & Watkins, 1991).

You might wonder how these changes in pain systems and endogenous opiates relate to the issues discussed earlier in the chapter. Do these changes have anything to do with the NE system, the BZ/GABA system, fear, and the like? They do. The intense fear and anxiety produced by uncontrollable aversive events are an important initiating step in the cascade of events producing many of the "noncognitive" consequences of uncontrollability. The ultimate cause of the behavioral outcome we measure (i.e., shuttlebox escape) might be something else set in motion by fear-produced activity in the BZ/GABA system, but fear is nonetheless involved early in the chain.

In keeping with this overall scheme, we find that BZs such as diazepam prevent the analgesia produced in rats by 80 to 100 inescapable shocks, and so fear is critical here as well (Maier, 1990). As you might expect, diazepam does not reduce the analgesia produced by fewer shocks. We have argued that analgesia in this instance is determined by interactions between the physical stressor and brainstem mechanisms, not by learning about uncontrollability. Thus, once again fear and anxiety are implicated. Intense fear may activate a brain opiate system that produces analgesia. In addition, the LC sends neurons to the spinal cord, which may be involved in producing analgesia at that level. There are enough connections between the systems we discussed earlier and pain mechanisms to expect with some confidence that they are all related.

TRANSMITTERS, NEUROMODULATORS, AND HORMONES

We have focused here on NE, GABA, and opioids because the evidence for their involvement is extensive and because this focus allowed us to make some general points. However, there is also good evidence that learned helplessness entails acetylcholine, serotonin, dopamine, and hormones such as adrenal corticosteroids. Experiments indicate that these substances are differentially altered by stressors that vary in their controllability, that pharmacological manipulation of these substances before exposure to uncontrollable stressors alters the impact of the stressor on some behavior, and that the behavior can be produced by the reverse pharmacological manipulation.

What are we to make of this evidence for the potential involvement of such an overwhelmingly large and diverse number of systems? This state of affairs is especially distressing for simplophiles such as ourselves. It may be worthwhile to ask whether there might not be a key player—some process, system, neurochemical, or brain region, for example—from which all or many of the other changes flow. Our ensuing discussion is purely speculative, but we feel it is important to convey to you that simplification is, at least in principle, possible.

CORTICOTROPIN RELEASING HORMONE (CRH)

We start by asking whether there is anything that seems to integrate the organism's complex array of physiological responses to stressors. In other words, is there a set of physiological changes produced by *all* challenges to the organism's well-being? This is how stress has long been defined, as all the peripheral changes that prepare the organism for "fight or flight" (Selye, 1956).

These changes have two basic components: activation of the pituitary-adrenal axis and of the autonomic nervous system. *Adrenocorticotropic hormone (ACTH)* and other products (e.g., beta-endorphin) are released into the circulation from the anterior pituitary, and ACTH stimulates the synthesis and release of glucocorticoids such as cortisol (in humans) or corticosterone (in rats) from the adrenal cortex. Glucocorticoids have a variety of general metabolic effects throughout the body and are thought to be the basis of many of the body's adaptive responses to threat. Activation of the sympathetic arm of the autonomic nervous system leads to the release of the catecholamines epinephrine and norepinephrine into the circulation by the adrenal medulla, and norepinephrine from sympathetic terminals that innervate a variety of organs. This produces altered activity in many peripheral organs such as the heart and blood vessels. The catecholamines released from the adrenal medulla and specific sympathetic neural activity are responsible for the increased heart rate and blood pressure that occur during stress.

How does the brain activate these changes? The pituitary gland sits at the base of the brain and receives a blood supply from the brain called the hypophysial (pituitary) portal blood system. This blood supply comes from the median eminence of the hypothalamus, and it has long been known that the hypothalamus releases some substance into the hypophysial portal blood system that induces the synthesis and release of ACTH from the anterior pituitary. This substance, called *corticotropin releasing factor (CRF)* or *hormone (CRH),* is manufactured by cells in the *paraventricular nucleus (PVN)* of the hypothalamus (Vale, Spiess, Rivier, & Rivier, 1981). The regulation of ACTH release from the pituitary involves influences other than CRH, but it is fair to say that CRH is the dominant controlling factor. This conclusion is supported by the finding that antiserum to CRH almost completely blocks the pituitary-adrenal response to stress (Rivier, Rivier, & Vale, 1982). So the brain activates the neuroendocrine pituitary-adrenal cascade by releasing CRH from the PVN.

How about the activation of the sympathetic nervous system? Here the situation is more complex, and there are multiple controls. However, they are not unrelated to what we already know. First, the PVN sends fibers directly to nuclei in the brainstem and spinal cord that are involved in sympathetic nervous system regulation. Some of these even come from the same region of the PVN where CRH is produced and may contain CRH. Moreover, reciprocal projections exist between brainstem autonomic nuclei such as the nucleus tractus solitarius and PVN CRH-containing cells (Cunningham & Sawchenko, 1988). Nuclei such as the nucleus tractus solitarius also receive input from visceral organs. The PVN and its CRH system are well situated to be a major site of integration of visceral input and output.

Consistent with the above argument, if very small amounts of CRH are injected into the brain, a pattern of sympathetic nervous system changes is produced that is highly similar to those produced by stress (see Fisher, 1991, for a review). There is an increase in plasma levels of epinephrine and norepinephrine, increased blood pressure, and increased heart rate. Moreover, the details of how the cardiovascular changes are produced by CRH are quite similar to how stress produces them. CRH shunts blood from the mesentery to skeletal muscle and increases cardiac output (Fisher, 1991). The effects of CRH that are produced by injecting it into the brain are *not* mediated by leakage of the CRH into the periphery or by activation by the CRH of the pituitary-adrenal system. So intravenous injections of antiserum to CRH do not alter the ability of CRH administered into the brain to stimulate sympathetic activity (Brown & Fisher, 1985). Anti-CRH serum administered peripherally neutralizes all peripheral CRH, so any effect remaining must be centrally mediated. And removal of the pituitary does not reduce the effects of centrally administered CRH on sympathetic outflow (Fisher, Jessen, & Brown, 1983).

Some of the impact of CRH on autonomic outflow from the brain may be of extrahypothalamic origin. CRH-containing neurons (Swanson, Sawchenko, Rivier, & Vale, 1983) and CRH receptors (De Souza, 1987) are not restricted to the hypothalamus and occur in numerous structures known to be involved in processes related both to stress and to autonomic function. The amygdala (see below) may be of special relevance here. It contains large amounts of CRH, and its various projections provide multiple routes by which CRH can produce its effects on autonomic function.

Not surprisingly, the role of CRH in mediating the behavioral consequences of stressor exposure is less clear (see Cole & Koob, 1991, for a review). Administration of CRH directly into the brain produces some behavioral changes that are reflective of anxiety and are similar to behavioral changes produced by stressors (e.g., Britton, Koob, Rivier, & Vale, 1982), but it is unknown whether CRH might produce helplessness effects. Moreover, administration of CRH antagonists or antiserum to CRH can block some of the behavioral effects of stressors such as restraint (Berridge & Dunn, 1987), but whether helplessness effects are blocked is unknown.

But what of NE systems, the LC, the BZ/GABA complex, and so on? Interestingly, CRH has known interactions with each of these. LC neurons turn out to make contact with the terminals of CRH-containing neurons, and CRH administration into the brain increases both the activity of NE systems (Dunn & Berridge, 1987) and the firing rate of LC neurons (Valentino, Foote, & Aston-Jones, 1983). Moreover, a number of stressors have been shown to produce increases in CRH concentration in the LC (Chappell et al., 1986), and CRH antagonists reduce or prevent the increase in LC firing rates produced by stressors (Valentino & Wehby, 1988). Clearly, the impact of stressors on the activity of the NE LC system could be mediated by CRH release at the LC.

Conversely, some of the behavioral effects of CRH could be mediated by its effects on NE systems. Some of the anxiogenic effects of CRH are blocked by antagonists of NE receptors (Cole & Koob, 1988), and others are blocked by the BZ-receptor antagonist Ro15-1788 (Britton, Lee, & Koob, 1988). CRH may therefore serve as an initiating event that acts on other systems, which in turn mediate behavioral and emotional outcomes such as fear and anxiety.

Our initial discussion of CRH focused on the PVN of the hypothalamus. The PVN is in a good position to respond to visceral inputs and the like and to send messages regulating endocrine and autonomic outflow. It is easy to see how it could be a site of integration for somatic inputs and outputs. However, it is difficult to see how the PVN could be a site of integration for the more "cognitive" or learned aspects of stressor phenomena. For example, how could the PVN be directly sensitive to a dimension such as stressor controllability? It is intriguing that the amygdala has proven to be a major site containing CRH. The amygdala is a major component of what is called the limbic system. This system provides a kind of interface between the neocortex and regions within the brainstem and spinal cord that control somatomotor, visceromotor, and neuroendocrine outflow from the brain. The amygdala has direct anatomical connections with the neocortex on the one hand, and the PVN and autonomic nuclei in the brainstem on the other.

The amygdala is considered a key region for mediating the experience and expression of fear and anxiety. Its stimulation produces fearlike behavior as well as elevated plasma catecholamines and glucocorticoids, whereas its destruction eliminates conditioned fear. For example, destruction of the amygdala reduces the heart rate increase that occurs to a tone that has been associated or paired with shock, but it does not reduce the heart rate increase produced by the shock itself (Iwata, LeDoux, Meeley, Arneric, & Reis, 1986). In other words, the amygdala seems to be involved with conditioned fear but not with the reflex response to shock.

The amygdala projects to many target regions, and these different target regions might then be, in turn, responsible for the expression of different aspects of fear (Gloor, 1978). It can be noted here that there is a major CRH output system from the amygdala (Gray, 1989), that the amygdala has a high density of BZ receptors (Niehoff & Kuhar, 1983), and it has reciprocal connections with the LC and the raphe nuclei. Moreover, as already stated, it communicates to the hypothalamus and brainstem and spinal cord autonomic nuclei. Finally, the amygdala projects to regions of the brain (the periaqueductal gray) that contain opiate receptors and endogenous opiates and are involved in the descending control of pain.

The amygdala is in an excellent position to translate learned aspects of a stress experience into behavioral, endocrine, and autonomic changes. Perhaps the hypothalamic areas respond directly to visceral aspects of stressor exposure, thus controlling reflexive or unconditioned responses to these stressors. And perhaps the amygdala acts as an interface adding learned features such as controllability. Perhaps CRH systems are key early events in this process. Maybe controllability has important effects on the loops we have suggested. If so, the widespread changes produced by controllability are no longer so surprising.

ISSUES OMITTED

This chapter has been highly selective, leaving many topics unmentioned so far. We note in passing the most important of these.

Acute versus chronic exposure. All of the discussion in this chapter has pertained to the effects of a single session of exposure to a stressor differing in controllability. This follows from the existing research literature. However, the stressors in real life are often chronic, persisting for long periods of time or recurring frequently. It is therefore reasonable to ask whether chronic or repeated exposures to an uncontrollable stressor produce the same biological changes as do acute exposures, and whether the same biological mechanisms are responsible for any behavioral changes we may observe after such chronic exposure.

As a general rule, biological systems undergo *compensatory* changes when repeatedly challenged. That is, there are usually mechanisms in place that can be recruited to oppose any alteration from baseline or normal functioning that the perturbing factor might produce. For example, we have already noted that inescapable shock increases the utilization of NE in the brain to the degree that utilization outpaces the synthesis of new NE, resulting in a net depletion. But if the subject is exposed to repeated daily sessions of inescapable shock, the shock no longer depletes NE (Weiss, Glazer, & Pohorecky, 1976). Instead, the activity of the enzyme that limits the rate of synthesis of NE (tyrosine hydroxylase) increases, so that now after chronic exposure NE synthesis can keep up with its utilization. So one can expect that most, if not all, biological consequences of uncontrollable stressors will shift from acute to chronic exposure. So too will some of the behavioral consequences.

Receptor function. Most of our discussion has focused on alterations in neurotransmitters and hormones. However, these substances exert their effects by acting at receptors, both postsynaptic and presynaptic. Receptors are not fixed and static entities but dynamic sites that change rapidly in response to fluctuations in the neurotransmitters, modulators, and hormones to which they are sensitive. Both the number of receptors expressed on the cell membrane and the affinity of the receptor itself for the substances that bind to it can change quickly (on the order of minutes), and these changes can persist for relatively long periods of time (days, perhaps weeks).

A single session of inescapable shock can produce receptor changes. Weiss, Woodmansee, and Maier (1992) found that alpha-2 NE receptors in the LC are upregulated after a single session of inescapable shock and that this change persists for at least 3 days. The behavioral changes produced by uncontrollable stressors might be a product of receptor changes rather than of alterations in neurotransmitter function per se. Moreover, not only do receptor numbers and affinity change, but the coupling of the receptor to further "downstream" processes in the neuron can also change. Thus, it is even possible that receptor numbers and affinity do not change, but the binding of the neurotransmitter to the receptor can have an altered effect on the cell. Much of the "action" is probably occurring at these levels.

Modulatory impact of organismic variables. There are a number of characteristics of animals (including human beings) that determine exactly how uncontrollable stressors impact on psychology and physiology.

1. *Individual differences.* Not all animals exposed to an uncontrollable stressor show learned helplessness effects. For example, only about two-thirds of rats exposed to inescapable shock later show poor escape learning. An important issue is whether one can identify factors that distinguish animals that are and are not susceptible to these effects. One important factor seems to be dominance status. The animal's preexisting tendency to be dominant can be used to predict who will and who will not be susceptible. Surprisingly, however, it is the submissive animals that are not susceptible (Fleshner, Peterson, & Maier, 1992).

2. *Sex.* The sex of the subject modulates the impact of the uncontrollable stressor, as does the hormonal status and estrous stage of the female (Ryan & Maier, 1988).

3. *Stage of life.* Uncontrollable stressors may have different effects at different stages of development. There may be times when the impact is much more profound than at other times.

WHAT WE KNOW

A remarkable amount of knowledge concerning the biology of learned helplessness has been produced in a short time. After all, the original studies by Weiss of the neurochemical consequences of shock controllability are only twenty years old. Many pieces of the puzzle have been identified, and a conceptual outline is starting to emerge. We know in some detail about the involvement of NE, the BZ/GABA complex, and the endogenous opiates. The big picture seems to be that animals (and presumably people) learn about the controllability of aversive events they encounter and that this learning in turn alters the amount of fear they experience. Feedback from the controlling response and its prediction of safety may be key here (Chapter 2). Learning that the stressor is uncontrollable may increase fear; learning that the stressor is uncontrollable may reduce fear; or both may be possible. The BZ/GABA system, CRH, and the amygdala may be especially important in these processes.

We think these discoveries are noteworthy because all of the "noncognitive" consequences of uncontrollable aversive events that have so far been studied can be reduced or prevented by drugs that act on the BZ/GABA system in such a way as to reduce fear. This is not true of manipulations that alter other systems. These initial changes in the BZ/GABA system then alter other systems (e.g., NE), and all can produce behavioral changes. So a given behavioral consequence of uncontrollability, such as decreased social interaction or deficits in shuttlebox escape, could be produced by changes in any or all of these systems.

However, cognitive changes can flow from what is learned about the stressor rather than from these physiological changes, which appear more related to the emotional and motivational impact of the uncontrollable stressor. Of course, this learning must somehow be represented in the chemical language of the brain, and this has not yet been extensively investigated. As a summary statement concerning what we know, we have identified some of the biological players in learned helplessness as well as started to map out which behaviors relate to which players.

WHAT WE DON'T KNOW

To switch to another metaphor, we know some of the notes, but we don't understand the symphony. How are the diverse biological changes orchestrated through time? Do some occur first, others second, others third, or are even more complex sequences involved? Do the different alterations have different time courses of decay? Is there an orchestra leader, and if so how does this leader work?

This process will not be an easy one to unravel. We doubt that a single serial cascade is at work here. Multiple *parallel* cascades are more likely. Any uncontrollable stressor is complex and multidimensional, and its different dimensions may influence different sets of neural systems. The analgesia produced by inescapable shock is a good example. The shock stimulus itself, as a sensory event, directly drives circuitry in the brainstem and spinal cord that produces pain inhibition. This process occurs without the mediation of cognitions and happens even if the animal is totally unconscious and anesthetized. However, other circuitry higher in the brain is responsive to what the animal learns about the shock it has received and is not activated by the shock per se. Moreover, the two sets of circuits are activated at different times and can interact with each other in complex ways. Obviously, it is not difficult to discover if a particular system (defined neurochemically or anatomically) is sensitive to controllability. However, it will take a great deal of work to figure out the structure of the symphony if our description of its organization is generally correct.

Most of the research we have reviewed here used a single stressor, electric shock. However, stressors differ in intensity and character. To what extent do different uncontrollable stressors produce similar neurochemical changes? Conversely, different laboratories use inescapable shocks with vastly different parameters. To what extent are the results that emerge comparable?

There is also considerable uncertainty regarding the mapping of this cascade of biological changes into behavior. There are many biological changes and many behavioral phenomena that result from exposure to uncontrollable stressors, but there has not been much effort to determine which are responsible for which. It is quite possible that one of the biological changes, say depletion of NE in the LC, is responsible for mediating one of the learned helplessness effects but not the others. All combinations of outcomes are possible. A given biological change could be responsible for many behaviors, a given change could be involved in some behaviors but not others, a given behavior could be influenced by more than one of the biological changes, and so on. There could be even greater specificity. For example, the forebrain projection of the LC might be involved in mediating attentional changes produced by uncontrollable stressors, whereas the cerebellar projections of the same nucleus might be responsible for motor changes. It will be a great challenge to unravel the connections and form a coherent map from biology to behavior.

Not all behavioral consequences of stressors are sensitive to the controllability of the stressor. For example, exposure to inescapable shock leads to a massive reduction in the rat's daily running activity (rats that have free access to a running wheel spend large amounts of their active period running in the wheel). This can persist for weeks (Desan, Silbert, & Maier, 1988). However, escapable shock produces the same outcome. Thus, we do not know what makes a behavior sensitive to stressor controllability.

Finally, much of the interest in the biology of learned helplessness has been generated by an interest in helplessness as a model of psychopathology, usually depression. Investigators have often been interested in determining whether uncontrollable stressors produce biological changes that resemble those hypothesized to underlie depression, rather than in studying learned helplessness per se. Does the biology of learned helplessness resemble the biology of depression, or the biology of something else? To answer this question, we must have a good knowledge of the biology of depression, yet this topic is far from complete and is itself controversial.

In Chapter 6, we discuss in detail the link between learned helplessness and depression. We close here with the comment that learned helplessness may have as much to do with anxiety as depression (see Willner, 1985, p. 408). At least on a biological level, anxiety and depression appear to fall along the same continuum and share a common substrate (Paul, 1988). Further work is needed to see whether learned helplessness ideas can shed some light on the relationship between anxiety and depression.

NOTES

1. You may remember during the Persian Gulf War that U.S. soldiers who might have been exposed to nerve gas were given syringes containing Valium.

This is because nerve gas kills by preventing inhibition in one's nervous system. The person dies of convulsions. Valium, by increasing inhibition, counteracts this process.

2. Cross-tolerance refers to a phenomenon in which repeated exposure to one agent leads to the development of tolerance to a *different agent*. Two agents that produce cross-tolerance must have a common site of action, and so cross-tolerance with the opiate morphine was considered to be a criterion for whether the other agent (the stressor in this case) involves action at an opiate site.

3. Clinical lore has long held that narcotics use reflects one's attempt to cope with an uncontrollable world. Perhaps involved in this link is a heightened sensitivity to these drugs.

4

Learned Helplessness in People

As we spelled out in Chapter 2, the controversy with regard to animal helplessness revolves around the adequacy of the learned helplessness model to explain the deficits produced in the laboratory by uncontrollability. In contrast, researchers investigating helplessness in people have proceeded differently, and controversy with regard to human helplessness reflects different issues. Human helplessness research started with an explanation for why people show deficits following uncontrollability: the cognitive account known as the learned helplessness model. The task of the researcher has been to produce in the laboratory the phenomenon explained by this model.

Human helplessness research has thus developed differently than the animal research, simply because the animal research came first. The animal studies are a good example of inductive inquiry, whereas the human studies have been a good example of deductive work. Animal researchers began with some intriguing facts, and they proposed a theory to account for them. In contrast, human investigators of helplessness began with some intriguing hypotheses, and they gathered facts to test them.

The animal paradigm we described in Chapter 2 provided the triadic design, operationalizations of uncontrollability and helplessness, and an explanation for human deficits following uncontrollable events—all before these deficits had been documented. The first studies of human helplessness assessed the adequacy of the animal paradigm as it might be applied to people. Researchers soon discovered that it did not provide the sophistication necessary to accommodate the full reaction of people to uncontrollable events. The early studies provided general support for learned helplessness in people while at the same time producing anomalous facts that the model could not explain. Subsequent researchers were forced into an inductive tack to explain these anomalies and to integrate them with those aspects of human helplessness that were accounted for by the learned helplessness hypothesis.

In this chapter, we describe the early studies of human helplessness. We do not hesitate to detail the quirks that emerged from this research. We can afford to do so, because a way to explain many of them eventually became apparent. In light of anomalous data, the learned helplessness model as applied to people was revised, and in the next chapter, we discuss this reformulated theory.

CRITERIA OF LEARNED HELPLESSNESS

As we explained in Chapter 1, learned helplessness has various meanings, so identifying it among people may not always be simple. Thus, we begin by reviewing again the senses in which "learned helplessness" is used. It may refer variously to deficits in thoughts, feelings, and actions; to the operations that produce these deficits (i.e., exposure to uncontrollable events); or to the cognitive account of how the operations lead to the deficits. Adding to this richness of meaning is the tendency of some theorists to use learned helplessness as a label for complex failures of adaptation to which the laboratory phenomena may be analogous (Chapter 7).

We recognize all of these senses in which learned helplessness is used. And we expect that different instances of helplessness may vary in the degree to which they embody the notion. Good examples of learned helplessness are those that reflect several of the meanings: deficits, cognitive mediation, and uncontrollable events as an antecedent. Poor examples reflect only one of the aspects of helplessness and thus demand caution when we speak about the other aspects.

Most laboratory studies of human helplessness fall between the "good" and the "poor" examples. Uncontrollability is typically present, because this is under the control of the experimenter. And as we discuss below, deficits are reliably produced by uncontrollable events. However, showing that the route from uncontrollability to deficits entails the specific cognitive processes hypothesized by the learned helplessness model has been the sticking point of this research.

OPERATIONALIZING LEARNED HELPLESSNESS
IN THE LABORATORY

As we already noted, the very first learned helplessness experiments using human subjects were modeled closely on those using animals. Subjects were exposed to aversive events, such as bursts of loud noise, electric shocks, or difficult problems. A triadic design was used. Subjects in the *controllable condition* had available to them some response that would terminate the aversive event. Subjects in the *uncontrollable condition* were exposed to these events but without any control over their offset. (In some experiments, following the example of animal research, subjects in the uncontrollable condition were explicitly yoked to those in the controllable condition, receiving the identical amount of aversive stimulation experienced by these subjects, with the critical difference, of course, that they had no control. Other designs did not employ this elegant procedure.) Completing the triadic design, subjects in the *no-pretreatment comparison condition* were exposed to no aversive events, controllable or uncontrollable.

All subjects were then tested on some task reflecting one or more of the disruptions attributed to learned helplessness. As in animals, learned helplessness was inferred when the subjects in the uncontrollable condition showed difficulties on the test task relative to those in the other two conditions. Numerous experiments with such a design have been conducted (see reviews by Abramson, Seligman, & Teasdale, 1978; McFerran & Breen, 1979; Miller & Norman, 1979; Roth, 1980; Wortman & Brehm, 1975). Although not always successful, many of them have found that people who experience uncontrollable events in the laboratory show disruptions in their subsequent thoughts, feelings, and actions.

An Illustrative Study

Let us consider a study reported by Hiroto and Seligman (1975), which shows both what is reasonable about such operationalizations and what is questionable. To set the stage, appreciate that when this study was conducted, only a handful of laboratory investigations of human helplessness had been reported in the literature (e.g., Fosco & Geer, 1971; Hiroto, 1974; Roth & Bootzin, 1974; Thornton & Jacobs, 1971, 1972). Without getting into details, suffice it to say that many of these studies were methodologically suspect (see the critique by Wortman & Brehm, 1975), and so the field as a whole was still unconvinced that there was a phenomenon among people analogous to learned helplessness among animals.

Hiroto and Seligman (1975) called attention to the most important aspect of helplessness, at least at that time, and that was the degree to which helplessness "learned" in one situation generalized to different situations. There was no doubt that when a person experienced uncontrollable events in one setting, he became passive and listless in that setting (e.g., MacDonald, 1946). But such a phenomenon was readily explained in terms of environmentalist theories: particular stimuli in that setting became associated with lack of contingent reward, and as these continued to be encountered, the person stopped responding as a result of mundane extinction. What made the idea of learned helplessness intriguing was the suggestion that the "expectancy of independence [between responses and outcomes] is an internal state of the organism that is broadly transferred" (Hiroto & Seligman, 1975, p. 311). Said another way, learned helplessness was presumably akin to a trait—stable and pervasive. This had not been demonstrated satisfactorily with human subjects.

Hiroto and Seligman (1975) were struggling against the same peripheralist explanations against which animal researchers had to defend their cognitive theory (Chapter 2). This explains why these researchers designed their study as they did, explicitly varying the pretreatment as well as the test task. Thus, the pretreatment task was either: (a) an *instrumental pretreatment*, in which subjects were called upon to press buttons to turn off a "slightly unpleasant" tone; or (b) a *cognitive pretreatment*, in which subjects were asked to solve a series of concept-identification problems, deciding which of various abstract stimuli exemplified the concept (e.g., "a big red square") that the experimenter had in mind. And the test task was similarly varied as either: (a) an *instrumental test task*, in which subjects had to move a lever from side to side to escape or avoid a 90-decibel tone judged to be "moderately aversive"; or (b) a *cognitive test task*, which consisted of twenty anagrams (scrambled words), all with the same pattern of solution.

The experiment varied all possible combinations of pretreatment and test task within an overall triadic design: that is, controllable pretreatment, uncontrollable pretreatment, and no-pretreatment comparison. Comparison subjects listened to the unpleasant tones, but not with the instruction that they might be able to control them; or they looked at the concept-identification stimuli, but not with the instruction that they try to solve them.

Hiroto and Seligman (1975) expected that subjects experiencing an uncontrollable pretreatment would show a decrement at the similar test task (i.e., instrumental or cognitive) relative to the controllable pretreatment and comparison group. That much was already established in the published literature. The more interesting question was whether experience with an uncontrollable instrumental task would produce deficits with a cognitive test and vice versa. If comparable deficits were indeed produced, then the argument that learned helplessness was an internal state of some generality, and not simply a circumscribed response to certain environmental cues, could be mounted.

This is exactly what the researchers found. On a variety of measures of test-task impairment—latency to solution, failures to solve, number of trials to catch on to solution—uncontrollability produced problems for the subjects, regardless of the type of test task. (There was one exception: the cognitive-cognitive conditions did not yield significant results, although they were in the expected direction. However, this was not a critical comparison, because the pretreatment and test task were the same.)

Using the jargon popular at the time, Hiroto and Seligman (1975) concluded that "cross-modal helplessness" had been produced, arguing against a peripheral interpretation of the results. They further concluded that the phenomenon observed in their study was "directly parallel to learned helplessness [as produced] in dogs, cats, and rats" (p. 325).

From the vantage of the 1990s, we no longer see these so-called instrumental versus cognitive tasks as drastically different; both can be readily described as abstract problems to be solved in the context of a psychology experiment. But remember that in 1975, most psychologists adhered to a very strict distinction between "behavior" (involved in the instrumental tasks) and "cognition" (tapped in the cognitive tasks), and thus the Hiroto and Seligman results were striking. Indeed, psychologists today readily speak of all such laboratory tasks in cognitive terms. This is due in no small part to studies like this one, which showed that central processes are entailed in all of them, regardless of their surface details.

In their discussion, Hiroto and Seligman (1975) defended the helplessness interpretation of their results against peripheral alternatives, just as animal researchers were defending their results. Once these were vanquished, all that remained standing was the cognitive interpretation of the learned helplessness model. It won by default, because at the time there were no cognitive competitors. The rest of the story of human helplessness saw the debate move onto cognitive grounds.

Few today believe that human helplessness might be produced by peripheral mechanisms, such as incompatible motor movements. Clearly something central is involved here, but its exact nature continues to be the subject of hot debate. Note that Hiroto and Seligman (1975) included no measures of the cognitive processes presumably mediating the effects they observed. They were content to infer that subjects had acquired an expectancy of response-outcome independence that generalized to other situations. "We suggest . . . that learned helplessness may involve a 'trait-like' system of expectancies that responding is futile" (p. 327).

The Context of Human Helplessness

Does the typical paradigm for human helplessness really capture the phenomenon as helplessness theory demands? Let's consider some of the criticisms of the methodology of this paradigm.

Unlike animal subjects in helplessness experiments, which are taken from their home cage, placed in a restraining device, and shocked—quite independently of anything they may or may not do—the human subject must engage in a great deal of instrumental behavior before being placed in a situation in which helplessness is induced.

If this subject is a college sophomore participating in the helplessness experiment in order to fulfill the course requirements for Introductory Psychology, consider all that she must do before being exposed to uncontrollable events. She must:

- Register for the course.
- Find her way to the lecture.
- Attend to the professor who explains the participation requirement.
- Sign up for the helplessness experiment.
- Find her way to the right laboratory at the correct time.
- Conduct herself in a decorous manner so that the experimenter does not dismiss her before the experiment begins.
- Read an informed consent form, which explains in more or less detail the procedures of the experiment and the discomforts it may entail.

- Agree to participate.
- Understand the experimenter's instructions.

And only then can the helplessness experiment begin.

If uncontrollability is operationalized by uncontrollable events imposed on the subject, she need do nothing more at this time in order to experience them. However, in many experiments, subjects are required to make further responses in order to experience uncontrollability. In any of a number of studies, for example, uncontrollability is operationalized in terms of concept-identification problems, as we saw in the Hiroto and Seligman (1975) study we just described. If the "right" or "wrong" feedback does not follow any rule but instead a random schedule, their solution can be regarded as uncontrollable.

Notice, however, that the subject must first do something—make a choice—before she is given random feedback. Unlike animals exposed to shock, or human subjects given bursts of noise through headphones, the subject attempting to solve such discrimination problems only experiences the uncontrollable feedback if she first attempts to solve the problem.

In other words, the experience of uncontrollability is contingent upon her behavior. We imagine that a subject who did not make any choice whatsoever would thwart the entire experiment, and we know of no instance in which this has actually occurred. Subjects will make a choice. They may do so relentlessly, carelessly, or listlessly, but they will make a choice. They understand—despite anything else that might be going on—that the experiment will not end until they make the choice that is required of them.

Human helplessness experiments, particularly those that operationalize uncontrollability via unsolvable problems, are not strictly parallel to the animal experiments. Right from the start, with the very first attempts to demonstrate learned helplessness using human subjects, it should be clear that any helplessness produced would be circumscribed. It should also be clear that human subjects might attribute the uncontrollable events to a variety of actions on their part: "if only I hadn't shown up for the experiment" . . . "if only I hadn't signed the consent form" . . . "if only I hadn't decided to participate in experiments at all" . . . and so on.

Could a subject thinking along these lines ever arrive at a general belief in response-outcome independence? Probably not. Once this is acknowledged, we can skip to the second stage of human helplessness theorizing (Chapter 5); here it is explicitly recognized that human helplessness is not the same as animal helplessness because it has boundary conditions determined by the person's interpretation of the setting in which she encounters uncontrollability.

We observe in Chapter 7 that there may exist out-of-the-laboratory instances of human helplessness in which the person believes in complete response-outcome independence, as in reactions to victimization. However, we further observe that it is no easy task to demonstrate that these instances of profound helplessness are driven mainly by cognitive factors. The role of trauma is difficult to ascertain independently of the role of uncontrollability. We are not particularly bothered by the circumscribed nature of human helplessness in the experimental laboratory. Many instances of out-of-the-laboratory human helplessness are bounded as well. And it is in the laboratory that we can best disentangle trauma and uncontrollability.

The Appropriate Comparison Group

In animal helplessness studies, it seems a simple matter to arrange the appropriate controls. The triadic design can be implemented in only one way. But it is not so simple with human subjects. Take in particular the no-pretreatment comparison condition that we mentioned earlier. What should these subjects be doing to bolster the argument that uncontrollability is responsible for deficits shown by helpless subjects?

In the animal experiment, subjects are put through the identical experience of their counterparts in the controllable and uncontrollable conditions, except that they are not exposed to the aversive events. In other words, they are removed from their cage, placed in a restraining apparatus, and held for the amount of time it takes to deliver shocks to subjects in the other two groups. They are then returned to their home cage, to be tested 24 hours later.

What about the no-pretreatment condition with human subjects? A variety of comparison groups have been used. In each case, one can question just what it is that these groups control. The researcher's intent is to hold all things constant except the experience of controllable or uncontrollable events. Some investigators, like Hiroto and Seligman (1975), have dealt with this problem by allowing subjects to examine or handle the pretreatment stimulus material. They do so for however long the subjects in the other groups work at the pretreatment problems.

While this procedure may hold certain experiences constant, it introduces a possible confound. What is a subject to think when he is given what looks like a problem, but then is not asked to solve it? Perhaps he will try to solve it anyway. Perhaps he will try to memorize its details. Regardless, he will try to make sense of what is going on. He may well end up confused, bored, or challenged, and his intended purpose as a comparison subject is not served.

Other researchers give their no-pretreatment subjects filler tasks: questionnaires to be completed, slides to be rated, and so on. A third approach is to have the subjects sit and wait. And a fourth way in which researchers implement the no-pretreatment comparson condition simply starts with the test tasks. What can we make of all this? We must take a broad view of these paradigms. Is there convergence across the comparison groups? As it turns out, the learned helplessness experiments conducted indeed show the same results with different comparison groups.

A META-ANALYSIS OF HUMAN HELPLESSNESS STUDIES

Hundreds of human helplessness studies have been conducted over the past two decades. It is a daunting task to bring some order to their results, because they vary along all sorts of procedural dimensions such as those discussed above. However, the answer to the status of human helplessness lies in their entirety, not in one particular study or another. How can we draw some general conclusions about this literature?

Meta-analysis provides one answer by treating the results of a given study as data in their own right and then combining these in a way that takes into account the power of designs as well as the strength of obtained effects. Individual studies are treated as independent observations and then combined to offer conclusions. Is there an overall effect? And if so, what is its magnitude?

Villanova and Peterson (1991) undertook a meta-analysis of learned helplessness experiments with human subjects. Studies were located by computerized abstract searches; "Learned Helplessness" is a key term in both *Psychological Abstracts* and *Index Medicus*, which means that the searches were relatively thorough. References in these articles were followed up in a second wave. We were interested in studies that measured performance at a test task following a helplessness induction. Some studies use dependent measures other than problem solving, and we mention these in a subsequent section, but these are too few and varied to undertake a meaningful meta-analysis. All studies used some version of the triadic design. Studies were then selected for inclusion based on, first, their availability in English and, second, their reporting of the statistics necessary for a meta-analysis: specifically, sample size, means for different conditions, and corresponding standard deviations. In all, 132 studies were included in the meta-analysis, including thousands of different subjects.

The overall conclusion from the meta-analysis is that indeed, people's experience with uncontrollable events disrupts their performance at test tasks, relative to both controllable conditions and no-pretreatment comparison conditions. The magnitude of this effect is what statisticians refer to as a moderate one. We should be explicit here that "moderate" in this sense does not mean trivial or disappointing. The most robust results in the social sciences attain only a moderate effect size, simply because human behavior has numerous determinants, which means that the contribution of any given cause—in this case, the experience of uncontrollability—is necessarily bounded. Said another way, the learned helplessness effect in people appears to be as robust as most findings in the social sciences.

Further calculations by Villanova and Peterson suggested that the effect in people may be even stronger than the analogous effect in animals, and this conclusion bears underscoring. Animal helplessness, because of its historical priority, is understandably used as the benchmark against which to measure human helplessness. But many who discuss helplessness in animals versus people go one step further to argue that the effect in animals is strong whereas the effect in people is probably more fragile and thus less impressive. Our results imply that such conclusions are wrong. They probably stem from the more dramatic descriptions of animal helplessness (not to mention the intriguing ability of most people to empathize with the plight of laboratory animals but not with that of other human beings). But dramatic effects are not necessarily the same as robust ones.

Another aspect of the meta-analysis was an investigation of factors that might influence the magnitude of obtained helplessness effects. Granted the overall effect, were some aspects of a study more associated with larger effects than others? This is not a trivial exercise, again because of the nature of the applications of helplessness ideas. It is widely asserted that certain sorts of people are more at risk for helplessness and that certain sorts of uncontrollable experiences are more apt to produce disruption. But what do the basic laboratory studies show about these assertions?

It was only possible to investigate factors that showed some variation across studies. If only a single study had a given wrinkle, it was not meaningful to compare that study's effects against all others. But Villanova and Peterson did identify a number of possible moderators:

1. Status of the journal in which the article appeared (operationalized as refereed or not), under the assumption that "better" journals would have "better" studies and hence pose a more stringent test for the phenomenon
2. Sample characteristics: whether subjects were children, adolescents, college students, or adults, and whether they were psychiatric patients or not
3. Sex: whether subjects were males or females
4. Type of event in helplessness induction: positive versus negative versus neutral
5. Type of test task: anagrams, concept identification, button pressing, or hand shuttlebox
6. Comparison group: yoked or not
7. Task importance: manipulated as important or not

None of these variables influenced the magnitude of helplessness effects. Although "null" results—even from a meta-analysis—should be interpreted cautiously, this finding may be as important as the fact that a helplessness effect exists in the first place.

These results further attest to the robustness of human helplessness. They also caution against glib conclusions about factors that make helplessness among people more versus less likely. They appear to pale in comparison with the sheer fact of uncontrollability.

Our results also suggest that different types of people, at least as studied in the 132 experiments, are not differentially susceptible to laboratory helplessness. This is also an important implication, because we might wish, for example, to use helplessness ideas to explain the greater likelihood of women becoming depressed (Chapter 6). But the present results suggest that we cannot speak of women showing a general *vulnerability* to helplessness. Helplessness may produce the sex difference in depression, but not because of anything that women bring to situations characterized by uncontrollability. The same is true for psychiatric patients, people of different ages, and so on. If there is a group that shows more helplessness outside the laboratory, perhaps it is simply because these people have experienced more uncontrollability, as opposed to being differentially sensitive to its effects.

This point might help explain the largely contradictory literature on the relationship of personality characteristics to laboratory helplessness. Any of a number of studies have been conducted that divide subjects into two groups based on their responses to some measure of an individual difference, such as locus of control or sex-role orientation. Then these subjects are put through some variant of a triadic design, with the hypothesis that the personality characteristic will interact with uncontrollability to produce disruption. Sometimes this happens, and sometimes it does not. Our sense is that it usually does not.

There is a shortcoming of the research we have just reviewed. These studies do not tease apart a cognitive impairment from a sheer motivational one, because the studies as originally conducted did not use procedures that distinguished these. We are left with the conclusion that uncontrollability disrupts task performance, but we cannot say with conviction that this is due to a disruption of problem-solving attempts (a motivational deficit) or an inability to see a solution when it presents itself (a cognitive deficit). Studies like Hiroto and Seligman's (1975) have tried to disentangle these, using response latency as a measure of motivation and the number of trials to reach a solution as a measure of cognition, but it is difficult to justify these as completely independent. Indeed, in the typical experiment, they are highly correlated.

OTHER ASPECTS OF HUMAN HELPLESSNESS

Studies with animals find learned helplessness to be marked not just by impaired problem solving but also by a host of other consequences. What do the parallel studies with people show? By and large, the pertinent investigations demonstrate that the impairments associated with human helplessness in the laboratory are analogous to those documented for animal helplessness.

Time Course

Like animal helplessness, human helplessness shows a time course. In other words, the effect goes away with the passage of time. This has not been extensively investigated, so the exact parameters of the time course are not yet known. But we can still conclude with certainty that human helplessness as induced in the laboratory eventually wanes, even when the test task is highly similar to the pretreatment situation (e.g., Young & Allin, 1986).

Emotional Consequences

Relative to subjects not exposed to uncontrollable events, those who have experience with uncontrollability report such negative emotions as anxiety, depression, and anger (e.g., Breier et al., 1987; Gatchel, Paulus, & Maples, 1975; Griffith, 1977; Smolen, 1978; Teasdale, 1978; Tuffin, Hesketh, & Podd, 1985). Some studies discern a succession to these feelings, so that anger and anxiety appear first in response to uncontrollability, eventually to give way to feelings of depression as the extent of uncontrollable events increases (e.g., Pittman & Pittman, 1979, 1980). Mikulincer and Caspy (1986) found that subjects who work at uncontrollable problems are apt to report a subjective feeling of helplessness, which means that the helplessness model has some descriptive validity.

Taken together, these negative feelings parallel the emotional disruption that has been observed in helpless animals (Chapter 2). What is not clear is whether this disruption deserves to be characterized as a deficit, as it sometimes is described among animals. Anxiety and depression are active emotions in their own right, not simply the absence of feelings as the term "deficit" implies. Humans made helpless in the laboratory are not emotionally stuporous but rather dysphoric.

Reduction of Aggression

Animals made helpless by uncontrollable events become less aggressive, and there are some hints from a handful of studies with people that the same consequence occurs among them as well (e.g., Dengerink & Myers, 1977; Sherrod, Moore, & Underwood, 1979). One interesting wrinkle on this conclusion is that Trice (1982) found that following uncontrollability, subjects increased their liking for hostile humor, while showing a decrease in their liking for innocent humor. Preference for tendentious humor has long been interpreted as vicarious satisfaction of aggressive drives (Freud, 1905), so perhaps this finding means that uncontrollability drives aggression underground, or at least into symbolic realms. One imagines, though, that if pushed to an extreme, uncontrollability would deaden all responses to humor, granted the incompatibility between negative emotions and the ability to appreciate humor.

Physiological Consequences

Uncontrollability among animals produces a host of somatic effects (Chapter 3), and some researchers have explored the physiological correlates of helplessness among people. The establishment of a parallel between animal and human studies is hampered by the fact that researchers have looked at different physiological indices among animals versus people. Human subjects cannot be "sacrificed" and subjected to fine-grained biochemical analyses. As a consequence, what we know about the physiology of human helplessness is limited to surface measures of galvanic skin response, heart rate, and the like.

So, we know that helplessness in people is associated with lower tonic skin conductance levels, smaller phasic skin conductance responses, higher levels of plasma adrenocorticotropic hormone, and more spontaneous electrodermal activity (e.g., Breier et al., 1987; Gatchel & Proctor, 1976). These characteristics are usually interpreted in terms of increased arousal, implying a parallel with the increased fear and anxiety that accompany learned helplessness in animals (Chapter 3).

Immunization and Therapy

Two other aspects of animal helplessness also have good parallels in the human research. People can be "immunized" against the effects of uncontrollable events by providing them with previous experience with controllability (e.g., Altmaier & Happ, 1985; Dyck & Breen, 1978; Eckelman & Dyck, 1979; Hirt & Genshaft, 1981; Jones, Nation, & Massad, 1977; Prindaville & Stein, 1978; Thornton & Powell, 1974).

And people made helpless by uncontrollable events in the laboratory can have their deficits reversed by various modes of "therapy" that encourage people to see connections between their responses and outcomes (Klein & Seligman, 1976). In animals, therapy took the form of dragging the helpless animal back and forth across the shuttlebox until it noticed the contingency between movement and shock termination (Chapter 2). In people, "therapy" need not be so literal but rather can be done more abstractly, by instructing people in the fact of contingency (Thornton & Powell, 1974), bolstering their self-esteem (Orbach & Hadas, 1982), improving their mood (Kilpatrick-Tabak & Roth, 1978; Raps, Reinhard, & Seligman,

1980), encouraging different explanations for their initial failure (Miller & Norman, 1981), and the like.

As we have concluded already about problem-solving deficits produced by uncontrollability, these studies are entirely consistent with the predictions of the helplessness model, but they do *not* show that deficits are produced by the exact cognitive mechanisms specified by the helplessness model. In other words, immunization and therapy effects could be produced by any of a number of mechanisms, which may or may not involve contingency perceptions and expectations.

Vicarious Helplessness

There are several aspects of human helplessness that have no counterpart among animals, and one of the most intriguing of these is that people can learn to be helpless through the observation of another person encountering uncontrollable events (Brown & Inouye, 1978). This is merely a special case of so-called vicarious learning, or modeling (Bandura, 1986), yet it is a finding of considerable interest. For one thing, if theorists needed yet another reason to suspect that learned helplessness was not simply a peripheral phenomenon, then the fact of vicarious helplessness provides it. Vicarious learning can only take place in a central—cognitive—fashion. In addition, vicarious helplessness greatly extends the range of topics outside the laboratory to which helplessness ideas might apply. An individual need not directly experience uncontrollable events in order to become helpless; it may be sufficient to see their effects on others. With the advent of the global television community, we can argue that more people are exposed to more uncontrollability than ever before in history (Chapter 7).

Group Helplessness

Another aspect of human helplessness with no parallel among animals is the demonstration by Simkin, Lederer, and Seligman (1983) that small groups can be made helpless by asking the group as a whole to work at unsolvable problems. On later tasks, the group as a whole acts in a helpless fashion, failing to solve problems readily mastered by other groups not previously exposed to uncontrollability. Interestingly, this group-level helplessness is not strictly a function of the helplessness of the individual members. In other words, helpless groups are not necessarily composed of those who act helplessly on individual tasks; those who act helplessly on individual tasks do not necessarily make for a helpless group.

Helplessness at a group level has the same important implications as vicarious helplessness. It challenges the notion that helplessness is somehow produced by trauma per se. And it greatly extends the range of topics to which helplessness ideas might apply. Might we be able to speak of complex organizations or even whole cultures and societies as helpless?

THE GENERALITY OF LEARNED HELPLESSNESS AMONG PEOPLE

The Hiroto and Seligman (1975) study we discussed earlier made the bold statement that induced helplessness was traitlike, and within the confines of the study, this conclusion was justified. In terms of arguing against a peripheral interpretation of human helplessness, this study was successful in making its case. But as we have earlier argued, just on the face of it we know that human helplessness as produced in the experimental laboratory cannot be completely general. It must have limits across time and situation.

Some studies showed exactly this. For example, Cole and Coyne (1977) found that helplessness induced in one situation did not generalize to all other possible situations (see also Douglas & Anisman, 1975). And we have already noted that human helplessness has a time course, present immediately after an experience with uncontrollability but not when the subject is tested hours or days later.

Granted that human helplessness is bounded in time and space, is there any way to determine the boundary conditions? Researchers have looked at various potential influences and most frequently settled on how the helpless subject interprets the causes of the original uncontrollable events. This interest in causal attributions was consistent with larger trends in psychology that emphasized them, as we explain in Chapter 5. They fit with the view of the person as a rational being, acting in accord with his or her interpretation of the world. If someone thinks that uncontrollability was produced by highly general causes, these causes—logically—will be present in other times and places, and so too will the uncontrollability. Hence helplessness should be general. And if uncontrollability is produced by circumscribed causes, then there is no justification for believing that it will again be present, and helplessness should be bounded.

A number of studies have supported this interpretation, showing that when subjects are induced in a helpless experiment to explain uncontrollable events in one way or another, the generality of the induced deficits sensibly is influenced by the attribution the subject entertains. So when subjects make stable explanations for laboratory failure, their subsequent disruption lasts longer than when they make unstable explanations (e.g., Brewin & Shapiro, 1985; Mikulincer, 1988b; Weiner, 1979). Analogously, subjects who are encouraged to make global explanations for failure show more widespread deficits at test tasks than subjects who make specific ones (e.g., Mikulincer, 1986; Mikulincer & Nizan, 1988; Pasahow, 1980). Such studies provide the impetus for the attributional reformulation of the helplessness model, which we take up in detail in the next chapter.

For now, let us note that these studies take the cognitive interpretation of human helplessness even further. They help to end any controversy about the production of human helplessness by peripheral mechanisms. The issue becomes whether human helplessness is produced by the cognitions suggested by the helplessness model or by other ones.

COGNITION AND SELF-REPORT

Animal researchers sometimes envy their colleagues who study people, at least when the topics of concern are cognitive factors. As detailed in Chapter 2, one must use ingenious procedures to infer what animals might be thinking. With human subjects, cognitive research seems so much easier. One can simply ask people what they are thinking.

Yet human researchers have learned the hard lesson that nothing is simple when it comes to studying cognitive theories like the learned helplessness model. Of course, one can ask subjects if they feel helpless, if they believe that responses and outcomes are unrelated, or if they expect future events to elude their control. Many researchers have done exactly this.

The problem is that results prove inconsistent (see Alloy, 1982b; Coyne & Gotlib, 1983; Tennen, 1982). Some studies indeed find that reports of certain thoughts and beliefs accompany deficits following uncontrollability, exactly as the learned helplessness model proposes. But other studies find deficits in the apparent absence of these thoughts and beliefs. At least part of the reason for inconsistent reports about "cognition" in human helplessness lies in the procedure of simply asking subjects what they are thinking.

A curious state of affairs results from this procedure. Depending on the researcher's particular bias, self-report data are either accepted or dismissed, according to what they seem to imply about cognition in learned helplessness. There is nothing malicious in this tendency, but neither is it good science. We have been guilty of it ourselves, and so have other researchers in the helplessness tradition—advocates and critics alike.

Self-report data are obviously nonfalsifiable if one stresses their strength when they support one's preconceptions but their weakness otherwise. Needed is an a priori statement about the pros and cons of self-report data in learned helplessness research. Then studies can proceed.

Here are some general statements about the role of self-report in learned helplessness investigations. We hope that other researchers will agree with our points. Regardless, we urge all to examine their particular beliefs about how best to study the cognitive factors associated with responses to uncontrollable events.

1. The cognitive variables of concern to the helplessness model are theoretical constructs, not actual things. The distinction drawn by MacCorquodale and Meehl (1948) between variables regarded as merely theoretical versus those regarded as real helps the researcher understand how to use self-report data to evaluate helplessness predictions. We suggest that notions like expectations reside more in our theories than literally in our subjects; accordingly, they are a way for us to make sense of what the subjects do. There are precedents for this in the other sciences: consider gravity, heredity, and the atom as purely theoretical constructs.

The methodological implication of regarding helplessness constructs as hypothetical abstractions is that their meaning is not exhausted by any single operation. And this of course includes self-report. Instead, a variety of operations bear on our judgment that a particular construct should be invoked. One should not make the mistake of regarding any one of these—or even their aggregate—as the construct itself.

Self-report is one way to assess cognition, but it is not the only way. By this logic, other measures are also pertinent. A person's listless performance at a test task may be the basis for inferring that she believes the solution to be beyond her control. Or it may not be, because no measure bears a one-to-one relationship with a theoretical construct. Certainly it would be circular to use listless behavior as the sole evidence for cognitive variables hypothesized to produce the listlessness.

It is incumbent upon the researcher to use several measures, of which self-report is but one, and look for what the patterns of these measures convey. And the researcher needs to recognize that a given measure may not be appropriate or optimal for capturing certain constructs. In sum, the task of the human researcher is really the same as the task of the animal researcher, despite the fact that human subjects can talk and complete questionnaires.

2. Content variables are more sensitive to study with self-report than process variables. The learned helplessness account of responses to uncontrollable events is phrased in cognitive terms. A rough distinction within the general realm of cognitive language is between *cognitive content* and *cognitive process* (Scott, Osgood, & Peterson, 1979). Cognitive content refers to particular thoughts, beliefs, and expectations, whereas cognitive process refers to particular sequences leading to and from the various contents. The learned helplessness model assigns importance to the expectation—"Future events will be uncontrollable"—and to the process that brings about this expectation: uncontrollable events → perception of response-outcome independence → expectation of future uncontrollability.

The content-process distinction implies that subjects can report with more validity on content than on process. I know that I love you and can tell you so, but I do not really know why. When I count the reasons, I am probably not telling you *how* I fell in love. Nisbett and Wilson (1977) compellingly argue that subjects in psychology experiments will answer questions posed to them about process, but in so doing, they "tell more than they know" because they do not have access to mechanisms. Researchers who put an explanatory burden on these answers will be disappointed.

This happens frequently in learned helplessness research, although it may be difficult to recognize because questions about process may masquerade as questions about content. For example, a subject given unsolvable concept-identification problems who then works somewhat unsuccessfully at a series of solvable anagrams may be asked to indicate on a 7-point scale the degree to which he believed that solutions to the concept-identification problems were beyond his control. He circles the "7," indicating that he believes them to be uncontrollable.

We would not argue with the researcher who regards this self-report as a valid indicator of what the subject believes at the moment he answered the question. But many researchers take a further step with this datum. They may argue from it that the perception of uncontrollability *mediates* his poor performance at the anagram problem. In other words, they assume that the subject's self-report is an indicator of process. And this is not justified.

Self-report can provide important information about some cognitive processes, but the study must be designed appropriately. In the preceding example, had the researcher asked the subject about his belief in the uncontrollability of the concept-identification problems in the course of his attempts to solve them, *then* it would be much more plausible to make an inference about the mediating role of this belief. A critical factor here is the timing of this question (cf. Tiggemann & Winefield, 1987). Investigations of process often demand that measures be made across time, not simply at the end of the process.

Fiske and Taylor (1984, chap. 10) make precisely this point in their general discussion of how to study cognitive processes. In what are called process-tracing measures, assessments are made of hypothesized mechanisms *across time,* stopping the putative sequence at different points to assess cognitive content and then using these assessments to infer cognitive process.

Learned helplessness research with human subjects has not frequently used this procedure, although it is superior to the strategy of assessing all cognitive factors at the end of the experiment. The reason is one of simple economy. The ideal strategy of interrupting subjects at different stages in the induction of learned helplessness requires a separate group of subjects for every interruption. The learned helplessness model is straightforward, but it does posit a number of discrete stages. No study has simultaneously studied human helplessness at each of these, which may seem incredible granted the literally hundreds of human helplessness studies. But each particular study is conducted under restraints, and researchers invariably take shortcuts.

Performance deficits following uncontrollable events are the most striking aspect of the learned helplessness phenomenon, and investigators therefore design their studies to highlight these deficits. It is unfortunate that the cognitive processes that give rise to these deficits are therefore accorded secondary status and not investigated in the most rigorous way. In this chapter, we discuss only a small minority of specific learned helplessness investigations, because so many studies shed no light on *why* uncontrollable events disrupt a person's performance. That they have this effect was established early in the 1970s. Why they do so is still not clear in the 1990s.

3. Cognitive content cannot be studied without using terms meaningful to the subject. Learned helplessness theory borrows a number of terms from ordinary language to explain the process by which uncontrollable events are disruptive: expectation, attribution, controllable, uncontrollable, even helplessness itself. These terms have been carefully defined within helplessness theory. For example, Seligman (1975) devoted fully twelve pages of his book *Helplessness* to defining controllability, and we have probably used up even more pages in this book in defining our terms.

However, in a typical helplessness experiment, subjects are asked to respond to questions using these terms *without the accompanying definitions.* We assume that the technical definitions are somewhat at odds with the ordinary language use of these terms, or else we would not spend so much time explaining what they mean. But isn't it ironic that we somehow assume that subjects will know what we mean when we ask them in the course of a helplessness experiment how much "control" they perceive over particular events?

Let us consider as an example a study reported by Oakes and Curtis (1982, experiment 1), in which subjects participated in 100 trials of a target-shooting task. Those in the contingent groups had their successes or failures accurately identified by the sounding of a tone; those in the noncontingent groups were yoked to subjects in the contingent groups—that is, they heard a predetermined pattern of tones regardless of their actual performance. All subjects were then administered solvable anagrams.

Following the anagram test task, subjects completed a questionnaire that tried to ascertain their thoughts during the target-shooting task by asking them to indicate:

1. To what extent did you believe you could be successful? (1–7 scale)
2. To what extent did you believe the task of hitting the bullseye could or could not be done? (1–7 scale)
3. To what extent do you feel each of the factors listed below was responsible for determining your success or failure? Please give your estimates in percentages of the total responsibility attributable to each factor. (Listed were difficulty level of task, your own effort, chance or luck, and experimenter control.)

Someone familiar with the learned helplessness literature has no difficulty understanding what these questions intend to operationalize. But given that they were answered by introductory psychology students, are these good operationalizations?

According to Oakes and Curtis (1982), Question 1 assessed "feelings of helplessness" (p. 396). But this is reasonable only if people's expectations of success are identical to their expectations of response-outcome contingency, and they certainly are not. Thus, someone may expect to do well because the experimenter looks lenient.

Question 2 supposedly measured "awareness of noncontingency" (p. 395). This operationalization is a better one, on the face of it, but we can still be skeptical and speculate that perhaps subjects believed that the task could be done successfully by someone with military training but not by themselves. How then should they answer this question? They might say that the task was able to be done, but this does not reflect their belief that the task was noncontingent on their own behavior.

Question 3 also was intended to reflect "awareness of noncontingency" by the amount of responsibility attributed to experimenter control (p. 395). This interpretation does not follow at all. Why does attribution to task difficulty not get at noncontingency? This seems to be how Question 2 operationalizes the notion. And why does attribution to effort not get at noncontingency? And why do subjects not have the option of saying that the response needed to succeed is not in their repertoire?

Our point is not to single out this particular study for criticism so much as to illustrate the difficulty that any researchers face in trying to measure the cognitions mediating learned helplessness. Indeed, quite a controversy exists within experimental psychology regarding the understanding that people have of such concepts as correlation and contingency. Our reading of this controversy shows that people's behavior is sensitive to even subtle variations in the statistical structure of events. At the same time, though, they are clueless regarding the abstract meanings of statistical notions. (Anyone who has ever taught elementary statistics to college students will confirm this conclusion.)

Researchers must not expect a subject's self-report to be already phrased in theoretical language. Subjects may use words quite differently than do learned helplessness theorists. For example, in a study conducted by Peterson (1991), subjects described bad events that had occurred to them and rated them in terms of their uncontrollability and their likelihood of future recurrence. According to theory, these ratings should be at least somewhat redundant, in that "uncontrollable" events by definition are apt to recur no matter what steps the person takes. But results showed them to be completely independent. "Uncontrollable" events were not necessarily regarded as likely to recur, nor vice versa.

The meanings assigned by everyday subjects to our theoretical constructs must be recognized as possibly idiosyncratic. "Control" or "success" as used by research subjects may tap into notions of contingency, but they may just as plausibly reflect intentionality and morality. Stated another way, researchers and subjects should be using the same terms. In the typical learned helplessness experiment, insufficient attention is paid to meeting this requirement.

4. Alternative explanations should be played off against each other as well as against the null hypothesis. The learned helplessness hypothesis describes sufficient conditions for maladaptive passivity. It does *not* make any claims that the process it describes is a necessary condition. There is considerable irony, therefore, that many supposed challenges to the helplessness model proceed by demonstrating that helplessness may be brought about by processes different from those posited by the helplessness model. Researchers then conclude that the model is wrong.

Such demonstrations may be valuable in their own right, but they have no direct pertinence to learned helplessness because they rest on faulty logic. The way to falsify a theory phrased in terms of sufficient conditions is to show that these conditions do not produce the hypothesized result. One cannot do so by showing that other conditions do produce the result.

We are quite willing to believe that the helplessness account of deficits following uncontrollability is wrong—indeed, our present conclusion is that the status of this hypothesis remains unclear. But the most compelling way to argue for its wrongness is by playing off rival hypotheses: the learned helplessness model versus some other account that makes an opposite prediction. In the remainder of this chapter, we describe and evaluate some of these other hypotheses.

OTHER EXPLANATIONS

We turn now to explanations of how people respond to uncontrollable events that differ from the learned helplessness account. As we have already emphasized, these tend to focus on alternative mediators of the debilitating effects of uncontrollability. The status of these alternatives is as unclear as the status of the helplessness model itself, because of the aforementioned difficulties in establishing the right way to go about ascertaining cognitive constructs.

Reactance

Learned helplessness researchers were not the first investigators to put people in situations that frustrated their attempts to solve problems. A long tradition of studies of this type exists, and here we see the construct ostensibly being investigated identified as frustration, failure, threat, partial reinforcement, or stress. In the 1960s, one more version of such investigations was popular under the rubric of *psychological reactance.* According to this idea, in situations in which their choices or freedoms are threatened, people respond by an increase in their motivation to restore that freedom or choice (Brehm, 1966, 1972). This motivational state is called reactance.

Reactance has typically been investigated by imposing outcomes on people rather than letting them choose from among alternatives, or by removing a choice from them. Influencing the magnitude of aroused reactance are such factors as:

- one's initial expectation of freedom;
- the strength of the threat;
- the importance of the threatened freedom; and
- the implication that the threat carries for other freedoms.

Among the consequences of reactance are an exaggeration of the attractiveness of the denied choice and—important for our purpose here—increased efforts to attain or participate in the threatened or eliminated behavior.

Reactance makes contact with the learned helplessness paradigm because uncontrollable events may arouse it. When control is expected and valued, then its removal, as it were, should threaten the person and arouse his motivation to restore the freedom, to regain control. Reactance theory thus makes a prediction diametrically opposed to that of the helplessness model, namely that uncontrollable events should lead to increased motivation to solve problems.

We have already noted that ample evidence suggests that uncontrollability leads to impaired problem solving, so it is clear that reactance theory does not replace helplessness theory. However, in some studies reactance effects, rather than helplessness effects, are produced by uncontrollability, which means that depending on the circumstances, one or the other may take place.

Wortman and Brehm (1975) argued that both theories can be true, that one's response to uncontrollability is reactance or helplessness depending on the amount of experience one has with uncontrollability. When one first encounters uncontrollable events, he experiences reactance, which shows itself as his enhanced efforts to solve problems. As his experience with uncontrollability continues, eventually his reactance motivation dissipates, and he becomes helpless, evidencing the familiar impairment of problem solving. The exact point at which reactance gives way to helplessness varies; one of the influences is the importance of the threatened freedom. More important tasks are more likely to give rise to longer periods of reactance.

The reactance-helplessness integration has several virtues. It is consistent with common sense. Imagine a vending machine that seems not to work. Our first reaction to the "uncontrollability" of the device is to keep pushing its buttons. We may do so with great vigor, particularly if we really want a candy bar. Sooner or later, though, our continued failure produces a lack of motivation to keep trying. We become helpless.

Wortman and Brehm (1975) suggested that their proposed integration explains immunization effects by giving the individual the expectation of freedom and hence sustaining reactance motivation when this is threatened. This seems less circuitous an interpretation of immunization than that favored by the helplessness model, which holds that an expectation of response-outcome contingency somehow "interferes" with recognizing its lack. The mechanism of this interference is never really specified, and one would think that the person or animal, simply by living in the world, should always expect response-outcome contingency, which means that helplessness effects should not be produced as readily as they are.

The integrative model also expects that helplessness effects should be somewhat bounded, which, as we have seen, is not readily explained by the helplessness model. Uncontrollable events, whether they produce reactance or helplessness, should foreshadow similar reactions in other domains of life only to the degree that the individual sees the new tasks as similar to the old ones. Here we are led again to the importance of taking into account how the individual interprets the original situation.

Let us turn from the theoretical virtues of this theory to the evidence that bears on it. Some studies show the hypothesized temporal pattern. We earlier mentioned studies of the emotional consequences of experience with uncontrollability, and when these have taken a look at the sequence in which negative emotions emerge, anxiety and anger precede depression and feelings of helplessness (Pittman & Pittman, 1979, 1980). This is exactly what we would expect if reactance were aroused prior to the development of helplessness.

And when the amount of experience with uncontrollable events is systematically varied, some studies have found that less experience with uncontrollability leads to a facilitation of problem solving at the test task, whereas more experience with uncontrollability leads to impairment (e.g., Mikulincer, 1988a; Mikulincer, Kedem, & Zilkha-Segal, 1989; Winefield & Jardine, 1982). Manipulations of the importance of the situation to the person are more likely to result in facilitated performance (e.g., Roth & Kubal, 1975). That is, helplessness develops more readily when the tasks involved are not important to the individual.

But the reactance-helplessness integration also has several drawbacks. It is not clear just where to expect the line between reactance and helplessness. Uncontrollable events, even of the most minimal degree, tend to produce helplessness rather than reactance, as we noted in reporting the results of the meta-analysis. Perhaps what is needed is a systematic study of the parameters of the pretreatment, but few researchers have had the patience to do this. As it stands now, it is difficult to predict just when reactance will appear in a helplessness experiment.

Perhaps the problem is that many laboratory tasks are unimportant to the subjects, which means they readily relinquish their attempts to restore the threatened freedom. This is not a problem with the model, but neither does it mean that we have to take Wortman and Brehm's theory too seriously in accounting for human helplessness as produced in the laboratory. It may simply apply to an occasional laboratory curiosity. Is their theory more relevant outside the laboratory, where tasks are more important? Presumably, but again, the evidence seems pretty convincing that uncontrollability, across a wide range of degrees, is debilitating, not facilitating.

Another criticism of the integrative model is that it is irrelevant in understanding our responses to uncontrollability. Perhaps reactance is an immediate reaction to our thwarted attempts to solve problems, but not to events we perceive as uncontrollable. Contrast the subject who says "I am not yet solving this problem" with the one who says "This problem is unsolvable." The first subject will show reactance, presumably, and the latter will show helplessness. But it is only the second subject who is reacting to uncontrollability (as she sees things). Said another way, reactance may be the motivational state that accompanies the learning of response-outcome contingencies; once the individual learns that responses and outcomes are unrelated, the processes identified by the helplessness model come into play.

Hypothesis Testing

Another alternative to the helplessness model's account of impairment following uncontrollable events was proposed independently by Levine, Rotkin, Jankovic, and Pitchford (1977) and Peterson (1976, 1978, 1980). Their suggestions took off from Levine's (1971) concept-identification theory. This was a natural point of examination because the concept-identification problems originally developed by Levine to test his theory have been frequently used by helplessness investigators, such as Hiroto and Seligman (1975), to induce helplessness.

As we earlier described, these problems present subjects with abstract stimuli that vary along several dimensions, such as shape, size, or color. The subject is shown a series of these stimuli and in each case is asked to indicate whether or not it is an instance of the concept to be acquired. Obviously on the first few trials the subject has no idea and can only guess. But the "right" or "wrong" feedback provides useful information that the individual uses in making his subsequent responses until eventually the concept is acquired.

A subject might be shown a large yellow square, for example, and he guesses that it is an instance of the concept. He is told that he is correct, and then on the next trial when he is shown a small yellow square, he again says yes, but this time he is told that he is wrong. Several simple possibilities for the concept in question can now be ruled out—for example, the concept is not all yellow stimuli, and it is not all squares. Perhaps it is all large stimuli as opposed to small ones. Because these stimuli vary along a finite number of dimensions, the subject eventually acquires the concept, although of course the ease or difficulty of doing so depends on how complex the concept indeed is.

So what happens when the right or wrong feedback is random—given independently of what the subject says? The problem is unsolvable, and following attempts to solve such insolvable problems, the individual will reliably show impairment at other problems, even when these admit to a solution. What transpires in between? The helplessness model proposes that the subject somehow abstracts a belief in response-outcome independence and then generalizes this expectancy of helplessness to the new situation, where it produces difficulties for him.

But Levine's concept-identification theory suggests another process. According to Levine, people solve problems like this—indeed, any problem—by starting with a set of admissible solutions. This set of solutions may be provided by explicit instructions—"the solution has something to do with the stimulus patterns"—or it may be inferred from the problem itself. Subjects actively entertain a particular hypothesis about the solution as they respond to instances. To the degree that the hypothesis results in "right" feedback, the individual stays with it. When it leads to "incorrect" feedback, the subject switches.

This view of concept identification as hypothesis testing is based on the view of people as active problem solvers, exactly the vision that guided the so-called cognitive revolution within psychology. As we described in Chapter 1, the learned helplessness model was crucial in bringing animal learning into this revolution, but here we can criticize helplessness theory for not going far enough, because the model brought with it its associationistic ancestry. In other words, the theory assumes that people rather automatically abstract response-outcome contingencies given the appropriate exposure to them. No mention is made of how the individual does this. Levine suggests that all learning, including that of response-outcome relationships, is mediated by hypothesis testing of the type we just sketched.

Meanwhile, we return to the helplessness laboratory and the individual given random feedback in his attempts to solve problems. According to Levine's theory, this random feedback negates the hypotheses that the problem solver successively entertains. One by one, he discards the large stimuli, the yellow ones, and the square ones.

People usually start with simple hypotheses and stay with them unless feedback from the world suggests that they are inadequate. Then people move to increasingly complex ones. Levine et al. and Peterson suggested, therefore, that uncontrollable events disrupt the subject's problem solving in the laboratory not because they lead her to believe in her own helplessness but because they alter the pool of potential hypotheses for problems, leading her during the pretreatment problems to entertain ever more complex possibilities. The greater the degree of pretreatment, the more of her hypotheses are disconfirmed and the more extreme and esoteric her remaining hypotheses become. When she brings these expectations—not of response-outcome independence but of difficult solutions—to the test task, she is hampered in accordance with the actual simplicity of the solution of the test task.

So Levine et al. and Peterson both showed that uncontrollable events disrupted test-task performance to a greater degree when the test task had a simple solution than when it had a more complex one. Indeed, complex test tasks were not impaired by uncontrollability, presumably because subjects were expecting complex solutions and immediately started to test complex hypotheses. There is no way that this result can be interpreted in terms of helplessness theory, which, if anything, would predict that more difficult test tasks would show the greatest disruption, in parallel to the animal results showing that effortful test tasks are most sensitive to the debilitating effects of uncontrollability (Chapter 2).

Like the reactance-helplessness integration proposed by Wortman and Brehm (1975), the Levine et al. and Peterson account does not say that the helplessness model is wrong but rather that it may not be what is typically going on in the laboratory. This alternative is able to explain why subjects keep working at psychology experiments in the wake of uncontrollability, which, as we have noted, is a problem for the helplessness model, which in its most stark form seems to imply that uncontrollability should produce an entirely listless individual rather than what actually happens—someone who cannot solve problems. This alternative can also handle reactance effects when they do occur and make sense of immunization (which legitimizes the pool of solutions for the test task) as well as therapy (which relegitimizes solutions that will work).

What are the limits of the hypothesis-testing account? Peterson (1980) surveyed disparate lines of research all implying that individuals in a psychology experiment are unlikely to consider the possibility that the events encountered therein are without meaning or pattern. Subjects who see strings of random numbers discern patterns. They detect contingencies between responses and outcomes when none is present. They expect the most clearly chance events—such as throwing dice or spinning a roulette wheel—to be something they can control. They conscientiously follow the most absurd of experimental directions. Extrapolating from these findings, how likely is it that people expect problems in a psychology experiment to be without a solution?

Peterson (1980) explored this question in several experiments. In one, he gave subjects concept-identification problems with random feedback but then asked subjects what they thought the concept was that governed the feedback. *Not a single subject* suggested that the problem was indeed without a solution. Instead, each suggested highly complex hypotheses. In another experiment, Peterson followed the same procedure with one critical exception. He suggested to subjects in their original directions that some of the problems they would be asked to solve might not have solutions. When this was said, subjects then were able to say that unsolvable problems really were unsolvable. (This was not a general demand, because solvable problems were still identified by subjects as solvable). And further consistent with the hypothesis-testing explanation, when these instructions were given to subjects, thereby legitimizing response-outcome independence as a possible description of the state of affairs in the experiment, problem solving at complex tasks was indeed disrupted by the prior experience with uncontrollability.

Can we take this notion outside the laboratory? Certainly. There will be domains of life in which the "hypothesis" of no control is entertained reluctantly or infrequently. Social psychologists over the years have documented a variety of such occurrences. Consider the *just world effect* (Lerner, 1980), where people blame victims for their misfortune, perhaps to keep their belief consistent that the world is a place where outcomes follow responses in a fair and coherent way. Taylor (1989) has cataloged a variety of benign illusions about control. Other researchers have shown that people misjudge the likelihood of negative events, consistently underestimating many of them in accordance with certain cognitive biases.

On the other hand, when bad events do occur, people's assumptions about the coherence in the world are indeed challenged, perhaps to the point where they consider the possibility that these things happen, sometimes independently of what one does. Janoff-Bulman (1989), for example, has studied the effects of various forms of victimization on one's beliefs about the world, and her results show that a variety of victims now consider the possibility of future victimization. The generality of the hypothesis-testing account has limits, but the view of contingency detection as hypothesis testing remains viable and may someday replace the simpler and more "automatic" view assumed by the helplessness model.

Egotism

Another alternative explanation of debilitated performance following uncontrollability focuses on *attributional egotism* (Snyder, Stephan, & Rosenfield, 1978). According to this theory, uncontrollability leads to poor performance through an effect on motivation. However, whereas the learned helplessness model proposes that an individual's decreased motivation is an inherent, automatic response to the expectation of response-outcome independence, the egotism theory suggests that his low motivation is a defensive strategy. The person not able to control some important outcome stops trying in order to protect himself from the conclusion that he lacks the ability needed to solve the task at hand. If he isn't trying, then he can attribute his failure to his lack of effort, presumably a less ego-threatening attribution than one that points to his inability. So, according to the egotism hypothesis, learned helplessness as produced in the experimental laboratory really is a way of sustaining self-esteem in the wake of failure.

Several studies have been reported in favor of the egotism notion. In the typical learned helplessness design, Frankel and Snyder (1978) followed uncontrollable problems with a test task described as either moderately or highly difficult. In point of fact, it was the same test task. But when a task was described as highly difficult, the thinking was that a subject would not need to retreat into low effort in order to save face in the case of subsequent failure. The ostensible difficulty of the test task should provide that rationale, and so there is no corresponding decrease in effort. This is what Frankel and Snyder (1978) indeed found. The performance decrement following uncontrollability was eliminated in this case, although not for subjects who thought they were working on a moderately difficult problem.

This study sounds similar to those we have already described by Levine et al. and Peterson in support of their hypothesis-testing explanation of helplessness effects, so let us draw out the distinction. Where Levine et al. and Peterson actually varied the difficulty of the test task, Frankel and Snyder did not, instead manipulating by instructions a subject's expectation about the difficulty of the test task. In either case, though, the helplessness model would not make the same predictions that these alternatives did.

Another study supporting the egotism hypothesis provided subjects in a learned helplessness experiment with a plausible excuse for possible poor performance during the test task: the playing of music during the test task and the explicit comment by the experimenter that the music might be distracting (Snyder, Smoller, Strenta, & Frankel, 1981). Again, this manipulation had the effect of eliminating problem-solving deficits. Other subjects not given this potential excuse fared poorly on the test task, apparently because this was their only way to save face in the case of their possible failure.

Frankel and Snyder draw a parallel between their egotism hypothesis and earlier work done with individuals who were greatly fearful of failure (e.g., Feather, 1961, 1963). Subjects with a great deal of performance anxiety did better at a task when it was described as difficult than when it was not, again with the rationale that the difficulty of the task provided a face-saving excuse just in case the subjects happened to fail. There was no shame in doing poorly at a clearly difficult task, and so subjects expended maximum effort with minimal fear.

These ideas are similar to Norem and Cantor's (1986) notion of *defensive pessimism*, a strategy used by some individuals as a way of curbing anxiety about an impending performance. The defensive pessimist loudly proclaims her likely failure—her helplessness—but then proceeds to do perfectly well at the task. In a clever experiment, Norem and Cantor interrupted the strategic use of pessimism by such subjects by giving them a pep talk prior to a problem. But when the subjects were assured that they would do well, they then performed poorly! In contrast, subjects not so encouraged did well.

How do we evaluate the egotism hypothesis and its cognates? On the one hand, we are convinced that some of the time, some of the people indeed respond to uncontrollability with such face-saving, anxiety-reducing strategies. That these may end up producing poor performance does not necessarily argue against their strategic intent. After all, maintaining a view of oneself as competent is probably more important than possible success at an isolated laboratory task.

The egotism hypothesis has the virtue of being able to make sense of many of the studies showing that helplessness effects are influenced by the sorts of attributions that people make for original uncontrollable events. To the degree that test tasks and pretreatment are diagnostic of one another, one would expect helplessness effects to occur, and the egotism hypothesis would say that this is because the person tries to save face at similar tasks following a failure at others. There is less of a motivation to do so when the tasks are dissimilar.

The egotism hypothesis also explains immunization effects. Presumably, they are effective because they provide subjects with evidence that they do have sufficient ability, despite the apparent challenge to this belief represented by uncontrollable events encountered during the pretreatment.

However, we think the egotism hypothesis has a problem explaining therapy effects. It implies that subjects should mightily resist such efforts. This interpretation follows from the hypothesis that the "helplessness" of the individual is motivated. The therapist must induce the subject to give up this strategy, not merely show him that he is mistaken about response-outcome noncontingency.

The egotism hypothesis is clearly at odds with the helplessness model, but one might wonder about its relationship to the attributional reformulation, to be discussed in Chapter 6. Both argue that subjects engage in active interpretations of the uncontrollable events they encounter. Both end up predicting that an attribution to low effort is less damaging than one to low ability, because the former does not imply as much about future performance as does the latter. But the egotism hypothesis still differs from the reformulated model in an essential way, and that is by its assumption that a person's helplessness is motivated.

Helplessness theory has never made this assumption, and we doubt that it is—in general—a useful assumption (Peterson & Bossio, 1989). As we have acknowledged, the egotism hypothesis may well explain what goes on inside or even outside the laboratory some of the time for some of the people, but we think it implausible that this is generally how people respond to uncontrollable events. If it were, then people would probably have an easier time than they do shaking off the effects of uncontrollability, but as we have seen, this takes a reliable toll in laboratory experiments as well as in the real world (Chapter 7).

If we wish to be highly skeptical of the egotism hypothesis and the studies reported in support of it, we can make the same criticism of this literature as we did of the original helplessness experiments. Theorists make inferences about underlying cognitive processes and contents without attempting to grapple with their measurement. This problem of making distant inferences about underlying thoughts means that theorists are standing at a distance from what they are theorizing about, and arguing that subjects must be thinking so-and-so if they act in such-and-such a way. As we have argued, this leaves the validity of the mediating cognitions suspect.

Similarly, the egotism hypothesis predicts that the greatest difficulty in problem solving in a helplessness experiment should be with purely motivational indices, not cognitive ones (seeing the solution), but this has not been explicitly investigated. The egotism

studies have measured persistence, obviously a motivational construct, but they haven't further shown that cognitive impairment
simultaneously does *not* exist. We hasten to add that the egotism
hypothesis and its supporting studies are no more suspect on this
ground than the helplessness model and its studies. This is a generic problem with the field.

Some researchers have tried to address more closely the egotism
hypothesis. Kofta and Sedek (1989), for example, contrasted it with
the helplessness model by asking what each identifies as the critical
aspect of the pretreatment that leads to an individual's debilitated
performance at the test task (see also Barber & Winefield, 1987). The
helplessness model clearly points to the uncontrollability of the pretreatment—the independence of responses and outcomes. The egotism hypothesis in contrast does not emphasize uncontrollability as
critical but instead failure. Uncontrollability per se does not threaten
someone's self-esteem—hence there is no need to protect against it.
Rather, it is failure—actively trying to achieve some goal (solve a
problem) and then falling short of this intent—that produces later
decrements in performance because failure threatens oneself in a
way that uncontrollability per se does not.

One critical way to test between the learned helplessness model
and the egotism hypothesis is therefore by separating uncontrollability and failure, to see which theory proves correct. We already
know from the meta-analysis that appetitive helplessness exists—
that is, when uncontrollable success is experienced during the pretreatment, then debilitated problem solving still appears during the
test task. Just on the face of it, this argues in favor of the learned
helplessness account. But such studies were not necessarily designed to distinguish uncontrollability and failure.

Instead, let us examine a study by Kofta and Sedek (1989) that
explicitly did this. They used a series of concept-identification problems during the pretreatment, as is now familiar. Feedback "right"
or "wrong" was delivered randomly, so that half the time a subject's answers were right and half the time wrong. In one condition,
the subjects were told that the tasks measured "something related
to logical thinking and the ability to draw conclusions" (pp. 4–5)
and that they would be given information about their overall performance at the very end of the experiment. In another condition,
the subjects were told that the tasks measured "some important
aspects of intelligence" (p. 5) and that they would be given information about their performance after each problem; in each case,

they were told that they had failed to solve the problem. In a third condition, subjects received the same instructions as those in the first condition, and the feedback on individual trials was accurate.

The second condition obviously sets up the conditions in which the processes hypothesized by the egotism view should operate. Checks—in the form of a questionnaire administered at the very end of the experiment—confirmed the intended manipulation of failure; subjects in the second condition reported that their performance was indeed poor at the pretreatment and furthermore that their mood was poor. Subjects in the first and third condition did not differ from one another on perceived failure, and both were substantially lower in perceived failure than those in the second condition.

In terms of test-task performance, which entailed pushing buttons in order to terminate a series of unpleasant noises, subjects in the two uncontrollability conditions showed impairment relative to the control condition, both in their latency to solve and in the total number of their failures. These two groups did not differ from one another, meaning that the addition of manipulations designed to highlight egotism had no discernible effect. As Kofta and Sedek concluded, these results are highly inconsistent with the egotism account yet completely compatible with the helplessness model. Uncontrollability was the critical feature of the helplessness induction, not failure.

At the same time, some of the questionnaire responses were at odds with the helplessness model. Noncontingent events did not produce a lowered mood among subjects in the first condition— although the failure manipulation did. Further, the manipulations did not affect ratings of the controllability of the test task, despite the fact that reliable performance decrements had been produced. Subjects did perceive uncontrollable pretreatment tasks as more uncontrollable, but this expectation was not generalized to the test task, as the helplessness model predicts. Neither did ratings show any difference with respect to an item asking about the role of increased effort, which the egotism model would predict would show differences among groups. Here we have what is becoming a familiar finding: performance deficits in the absence of corresponding differences in a subject's reported thoughts and expectations.

This study questions the ability of the egotism hypothesis to replace the helplessness model, but it does not show that it is completely without merit. Enhanced persistence at difficult test tasks remains a finding not accommodated with the helplessness approach. What we can say at the present is that both failure and uncontrollable events influence a person's subsequent performance, although the exact processes by which they do so remain unclear.

State versus Action Orientation

Kuhl (1981) proposed yet another cognitive interpretation of helplessness effects. He agrees with the helplessness model (and the bulk of the research results) that uncontrollability leads to debilitated performance, but he proposes a different cognitive mechanism that places less emphasis on the expectation of future helplessness as hypothesized by helplessness theory.

Instead, Kuhl argues that "helplessness" effects can be better explained by constructs already articulated and investigated within the tradition of achievement motivation. He suggests that the immediate response to failure (uncontrollability) is a heightened motivation to do well at a subsequent task. Here he agrees with the Wortman and Brehm (1975) idea about reactance being produced by experience with uncontrollable events. Consistent with this assumption are reports (e.g., Miller & Seligman, 1975) that ostensibly helpless subjects approach the test task with initial vigor, which is exactly what the helplessness model does not expect. It is only when they fail to achieve success at the task that they then give up.

But why should a subject not be able to do well at a test task, if her motivation to do so is intact and she does not expect that she will do poorly? Kuhl introduces a contrast between two psychological approaches to problem solving: state orientation versus action orientation. *State orientation* is a focus on the past, present, and/or future state of the person: how am I feeling, why am I having trouble, what are the implications of this experience for my well-being, and so on. Because it is task-irrelevant, state orientation interferes with the person's performance, at least when the task is difficult. In contrast, *action orientation* is an unimpeded approach to problem solving; here the person focuses on the problem at hand and the various ways that it might be solved.

Thus we have yet another alternative explanation of performance impairment following uncontrollability. Although failure per se may enhance a person's motivation, if the failure also produces a sufficient state orientation, it will override her enhanced motivation and interfere with her task performance. Said another way, helplessness effects are produced not by perceptions of response-outcome independence but rather by a host of irrelevant thoughts on which the person ruminates. It is rumination that then creates her difficulties.

Interestingly, Kuhl's argument says that helplessness is very much a cognitive phenomenon but that it is not particularly important just what type of cognitive activity is occurring. As long as it is not problem focused, it is apt to be disruptive. In contrast to the learned helplessness reformulation, this theory suggests that attributional activity per se is disruptive, because it distracts the person from the business at hand. Consistent with this notion is research by Diener and Dweck (1978) finding that children were disrupted by uncontrollable problems to the degree that they offered any type of causal attributions for their failure.

Kuhl suggests that helplessness produced by state orientation be called functional helplessness. In contrast, the helplessness of concern to the learned helplessness model is deemed motivational helplessness, and it is mediated by expectations of uncontrollability. Kuhl implies that in typical laboratory studies, motivational helplessness is apt to be found only when test tasks and pretreatments are highly similar, in which case the person might well generalize a belief in response-outcome independence abstracted in the first situation to the second. But in other experiments, where test task and pretreatment are dissimilar, he argues that such transfer of expectation is unlikely and that observed deficits are probably functional helplessness. And out of the laboratory, he further argues, functional helplessness is the norm, not motivational helplessness:

> The student who has had an experience of uncontrollability at a math test may burn his or her dinner, behave awkwardly toward friends, and be less assertive than usual in expressing his or her needs in a group. The [functional helplessness] theory maintains that behavioral effects of this generality cannot be attributed to generalized expectancy . . . The student is not likely to have problems dealing with friends because she or he infers an inability to deal with them from an inability to pass the test. The problems in dealing with friends are more likely to arise because she or he is still preoccupied with the *state* created by the flunked test. (Kuhl, 1981, p. 160)

In support of his theory, Kuhl reported several experiments. In one, following a typical helplessness induction, subjects in some groups had an additional experience interpolated before the test task. One condition was intended to accentuate a state orientation; subjects were asked to respond to a questionnaire asking about their reasons for failure, descriptions of their emotional state, and an evaluation of the experimental situation. Another condition was intended to accentuate an action orientation; subjects here were asked to engage in a nonachievement task—reading an essay and offering an opinion about how interesting and informative it has been. Subjects in another condition had no interpolated task but proceeded directly to the test task, which entailed finding specific symbols in a complex array.

Relative to subjects without initial uncontrollability, those with an induced state orientation showed disruption at the test task, whereas an induced action orientation did not. These findings are consistent with Kuhl's theory. Ratings of perceptions of uncontrollability did not support the helplessness model's notion that these effects are generalized and mediate disruption. However, a problem with this experiment is that among subjects in the uncontrollable condition without intervention—that is, a standard helplessness condition—no disruption relative to control subjects was produced. In other words, Kuhl did not demonstrate that his procedure could produce a helplessness result, which is obviously a problem in using his other findings to support an alternative interpretation of helplessness effects.

Cognitive Exhaustion

A variant of Kuhl's notion of state orientation induced by uncontrollability has been proposed by Sedek and Kofta (1990), who argued that experience with uncontrollable events initially sets off a great deal of cognitive activity, as the person attempts to solve the problem presented and to make sense of his inability to do so. However, the effect of noncontingency is to make these efforts necessarily unsuccessful. Like the hypothesis-testing alternative we have already described, this view says that people entertain and evaluate various possibilities as descriptions of the state of affairs they are encountering. In the case of random feedback, the person does not continue proposing and evaluating hypotheses endlessly. He eventually switches into a state these researchers identify as cognitive exhaustion, where he simply stops thinking. It is this state of cognitive demobilization that then produces cognitive impairment on subsequent tasks. (Barber & Winefield, 1986, sketched yet another version of this explanation by stating that helplessness effects occur when subjects stop paying attention to stimuli.)

Sedek and Kofta reported an experiment that tried to test this account. In their helplessness induction, they arranged matters so that random feedback was explicitly contradictory—that is, subjects were given explicitly opposite feedback on identical stimuli in a concept-identification task—versus just random feedback. Then subjects worked on a simple test task followed by a difficult one. No disruption was found for the first task, presumably because it was readily solved, even by a cognitively exhausted individual. There was disruption at the second, more difficult task, but only when subjects had received explicitly contradictory information during the pretreatment. Subjects reported feeling uncertain, unable to pay attention, and having lowered expectations about their success.

We think the cognitive exhaustion hypothesis is not as crisply supported by these results as Sedek and Kofta hoped. Certainly one can confuse subjects by providing them with contradictory information; that this then leads to their poor performance later on at a difficult—effortful—task is reasonable, too. But does this prove that exhaustion is the critical mediator in all helplessness experiments? Hardly, particularly when the researchers failed to produce helplessness effects in what was the most standard condition. Perhaps the introduction of the easy test task broke up the helpless effects for these subjects, but not for the confused subjects. Further work is needed to evaluate this alternative. Its most attractive part is its proposal that the cognitive deficit in learned helplessness is precisely that—a failure to think—which may well explain why attempts to characterize this deficit have met with so little success. There literally is nothing to characterize!

Secondary Control

One more alternative account of reactions to uncontrollable events was proposed by Rothbaum, Weisz, and Snyder (1982). Where helplessness theory interprets passivity, withdrawal, and submissiveness as prima facie evidence of diminished personal control (Chapter 1), Rothbaum et al. suggested instead that these ostensible signs of helplessness may reflect alternative forms of control.

Central to Rothbaum et al.'s model is a distinction between *primary control*, defined as an individual's ability to bring the environment into line with her wishes, and *secondary control*, defined as an individual's ability to bring herself into line with the environment. Primary control has been the concern of helplessness theories and most other explanations of how people respond to bad events (Peterson & Stunkard, 1989). According to Rothbaum et al., attempts at primary control may be the person's first and preferred response to uncontrollability. But secondary control may succeed when primary control fails. If the person is able to accept uncontrollable events and derive meaning from them, then he will not be disrupted by them. What looks like helplessness may well be an attempt to sustain secondary control over events that elude primary control.

Rothbaum et al. describe several different forms of secondary control. Each is marked by characteristic causal explanations, and what is interesting in each case is that these attributions are the same ones that we interpret as exacerbating a lack of control (Chapter 5). "Predictive control refers to the ability to predict aversive events to avoid disappointment" (p. 13). To always expect the worst is not to be disappointed when the worst occasionally or even frequently happens. Note the similarity to Norem and Cantor's (1986) notion of defensive pessimism, which we described earlier. Predictive control is characterized by attributions of deficient ability and is exemplified by the individual who continually downgrades his own skills and accomplishments.

A second form, illusory control, occurs when people align themselves with chance or fate. Again, explanations in terms of luck and the like are typically seen as reflecting a capricious world. But Rothbaum et al. argue that illusory control reflects just the opposite. Although people with illusory control are obviously not directly influencing events, they nevertheless believe that events are orderly. Fate deals the cards, but it is possible to synchronize oneself with fate.

A third form of secondary control is vicarious control, similar to illusory control except that the individual achieves control by associating himself not with chance but with powerful groups or individuals: religious or political leaders, certain professions or hobbies, athletes, God, rock-and-roll musicians, and so on. Identification with individuals or groups powerful enough to control outcomes that one cannot influence oneself is the psychological mechanism highlighted by Erich Fromm (1941) in his well-known *Escape from Freedom*. According to Fromm, totalitarian movements like fascism are appealing to individuals who cannot or will not achieve freedom by their own efforts (primary control). The important point in this context is that attribution to "other people" is usually seen as the relinquishing of control; once again, Rothbaum et al. argue that it is a means of gaining and maintaining control.

Collectively, these and other forms of secondary control are called interpretive control, which people are motivated to achieve when primary control fails. Individual search for meaning and understanding following bad events, and the finding of an answer—regardless of its nature—may be adaptive. By this view, expectations of uncontrollability, causal explanations, and even passive withdrawn behavior may be useful strategies. Labeling them helplessness is to miss their purpose.

Rothbaum et al.'s ideas are no doubt reasonable in some cases. The trick is to distinguish these cases from others and then to decide which is the rule and which is the exception. Research to date has not attempted this, but the appropriate investigation would look at the degree to which "helpless" behavior is motivated: persistent and effortful. Do ostensibly helpless individuals prefer situations where failure is inevitable? It would also look more closely at what people believe about such causes as deficient ability, chance, or powerful others. Are these seen as comforting or distressing?

The logic here can become quite convoluted. If passive behavior is found not to be persistent, does this vindicate the helplessness model and other theories that regard passivity as isomorphic with diminished control, or can it then be argued that ostensibly "helpless" helplessness is really a tertiary form of control? Rothbaum et al.'s two-process theory may be nonfalsifiable. Regardless, if the general thrust of this section is that people's thoughts about uncontrollable events can be quite complex, then Rothbaum et al.'s observations well illustrate this point.

WHAT WE KNOW

Researchers began their investigations of learned helplessness in people with the general question of whether something akin to the phenomenon previously documented among animals exposed to uncontrollability had a counterpart among human beings. Our first conclusion is that it does exist. Uncontrollable events, operationalized in a variety of ways, reliably lead to disruption at subsequent problem-solving tasks. Uncontrollability also has effects on people's emotions, aggression, and physiology. Helplessness effects among people have a time course. They can be minimized by immunization and reversed by therapy. All in all, these findings from studies with human subjects attest to a strong analogy with the animal phenomenon.

Our second conclusion is that learned helplessness among people has boundary conditions. (So too does animal helplessness, although recognition of this aspect of animal learned helplessness was not what led researchers to demonstrate it among people.) Although helplessness effects are somewhat general—after all, this is what it means to be helpless—there are clear limits to generality across time and situation. Among the reliable influences on this generality are the individual's causal attributions about the original uncontrollable events. As we discuss in the next chapter, the role of attributions was the point of departure for the reformulation of helplessness theory along attributional lines.

Our third conclusion is that human helplessness has some variants with no clear counterpart among animals. People can acquire helplessness vicariously, by observing others. And groups of people as a whole can be made helpless by uncontrollability; further, group helplessness is not reducible to the helplessness of the individual members. Neither of these phenomena has been the subject of much research beyond their initial demonstration, but we highlight them as particularly intriguing, opening the doors to all sorts of possible applications of helplessness ideas outside the laboratory.

Finally, our last conclusion is that helplessness among people is under the sway of central factors. Early studies with human subjects geared up against the same sort of peripheralist interpretations suggested for the animal phenomenon, but it was soon quite obvious that human helplessness entailed some sort of mentalistic mediation. There were simply too many effects, obvious and subtle, readily explained in central terms that were impossible to explain by reference to notions like incompatible motor responses or biochemical trauma.

WHAT WE DON'T KNOW

Although there exists a learned helplessness effect among people in that they perform poorly at test tasks following uncontrollability, we do not yet know if this reflects both motivational and cognitive disruptions, as the helplessness model holds, or just one sort of deficit. Researchers to date have not been sufficiently clever in devising independent operationalizations of these deficits.

As we have repeatedly emphasized, we also do not know the exact nature of the mediation of human helplessness as produced in the laboratory. The helplessness model proposes that expectations of uncontrollability acquired during pretreatment and generalized to the test task produce helplessness effects, but research has not conclusively shown that this is indeed what happens. Making this difficult are the considerable pitfalls in studying cognition in the typical learned helplessness paradigms. We discussed some considerations that might aid investigation of the cognitive mediation of helplessness effects, but few studies to date qualify as laudable by the criteria we suggest.

Relatedly, we are not sure how to evaluate the rather large number of alternative explanations of helplessness effects. All these explanations propose a different mediation than does the helplessness model. In each case, we suggested that they capture something important about responses to uncontrollability, but at the same time we do not think that any represents a death knell for the helplessness model. Some have their own conceptual or empirical problems. All run into the same problems as does the helplessness model of verifying the existence of elusive cognitive constructs. Most do not address one another but rather direct their critical energy at the helplessness model alone. Can they all be correct? Maybe, but not in a mushy eclecticism in which all possibilities are accorded equal status. Contrast the cognitive exhaustion explanation, which attributes disruption to insufficient thinking, with the state orientation explanation, which points the finger at too much thinking!

Needed, we imagine, is a series of very careful studies of how people respond to uncontrollability, over the range of parameters stressed by these alternative theories. In particular, these studies should take time into account, because most of the alternative explanations hypothesize about processes that unfold as experience with uncontrollability increases. Perhaps more sophisticated strategies for studying cognitive content and process need to be devised; the animal literature reviewed in Chapter 2 might provide some useful hints concerning operationalizations. Until this happens, the biggest unknown of human helplessness will remain the details of what and how the helpless person thinks, and when he does so.

5

The Attributional Reformulation

As it was first articulated, the learned helplessness model hypothesized that experience with uncontrollable events leads to difficulties in motivation, cognition, and emotion (Chapter 2). Mediating this effect is a person's expectation that responses and outcomes are independent. This expectation arises through his attempts to master events that elude his control, and it is generalized into new situations to produce the problems that constitute the learned helplessness phenomenon (Chapter 1).

Our purpose in this chapter is to describe the theoretical and empirical reactions to the shortcomings of the very first studies of human helplessness, as we described in the previous chapter. These reactions stressed cognitive factors. Any of a number might have received attention, but most investigators zeroed in on how the helpless individual construed the causes of the original uncontrollable events that produced his helplessness. The original helplessness model was therefore revised to include causal explanations, and what ensued was a more powerful account of how people respond to uncontrollable events. In particular, the revised theory was able to explain individual differences in response to uncontrollability, because people bring habitual explanatory styles to bear on the events they experience.

HISTORICAL BACKGROUND: ATTRIBUTION THEORY AND THEORIZING

Psychology's interest in the individual's causal interpretation of events can be traced to Fritz Heider's (1958) *Psychology of Interpersonal Re-*

lations. In this highly original work, Heider called for the study of what he termed naive psychology: how everyday people make sense of their world. Naive psychology includes the way that people understand the causes of behavior: their own and that of their fellows.

Heider falls within the gestalt psychology tradition, and several of his emphases thereby become clear. First, he believes that people look for meaning in their experiences. The meanings they assign determine their subsequent thoughts, feelings, and actions, just as one's interpretation of a visual object determines one's subsequent perception. Second, he believes that people's interpretations are characterized by balance or harmony. The effect is that people generalize their interpretations beyond immediate experience. Third, Heider believes that people's "cognitive" interpretations are analogous to their more "perceptual" ones.

This last point is subtle, but it has important implications, so we will state it in a different way. Although concerned with how people make sense of complex behavior, Heider often theorizes from the viewpoint of a perception psychologist. When he speaks of someone's point of view, he means this in an almost literal sense. In observing someone's behavior, we see that it has causes (Michotte, 1963). As noted in Chapter 2, the experience of events under particular conditions gives rise to a causal perception. A student raises his hand, and *thus* the teacher calls on him. Someone experiences boredom, and *thus* she flips the television channel.

According to Heider, then, when people make sense of behavior, they do so in terms of causes. Of course, other ways of construal are possible, for instance, interpretations in terms of ultimate goals. But a teleological explanation is not grounded in perception and may not be as basic as a causal explanation. We agree with Heider that everyday people are concerned with the causes of events. There has been some disagreement on this point (Wortman & Dintzer, 1978), but the evidence seems overwhelming that a concern with causality is a basic aspect of human nature.

Another important consequence of Heider's analogy to perception is that the fundamental distinction within causal explanations is between internal and external causes. This distinction corresponds to the distinction between the perceiver and the perceived, between the self and the world, between the inside and the outside of our skins. Some contemporary writers have observed that the internal-external distinction is problematic. There seem to exist ambiguous cases, like headaches. But at least some of these difficulties can be resolved by remembering Heider's perceptual emphasis. Is a cause seen as imposed from without, or is it seen as emanating from within? The perspective of the individual is critical, and headaches may be either internal or external, depending on who is experiencing them.

Many of us have had the misfortune to break an arm or leg. At least in the old days, a plaster cast was used to immobilize our limb while it healed. When the cast was first set, it was external to the self and occupied a great deal of our attention. After time passed, it became internal and occupied little attention. To further the analogy with literal perception, a figure-ground reversal occurred, as the cast was assimilated to the self. The point here is that a cast can be construed as external, or it can be construed as internal, but it is not ambiguous. It is one or the other, depending on other factors.

Popularized by Jones and Davis (1965) and Kelley (1967, 1972), Heider's ideas eventually took hold in the larger field of psychology, and particularly in social psychology. They form the foundation of what is now called *attribution theory*, a loosely defined approach to understanding people's behavior by taking into account their causal beliefs. Attribution theory and research usually distinguish between internal and external causes. Other distinctions have been added, but the internal-external one remains important (Weiner, 1986).

Why has attribution theory been so popular? Part of the answer refers to the Zeitgeist. The 1960s and 1970s saw a waning of interest in empty organism approaches to psychology and a corresponding increase of interest in ways that people "process information" from the world (Gardner, 1985). Two related metaphors of human nature became dominant: person-as-scientist and person-as-computer. Attribution theory is compatible with each. Like scientists, people try to understand the world. Specifically, they try to identify causes that allow them to predict and control future events. Like computers, people take in information, transform it according to rules, and produce some result. It was easy for psychologists to translate stimulus-response language into input-output language; the added benefit of this was a rich vocabulary for conceiving what went on in between.

The other reason attribution theory has been popular is quite simply that it captures what is really going on. It may not be fashionable in these days of relativism to say that science is the business of understanding reality. But if nothing else, this is a good working assumption, probably one that all scientists adopt in the course of everyday science. So we assume that people really are attentive to the causes of behavior and that their causal interpretations really do determine the way they act. We conclude that attribution theory is popular in no small way because it works well.

Attribution theory has been the province of social psychology, which means that it has been studied from a social psychology stance, emphasizing the situational determinants of causal attributions. As described in the last chapter, studies of this kind challenged the original learned helplessness model as it applied to people, because situationally manipulated attributions affected induced helplessness above and beyond any manipulations of controllability.

But the real benefit of introducing attribution theory to the learned helplessness model is that it allows us to explain individual differences. Different people offer different causal explanations for the same events, and thus they react in different ways. Because individual variation is not the typical concern of social psychology, an attributional account of learned helplessness goes beyond social psychology to speak to issues important in personality psychology and psychopathology.

CAUSAL EXPLANATIONS AND LOCUS OF CONTROL

We need to address specifically the relationship between internal versus external causal explanations as proposed within attribution theory and internal versus external *locus of control* as proposed within Rotter's (1966) social learning theory. Some theorists have regarded these concepts as essentially the same, whereas other theorists (including us in previous incarnations; e.g., Peterson & Seligman, 1984) have regarded them as completely different. At the present time, we have a more complex view. Causal explanations and locus of control overlap with each other, yet they are distinct to some degree. Neither the similarity nor the difference can be appreciated without reference to the other (Peterson & Stunkard, 1989, 1992).

Julian Rotter's (1954) social learning theory defies categorization. It is a learning theory in that it is concerned with how people come to behave in a particular way in response to particular stimuli, but Rotter's major influences were the psychoanalytic theorist Alfred Adler and the field theorist Kurt Lewin. Because Heider was also influenced by Lewin's ideas, we can expect at least some convergence between social learning theory and attribution theory. According to Rotter (1966), reinforcement does not automatically strengthen the behaviors that precede it. An individual will increase the likelihood of some response only to the degree that he expects the response to be followed by reinforcement in the future. This expectation in turn has two determinants.

First, the specific characteristics of the response and the reinforcement shape the expectation of a future link between the two. If Suzie Student receives an A grade in organic chemistry, she does not repeat the course the next term, even though the A grade was the highlight of her academic career. There is good reason for her to expect that a repeat performance would not be reinforced.

Second, people have a general belief about the locus of rewards. Some people believe that rewards originate within: from their own efforts and abilities. Others believe that they originate without: from situations, chance, or other people. These two extremes define the endpoints of Rotter's locus-of-control continuum: internal versus external, respectively. All things being equal, the internal individual is more likely to form the expectation that reinforcement will follow particular behaviors than the external individual. But as Rotter (1975) has carefully explained, quite often all things are not equal. Particularly in situations in which the causal structure is well known, the personality difference is apt to be irrelevant.

Compare playing slot machines in Atlantic City with taking a driver's license test in Philadelphia. In the former case, most people believe that "chance" determines reinforcement, whereas in the latter case, most people believe that "effort" and/or "skill" predominates. One would not expect locus of control to be overwhelmingly important in determining expectations (and hence behavior) in these situations. Internals will play the slots, eventually stopping when excitement has run its course, whereas externals will practice for their driver's license test, eventually stopping when they pass.

The similarity between locus of control and causal attributions is that both are cognitive constructs that explain variations in our behavior. Both refer to the relationship between our actions and outcomes. Both may influence the vigor or passivity with which we live.

The difference is that locus of control is a belief about the nature of reinforcement—that is, about rewards and punishments in the world. Causal attributions are judgments about the causes of events. Although related, these are not the same. Empirically they may be independent. An individual with an internal locus of control may offer external causal explanations—"If I am charming, I will be offered the job, but whether or not I am charming depends on the mood of the interviewer"—or vice versa.

A more exact parallel exists between causal attributions and Rotter's notion of expectation than between attributions and locus of control. This expectation lends itself to attributional language, because it is a belief about whether responses lead to (cause) reinforcement. Locus of control is merely one determinant of this expectation, and so it exists at a different conceptual level than causal attributions.

THE REFORMULATED LEARNED HELPLESSNESS MODEL

In 1978, Lyn Abramson, Martin Seligman, and John Teasdale presented a "critique and reformulation" of the learned helplessness model as applied to people. Their chief modification was to assign to causal attributions a mediating effect in the process by which uncontrollable events produce deficits. This paper appeared in a special issue of the *Journal of Abnormal Psychology* devoted to learned helplessness as a model of depression, and probably as a result, the attributional reformulation has been examined mainly as an account of depressive disorders (Chapter 6). However, helplessness theory as a whole was revised in this reformulation, not just its application to depression.

As we described in the last chapter, a number of laboratory studies showed that an individual's causal explanations for uncontrollable events influence reactions to them. And as described in the present chapter, attribution theory and attribution theorizing were ripe for combination with the original helplessness model.

Abramson et al. (1978) introduced the reformulation by pointing to two major problems encountered in applying helplessness theory to people. The first problem was that the theory did not distinguish between cases in which outcomes are uncontrollable for all people and cases in which they are uncontrollable only for some people. The first of these cases they called *universal helplessness* and is exemplified by the parent with a fatally ill child. Nothing he or she can do will make the child healthy again, and nothing that anybody else can do will help either. The second of these cases is *personal helplessness* and is exemplified by the student who is failing calculus. Although she or he cannot solve the problems on homework assignments or examinations, other people in the class have no difficulty doing so.

What difference does it make if someone experiences universal helplessness or personal helplessness? In both instances, the individual perceives no relationship between behaviors and outcomes. In both instances, the expectation of future noncontingency results in debilitation. But in the case of personal helplessness, the individual engages in self-recrimination. "If only" rumination occurs, and the person's self-esteem plummets. In the case of universal helplessness, the person's self-esteem is left intact.

The second problem with the original helplessness theory is that it does not explain when helplessness deficits will be generalized. According to the original theory, the helpless person expects responses (in general) and outcomes (in general) to be unrelated. The implication is that helplessness deficits following uncontrollability are highly general. Common sense as well as the laboratory studies reviewed in the previous chapter argue against this implication.

While there are instances of general helplessness, they seem most likely to occur in highly unusual situations, like the aftermath of concentration camp internment or a natural disaster. We would not wish to reserve "learned helplessness" only for these instances of highly generalized passivity. Unfortunately, the original theory does not explain the more typical instances of debilitation following uncontrollability: somewhat general, somewhat circumscribed helplessness.

Abramson et al. (1978) resolved these two problems by proposing that helpless people make causal explanations for the uncontrollable events they encounter. These causal explanations affect self-esteem as well as the generality of deficits. In other words, when people encounter important events that elude their control, they ask "why?" Their answer affects the way in which they respond to these events.

Figure 5-1 diagrams the hypothesized sequence of events leading from noncontingency to a person's helpless behavior. Note that helplessness theory, as applied to people, has become more complex in its depiction of the cognitive processes involved. A person need not actually experience repeated events in order for them to produce helplessness. All that is needed is for the person to expect that events will be uncontrollable. Abstraction of response-outcome relations is unnecessary for a person to expect that responses and outcomes are unrelated. This expectation may come from a variety of sources besides induction: for instance, observation of others, cultural stereotypes, specific information to this effect, and so on (Chapter 4).

Once someone expects responses and outcomes to be independent, he seeks a causal explanation for this noncontingency. This explanation *influences* his expectation of future noncontingency, which in turn *determines* the nature of helplessness deficits. We chose our language here carefully. Causal explanations "influence" expecta-

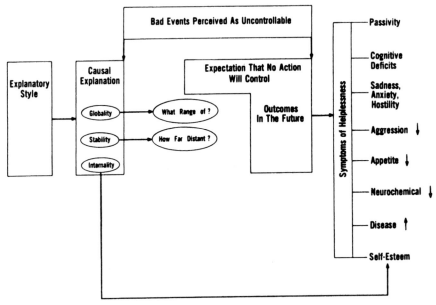

Figure 5-1. The attributional reformulation. *Source:* Peterson, C., and Seligman, M.E.P. (1984). Causal explanations as a risk factor for depression: Theory and evidence. *Psychological Review* 91:347–374. © 1984 by the American Psychological Association. Reprinted by permission of the publisher.

tions, which means that they are but one of several determinants. Causal explanations are neither necessary nor sufficient for an expectation of future noncontingency because other factors can override their influence on expectations. Expectations in turn "determine" helplessness, which means that they are causes. Expectations are sufficient for helplessness deficits.

The helplessness reformulation has focused research attention on causal explanations on the one hand and on outcomes reflecting helplessness on the other hand. Not nearly as much attention has been paid to the hypothesized cognitive process depicted in Figure 5-1.

Abramson et al. suggest that three parameters of causal explanation are important. First is the familiar distinction between *internal* versus *external* causes (see Table 5-1 for examples of such explanations as they might be offered for a romantic rejection). An internal explanation for uncontrollable events is associated with personal helplessness, because the uncontrollability is attributed to something about the particular person. In contrast, an external explanation is associated with universal helplessness, because the uncon-

Table 5-1. Examples of Causal Explanations for
Romantic Rejection.

Internal
    Stable
        Global: "I'm unattractive."
        Specific: "I'm unattractive to him/her."
    Unstable
        Global: "My conversation is sometimes boring."
        Specific: "My conversation bores him/her."
External
    Stable
        Global: "Romance is difficult for other people."
        Specific: "Romance is difficult for him/her."
    Unstable
        Global: "People sometimes have rejecting moods."
        Specific: "He/she was in a rejecting mood."

---

trollability is attributed to something about the situation or circumstance that would affect anybody placed in it. Thus, whether someone makes an internal or external explanation for uncontrollability affects her subsequent self-esteem. Internal explanations make the loss of self-esteem likely, whereas external explanations tend to leave self-esteem intact.

The second parameter of concern is a distinction between causes that are *stable* over time versus those that are *unstable* (again, see Table 5-1 for examples). Suppose you fail your first examination in a college course. Contrast your expectations for future success or failure at college tests if you explain your poor grade as due to a headache (presumably an unstable cause) versus if you attribute your failure to stupidity (presumably a stable cause, whether your own or that of college teachers). In the former case, passivity and other helplessness deficits will tend to be short-lived, because your headache will go away. In the latter case, helplessness will tend to persist, because stupidity is forever.

In a series of intriguing studies, Wilson and Linville (1982, 1985) used exactly this line of reasoning to guide an intervention that improved the grades of college students. Students were told that their grades would probably improve over the course of their college career. In other words, they were encouraged to explain their initial failures and disappointments with unstable causes. These students, in contrast to those not given this intervention, indeed improved their grades.

The third parameter of causal explanations identified by Abramson et al. distinguishes between causes that are *global* (affecting a variety of outcomes and situations) and those that are *specific* (affecting few outcomes and situations). Table 5-1 provides examples of these types of causal explanations. Just as stable explanations affect the generalization of helplessness deficits across time, global explanations affect generalization across situations. Again, imagine you are a student who has failed your first college exam. "Stupidity" is a global cause, relevant to history exams, English papers, and calculus problems. If this is how you explain your exam failure, widespread debilitation is apt to follow. In contrast, if you explain the failure with a more circumscribed cause ("I'm not good at multiple-choice tests" or "Chemistry is a difficult subject"), you will have less widespread difficulties, exactly in proportion to the specificity of the cause.

As we described earlier, almost all attribution theorists embrace Heider's (1958) distinction between internal versus external causes. And following the theoretical insights of Bernard Weiner (1972, 1974), most recent attribution theorists also distinguish between stable versus unstable causes. The globality versus specificity dimension was first introduced by Harold Kelley (1967, 1972) under the rubric of a cause's degree of distinctiveness. As used by Abramson et al., this dimension reflects the typical concern of learning theorists with generalization and discrimination.

Thus, the attributional reformulation of helplessness theory allows the two problems with the original theory to be resolved. Universal versus personal helplessness (and the role of self-esteem) is explained by introducing internal versus external causal explanations for uncontrollability. Generality of helplessness deficits is explained by introducing stable versus unstable causal explanations (influencing generality across time) and global versus specific explanations (influencing generality across situation).

Some who have commented on the helplessness reformulation argue that additional parameters of causal explanation may be relevant and further that cognitive factors besides causal beliefs moderate the uncontrollability-helplessness link (see Peterson, 1991). Both arguments have merits, and we return to them at the end of this chapter. However, Abramson et al. (1978) proposed the attributional reformulation in the way that they did not to exhaustively catalog cognitive variables possibly relating to passivity but rather to shore up helplessness theory in exactly the areas where it had proved weak.

Abramson et al.'s revised theory paid a further dividend, though, by suggesting that people differ in terms of how they habitually explain events. This "attributional style" (later called "explanatory style" by Peterson & Seligman, 1984) allows for individual variation in response to uncontrollability. As noted earlier, this individual difference variable moves helplessness theory out of the experimental/social tradition of psychology and into the personality/clinical tradition (Cronbach, 1957). The application of helplessness ideas to failures of adaptation like depression was made much more plausible.

Explanatory style is one of two determinants of the particular causal explanation a person chooses when faced with uncontrollable events. The other determinant is the nature of the event itself. This point is not sufficiently appreciated, so here we draw out the logic involved. According to the reformulated model, particular causal explanations influence the loss of self-esteem following uncontrollability as well as the generality of helplessness deficits. These particular causal explanations in turn may stem from an individual's typical worldview ("there you go again"), or from the generally accepted cause of events of this nature ("you wrecked the car because you were careless"), or from some combination of the two.

What this means is that sometimes explanatory style is highly relevant to subsequent deficits, whereas other times it is completely irrelevant. The key here is the causal ambiguity of the uncontrollable events. For some events, there is high concensus about operative causes, either because the "real" cause is easily seen in the covariation among actual events or because a societally provided explanation is generally accepted. When there is a high concensus concerning causes, an individual's habitual way of explaining events is put on the back shelf.

However, for other events, there is a low concensus about causes. There is no agreed-upon right answer, either because the events are too singular to allow causal relationships to be abstracted or because potential causes are numerous and confounded with one another. In these cases, an individual's habitual way of explaining events takes the lead, because reality does not encumber it.

This point is a specific instance of a more general idea familiar to personality psychologists. Personality differences do not explain behavior in highly constrained settings. Weddings and funerals and certain psychology experiments, for instance, "demand" that people act in particular ways, regardless of their personalities. Less constrained settings allow a person's personality to influence his behavior.

We feel that some investigations of explanatory style have looked for its effects in situations that constrain its possible influence on the particular explanation people choose (and hence its influence on expectations of response-outcome independence and ultimately its influence on helplessness and other outcomes). Postpartum depression (e.g., Cutrona, 1983) and teacher stress (e.g., Hammen & deMayo, 1982) are two such topics where researchers have been less than successful in showing the relevance of explanatory style. But is this due to the theoretical shortcomings of the helplessness reformulation or to the particular topic chosen for investigation? In both cases, there seems to be a considerable basis in reality to the distress that someone experiences; explanatory style is therefore apt to be irrelevant.

There is danger here of dismissing studies after the fact as inappropriate simply because they fail to confirm predictions of the reformulation. This is not good science. One must decide the appropriateness of a topic vis-à-vis explanatory style on other grounds.

First, is there sufficient variation in the outcome measure? In other words, is there anything to be explained? If most people are responding in the same way, an individual difference variable like explanatory style is not needed; there's nothing for it to do.

Second, is there sufficient variation in the causal explanations offered by the research subjects? If not, then causality is unambiguous, and explanatory style again has nothing to do. The most cautious research should therefore measure both explanatory style and causal explanations, because variance in explanatory style does not guarantee variance in causal explanations. Studies that fail to find a correlation between explanatory style and outcomes are ambiguous in the absence of measures of particular explanations.

Third, are measures of the particular explanations that people make reliable? Even if there is substantial variation across individuals in the explanations they make for uncontrollable events, this does not guarantee reliable measurement. The assessment of causal explanations can be influenced by such subtleties as the phrasing of questions (Elig & Frieze, 1979), and it seems best to use multiple measures to cancel out these extraneous factors. Again, this is not always done in research, and nonsignificant findings become difficult to interpret.

In a 1984 review of studies applying the model to depression, Peterson and Seligman fine-tuned the reformulation by clarifying certain issues and introducing some new terminology. Following are the major modifications.

First, Peterson and Seligman switched from attributions and attributional style to causal explanations and explanatory style. This makes the language of the reformulation more precise. "Attribution" means the ascription of any property to any object or event. But the helplessness reformulation is specifically concerned with just one type of attribution: how people assign causes to events involving themselves.

Second, Peterson and Seligman made it explicit that causal explanations and explanatory style are to be regarded as theoretical notions, not literal things (MacCorquodale & Meehl, 1948). When we say that people make causal explanations for the events they experience, we are not saying that these explanations may be phenomenologically real; we are not saying that their meaning is exhausted by a single operation. Instead, a causal explanation is a way for the theorist to make sense of observable behaviors. It is akin to concepts like natural selection, life, Eros, preference, and reward. Theoretical notions like these can (and should) be measured in a variety of ways with different converging operations.

This clarification protects helplessness theorists and researchers from putting all of their theoretical eggs in the same methodological basket. Some attribution theorists, like Heider (1958), seem to treat causal explanations as phenomenologically real. The consequence is that they can be measured only by asking individuals to introspect upon and to report in words their causal beliefs. If this were the only reasonable way to assess causal explanations and explanatory style, then research that relies on other strategies would not turn out to be as coherent as it is.

Third, Peterson and Seligman switched from an emphasis on personal versus universal helplessness to one on internal versus external causal explanations. This does not at all change the helplessness reformulation. Abramson et al. (1978) noted that the two contrasts end up making the same distinction among helpless people. Someone cannot experience universal helplessness and make internal explanations; someone cannot experience personal helplessness and make external explanations (Schwartz, Burish, O'Rourke, & Holmes, 1986).

Why the change then? It was not self-conscious. Instead, it came about as we became increasingly concerned with the cognitions that mediate helplessness deficits, particularly for depressed individuals. We looked less at helplessness per se and more at causal explanations and explanatory style. It became easier to speak of the internal-external distinction, because it was on focus, than on the personal-universal distinction, because it was not.

In addition, depressed people tend not to experience universal helplessness. Self-blame and recrimination are an important part of depression, at least in Western cultures, and thus the personal versus universal helplessness distinction is not all that useful in describing depressives. As the helplessness reformulation is applied to other failures of adaptation, like victimization, perhaps the original distinction will return to fashion.

Fourth, Peterson and Seligman started to speak not of uncontrollable events but of bad events. The helplessness model, both in its original and reformulated versions, holds that uncontrollability is the critical factor producing deficits. Traumatic events may indeed disrupt an animal or person, but if the trauma per se does the damage, then this is not what we mean by learned helplessness. The triadic design (Chapter 2) is used precisely to disentangle uncontrollability from trauma.

Although deficits can be produced by noncontingent reward, so-called appetitive helplessness is nonetheless not as frequently encountered as aversive helplessness. In the case of people, at least, this probably reflects people's insensitivity to noncontingency when success occurs. Most people expect to succeed at most tasks they confront, and when they do win reward, they fail to entertain the possibility that the reward was *not* contingent on their actions. We remember a television interview with a professional basketball player who made a 70-foot shot at the buzzer to win a game. "Were you surprised the shot was good?" asked the interviewer. The player looked at him scornfully: "*All* of my shots are good."

Another reason leading to the distinction between uncontrollable events and bad events is the incorporation of causal explanations into the helplessness model. Attribution researchers have shown over and over that success and failure are attributed differently; further, a particular attribution for success ("I did well because I'm smart") has a different meaning and different psychological consequences than the same attribution for failure ("I did poorly because I'm not smart"). We could not speak about causal explanations for uncontrollable events in general. We had to distinguish good events from bad events.

Many bad events are a subset of uncontrollable ones. Certainly an internal, stable, and global explanation for a bad event is another way of saying that it is difficult to envision controlling it in the future or other circumstances. On the other hand, some bad events are perceived as controllable (Peterson, 1991). We need to be more careful about this distinction than we have been. Researchers have shown that it makes a difference (Brown & Siegel, 1988; Sellers & Peterson, 1991).

These four clarifications bring the helplessness reformulation up to date. In the remainder of the chapter, we describe the research that the reformulation has generated. Many of these investigations look at explanatory style. We suspect that this individual difference has been responsible for attracting many researchers to the helplessness reformulation. One of the striking things about bad events is how they produce a variety of reactions among people. The helplessness reformulation not only explains this range of responses but also allows the researcher to predict where people will fall along it.

A related reason for the popularity of the helplessness reformulation is that we have developed two means of measuring explanatory style. Both are simple and cheap, reliable and valid. Theories attract the attention of researchers only if the researchers can do something with them. The helplessness reformulation gives researchers a choice.

ASSESSING EXPLANATORY STYLE

Our two ways of assessing an individual's explanatory style are a self-report questionnaire called the Attributional Style Questionnaire (ASQ) and a content analysis procedure called the CAVE technique (content analysis of verbatim explanations). We describe these in turn. (We have also developed a version of the ASQ for children, which we dub the CASQ; Seligman, Peterson, Kaslow, Tanenbaum, Alloy, & Abramson, 1984. Because the CASQ has been used mainly to investigate depression among children, we postpone its discussion until Chapter 6.)

Other researchers have developed similar measures of causal explanations and explanatory style, opting either for a questionnaire or for content analysis. Few if any studies have explicitly compared these measures with the ones we use, but we assume there is some overlap.

The ASQ

The ASQ[1] was originally used by Seligman, Abramson, Semmel, and von Baeyer, (1979) and later described in detail by Peterson, Semmel, von Baeyer, Abramson, Metalsky, and Seligman (1982). Respondents are given the following instructions:

> Please try to vividly imagine yourself in the situations that follow. If such a situation happened to you, what would you feel would have caused it? While events may have many causes, we want you to pick only one—the cause if this event happened to *you*. Please write this cause in the blank provided after each event. Next we want to ask you some questions about the cause. To summarize, we want you to:
>
> 1. Read each situation and imagine it happening to you.
> 2. Decide what you feel would be the *major* cause of the situation if it happened to you.
> 3. Write one cause in the blank provided.
> 4. Answer three questions about the cause.

(Early versions of the ASQ asked respondents about the importance of events, under the assumption that this variable would moderate correlations with deficits. However, this proved not to be the case, perhaps because the ASQ events are mostly of equal importance to respondents.)

The ASQ presents subjects with six bad events (e.g., you meet a friend who acts hostilely toward you; you can't get all the work done that others expect of you) and six good events (e.g., you do a project that is highly praised; your boyfriend or girlfriend is treating you more lovingly). We ask the subjects to rate the cause of each event on 7-point scales according to its internality versus externality, stability versus instability, and globality versus specificity.

So, for each cause, subjects answer the following questions:

> Is this cause due to something about you or something about other people or circumstances?
>
> In the future will this cause again be present?
>
> Is the cause something that just influences this situation or does it also influence other areas of your life?

Ratings are made in the direction of increasing internality, stability, and globality, and they are averaged across the good and bad events separately. We sometimes form a composite explanatory-style score by combining scores from the three dimensions.

Tennen and Herzberger (1986) reviewed the available evidence bearing on the reliability and validity of the ASQ, drawing several conclusions, which we repeat here. First, a variety of subject samples can complete the ASQ without difficulty. Second, the internal consistencies of the individual dimensions are moderate, with alpha coefficients ranging from .40 to .70. Third, the internal consistencies of the composite scores are much more satisfactory, with alpha coefficients of .70 or more. Fourth, the test-retest reliabilities are respectably high over periods of weeks to months ($r's = .60$ or above). Fifth, a variety of evidence, mostly from studies of depression, supports the construct validity of the ASQ. We review this evidence ourselves, in the present chapter and in Chapter 6.

With respect to the ASQ, we need to scrutinize several matters further. In our recent research, we have bolstered the reliability of the ASQ's individual dimensions by increasing the number of events for which causes are offered (Peterson & Villanova, 1988). This is a psychometrically straightforward strategy and yields reliabilities for the individual dimensions in the .70 to .85 range. However, we thereby move some distance from the validity evidence of the original ASQ.

Some might wonder if subjects completing the ASQ know what is being measured. If some number of subjects can see through the purpose of this test, this might bias their answers, because clearly there is a "desirable" way to respond to questions. Here we can rest comfortably, though, because Schulman, Seligman, and Amsterdam (1987) specifically investigated the transparency of the measure, finding that even subjects given explicit instruction in what the test was trying to measure could not produce these answers. Nor did a promised reward of $100 for producing the "best" score, given these instructions, influence how subjects answered.

Explanatory style for good events is not well understood. However, researchers find that causal explanations for good events occasionally relate to variables like depression, usually in a fashion opposite to causal explanations for bad events. That is, external, unstable, and specific explanations for good events sometimes correlate with depression (Peterson & Seligman, 1984). And explanatory style for good events is usually independent of explanatory style for bad events (Peterson, Semmel, et al., 1982), which means that their opposite patterns of correlation are not due to the confounding of the one style with the other.

Another matter concerns the relationship among the three dimensions of explanatory style. In many studies using the ASQ, internality, stability, and globality are substantially correlated (within good events and within bad events). In studies with expanded versions of the ASQ, internality often stands alone, and stability and globality continue to be highly entwined. Does this mean that explanatory style should be described in terms of one or two dimensions rather than three?

When learned helplessness theory was revised along attributional lines, the three dimensions of causal explanation were proposed to encompass concerns of the academic psychologist (i.e., locus, time, and space). Naive psychologists may construe matters differently (Heider, 1958). And as we have seen, other theorists have proposed additional dimensions along which explanations can be described.

The eventual answer to this question about the dimensionality of explanatory style will determine the way we regard composite scores (Peterson, 1991). To date, we have treated composites as simply reliable predictors of future helplessness. If explanatory style proves multidimensional, we can still form composite scores. However, the "reliability" of the composites will then be moot. Expectations will be reinterpreted as multidimensional, and perhaps configural scoring of the ASQ will be indicated. In any event, research to date using composites has made it impossible to test the differential predictions about the individual attributional dimensions (Carver, 1989).

A final issue with regard to the ASQ has to do with the causal ambiguity of the hypothetical events. Before the ASQ took its final form, we conducted pilot tests to find events that would elicit a range of explanations by the respondents. For some events, there is a consensus about operative causes. Explanations for these events are not psychologically interesting. For example, one of the events on the ASQ asks subjects to imagine that they have been unsuccessful in looking for a job. Whenever the nation's economy is poor, we fear that we need to replace this question, because so many subjects offer the same cause for this event: "There are no jobs to be found." The need for caution in choosing our events is obvious.

The ASQ can be regarded as a projective test in the sense that it works best when the subject's explanations are not overly constrained by the presented events. (Note: We do not mean to imply that causal explanations are unconscious.) We have mentioned two constraints: reality and a high consensus about operative causes. Another constraint occurs when the event is completely irrelevant to the subject. Tennen and Herzberger (1986) argued that questions about dating or school grades are probably irrelevant to samples of expectant mothers or elderly individuals; however, some studies have administered the ASQ to such samples. We suspect that subjects will answer "off the top of their head" and reveal nothing interesting about themselves (Taylor & Fiske, 1978).

The CAVE Technique

When helplessness theory was revised to include causal explanations, some critics suggested that people did not necessarily offer spontaneous causal explanations for the events they encountered (Wortman & Dintzer, 1978). If valid, this criticism is a serious one. However, as we noted earlier, current opinion holds that people do explain without prompting many of the events they encounter (Weiner, 1985). In particular, events that are aversive, surprising, and/or unusual elicit an "attributional search" (Wong & Weiner, 1981). Note that these are exactly the kinds of events that should produce learned helplessness in and out of the laboratory. As philosopher Charles S. Peirce (1955) observed, the purpose of thought is to allay doubt. (The fact that people are less likely to make causal explanations for good events may explain why bad events are more harmful to a person's well-being than good events are beneficial. Perhaps if one is to savor a good event, he must be "mindful" of its possible causes; Langer, 1989.)

As you might imagine, we have been interested in causal explanations for a long time, and so we see them everywhere: in letters, newspaper editorials, therapy transcripts, term papers by our students when they hand them in, excuses by our students when they don't, television interviews, advice columns, song lyrics, sports stories, political speeches, personal ads, billboards, religious writings, and even bathroom graffiti. Indeed, we were struck by the similarity between these spontaneous causal explanations and the open-ended responses written by subjects on the ASQ.

The main difference between the spontaneous causes we see all around us and the elicited causes we see on the ASQ is that the latter are followed by ratings for internality, stability, and globality. It was a small step to wonder if we could rate the spontaneous causal explanations we encountered in verbal material. If this could be done reliably, and if different explanations by the same speaker converged, then we would have an alternative way of assessing explanatory style. To varying degrees, this content analysis procedure introduces noise into the measurement of explanatory style. But then again, it allows us to study "subjects" quick, dead, or otherwise unavailable—so long as they have left a written record containing causal explanations for events in their lives.

Thus was born the CAVE technique (Peterson, Luborsky, & Seligman, 1983). Although not as extensively developed as the ASQ, this procedure has been successfully employed in more than a dozen investigations. An overview of the technique follows (Peterson, Schulman, Castellon, & Seligman, 1992).

First, some verbal material is more suitable than others. The researcher must be careful not to analyze verbal material in which factors other than an individual's projected explanatory tendencies predominate. Psychotherapy transcripts have proven highly suitable. Perhaps surprisingly, so too have sports page quotes.

In contrast, one of us (CP) has read one hundred essays by high school seniors submitted in support of a college scholarship application, in the hope of coding explanatory style and then relating it to subsequent academic performance. However, these essays proved useless. Each student wrote about personally relevant matters ("describe an incident in which you did something you knew to be wrong"), but the desire to present a desirable image (understandable, granted the ultimate purpose of the essay) resulted in virtually no negative events being acknowledged. Accordingly, there were few causal explanations. Among those that were made, there was little variation across students.

Given that suitable verbatim material is available, the second step is to extract causal explanations from it. These explanations can be difficult to identify, so we recommend a conservative strategy: extract only clear examples. Borderline instances of causal explanations (like attributions of responsibility) may be psychologically informative, but the CAVE technique is more reliable when only clear causal statements are used.

To identify a causal explanation, one first locates a good or bad event that has happened to the speaker. Again, we recommend being conservative. Unless an event strikes us as clearly good or bad (e.g., "I was offered the job I really wanted") or the subject indicates a clear evaluation ("The evening was horrible"), we steer away from events of ambiguous valence.

Once we locate an event, we search for a causal explanation. Certain phrases are clues: "because"; "as a result of"; "since"; "this led to it"; and so on. The bottom line, however, in determining whether an attribution is a causal explanation is whether the attributed factor precedes the event in question and covaries with it (from the perspective of the speaker or writer). If the attributed factor were absent, would the event not occur? If the event were not to occur, would the attributed factor have been absent? Using these conservative extraction criteria, independent judges agree 90 percent of the time about the presence of particular causal explanations (Peterson, Bettes, & Seligman, 1985).

The final step is to rate the causal explanations. An event and its explanation are copied onto index cards and shown to independent judges who are blind to other information about the speaker or writer. They are instructed about the ASQ and asked to rate each cause with 7-point scales according to its internality, stability, and globality (from the perspective of the subject, not their own). The number of judges is arbitrary, but we have usually used three or four. Obviously, the more judges, the higher the reliability of the ratings.

When we first developed the CAVE technique, we gave our judges extensive instruction and practice. A coding manual was developed. With four judges, the reliability of ratings of particular attributions along each dimension was highly satisfactory: .80 to .90, as estimated by Cronbach's (1951) coefficient alpha.

But then we asked judges with no training at all to rate extracted causal explanations. With just the ASQ instructions, they agreed just as highly with one another and the trained judges as did the trained judges among themselves! Granted the ease with which subjects complete the ASQ, perhaps this is not so surprising. Regardless, the simplest and most reliable step of the CAVE technique is the rating.

As measured with the CAVE technique, are the causal explanations offered by individuals consistent with respect to internality, stability, and globality? Four studies suggest that they are. In the first, sixty-six college students described in writing the two worst events that had occurred to them in the preceding year (Peterson, Bettes, & Seligman, 1985). Causal explanations for these bad events were extracted and rated by four judges for internality, stability, and globality.

The ratings were collapsed across judges, and those for the first bad event were correlated with those for the second bad event. In all cases, the correlations were positive. For internality: $r = .25$ ($p < .05$). For stability: $r = .49$ ($p < .001$). And for globality: $r = .33$ ($p < .01$). The consistency of explanatory style exceeds that of many individual differences (Mischel, 1968). If we had explanations for more than two events, consistency would have been even more evident (Epstein, 1980). For instance, if subjects had written about ten bad events, the Spearman-Brown formula projects consistencies of .77 for internality, .91 for stability, and .83 for globality.

The second relevant study supports this extrapolation. We applied the CAVE technique to the verbatim statements made by forty patients in psychotherapy (Peterson & Seligman, 1984). At least five explanations for bad events were extracted in each case, so we were able to calculate the alpha coefficients corresponding to the internality, stability, and globality ratings of these explanations. The figures were respectably high: .64 for internality, .64 for stability, and .60 for globality.

The third study extracted causal explanations from open-ended interviews conducted with ninety-nine men in which they described their most difficult experiences during World War II (Peterson, Seligman, & Vaillant, 1988). Fifty-nine of these men offered ten or more explanations for bad events, so we ascertained consistency by looking at the first ten explanations of these individuals. As estimated by coefficient alpha, the consistencies were moderate: .48 for internality, .40 for stability, and .46 for globality. These are lower than those from the other two studies we just described, and we think that they result from the particular events described (war experiences). Perhaps the commonality of these experiences reduced the range of explanations offered for them. Still, an explanatory "style" was evident.

The fourth study used the CAVE technique to identify and score causal explanations appearing in the TAT protocols of 108 college students (Peterson & Ulrey, 1991). Seventy-four of these students offered at least four causal explanations, and their consistencies, estimated by coefficient alpha, were .56 for stability and .55 for globality. (Internality was not scored because the causal explanations were made about the protagonists in the TAT pictures, with whom the subjects may or may not have been identifying.)

Is explanatory style as assessed by the CAVE technique stable over time? The most impressive demonstration is by Burns and Seligman (1989), who obtained written material (letters and diaries) spanning five decades from thirty individuals. Composite explanatory style for bad events coded from early material correlated significantly and substantially with explanatory style coded from later material ($r = .54$, $p < .002$).

The evidence for the construct validity of the CAVE technique is not nearly as extensive as that for the ASQ. The two measures seem to converge, but only to a moderate degree (Peterson, Bettes, & Seligman, 1985). We treat the CAVE technique and the ASQ as alternative measures of explanatory style, but we also believe that they are not equivalent. Remember that the ASQ inquires about hypothetical events, whereas the CAVE technique usually assesses actual events that happened to the speaker. As a result, the respective strengths and weaknesses of each procedure differ. Causal explanations for actual events are closer in time to the difficulties that follow bad events. In this sense, the CAVE technique has greater ecological validity than the ASQ. On the other hand, it seems clear that the actual internality, stability, and globality of causes will dilute the CAVE technique more than the ASQ. In this sense, the ASQ probably has greater predictive validity than the CAVE technique (Schulman, Castellon, & Seligman, 1989).

We have not played off the two techniques in our research to date, although it is important that we eventually do so. Instead, we have usually used one technique or the other, whichever has been the more convenient, and looked for convergence across our different investigations. In our studies of depression (Chapter 6) and illness (Chapter 8), for instance, the ASQ and the CAVE technique yield comparable results. Nevertheless, the difference between the two measures should be kept in mind.

EMPIRICAL STUDIES OF EXPLANATORY STYLE

The helplessness reformulation has generated several hundred empirical investigations, most of which are concerned with explanatory style. And of these, most looked at the link between explanatory style and depression. We discuss these studies of depression in Chapter 6. In this section, we give an overview of the "other" investigations of explanatory style. Our coverage is necessarily selective and focuses on studies using the ASQ or CAVE technique. Although our own investigations end up being emphasized, we believe that they at least exemplify the sorts of studies conducted to date.

Does Explanatory Style Predict Causal Explanations?

By definition, explanatory style should predispose the causal explanations a person makes. All things being equal, someone with an internal style should offer internal explanations for bad events that are encountered, someone with a stable style should offer stable explanations, and so on. This hypothesis can be cast in three different forms.

The weakest of these is that measures of explanatory style are internally consistent. Remember that the ASQ and the CAVE technique index style by aggregating explanations for a variety of events.

Were explanatory "style" unrelated to particular explanations, the reliability of these measures would be nil. This is not the case, so explanatory style predicts explanations in this sense.

Another form of the hypothesis looks at the relationship between ASQ scores and explanations assessed by the CAVE technique. As noted in our earlier section on assessment, scores from these two procedures indeed correlate as we would expect. A study of college students writing about the "two worst events" in the last year (Peterson, Bettes, & Seligman, 1985) and a study of depressed patients describing the circumstances that brought them to psychotherapy (Castellon & Seligman, 1985) both found that explanatory style measured with the ASQ agreed with explanatory style measured with the CAVE. In both cases, correlations were in the .30 range. However, discriminant validity of the individual dimensions was not evident. In other words, although a given dimension as measured by the ASQ correlated with the corresponding dimension as measured by the CAVE, so too did it correlate with the other dimensions, and vice versa.

A third and perhaps the most important form of the hypothesis is that measures of explanatory style from hypothetical events predict causal explanations of actual events. In several studies testing this version of the question, the measure of explanatory style has been the ASQ, and the actual events have been failure at a laboratory task or a stressful life event befalling the subject in the recent past. In either case, causal explanations are elicited for these actual events and rated by the subject as in the ASQ.

In a representative study, Cutrona, Russell, and Jones (1985) administered the ASQ to eighty-five women in their third trimester of pregnancy. At this time, the women were also asked to describe up to three stressful events that had occurred to them in the past two years. For each event, the "one major cause" was reported and then rated for internality, stability, and globality. Two weeks after giving birth, these women again made explanations for the three most stressful events involved in childcare, the three most common symptoms of "maternity blues" (tearfulness, anxiety, and irritability), and the most upsetting event of the past two weeks. Again, subjects rated each explanation along the dimensions of interest to the helplessness reformulation. Finally, eight weeks after giving birth, the women again made explanations for stressful aspects of childcare.

According to Cutrona et al. (1985), their results do not support the hypothesis that explanatory style predicts explanations of actual events. We disagree. Inspection of Table 5 in their research report shows that all but one of the correlation coefficients they computed between explanatory style and actual explanations are in the predicted direction. About half are statistically significant. Granted that explanations for events like childcare and postpartum symptoms are apt to have a large reality component, we feel that explanatory style fares quite well in predicting actual explanations by these women (see also Gilmor & Reid, 1979; Gong-Guy & Hammen, 1980; Metalsky, Halberstadt, & Abramson, 1987).

Let us address an issue that is critical in understanding much of the controversy surrounding studies of explanatory style. Because explanatory style is an individual difference, most studies compute correlations between explanatory style and other measures. These correlations are invariably in the predicted direction, and some number of them achieve statistical significance. No one would disagree that these statements summarize this body of research. However, considerable disagreement occurs over how to interpret the magnitude of these statistically significant correlation coefficients. In other words, how big is big? When should correlation coefficients be taken seriously, and when should they be dismissed?

This issue came to a head some years ago when Mischel (1968) reviewed the empirical literature bearing on the cross-situational consistency of personality characteristics. Most findings were bound by an $r = .30$ limit, which Mischel dismissed as too small for psychologists to bother with. His conclusions have been widely influential in psychology, and we find many of the criticisms of our research with explanatory style strangely reminiscent of his more general critique of personality psychology.

However, this is no longer the 1960s, and we should trade in simple criticisms for a keener understanding of how to evaluate correlational research. Within mainstream personality psychology, Mischel's criticisms have been rebutted. Unfortunately, the rest of psychology has not yet heard how this story ended. A full review of the recent history of personality psychology is not appropriate here (but see Peterson, 1992b). Let us draw two conclusions from this history that specifically pertain to our present discussion.

First, personality psychologists have come to appreciate the need to aggregate measures of individual differences into composites. This has long been recognized on the "questionnaire" end of personality research; all such measures have multiple items in order to achieve a reliable score. Only recently has the same mentality been applied on the "behavior" end of research (Epstein, 1980, 1983, 1984). In other words, multiple items reflecting the behavior to be predicted by a personality questionnaire are also needed for reliability. Research that measures behavior (read actual causal explanations) in but one or a few ways runs the risk of poor results, not because people are inconsistent but because studies are procedurally inadequate.

Second, the dismissal of .30 correlation coefficients as "too small" is unwarranted. Most of us know that if we square a correlation coefficient, the resulting figure is the percentage of variance in one variable accounted for by the other variable. Nine percent of the variance doesn't seem like very much, and we can be persuaded that other considerations are much more important.

But let's slow down and examine the argument here. What does it mean to account for 9 percent of the variance? Rosenthal and Rubin (1982) show that a .30 correlation coefficient reflects the same proportion of variance as a medical treatment that reduces our risk of death from 65 percent to 35 percent. And Funder and Ozer (1983) calculate the percentage of variance accounted for by situational manipulations in the well-known Milgram (1963) study of destructive obedience and the Darley and Latane' (1968) investigation of bystander apathy. In both cases, it's about 9 percent, again, the same proportion of variance associated with a correlation coefficient of $r = .30$. Because most of us would take quite seriously the medical treatment described, and because these social psychology studies are widely regarded as proving the power of situational determinants of behavior, the much-maligned .30 correlation is important after all (Peterson, 1991).

At any rate, we think these considerations help in the interpretation of studies looking at the relationship between explanatory style and actual explanations. Procedurally adequate studies that achieve correlations in the .30 vicinity constitute good support of the hypothesis. Procedural adequacy involves events with ambiguous causes, multiple measures of actual explanations, and a sufficient sample size (Peterson, Villanova, & Raps, 1985). Such studies exist. For instance, Peterson and Villanova (1988) administered to 140 subjects an expanded version of the ASQ that elicited explanations for twenty-four hypothetical bad events. One month later, the subjects returned and described the four worst events that had occurred to them in the past month. In each case, they described the "one major cause" and rated it for its internality, stability, and globality. These ratings were then averaged over the four events.

Explanatory style predicted actual explanations. Internal explanatory style correlated .32 ($p<.001$) with internal explanations, stable explanatory style .18 ($p<.05$) with stable explanations, and global explanatory style .36 ($p<.001$) with global explanations. However, it is one thing to show that internal explanatory style predicts the internality of actual explanations, and it is another thing to show that this correlation is higher than correlations between internal explanatory style and the stability or globality of actual explanations. Peterson and Villanova found that internal explanatory style and global explanatory style fared well by this criterion, but stable explanatory style did not. In particular, stability was entwined with globality. Thus, we conclude that explanatory style predicts actual explanations but that the discriminant validity of the particular attributional dimensions has not been fully demonstrated.

What Are the Correlates and Consequences of Explanatory Style?

According to the helplessness reformulation, explanatory style influences the boundary conditions of deficits following uncontrollability. A number of studies have looked at the relationship between explanatory style and various human ills. For the most part, these investigations correlate explanatory style with the magnitude of people's difficulties. Strictly speaking, this is *not* the exact hypothesis of the helplessness reformulation. Instead, research should look at the chronicity of problems and their pervasiveness as a function of explanatory style. To the degree that chronic and pervasive problems are also large-magnitude problems (and this is certainly a reasonable assumption), then these studies indeed bear on the reformulation. However, they cannot speak to the roles of the particular dimensions of explanatory style.

We note further that the most appropriate investigations of explanatory style and deficits use a longitudinal design: measuring explanatory style at Time One and difficulties at Time Two. This of course is dictated by our conception of explanatory style as a risk factor. Too many investigations, by others as well as us, test an extremely weak version of the reformulation by gathering all measures simultaneously. Cross-sectional investigations cannot answer questions about the direction of causality. Further, response sets and other procedural confounds can inflate correlations among simultaneous measures. One partial solution is to spread the research over time and assess the Time One level of whatever deficit one wishes to predict at Time Two for use as a covariate. If explanatory style predicts subsequent deficits even with baseline deficits held constant, then strong support for the risk factor conception is at hand.

We have just started to conduct these more stringent investigations ourselves, because these seem sensible only when cross-sectional studies are supportive. (Appreciate, though, that the lack of a simultaneous correlation does not mean that a correlation across time will also be zero. According to the reformulation, bad events must accrue before explanatory style does its damage.) In this section, we review the handful of longitudinal investigations as well as the more common cross-sectional studies. As we have already noted, the numerous studies of explanatory style and depression are reviewed in Chapter 6.

Laboratory Helplessness. Any of a number of experiments show that particular causal explanations affect laboratory helplessness in the expected ways, and some of these experiments were reviewed in the preceding chapter. Perhaps surprisingly, though, relatively few studies have looked at how preexisting explanatory style mediates the effects of uncontrollable events manipulated in a laboratory experiment. This is unfortunate because laboratory experiments allow the most fine-grained test of the reformulation and in particular of the specific roles assigned to the dimensions of internality, stability, and globality.

Although the available studies tell a coherent story, we are not happy with the available laboratory support for the reformulation. Although most studies are consistent with the reformulation in that a particular dimension of explanatory style is linked with a particular deficit following bad events in the laboratory, few of these studies explicitly ruled out the confounding effects of the other two dimensions. So Alloy, Peterson, Abramson, and Seligman (1984) linked global explanatory style to generalized failure following uncontrollability, using internality and stability for bad events as covariates in their analyses. Virtually no other study to date has been this refined.

Laboratory investigations of the helplessness reformulation have been underutilized to date. We speculate that this neglect stems from two related reasons. First, psychologists interested in personality dimensions like explanatory style are drawn to out-of-the-laboratory applications. Second, it is quite difficult (although not impossible) to investigate individual differences in conjunction with situational manipulations in laboratory experiments. Manipulations of situational factors must be strong enough to affect dependent measures but not so strong as to swamp the effect of individual differences. The choice of particular parameters is thus crucial, and many researchers lack either the skill or the patience to conduct such investigations. Needless to say, these are not good scientific reasons for neglecting laboratory studies, and we hope that in the future, experimentalists test the helplessness reformulation more frequently.

Helpless Behaviors. One of the curious things about learned helplessness research, at least as conducted with people, is that it is seldom concerned with helplessness per se. Research generated both by the original helplessness model and by the reformulated model looks at outcomes ostensibly reflecting helplessness, like anagram failure or depressed mood, but not at specific helpless behaviors. To remedy this shortcoming, Peterson (1986) studied the relationship between explanatory style and instances of helplessness that people display in their everyday life.

To identify candidates of helplessness for investigation, Buss and Craik's (1984) act-frequency approach was employed. This strategy in turn is borrowed from experimental psychology where it has been used to map the specific instances exemplifying abstract concepts. Subjects are asked to nominate possible examples of some concept (like fruit, or game, or helplessness). Other subjects rate the "goodness" of these instances as examples. Subjects agree highly whether particular instances are good or poor instances of a given concept. The good instances are regarded as prototypes that capture the essence of the concept in question.

Peterson (1986) followed this procedure to identify the prototypic behavioral instances of helplessness shown in Table 5-2. Note that many of these helpless behaviors are inherently social in nature: for example, refusing to do things on one's own; letting others make decisions; and using other people as crutches. Granted the concern of helplessness research with achievement, this characterization is unanticipated yet intriguing. It suggests that future investigations of helplessness look more specifically at its social context.

At any rate, Peterson (1986) developed a self-report questionnaire that asked subjects to describe how many times in the past month they had performed each of the helpless behaviors. The questionnaire was completed by seventy-five undergraduate students. To validate these answers, a friend of each subject completed a parallel questionnaire asking about the behaviors of this particular subject.

Table 5-2. Prototypical Examples of
Helplessness.

I didn't leave my house all day.
I didn't cook for myself.
I was unable to fix a broken object.
I gave up in the middle of doing something.
I didn't compete when given the opportunity.
I let someone take advantage of me.
I asked others to do something for me.
I didn't stand up for myself.
I let someone else make a decision for me.
I used another person as a crutch.
I refused to do something on my own.

Source: Peterson, C. (1993). Helpless behaviour.
Behaviour Therapy and Research. In press. © 1993 by
Pergamon Press Ltd. Adapted by permission of
the publisher.

Agreement was substantial, and so this "helplessness questionnaire" appears valid.

In the present context, two further findings should be pointed out. First, subjects' responses to the helplessness measure cohered. In other words, helplessness as measured is a psychological state of some generality. This, of course, is consistent with the original helplessness model and its conception of helplessness as a general set of deficits. Second, Peterson (1986) also asked the subjects to complete a version of the ASQ, and he found that helpless behaviors were more frequent among those who explained bad events with internal, stable, and global causes than among those who favored external, unstable, and specific explanations ($r = .23$, $p < .05$). And again this finding is consistent with the helplessness reformulation.

Further support comes from the work of Nolen-Hoeksema, Girgus, and Seligman (1986). We asked grade school teachers to rate the extent that their students performed "helpless" behaviors like preferring easy problems to difficult ones. The explanatory style of these students, assessed three months earlier with the CASQ, predicted these ratings. These findings converge with those of Peterson (1986) to show that explanatory style is linked to concrete instances of helpless behaviors.

Reactions to Life Events. Formally speaking, the helplessness reformulation is a diathesis-stress model of disorder. A preexisting weakness (pessimistic explanatory style) interacts with an environmental stressor (bad event) to produce difficulties for an individual. One particularly appropriate way to test the reformulation is by seeing how well it accounts for a person's reactions to bad life events. Several studies of this kind have been investigated; most look at depression as consequences and are therefore described in Chapter 6. However, some of these studies have looked at other consequences, and so we discuss them here.

In the study described earlier, Peterson and Villanova (1988) measured explanatory style of 140 undergraduates who returned one month later to describe the four worst events that had occurred to them in the meantime. In their descriptions, they rated the degree to which each bad event had long-lasting consequences and the degree to which each had broad consequences. Composite scores were formed by averaging these ratings across the four events.

Did prior explanatory style correlate with these composites? Stable explanatory style predicted long-lasting consequences ($r = .19$, $p < .05$), but so too did global explanatory style ($r = .18$, $p < .05$). In contrast, global explanatory style predicted pervasive consequences ($r = .38$, $p < .001$), and to a greater degree than did stable explanatory style ($r = .18$, $p < .05$). Internal explanatory style was related to neither chronicity nor generality of the consequences of bad events. The general pattern of these results is consistent with the helplessness reformulation, although the discriminant validity of the particular dimensions is not strongly supported.

Williams and Brewin (1984) studied people's reactions to failing a test for a driver's license. Although their investigation is limited by an extremely small sample size ($n = 30$), some of their findings are consistent with the helplessness reformulation. When men explained their failure with stable terms, they reduced their expectancy for future success at the test. (This did not happen for women.) Other findings from this study failed to support predictions. These researchers included an intriguing measure to operationalize persistence: how quickly subjects reapplied for another driving test following their failure. Reapplication was not correlated with explanations for failure, although it was predicted by a subject's pretest expectancy for success and incentive for success.

Anderson (1983) studied the effects of explanatory style on persistence following a failure. Using his own measure of explanatory style, he identified subjects who explained failure in terms of character deficits (in our terms: internal, stable, and global causes) versus subjects who explained failure with behavioral mistakes (i.e., internal, unstable, and specific causes). These subjects were then asked to make phone calls to recruit blood donors. Their initial call was to a confederate who refused to cooperate. Thus, all subjects failed in their initial request. Subjects were then given the names and phone numbers of more individuals to call. Consistent with the notion that pessimistic explanatory style leads to passivity, subjects who explained bad events with character deficits showed lower expectations of success, made fewer phone calls, and were less successful at obtaining volunteers than subjects who explained bad events with behavioral mistakes.

Another aspect of Anderson's (1983) study was a situational manipulation for the original failure. Again, subjects were induced to explain the refusal of the confederate either in terms of their character (lack of persuasiveness) or in terms of their behavior (incorrect strategy). Results paralleled those for preexisting explanatory style (Anderson & Jennings, 1980). Taken together, these results strongly support the helplessness reformulation as an account of how people respond to bad events in their lives.

Major, Mueller, and Hildebrandt (1985) looked at the relationship between causal explanations and how women coped with the aftermath of an abortion. Women who blamed their character (i.e., internal, stable, and global cause) for their pregnancy had more physical complaints and anticipated more negative consequences than women who blamed their behavior (i.e., internal, unstable, and specific cause). Major et al. (1985) also found that poor coping was predicted by the expectation that one would cope poorly, intentionality of the pregnancy, and meaningfulness of the pregnancy. Interestingly, women who were accompanied by their partner to the abortion clinic coped less well than women who went alone. This finding seems to counter conventional wisdom, although a straightforward attributional interpretation is possible. Perhaps the women who experienced this stressful event by themselves consequently inferred that they were more capable individuals.

In a cross-sectional study, Newman and Langer (1981) looked at how women responded to divorce. They distinguished between person attributions, by which they mean explanations in terms of either marriage partner, and interactive attributions, by which they mean the particular mesh of the two people in the marriage. Presumably, interactive attributions are much less stable and global than person attributions. Women who explained their divorce in these terms were indeed happier and more active following the divorce than those who employed person attributions.

A number of studies have looked at how causal explanations are related to people's reactions to physical injury or disease. Here the results are quite inconsistent (e.g., Abrams & Finesinger, 1953; Bard & Dyk, 1956; Bulman & Wortman, 1977; Mastrovito, 1974). The relevance of most of these investigations to the helplessness reformulation is unclear, because explanatory style is rarely assessed. Instead, particular explanations for the particular disease are ascertained; reality may confound these explanations to varying and unknown degrees. For example, Taylor, Lichtman, and Wood (1984) found no relationship between a woman's particular causal explanations and her adjustment following breast cancer. Consistent with the original helplessness model, though, these researchers found that someone's perceived control over her cancer did predict good adjustment. This effect was obtained whether the patient saw herself as in control (primary control) or her physician (secondary control).

In a related line of research, Steele and Southwick (1981) investigated the impact of fear-based appeals to reduce drinking as a function of how the alcoholism was explained. Drinkers who were told that alcoholism was an incurable (stable) disease were less persuaded to stop drinking than those who were told that alcoholism was the result of learned behavior (unstable). If this is a general finding, it has important implications for the way alcohol and drug treatment should be conducted; abusers should *not* be told that they suffer from a progressive disease, as is done in Alcoholics Anonymous and similar twelve-step programs. This only makes the problem to be solved more daunting than it already is (see Peele, 1989).

Finally, several studies have looked at how causal explanations affect the response of those whose loved ones have a serious injury or illness. Mothers of infants with perinatal complications expected greater caretaking problems when they blamed other people for their child's problem than when they blamed their own behavior (Affleck, Allen, McGrade, & McQueeney, 1982). To us, this result reflects differences in perceived controllability, but this is an inference. A more recent study by Tennen, Affleck, and Gershman (1986) supports our conclusion, because they found explicit support for the notion that perceived control by the mother of an at-risk infant predicts better coping.

In sum, the helplessness reformulation often seems a reasonable account of how individuals respond to bad events in their lives. At the same time, the particular roles assigned to individual dimensions of explanatory style have yet to be demonstrated. Further, single explanations for particular bad events show a much more variable relationship to responses, perhaps because of reality contamination. The ideal investigation of how explanatory style influences response to naturally occurring bad events needs to be longitudinal and prospective. There are logistic problems in mounting such a study, although the CAVE technique may solve some of these difficulties.

Self-Esteem.   The reformulation predicts that internal explanations for bad events are associated with loss of self-esteem. Empirical support for this claim comes from a variety of studies that have examined both particular causal explanations and explanatory style in both cross-sectional and longitudinal designs (e.g., Brewin & Shapiro, 1984; Devins, 1982; Fielstein et al., 1985; Girodo, Dotzenroth, & Stein, 1981; Ickes & Layden, 1978; McFarland & Ross, 1982; Rothwell & Williams, 1983; Weiner, 1979). However, it is not clear that internal explanatory style is more strongly related to poor self-esteem than stable or global explanatory style. Peterson and Villanova (1986), for instance, found that all three dimensions of explanatory style were correlated with self-esteem, but none more so than the others. Again, evidence for the discriminant validity of the particular dimensions is lacking.

Political Popularity.   In one of the most intriguing studies of explanatory style, Zullow and Seligman (1990) coded explanatory style from the nomination acceptance speeches of Republican and Democratic presidential candidates from 1900 to 1984. We also quantified the degree to which each candidate ruminated about bad events. A composite of explanatory style and rumination successfully predicted the outcomes of the subsequent elections: pessimistic ruminators in eighteen out of twenty-two elections were defeated. Indeed, the margin of defeat was a function of the degree of pessimistic rumination evidenced in the speeches, even when likely third variables such as incumbency and initial popularity in political polls were held constant. The American electorate apparently responds well to a hopeful message.

How Does Explanatory Style Originate and Change?

Although social psychologists have long been interested in the determinants of particular causal explanations, little is known about the determinants of explanatory style. The helplessness model is neutral on this issue. Nevertheless, a full account of how explanatory style influences learned helplessness must explain both how it originates and how it changes (Fincham & Cain, 1986). We will not always be content merely to describe the mechanisms that produce human ills. We someday would like to undo these processes when they occur and even to prevent them in the first place.

Kelley (1973) distinguished between two general determinants of particular causal explanations. The first is covariation information contained in the actual occurrences of events in the world. By induction, people can infer cause-effect relationships from this information. The more likely some event is to covary across time and situations with an outcome of interest, the more likely that event is to be considered a cause.

The second determinant of causal explanations that Kelley (1973) described is a causal schema: an already abstract belief about the causes of particular events. When people encounter these events, they draw on their causal schema to identify the causes. Presumably, a causal schema is imparted to an individual during socialization, through any of a number of means.

The distinction between these two general determinants of causal explanations blurs upon examination. "Pure" induction seems not to exist. When people judge the relationships among causes and effects, they do so in light of already-existing beliefs. And people are more versus less likely to rely on a causal schema according to its success in particular instances.

These determinants of causal explanations can be extrapolated to explain the origins of explanatory style. Repeated experience with events that lead one to make the same explanations should eventually produce a consistent explanatory style. Repeated exposure to a causal schema that encourages one to make the same explanations should similarly lead to a consistent explanatory style.

Several studies suggest that a history of bad life events is associated with pessimistic explanatory style (cf. Brewin & Furnham, 1986; Feather & Barber, 1983; Jackson & Tessler, 1984; Peterson, Schwartz, & Seligman, 1981). Notice the complexity here. Pessimistic explanatory style may lead a person into difficulties, which in turn will strengthen his tendency to explain bad events in a pessimistic fashion. A similar phenomenon seems to exist with respect to depression, where explanatory style can be both a cause and a consequence (Nolen-Hoeksema, Girgus, & Seligman, 1986).

A few studies have taken an explicit look at the origins of explanatory style. Nolen-Hoeksema (1986) studied young children to see when and how explanatory style emerged. She would pose negative events to them ("another kid doesn't want to play with you") and probe for causal explanations. Among four-year-olds, one frequent response was a solution to the bad events ("I'd tell the teacher"). Perhaps causal explanations start to be entertained when solutions fail.

A consistent style begins to emerge when children are about eight years old, which makes sense in light of what is going on with children's cognitive development (Fincham & Cain, 1986). Prior to age eight, children tend not to judge accurately their success and failure, and they tend not to think in terms of the stability and globality of causes. But once these abilities are present, an explanatory style indeed emerges that is related to outcomes as the helplessness reformulation predicts.

In another study, child-rearing variables were linked to adult explanatory style (Peterson & Bossio, 1991). This investigation began in the 1950s, when mothers of young children were given extensive interviews about how they treated their children. These children were then recontacted almost forty years later, when they completed a measure of explanatory style. We found that harsh and inconsistent treatment during childhood was associated with a pessimistic explanatory style during middle adulthood.

We think also that explanatory style can be learned as a whole. Research by Carol Dweck suggests that children come to explain their own academic failures in accordance with the causal attributions contained in the criticisms of their teachers (e.g., Dweck, Davidson, Nelson, & Enna, 1978; Dweck, Goetz, & Strauss, 1980). "Stable" criticisms by teachers ("you're hopeless") give rise to stable self-attributions; "unstable" criticisms by teachers ("you're not trying") give rise to unstable self-attributions; and so on.

In an intriguing study, Plous and Zimbardo (1986) ascertained the explanatory styles of psychoanalysts and behavior therapists. Each type of clinician explained events as one would expect given their training. Psychoanalysts favored dispositional explanations, whereas behavior therapists pointed to situational causes. It seems that part of professional education is the socialization of causal explanation. This conclusion can probably be generalized much more broadly; consider the explanatory styles fostered by grade school primers (see Dick and Jane offer unstable explanations for bad events), catechism classes, gossip columns, television shows, the Cub Scouts, bumper stickers, newspaper editorials, and rock songs.

Seligman et al. (1984) compared the explanatory styles of parents and their children and found that youngsters of both sexes explained events like their mothers did. The explanatory styles of fathers were unrelated to those of their spouses or their children. These subjects were mostly from traditional middle-class families, so we assume that both mothers and children spent more time with each other than they did with fathers. We would therefore expect to see similar explanatory styles. A longitudinal study here would be interesting, because it might reveal the direction of influence between mothers and children.

Some recent research suggests that explanatory style may be heritable. Schulman, Keith, and Seligman (1991) administered the ASQ to sets of identical twins ($n = 115$) and fraternal twins ($n = 27$). Correlations were quite high between ASQ scores for bad events among identical twins but not among fraternal twins, implying some sort of genetic influence. The magnitude of this influence is comparable to that demonstrated for other personality characteristics.

Let us be clear that "heritable" does not mean inherited as a whole. Rather, the term has a more technical meaning: variation in the characteristic (i.e., explanatory style) is correlated with genetic variation. Heritability is a property of a group of individuals, not any given person. That a characteristic is heritable does not at all rule out environmental influence or malleability. Finally, a characteristic may prove heritable not because it is directly influenced by genetics but because of an indirect influence. Future research will need to investigate the possibility that explanatory style proves heritable because of the influence of such factors as temperament.

Given that a person has a particular explanatory style, how and why does it change? Again, the helplessness model is neutral on this matter. And again, not that much is known about the process by which explanatory style changes. The evidence we reviewed earlier in this chapter shows that explanatory style is stable across time. Still, this stability is not 100 percent, which means that it is also somewhat malleable.

When Abramson et al. (1978) first described the helplessness reformulation, they discussed treatment strategies for depression implied by the helplessness model. However, this discussion was very general: "change unrealistic attributions for failure toward external, unstable, and specific factors, and change unrealistic attributions for success toward internal, stable, and global factors" (p. 70). Seligman (1981) later elaborated treatment implications, hypothesizing that explanatory style could be changed in at least two ways. First, the therapist underscores the possibility of causal explanations other than those chronically favored by the individual. Second, the therapist directly challenges the explanations the individual makes, as Ellis or Beck describe in their cognitively based psychotherapies.

WHAT WE KNOW

In this chapter, we described the reformulated model of learned helplessness proposed in 1978 by Abramson, Seligman, and Teasdale. We placed the model in its theoretical context; we explained how it has been investigated; and we detailed the important findings. Let us now try to draw some general conclusions about the reformulation. As in previous chapters, we organize our conclusions into the things we know versus the things we don't.

Here are the conclusions about which we are confident. First, people's causal explanations for bad events affect their response to these events in a variety of spheres: motivation, emotion, cognition, and behavior. Second, people have a characteristic explanatory style: a habitual way of explaining bad events that can be measured in several ways, reliably and validly. Our measures have come in for a fair amount of criticism, but we think that they are as satisfactory as most operationalizations of individual differences (Peterson, 1991). Of course, improvement is possible, but researchers keep using the ASQ. And the CAVE is becoming popular as well. Third, explanatory style predicts the vigor or passivity with which people behave in many domains, exactly as the learned helplessness reformulation predicts.

Our overall conclusion is therefore positive. With regard to its general claims, the helplessness reformulation is strongly supported by the available research. Causal explanations and explanatory style are concerned with an important aspect of the human condition.

In the context of this positive conclusion, an important qualification must be made. With regard to some of its specific claims, the helplessness reformulation is not so strongly supported. For instance, evidence for the discriminant validity of the particular dimensions of explanatory style is missing. The role of bad events has often not been investigated. The central construct in helplessness theory—expectation of future noncontingency—has been ignored in favor of its supposed determinants. The entire process hypothesized by the helplessness reformulation needs to be investigated more fully. A number of questions about the reformulation require further scrutiny, both theoretical and empirical. We now turn to these.

WHAT WE DON'T KNOW

Throughout this chapter, we have noted problem areas. Let's gather them together in one place. First, how is explanatory style related to other cognitive personality variables? Other theories suggest that factors besides causal explanations affect the way people respond to bad events. These constructs deserve further comparison and contrast with helplessness constructs. If they differ, perhaps they should be added to the model. For instance, the importance (and/or frequency and/or intensity) of the bad events that produce helplessness might dictate the magnitude of ensuing deficits. We would still hypothesize that stable and global explanations influence the chronicity and pervasiveness of deficits, respectively, but note that these parameters may be conceptually distinct from the magnitude of difficulties.[2] If constructs are redundant, perhaps they should be collapsed into the helplessness model to flesh out its theoretical meaning. So we have speculated that causal explanations and coping may be two sides of the same coin. Assuming this is the case, we would gain a better understanding of each by acknowledging their relationship.

Second, what are the fundamental dimensions along which to describe causal explanations? The helplessness reformulation proposes three. Research to date has had trouble demonstrating that they are distinct, so maybe a simpler view is indicated. We tentatively suggest two: locus and generality (Peterson, 1991).

Third, whatever happened to expectations? We have elsewhere stated that expectations are difficult to measure and hence we prefer to focus on causal explanations and explanatory style (Peterson & Seligman, 1984). This may be too glib. After all, other psychology research traditions measure people's expectations without much difficulty (e.g., Bandura, 1986; Rotter, 1966). The helplessness model, both in its original and reformulated versions, accords such importance to expectations that renewed attempts at operationalization are imperative. Perhaps so much attention has been devoted to causal attributions and explanatory style because these were new additions to the model. And once the ASQ and the CAVE technique were devised, these took on a life of their own, and the neglect of expectations continued.

Fourth, what is the significance of explanatory style for good events? We have not focused on style for good events in this chapter, but remember what is known. Style for good events often has the opposite relationship with outcomes as style for bad events. And style for good events is independent of style for bad events. Taken together, these two statements imply that research that looks at both good and bad style will be able to predict outcomes better than research that looks just at bad style. But we still don't know what good style means. Studies testing the reformulation have looked almost exclusively at bad events. Perhaps if researchers additionally looked at how people respond to good events, the significance of good style would become clear.

Fifth, how do situational factors interact with explanatory style to produce particular explanations? We feel that our general view on the matter is reasonable, but it is precisely that: a general view. What we need are fine-grained studies that look at both situational factors and explanatory style.

Sixth, what are the limits on the benefits of an optimistic explanatory style? Those who offer external, unstable, and specific explanations for bad events exhibit good cheer and perseverance in most domains, yet surely there are circumstances that demand sobriety and caution (Seligman, 1990). When taken to an extreme, our vision of psychological health is incomplete, even objectionable, because it implies that individual happiness and achievement are all that matter. In Chapter 1, we proposed that learned helplessness is very much a theory for the here and now, but we mean this in a descriptive sense only, hardly a prescriptive one. Perhaps we have an obligation to round out the meaning of explanatory style by investigating situations in which "optimism" fails.

Finally, let us comment on two other matters concerning explanatory style that we do not know enough about. The first poses a procedural question. Should we develop domain-specific measures of explanatory style? Researchers in related areas like locus of control and self-efficacy have tended of late to use questionnaires highly specific to the outcomes to be predicted. Some explanatory style investigators have followed suit (e.g., Atlas & Peterson, 1990; Peterson & Barrett, 1987). Prediction may be enhanced, although we do not know by how much. Several related issues are involved here. How general an individual difference do we wish to make explanatory style? And do gains we might make in prediction with domain-specific measures offset the difficulty in devising them? And do we wish to shrink the power of the explanatory style construct by limiting it to given areas of life?

The second entails a conceptual question. Granted that individuals who make internal, stable, and global explanations for bad events are at risk for various bad outcomes, what determines the particular outcome that ensues? Do the same individuals become depressed, fall ill, fail classes, quit jobs, and lose presidential elections? If so, then the specificity of explanatory style to any particular problem must be questioned. This matter is reaching a head in the depression literature, where the specificity of explanatory style to depression is being questioned. Of course, the prior question is how problems like anxiety, depression, illness, academic failure, and the like themselves covary in the population. If they tend to go together, then the fact that explanatory style foreshadows them all makes perfect sense.

But if they don't covary to an appreciable degree, additional considerations must be brought to bear in explaining the apparent ability of explanatory style to predict them all. As it is currently formulated, helplessness theory may only explain who falls victim to misfortunes for which they are predisposed by other factors (like low intelligence in the case of school failure or biochemical abnormalities in the case of depression). Perhaps the helplessness reformulation should be considered less a model of one or a few human difficulties and more a mechanism involved in all manner of problems. Regardless, our conclusion remains that the reformulation successfully identifies important constructs.

NOTES

1. Martin Seligman acknowledges the significant contribution of Mary Ann Layden to the development of the Attributional Style Questionnaire.

2. In its original form, the ASQ contained a scale that asked respondents to rate the importance to them of the event in question. This rating was eventually dropped because it proved highly redundant with the globality rating. However, importance and globality might prove more distinct when considered across a wider range of events than those used in the ASQ.

6

Learned Helplessness and Depression

The first reach outward for learned helplessness was toward depression, and to this day it remains the theory's most thoroughly researched application. This chapter's discussion of depression is divided into four parts. First, we describe it: what kinds there are and how to recognize them. Second, we take a look at the reformulated learned helplessness theory as it applies to depression. Third, we discuss the new evidence suggesting that modernity has brought an epidemic of depression in its wake. How does helplessness theory illuminate this evidence? Finally, we describe several issues of controversy surrounding the application of learned helplessness to depression.

WHAT IS DEPRESSION?

"Depression" is a broad term that encompasses fleeting moods and chronic disorders. One can make numerous distinctions concerning depression, but we prefer to focus on three: normal depression, unipolar depression, and bipolar depression.

Normal Depression

Pain and loss are inevitable aspects of being human. We don't get the jobs we want. We get rejected by people we love. Our parents die. Our stocks go down. We give bad lectures and write bad books. We ultimately must face our own death. When such losses occur, as unique as they may seem to us, how we react is fairly predictable. We feel sad and hopeless. We become passive and lethargic. We believe that our future looks bleak, that we lack the talent to make things better. The zest goes out of activities we usually enjoy, as we lose our appetites for food, company, sex, and even sleep. After a while, by one of nature's benign mysteries, we start to feel better. This is what we mean by *normal depression*, and for someone not to react to pain and loss in such a way would be cause for alarm.

The Depressive "Disorders"

Diagnosticians agree that there are two basic depressive disorders: unipolar depression and bipolar depression. In *unipolar depression*, the individual suffers depression without the experience of mania. In *bipolar depression*, the individual suffers bouts of both depression and mania. Mania has a set of symptoms very much the opposite of depression: euphoria, grandiosity, frenetic talk and action, inflated self-esteem, and insomnia. The existence of two mood disorders that seem to go in opposite directions has led the field to use the term "affective disorders" to embrace unipolar depression, bipolar depression, and mania.

Bipolar depression is distinct from unipolar depression. It has the hallmark of manic episodes, whereas unipolar depressives never experience them. And bipolar depression is considerably more heritable than its unipolar counterpart. In a summary of nine twin studies of affective disorders, Allen (1976) reported an overall concordance rate for identical twins of 72% for bipolar illness versus 14% for fraternal twins. For unipolar depression, however, the concordance was 40 percent for identical twins versus 11% for fraternals. Different concordance rates suggest different entities, with bipolar disorder being quite heritable and unipolar disorder only marginally so. A final line of reasoning that suggests a basic difference between bipolar and unipolar depression is that bipolar depression responds to lithium carbonate. Upwards of 80% of bipolars will have their symptoms of mania, and to a lesser extent, depression, alleviated by this medication. When bipolars are maintained on lithium preventatively, only 34% relapse, in contrast to 79% on placebos (Gelenberg & Klerman, 1978). The drugs that help unipolars (tricyclics and MAO inhibitors) do not much help bipolars (Gelenberg & Klerman, 1978). Such differential effectiveness of drugs suggests two different disorders. We will not discuss bipolar depression any further in this chapter, except to conclude that it is probably more related to unipolar depression in appearance than in mechanism.

How are unipolar depression, a certified disorder, and normal depression related? We believe that they are wholly continuous, the same phenomenon, differing only in the number and severity of symptoms. This view contrasts with the prevailing medical opinion that holds unipolar depression to be an illness and normal depression to be a transient demoralization that holds no clinical interest. This continuity-discontinuity question is both important and complex, and so we discuss it later on in detail. For now, we turn to how one recognizes depression.

The Symptoms of Depression

Depression, be it unipolar, bipolar, or normal, has a common set of symptoms manifest in one's mood, thought, behavior, and physiology. To be diagnosed as depressed, it is not necessary that an individual experience all possible symptoms. Indeed, no single symptom is necessary, but the more symptoms present and the more intense they are, the more certain we can be that someone's problem is indeed depression.

Mood. A depressed person feels awful: sad, unhappy, blue, downhearted, discouraged, sunk in a pit of despair. He may cry a lot, or he may be beyond tears. Almost universally, the fun goes out of his life. Formerly enjoyable activities become flat. Jokes no longer seem funny.

Sadness is not the only mood salient in depression. There is a strong relationship between depression and anxiety. Mildly and moderately depressed people are almost always anxious. Interestingly, severely depressed people may not be anxious at all. What makes sense of this pattern? Perhaps anxiety is an energizing response to danger, whereas depression is a de-energizing, conserving response. When danger threatens a person, his anxiety will be aroused and will fuel planning and action, for as long as he believes that some action might be able to help him. Once he expects with certainty that he will be helpless, anxiety may drop out and be replaced with depression. Depression demobilizes his planning and action and conserves his resources, when in reality nothing can be done. Anxiety and depression can coexist when an individual oscillates between the expectation that he will be helpless and the hope that he might be able to do something about his situation (Garber, Miller, & Abramson, 1980).

In addition to sadness and anxiety, hostility—actually its lack—is tied up with depression. Freud (1917) believed that depression resulted from hostility turned inward upon the self. There may be some truth to this suggestion, in view of how infrequently depressed people get angry at others. Still, we have a different view on the matter than did Freud. We don't believe that the anger has been transmuted inwardly so much as suspended. The absence of hostility among depressives is part of the global deficits in initiating voluntary action that characterize the disorder.

Thought. The way a depressed person thinks differs from the way a person who is not depressed thinks. Aaron Beck's (1967) theory of depression gives the most accurate description of depressed thought. We discuss it here because it is the closest theory to our own, and we will of course point out the differences along the way. Beck (1967) describes depressive thinking in terms of the negative *cognitive triad:* that is, negative thoughts about the self, ongoing experience, and the future. In addition, Beck argues that the depressive makes errors of logic. Among the six logical errors that Beck specifies are such habits of thought as arbitrary inference (jumping to conclusions from a single fact) and personalization (blaming oneself for bad events in which one actually played no role).

While Beck's depiction of depressive thinking seems accurate, it is a theorist's nightmare, and part of our task here will be to retain its descriptive accuracy while adding theoretical clarity (see also Brewin, 1989; Segal, 1988). There are several inadequacies to Beck's concepts as they are currently presented.

The question of causation is unclear. The pessimistic thoughts of a depressed person are a major symptom of his disorder. Are these just one symptom cluster among several, or are they the central symptom that causes the other symptoms? Beck (1967), in his early work, claimed they were causal. But Beck (1984) has more recently relegated them to a noncausal position in a major concession to the biological school. If cognitions are causal, how do they bring about the other symptoms of depression? The reformulation of the learned helplessness model of depression, which we spelled out in Chapter 5, treats a person's explanatory style as a preexisting disposition that can bring about the other symptoms of depression through its influence on expectations of helplessness.

Another inadequacy in Beck's theory is that the empirical relationship between the cognitive triad and the errors of logic is unclear. Does personalization (the tendency to blame oneself) cause a negative view of self or vice versa? According to the reformulation of the learned helplessness model of depression, these symptoms are derived from the individual's explanatory style.

Finally, the conceptual relationship among Beck's variables is unclear as well. How do the different errors in logic differ from one another? Cook and Peterson (1986) reported considerable disagreement among expert judges in classifying erroneous reasoning using Beck's categories. And why are there nine mechanisms in the theory (the triad plus six errors) rather than just three or six or whatever? In contrast, the reformulation of the learned helplessness model of depression is a parsimonious account that derives all of Beck's mechanisms from explanatory style.

Behavior and Motivation.   Depressed people show such behavioral and motivational symptoms as passivity, indecisiveness, and suicidal action. They often cannot get started on any but the most routine tasks, and they give up easily when thwarted. A depressed college professor cannot get the first word of an article written. When she finally does, she quits writing when the screen on her word processor flickers, and she doesn't go back to it for a month.

Depressed people cannot decide among alternatives. A depressed student phones for a pizza and when asked if he wants it plain or with a topping, he stares paralyzed at the receiver. After a minute of silence, he hangs up.

Depressed people obsess about death and may even attempt suicide. They generally have one or both of two motives. Either they find the prospect of going on with life as it currently is to be unbearable, or they want to accomplish something in the world—bring back love, get revenge, or have the last word in an argument. In either case, the link between depression and suicide is a strong one in our society. Perhaps eighty percent of those who kill themselves do so when severely depressed.

Physiology.   Depression is frequently accompanied by physical symptoms. As we mentioned, the appetites in general diminish. The desire for food, sex, and companionship wanes. The people we usually love we now just tolerate. Formerly enjoyable activities become boring. We have trouble falling asleep and staying asleep (particularly when anxiety accompanies our depression).

Body chemistry changes, in ways that parallel the bodily changes

Table 6-1. Parallels between Symptoms of Learned Helplessness and Depression.

	Learned Helplessness	Depression
Symptoms	Passivity	Passivity
	Cognitive deficits	Negative cognitive triad
	Self-esteem deficits	Low self-esteem
	Sadness, hostility, and anxiety	Sadness, hostility, and anxiety
	Loss of appetite	Loss of appetite
	Reduced aggression	Reduced aggression
	Sleep loss	Sleep loss
	Norepinephrine and serotonin depletion	Norepinephrine and serotonin depletion
Causes	Learned belief that responding is independent of outcomes	Generalized belief that responding will be ineffective
Treatments	Change belief in response futility	Cognitive and behavioral therapy
	ECT, antidepressants	ECT, antidepressants
	REM deprivation	REM deprivation
	Time	Time
Prevention	Immunization	Invulnerability factors

Source: Rosenhan, D. L., and Seligman, M.E.P. (1989). *Abnormal psychology* (2nd ed.). New York: Norton. © 1989 by W. W. Norton & Company, Inc. Adapted by permission of the publisher.

that take place when animals are made helpless (Chapter 3). Biogenic amines become less available, with norepinephrine and serotonin particularly affected. Endorphin levels rise, along with pain thresholds. And the immune system becomes less able to defend against disease (Chapter 8).

Learned Helplessness and Depression

This completes our brief overview of depressive symptoms. In 1975, Seligman argued that these symptoms mapped well into the symptoms of people and animals made helpless, and these similarities formed the basis of the original helplessness model of depression (see Table 6–1). Subsequent research investigated parallels between learned helplessness and depression with respect to causes, treatments, and preventions (see Peterson & Seligman, 1984, 1985).

The parallels between depression and learned helplessness are easy to appreciate with respect to people. But what about animals? Weiss and Goodman (1985) suggested that this question is best approached by keeping in mind the criteria used to diagnose human depression and then examining whether animals exposed to inescapable shock meet these criteria. The Diagnostic and Statistical Manual for Mental Disorders (DSM-III-R) lists nine such symptoms for diagnosing depression in people (American Psychiatric Association, 1987):

1. Depressed or irritable mood
2. Loss of interest in usual activities
3. Appetite and weight disturbance (increase or decrease)
4. Sleep disturbances (insomnia or hypersomnia)
5. Psychomotor disturbance (agitation or retardation)
6. Loss of energy or fatigue
7. Feelings of worthlessness
8. Evidence of decreased ability to think
9. Recurrent thoughts of death and suicide

Five symptoms are required for a diagnosis of depression. Depressed mood, feelings of worthlessness, and suicidal ideation are impossible to assess in animals, but the other criteria can be examined, and requiring that five of these six be present is indeed a stringent diagnostic requirement. Do inescapably shocked animals meet these criteria?

Loss of Interest in Usual Activities.   A variety of studies have examined the impact of uncontrollable versus controllable shock on natural rat activities. Many of these have centered on agonistic behavior. In the first of these, Maier, Anderson, and Lieberman (1972) determined whether prior exposure to controllable and uncontrollable shock would alter the level of "shock-elicited aggression." (Shock-elicited aggression refers to the fact that two rats will adopt aggressive postures toward each other and "fight" if they are exposed to brief foot shocks while in the same enclosure.) Prior inescapable shock reduced the level of aggression, while escapable shock did not.

Shock-elicited aggression might seem artificial and not representative of actual aggressive behavior. However, inescapable shock depresses more "natural" aggressive behavior as well. Williams (1982) allowed trios of two male rats and one female to establish a colony together for 8 weeks. One of the males will almost always become dominant in such a situation (the "alpha" male). If an intruder is introduced into the colony, the alpha male will typically attack the intruder. After the colonies had been left undisturbed for 8 weeks, the alpha males were removed and given escapable shock, yoked inescapable shock, or no shock. The rats were returned to their colonies and an intruder was introduced into each of the colonies 24 hours later.

The question of interest was whether the shock treatments altered the alpha male's tendency to attack the intruder. Escapable shock had no effect on the alpha's aggressive behavior. However, inescapable shock greatly reduced the alpha's tendency to attack the intruder. Here a more natural aggressive behavior was measured. Shock was not present in the test situation. Yet experience with uncontrollability led to a decrease in the activity.

In the Williams experiment, the nontreated non-alpha male paired with the inescapably shocked alpha male showed an increased tendency to attack the intruder. This suggests that inescapable shock might have reduced the alpha's dominance. Indeed, Rapaport and Maier (1978) examined this possibility directly. The dominance hierarchy of a set of rats was established by a series of round-robin tests in which every possible pair of rats was allowed to compete for access to a food cup that did not allow two rats to eat from it at once. This allowed identification of the rat winning the most encounters, the second most, and so on.

Retesting revealed that the hierarchy was quite stable. The rats were then given escapable shock, yoked inescapable shock, or no shock. Twenty-four hours later the dominance hierarchy was again assessed with the food competition test. Inescapably shocked rats moved down in the dominance hierarchy, now losing competitions that they would not previously have lost. They ran to the food as fast as before and ate normal amounts if a competitor was not present. Although motivated to attain the food, they submitted to any competitor that was present. Escapable shock had no effect.

These widespread effects of uncontrollability are not limited to agonistic behavior. Williams (1984) gave mother rats either controllable or uncontrollable shock 8 days after giving birth. Their maternal behavior was observed 24 and 72 hours after the shock treatment. The inescapably shocked mothers showed disrupted maternal behavior—they were slower to approach the nest when removed, stayed in the nest area for shorter durations, and had lower frequencies and durations of oral contact with their pups.

Experience with uncontrollable shock apparently disrupts a number of usual activities of the rat—aggression, dominance, and maternal behavior. These are the only behaviors that have been examined in published studies, but there is no reason to suppose that the impact is limited to them. For example, unpublished data from our laboratories reveal a suppression of sexual behavior as well. It is fair to conclude that uncontrollable shock does disrupt many of the usual activities of the rat for at least 24 to 72 hours. Knowledge of the limits of these effects waits for further research.

Appetite, Weight, and Sleep Disturbances.   Weiss (1968) has shown that prolonged and severe uncontrollable shock leads to many of the somatic symptoms that characterize depression. Animals that experience inescapable shock eat less and lose weight relative to escapably shocked subjects. Weiss and Goodman (1985) have more recently studied sleep patterns in animals that had received two sessions of severe inescapable shock. These animals slept less than did controls, with the greatest effect occurring in the early morning light part of the sleep cycle. The overall loss of sleep persisted for 5 days following the inescapable shock treatment, whereas the early morning waking effect persisted for many days.

Psychomotor Retardation and Loss of Energy.   In Chapter 2, we described data indicating that uncontrollable but not controllable shock reduces the organism's subsequent activity in the presence of shock. But animals that have received prolonged uncontrollable shock are also less active in situations that do not involve shock. For example, Weiss et al. (1981) gave rats a prolonged session of severe controllable or uncontrollable shock. The animals were later placed in a tank of water. They were fitted with flotation devices resembling "water wings" so that they could not sink. Weiss and his colleagues measured the animals' tendency to struggle (front feet moving and breaking the surface of the water) and to float (feet motionless). Rats that had experienced uncontrollable shock gave up struggling and became motionless far more rapidly than did control subjects. Moreover, rats that have experienced uncontrollable positive events later engage in less exploration when placed in novel environments (Joffe, Rawson, & Mulick, 1973). These findings imply psychomotor retardation and loss of energy.

Decreased Ability to Think.   We also reviewed evidence indicating that animals that have been exposed to uncontrollable shock have difficulty learning relationships between their behavior and outcomes, perhaps through an alteration in attentional mechanisms. Moreover, they are more affected than controls by the complexity of environmental contingencies (Maier & Testa, 1975) and give up sooner in problem-solving situations. This pattern in humans would lead to a label of "decreased ability to think."

Do these consequences of inescapable shock justify a "diagnosis" of depression? It is, of course, speculative to talk of depression in rats, because we think of depression as involving subjective sadness and distress. Yet the behavior of inescapably shocked rats shows a profile that would lead to a diagnosis of depression if the rat were a person. *All* of the DSM-III-R symptoms that could be assessed in an animal are present.

It should also be noted here that inescapably shocked rats show a pattern of neurochemical changes thought to be involved in human depression (see Chapter 3). And the drugs that break up depression in people break up learned helplessness as produced in animals. Tricyclic antidepressants and MAO inhibitors, as well as electroconvulsive shock, relieve helplessness in rats and dogs (e.g., Dorworth & Overꞓ ꞉er, 1977; Martin, Soubrie, & Simon, 1987; Porsolt, Anton, Blavet, & Jalfre, 1978; Sherman & Petty, 1980). Drugs that are not effective antidepressants are typically not effective against learned helplessness in animals either. Further, a variety of these antidepressive agents can also be used to prevent helplessness among animals in the first place (e.g., Petty & Sherman, 1980).

With respect to people, the only symptom of depression that has not been produced in the laboratory by uncontrollable events is suicidal ideation. One reason for this may be intensity; laboratory events are much milder than the real life events that spark suicide. Another reason is that suicide can be instrumental; it brings suffering to an end or accomplishes some other purpose. Any theory emphasizing helplessness is going to have trouble making sense of behaviors like suicide, no matter how maladaptive their consequences. By this latter line of reasoning, suicide may be a reaction to helplessness rather than a direct effect of it.

THE REFORMULATION OF THE LEARNED HELPLESSNESS MODEL OF DEPRESSION

If the mapping of symptoms and treatments between depression in the clinic and helplessness in the laboratory is this strong, why was the original learned helplessness theory in need of change? The main problem with the model is its incompleteness. Applied both to human helplessness in the laboratory and to natural depression, the model fails to account for boundary conditions. Sometimes laboratory helplessness is general (e.g., Hiroto & Seligman, 1975), and sometimes it is circumscribed (e.g., Cole & Coyne, 1977). Sometimes bad events precipitate depressive reactions in people (occasionally transient, occasionally long lasting), and sometimes they do not (e.g., Brown & Harris, 1978; Lloyd, 1980). What determines the chronicity and generality of helplessness and depression? Similarly, the original learned helplessness model does not explain the self-esteem loss frequently observed among depressives. Why should individuals blame themselves for events over which they perceive no control (Abramson & Sackeim, 1977)? The original model is silent about these matters.

As we explained in Chapter 5, Abramson, Seligman, and Teasdale (1978) addressed these shortcomings by revising helplessness theory to include the individual's explanations of the original bad events. In the wake of uncontrollability, people ask "why did this happen to me?" Their answer affects their reaction. With respect to depression, there is one particularly insidious pattern of making explanations: internal, stable, and global for bad events ("it's me; it's going to last forever; and it's going to undermine everything I do") and external, unstable, and specific for good events ("it just happened; it's going to go away quickly; and it's just an isolated occurrence"). Individuals who are prone to make such explanations are at risk for depression.

Here is why. As we saw, when an individual becomes helpless about some bad event, a set of symptoms that look very much like depression appears. If these symptoms last for weeks or months, we call them depression; if they disappear quickly, we call them a bad mood. If the symptoms pervade most of life, we again call them depression; if they are confined to one arena, we call them burnout or demoralization. So, when bad events strike, individuals who expect their causes to extend well into the future and across all their activities will be at risk for full-blown depression rather than just bad moods, burnout, or demoralization. Further, if the individual is prone to make internal explanations for failure, she will tend to lose self-esteem when she fails, adding yet another depressive symptom.

A key concept in the reformulated theory is explanatory style, the habitual tendency to offer the same sorts of explanations for diverse bad events. We need to take into account individual differences in dispositions to explain events in order to make sense of why different individuals have different reactions to the same events. Why do some people become helpless following unsolvable problems and others not (Alloy, Peterson, Abramson, & Seligman, 1984; Dweck

Table 6-2. Meta-analysis.

	Negative Events				Positive Events			
	Int	Sta	Glo	Composite	Int	Sta	Glo	Composite
Number of studies	90	75	61	42	54	43	33	30
Effect size	.36	.34	.37	.44	−.36	−.25	−.12	−.26
Probability	.0001	.0001	.0001	.0001	.0001	.001	.001	.001
File drawer statistic	12,729	10,254	9,760	6,678	5,114	2,038	262	1,149

Source: Sweeney, P. D., Anderson, K., and Bailey, S. (1986). Attributional style in depression: A meta-analytic review. *Journal of Personality and Social Psychology* 50:974–991. © 1986 by the American Psychological Association. Adapted by permission of the publisher and Paul D. Sweeney.

& Licht, 1980)? Why do some people become depressed following bad events and others not (Lloyd, 1980; Metalsky, Abramson, Seligman, Semmel, & Peterson, 1982)? The reformulation proposes that people susceptible to depression interpret these events in internal, stable, and global terms. If reality is ambiguous enough, a person may project his habitual explanations onto it. If these tendencies are toward internal, stable, and global causes for bad events, then that individual will tend to become depressed when bad events occur.

This is the central prediction of the reformulation, and we now turn to the evidence in support of it. We examine several types of converging evidence. Cross-sectional studies look at the link between explanatory style and depression measured at the same time. Longitudinal studies measure explanatory style and depression over time. And experiments of nature start with people whose explanatory styles are known and then determine who becomes depressed in the wake of bad events.

Cross-sectional Evidence

Sweeney, Anderson, and Bailey (1986) performed a meta-analysis of 104 studies involving over 15,000 subjects that tested the relationship of explanatory style to depression. These studies included 75 published articles and 29 unpublished papers and excluded articles from any of our laboratories. Their findings are consistent with the reformulation, for each dimension and for both positive and negative events. Table 6–2 shows the basic results.

The authors used two statistics to evaluate the size and significance of the predicted effects. The first was the *effect size:* the fraction of a standard deviation by which the depressed group differs on average from the nondepressed group, corrected for unreliability. The second was the *file drawer* statistic: the number of null findings that would have to be sitting around unpublished in the file drawers of different investigators to render the effect nonsignificant. As you can see by scanning Table 6–2, effects of moderate size are found for each of the six predictions. Depressed subjects make more internal, stable, and global explanations for bad events (by between .34 and .44 standard deviations) than do nondepressed subjects. And depressed subjects make more external, unstable, and specific explanations for good events (by between .12 and .36 standard deviations) than do nondepressed subjects. Each of these predictions is unambiguously significant and would take a staggering number of null findings to overturn. Helplessness research is popular, but not this popular! With the correlation now established, let us turn to some issues about the role of explanatory style in depression.

Depressed Patients Versus College Students. It is often said that the reformulation has not been tested sufficiently with real patients but is an artifact of the moody college sophomore who received the wrong color BMW for a birthday present. This criticism proves off base. While there are 52 studies of college students in this meta-analysis (as well as 24 studies of normal nonstudents), there are also 14 studies of depressed patients. The depressed patients show the same effects as above, only stronger. Similarly, it does not seem to matter if the subjects are explaining hypothetical events (e.g., the ASQ), real events (e.g., the CAVE), or events that have just happened to them in the laboratory; in each case the predicted depressive explanatory style emerges.

Specificity of Depressive Explanatory Style. Is the habit of explaining bad events by internal, stable, and global causes a general characteristic of psychopathology or is it specific to depression? This question boils down to the control groups that are compared with the depressive groups. There are a number of relevant studies. In one, Raps, Peterson, Reinhard, Abramson, and Seligman (1982) compared inpatients with unipolar depression to nondepressed schizophrenics, matched according to their length of hospitalization. Depressives explained bad events with more internal, stable, and global causes than did schizophrenics. The schizophrenics in turn resembled medical and surgical inpatients with respect to explanatory style, with one important exception: they were more external about bad events, as we would expect granted their paranoid ideation.

Riskind, Castellon, and Beck (1989) compared unipolar depressed outpatients (who were not anxious) with outpatients with generalized anxiety disorder, or GAD (who were not depressed), using the CAVE technique to infer explanatory style. They found a different pattern of explanations, with GAD patients having less pessimistic CAVE scores than unipolar depressives.

Still more evidence comes from a study by Eaves and Rush (1984). They used the ASQ as a diagnostic tool to differentiate between known depressed patients and nonpatient controls. The sensitivity of the ASQ, defined as the probability of a correct diagnosis of depression given that the patient is depressed (i.e., the percentage of true positives), was 61% for internality for bad events, 58% for stability for bad events, and 77% for globality for bad events. The specificity of the ASQ, defined as the probability of a correct diagnosis given that the patient is *not* depressed (i.e., the percentage of true negatives), was 94%, 94%, and 88%, respectively, for internality, stability, and globality for bad events. These figures compare favorably with the best biological tests of depression.

In addition, explanatory style for bad events correlated with the total amount of time the individual was depressed, the average length of his or her episode, and the length of the current episode for nonendogenously depressed individuals. This was particularly the case for the stability measure, which correlated .79 with the total time of depression, .76 with the average length of episode, and .71 with the length of the current episode (all p's $< .001$. These data suggest that stability for bad events reflects, and may predict, how long a depressive episode will last.

Seligman et al. (1988) found no differences in explanatory style between unipolar depressed patients and bipolar patients during their depressed phase. We also found no difference between melancholic and nonmelancholic depressives or between anxious and nonanxious depressed patients.

Studies exist showing that a "depressive" explanatory style is linked with a variety of psychopathologies, such as eating disorders, anxiety, pathological gambling, substance abuse, and the like. On the face of it, these studies seem to argue against the specificity of explanatory style to depression. However, in some if not all of these cases, the role of depression in these psychopathologies has not been ruled out in terms of being the real correlate of explanatory style. Indeed, epidemiologists estimate that the majority of those who are severely depressed have at least one other disorder (Sanderson, Beck, & Beck, 1990), so the issue of specificity is not as simple as it might seem.

Whatever the boundaries may be, we feel confident in saying that there is a depressive explanatory style; depressed individuals are more likely to offer internal, stable, and global causes for bad events and external, unstable, and specific causes for good events than nondepressed individuals. Further controversy about this point is idle, and we suggest that the field's attention should now be turned to whether this explanatory style plays a causal role in producing depression.

The reformulation claims that explanatory style is a risk factor for depression. Individuals who at this moment habitually explain the causes of bad events as internal, stable, and global will be at higher risk for later depression—even if they are not now depressed—than individuals with the opposite style. But the results of the meta-analysis, because they are mere correlations, are compatible with other, less interesting hypotheses. Perhaps depression causes pessimistic explanatory style, not the other way around. Perhaps some third variable like catecholamine depletion, or turning anger upon oneself, causes both depression and pessimistic explanatory style. Or perhaps the relationship is a mere tautology; part of how we know someone is depressed is because she says pessimistic things about herself. So the way we determine that she is depressed and the way we determine that she has a pessimistic explanatory style are by attending to the same phenomenon, even though we call it depression in one case and pessimism in the other.

These possibilities can be disentangled by looking at depression and explanatory style across time. In particular, the reformulation makes three predictions:

1. Individuals who are not depressed now but have a depressive explanatory style are at greater risk for becoming depressed in the future.
2. Individuals who are depressed now but have a nondepressive explanatory style will tend to become less depressed in the future.
3. Individuals who undergo a change in explanatory style (as in therapy or preventative procedures) will have their depression changed accordingly.

We now look at two research strategies that test the risk-factor hypothesis against the other hypotheses: longitudinal studies and experiments of nature.

Longitudinal Studies

Longitudinal studies look at the same individuals across time, taking the same set of measurements at various points. This allows us to find out if explanatory style at an earlier time influences susceptibility to depression later on, over and above how depressed the individual was at the earlier time. This is the way that predictions 1 and 2 in the previous paragraph can be addressed. There are three sets of longitudinal studies, with children, normal adults, and depressed patients.

Children. Susan Nolen-Hoeksema, Joan Girgus, and Martin Seligman (in press) carried out a five-year longitudinal study of 350 third graders and their parents, attempting to predict depression and poor school achievement from explanatory style. The main instrument we used was the Children's Attributional Style Questionnaire (CASQ; Seligman, Peterson, Kaslow, Tanenbaum, Alloy, & Abramson, 1984). The CASQ is a forced-choice instrument that we created when we found in pilot work that young children had trouble completing the adult ASQ, particularly the rating of globality. In this questionnaire just for children, hypothetical good or bad events involving the child are followed by two possible explanations. For each event, one of the explanatory dimensions is varied while the other two are held constant. Sixteen questions pertain to each of the three dimensions; half refer to good events and half to bad events. See Table 6–3 for sample items from the CASQ.

The CASQ is scored by assigning a 1 to each internal or stable or global response and a 0 to each external or unstable or specific response. Scales are formed by summing the three scores across the appropriate questions for each of the three dimensions, separately for good events and for bad events. The scores for each of the scales range from 0 to 8. CASQ subscales are only moderately reliable. More satisfactory reliabilities can be obtained by combining the subscales (again, separately for good events and for bad events). The alpha for the good events composite was .66 and for bad events, .50. The CASQ scales and composites are consistent in showing explanatory style to be a somewhat coherent individual difference among children, just as it is among adults.

Table 6-3. Sample Items from the CASQ.

Item	Valence	Varied	Held Constant
A good friend tells you that he hates you.	Bad		Stability; globality
a. My friend was in a bad mood that day.		External	
b. I wasn't nice to my friend that day.		Internal	
You get all the toys you want for your birthday.	Good		Internality; globality
a. People always guess what toys to get me for my birthday.		Stable	
b. This birthday people guessed right about what toys I wanted.		Unstable	
You get an "A" on a test.	Good		Internality, stability
a. I am smart.		Global	
b. I am smart in the subject.		Specific	

Source: Peterson C., and Seligman, M.E.P. (1984). Causal explanations as a risk factor for depression: Theory and evidence. *Psychological Review* 91:347–374. © 1984 by the American Psychological Association. Reprinted by permission of the publisher.

This large-scale study is based on a more modest one: a one-year longitudinal investigation of 168 third to fifth graders, with depression (as measured by the Children's Depression Inventory; Kovacs & Beck, 1977) and explanatory style measured at five time points (waves). We found consistent results for each wave (Nolen-Hoeksema, Girgus, & Seligman, 1986).

First, both explanatory style and depression were stable from wave to wave (r = .36 to .61, r = .46 to .71, respectively). Second, explanatory style and depression correlated within each wave (mean r = .29 to .48) Third, explanatory style at each earlier wave predicted depression at the next wave, partialing out depression at the earlier wave (partial r's = .29 to .37). This means that on average:

- Children with a depressive explanatory style who are not depressed tend to get depressed as time goes on.
- Children with a nondepressive style who are depressed tend to get less depressed.
- Children with a depressive explanatory style who are depressed tend to stay depressed.
- Children with a nondepressive style who are not depressed tend to stay nondepressed.

The next finding is also important, and typical of the results of longitudinal studies of explanatory style and depression. Depression at each earlier wave predicted explanatory style at the next wave, partialing out explanatory style at the earlier wave. This means that depression makes a person more pessimistic, just as pessimistic explanatory style makes her more depressed. This pattern of results, in which each factor has a causal influence on the other, is called reciprocal causation. It tends to be the rule rather than the exception in social and behavioral science, particularly with regard to thinking and mood (Teasdale, 1983).

Does this mean that explanatory style has no causal effect on depression, except insofar as prior depression causes both later depression and later depressive explanatory style? This seems unlikely to us, because we can point to two studies that show that inducing depressed mood does not change a person's explanatory style (Brewin & Harris, 1985; Mukherji, Abramson, & Martin, 1982). In other words, explanatory style and depressed mood do not always move in lockstep. But the reciprocal relationship between explanatory style and depression makes one more analysis of our results necessary, which brings us to the fifth finding. If depression at Time One brings about pessimistic explanatory style at Time Two, is it possible that pessimistic explanatory style at Time Two brings about depression at Time Three merely because depression at Time One influences depression at Time Three?

The results suggest that this is not the case. Explanatory style at time n predicts depression at time $n + 1$, partialing out depression at both time n and time $n - 1$, for each wave. This means that there is a genuine effect of depressive explanatory style on later depression, beyond any effects of earlier depression on later depression.

The large-scale study was a five-year replication with ten waves of measurement. Depression is consistently predicted by prior depression, by pessimistic explanatory style, and by bad life events. Each of these factors makes a separate contribution to predicting which third grader will experience depression by the end of seventh grade.

Adults. The parallel questions have been asked of college students by Zullow (1984). In his study, 154 students took the ASQ and the Beck Depression Inventory (BDI) in three waves over three months. The same pattern of results as with children emerged: depressive explanatory style predicted later depression over and above earlier depression (see also Golin, Sweeney, & Shaeffer, 1981).

More specifically, those at the severe end of depression were particularly hurt by a pessimistic explanatory style when it was coupled with a state orientation. As we discussed in Chapter 4, Kuhl (1981) characterizes thought patterns as either action oriented (directed toward productive future action) or state oriented (ruminating about how bad things are). Kuhl argues that ruminators are more prone to helplessness and depression than are action-oriented people. Zullow (1984) added a twist to this. It is people who ruminate *and* have a disposition to make internal, stable, and global explanations of bad events who are most prone to depression.

Explanatory style is a mere disposition to explain events in a patterned way; unlike a specific explanation, it does not exist in time. How, then, might it impact the person to bring about depression? This study gives us a hint as to what the pathway between explanatory style and depression might be. Ruminators are individuals who talk to themselves a lot. Depressive explanatory style provides a framework for specific content—"I'm stupid, talentless, unlovable, and incompetent." If a person both is a ruminator and has this depressive style, he will say such things to himself frequently. If he is a ruminator but has the opposite style, he will talk to himself frequently but about less depressing causes—"This is my unlucky day; she's difficult to please; my boss is in a bad mood." If he is not a ruminator but has a depressive style, he will not say depressing things to himself very frequently.

Zullow (1984) proposed that rumination bridges explanatory style and depression. What one consciously thinks is the final link in the chain that sets off depression. Internal, stable, and global attributions about bad events are sufficient to produce momentary depressive symptoms. And the more frequently one thinks in this way, the longer and more severe these symptoms. In Beck's language, automatic thoughts (obsessive thinking) that entail internal, stable, and global causes for bad events trigger depression. This line of reasoning is consistent with findings of Kammer (1983) and Dweck and Licht (1980). They find that not only do depressed adults and helpless children have a depressive explanatory style, but they also entertain more explanations of events. Depression may be the product not only of what you say (explanatory style), but how often you say it (rumination).

Also consistent with this line of reasoning are studies showing that people are particularly prone to think when confronted with aversive events (e.g., Wong & Weiner, 1981). When bad things happen to us, we think, and when lots of bad things happen, we think a great deal. This explains the strong link, perhaps, between stressful life events and depression, both as predispositions and triggers (Lloyd, 1980). These findings are often presented without much attention as to why the link occurs; we suggest that cognition fills the gap. Because being depressed is a bad event, we end up with cascading influences among bad events, depressed mood, causal attributions, and rumination.

Patients. Firth and Brewin (1982) reported a study that looked at the course of depression among patients undergoing antidepressive medication therapy. They found that those patients who explained recent life events as more unstable and controllable became less depressed over the next six weeks. Brewin (1985), citing similar recovery results (e.g., Cutrona, 1983), argued for a recovery model of the power of explanatory style. In particular, he emphasized that prediction of nondepression, given an optimistic explanatory style, is more uniformly confirmed than is prediction of depression given a pessimistic style.

The final longitudinal study involving patients is an unusual one, because it only involved one individual (Peterson, Luborsky, & Seligman, 1983). It made, however, a very accurate, fine-grained prediction of his behavior. This patient, Mr. Q, demonstrated precipitous shifts in mood (Luborsky, 1964, 1970) during his psychotherapy sessions (conducted over four years). More than 200 sessions with Mr. Q were tape-recorded, and a sample was transcribed, allowing a thorough content analysis of his explanations before and after his mood swings. Three types of sessions were analyzed: those in which Mr. Q became more depressed, those in which he became less depressed, and those in which no change in mood occurred. His explanations for bad events were extracted from these sessions before and after his mood swings and were rated for internality, stability, and globality, in the very first use of the CAVE technique.

We used several criteria to identify Mr. Q's swings to and from depression: (a) his own report of a shift in mood (e.g., "my mood just went down"); (b) the agreement of two independent judges reading the transcript of the therapy sessions that a mood swing had just occurred; and (c) the fact that the swing did not occur in close proximity to another swing (i.e., within fifteen minutes of the same session). Applying these three criteria resulted in a set of four swings in which Mr. Q became more depressed and five in which he became less depressed.

Explanations for bad events were extracted from the first 400 words

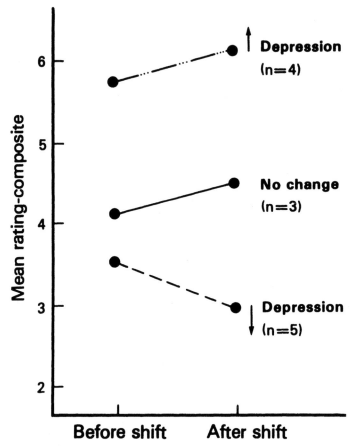

Figure 6-1. Causal explanations of Mr. Q. *Source:* Peterson, C., Luborsky, L., and Seligman, M.E.P. (1983). Attributions and depressive mood shifts. *Journal of Abnormal Psychology* 92:96–103. © 1983 by the American Psychological Association. Reprinted by permission of the publisher.

(spoken by Mr. Q) before each swing and from the 400 words following it. For comparison purposes, causal explanations were also extracted from randomly chosen 800-word segments of three sessions in which no mood swing occurred. Figure 6–1 shows the means for the different types of sessions.

The differences predicted by the reformulation were present before Mr. Q's mood swings. Highly internal, stable, and global causal explanations preceded an increase in depression, whereas much more external, unstable, and specific statements preceded a decrease in depression. There was no overlap between the ratings of causal explanations before swings to more versus less depression.

This is a fine-grained case study, but because it is not experimental, we must rule out some plausible third variables before we can argue that explanations, not some factor correlated with them, produced his mood swings. Various content characteristics of these same transcripts, including Mr. Q's statements about his anxiety, hopelessness, guilt, hostility, loss of self-esteem, and Oedipal conflict, were examined. These were not redundant with the causal explanation scores, rising and falling with the level of mood in a given session. In contrast, these explanations were different before swings.

This study shows that the reformulation of the helplessness model may be applied to single individuals with depressive symptoms. Ratings of the causal explanations for sessions in which swings to increased depression occurred did not at all overlap with those for sessions in which swings to decreased depression occurred, allowing perfect prediction.

In sum, these longitudinal studies are for the most part consistent with the prediction that depressive explanatory style precedes depressive symptoms. There are other studies that have been conducted that do not support this prediction (e.g., Peterson, Schwartz, & Seligman, 1981). Rather than discuss these studies point by point, we offer the comment that depression often proves highly stable, and longitudinal studies cannot work if there is not enough variation across time in depression for a person's explanatory style to have an effect. Said another way, explanatory style can only have an influence when given the opportunity to do so. Shared by the studies we have described is the fact that some people actually changed their status from depressed to nondepressed and/or vice versa.

There is a serious flaw in the studies we have discussed. They do not manipulate or assess bad life events. It is possible that people with a pessimistic style experience (or even bring about) more bad events, and thus it is simply bad events that are causing their depression. Moreover, according to Abramson et al. (1978), a depressive explanatory style per se is not sufficient for depression. It is only when bad events actually occur and the person interprets them in terms of internal, stable, and global causes that depressive symptoms are more likely to ensue. Because these studies did not look at bad events, they did not test this prediction. The studies in the next section test the stronger prediction that a preexisting depressive explanatory style followed by bad events makes depression more likely.

Experiments of Nature

The ideal way to test the helplessness reformulation with regard to depression is to measure the explanatory style of individuals and then to choose randomly half of them to experience some horrible event. Those subjects with a preexisting depressive explanatory style who then experience this event should—by prediction—be most likely to become depressed. The obvious ethical dilemma can be partly solved by a quasi-experimental method in which naturally occurring bad events take the place of experimental manipulation. We next report several sets of such studies. In the first, the bad event was an unsatisfactory grade on a midterm examination. In the second, the event was imprisonment. In the third, extending the logic of an experiment of nature, we look at the effects of therapy on explanatory style.

Midterm Studies.   Metalsky, Abramson, Seligman, Semmel, and Peterson (1982) carried out a prospective study of college students and their reactions to a low grade on a midterm. The participants were undergraduates in an introductory psychology class. At Time One, they completed the ASQ and a questionnaire asking about the grades for the class midterm with which they would be happy or unhappy. At Time Two, just prior to the midterm examination, their level of depressed mood was assessed with the Multiple Affect Adjective Check List (MAACL; Zuckerman & Lubin, 1965). At Time Three, immediately following receipt of their midterm grade, the students again completed the MAACL.

Our subjects were considered to have received a low grade if their midterm grade was less than or equal to the grade with which they said they would be unhappy. To test the predictions of the reformulation, explanatory style scores for bad events were correlated with standardized residual gain scores on the MAACL depression scale from Time Two to Time Three. What happened? Explanatory style for bad events predicted increases in depressed mood for students who received low grades—internality ($r = .34$, $p < .02$), stability ($r = .04$, ns), and globality ($r = .32$, $p < .02$)—but not for students who did well.

Recently, Metalsky, Halberstadt, and Abramson (1987) carried out a more elegant version of this study. In addition to replicating the basic finding just described, they examined the relationship between explanatory style and the actual explanation that students made for their failure on the midterm. The helplessness reformulation claims that a person's explanatory style affects depression by influencing the actual explanation given for failure. Metalsky et al. (1987) had students offer an explanation for how they did on the midterm. The researchers found that explanatory style predicted the particular explanation for the midterm failure. The particular explanation in turn predicted depressive reaction. Explanatory style per se had no effect on depressive reaction, over and above its effect on the particular explanation made. This experiment supports the causal chain postulated by the reformulated theory.

Prison Study. Does explanatory style predict depression following imprisonment (Bukstel & Kilmann, 1980)? For most individuals, imprisonment is inarguably a bad event. Prisons deny individuals control over even the most mundane aspects of their lives (cf. Goffman, 1961; Taylor, 1979). We would expect, then, that a common reaction to imprisonment is depression. Furthermore, we would predict that prisoners with a pessimistic explanatory style would be the most likely to become depressed after internment. We describe a preliminary study of this, in which individuals completed the ASQ upon their imprisonment. Then, shortly before their release, these same individuals completed the BDI (Peterson, Nutter, & Seligman, 1982).

Within one week following imprisonment at a maximum security prison in either New York, Ohio, or Pennsylvania, 245 adult males (ranging in age from seventeen to sixty-four years; average age, twenty-seven years) completed the ASQ. Within one week before their release, which varied from one month to one year, they completed the BDI. For 28 prisoners, BDI scores from the time of initial imprisonment were available. These averaged only 1.68, suggesting that subjects were not at all depressed at the time of imprisonment.

But at the end of their imprisonment, prisoners scored an average of 17.7 on the BDI, placing them in the moderately to severely depressed range. Furthermore, their depressive symptoms at the end of the imprisonment were strongly associated with their explanatory style at the beginning of their prison term. As expected, explanations for bad events were positively correlated with the development of depressive symptoms: internality ($r = .34$, $p < .001$), stability ($r = .36$, $p < .001$), and globality ($r = .35$, $p < .001$).

These experiments of nature confirm the reformulation and suggest that depressive explanatory style may predict who will become most depressed when tragedy or disaster strikes. The usefulness of this predictor is now being studied among bereaved relatives, among rapid-cycling bipolar depressives, and among women who have just given birth (Cutrona, 1983; O'Hara, Rehm, & Campbell, 1982; but cf. O'Hara, Neunaber, & Zekoski, 1984). There is a final group whose change in explanatory style provides an important experiment of nature: depressed patients undergoing therapy.

Therapy. Therapy fits our definition of an experiment of nature. The explanatory style and depression of patients can be observed before, during, and after therapy. The reformulation makes two predictions about therapy: (1) the change in explanatory style for the better (more external, unstable, and specific for bad events) should result in relief from depression; and (2) relapse should tend to occur among patients whose depression remits during therapy but whose explanatory style remains poor.

There are four kinds of treatments that are well documented in their relief of unipolar depression. Two are somatic: antidepressant drugs (most commonly tricyclics) and electroconvulsive shock. Two are psychotherapeutic: cognitive therapy and interpersonal therapy. In treatment with tricyclics and cognitive therapy, changes in explanatory style and depression have been tracked.

In one relevant study, unipolar depressed patients were randomly assigned to either tricyclic therapy, cognitive therapy, or both, and given twelve weeks of treatment (see Hollon, Shelton, & Loosen, 1991). Each treatment produced strong relief from depression. Explanatory style was measured by the ASQ at the beginning, middle, and end of therapy. What was the relation between the patient's relief from depression and his or her change for the better in explanatory style? In the tricyclic group, the correlation was nonsignificant. In the group getting both cognitive therapy and tricyclics, the relation was strongly positive ($r = .55$, $p < .001$). In the cognitive therapy group, the relationship was also very strong ($r = .77$, $p < .001$). Seligman et al. (1988) and Persons and Rao (1985) reported parallel strong correlations between relief from depression and improvement in explanatory style during therapy.

What do these results mean? As explanatory style changes for the better during cognitive therapy, patients become less depressed. But in drug therapy, improving someone's explanatory style was unrelated to symptomatic improvement. This suggests that cognitive therapy and drug therapy break up depression in different ways. Perhaps drug therapy activates patients, and cognitive therapy changes the way they look at causes.

But this finding, however suggestive it may be, is merely a correlation over time. Here is our hypothesis about the causal chain:

cognitive therapy produces a change for the better in explanatory style, which in turn causes depression to lift. As the data stand, this could be true. But it is also possible that the change in depression causes the improvement in explanatory style or that cognitive therapy changes something else, such as calling up good memories, which improves both explanatory style and depression. We are currently engaged in a detailed test of what the causal chain actually might be. Using each of the twelve therapy sessions from each of the patients in the study just described, we have indexed the amount and quality of therapy delivered, the explanatory style, and the depression level in each session. We are undertaking causal modeling to test the chain. What we hope to find is that following sessions in which a great deal of quality cognitive therapy is delivered, the person's explanatory style improves. When that happens, his or her depressive symptoms then remit.

There is also a hint that we can predict a relapse from someone's lack of improvement in explanatory style. Seligman et al. (1988) followed thirty-eight patients through cognitive therapy and one year of follow-up. The three patients who relapsed were among the four who had the least improved explanatory style at the end of therapy, even though their depression had remitted by the end of therapy. For the moment, this suggests that the conservative posture is not to terminate therapy until both depression remits and explanatory style improves.

The specificity of explanatory style change to cognitive therapy and not to tricyclics suggests that the specific active ingredient in cognitive therapy might be explanatory style change. In other words, the basic techniques of cognitive therapy may boil down to strategies for changing people's explanations. Recognizing automatic thoughts ("I'm a terrible mother and deserve to die") and marshaling evidence against them ("No, I'm just not a morning person") seem to change explanations of bad events from internal, stable, and global to more external, unstable, and specific. The search for alternatives ("Is it really true that you're a lousy student or might the professor have given low grades to everyone?") seems a search for less internal, stable, and global explanations. And another cognitive therapy technique—reattribution training—is explicitly geared toward explanatory style change.

In summary, cognitive therapy produces pronounced improvement in explanatory style. This improvement is durable; in a one-year follow-up, Seligman et al. (1988) found high stability of explanatory style gain. We speculate that change in explanatory style is the active ingredient of cognitive therapy. Perhaps future versions of cognitive therapy should be explicitly and specifically attributional (cf. Forsterling, 1985).

MODERNITY AND DEPRESSION

Let's recap before we move on. We began this chapter by looking at the symptoms of depression. We found that they matched reasonably well with the symptoms of learned helplessness. We argued, however, that the original theory was flawed in its claim that helplessness (as produced in the laboratory) was a model of depression. It failed to account for boundary conditions. By adding the premise of a depressive explanatory style, the theory could account for variations in depression across time and space. Explanatory style also predicted who would be at particular risk for depression, and we found that a good deal of evidence confirms this.

We do not have room for an exhaustive discussion of all the risk factors for depression (genetics, bad life events, fall and winter months, and so on), but there is a puzzling risk factor that the reformulated theory may illuminate. Indeed, it is the risk factor from which this book derives its subtitle, "A theory for the age of personal control." Something about modern life seems to have greatly multiplied the likelihood of depression, and it may be our glorification of the individual.

An Era of Melancholy?

There is growing evidence that we live in an era of melancholy. In the past, it has been notoriously hard to compare the prevalence of depression throughout history, but several recent studies have overcome such problems, particularly the differences in classification of depression over time (Jackson, 1986). In other words, the diagnosis of depression today means something different from its diagnosis fifty years ago, such that comparing tabled rates of depression from 1940 with those of 1990 is almost like comparing apples and oranges. The current studies, however, use a uniform classification scheme, derived from the structured diagnostic interviews associated with DSM-III-R, so that a case of depression in 1950 must meet the same criteria as a case today.

The ECA (Epidemiological Catchment Area) Study. In the late 1970s, the National Institute of Mental Health (NIMH) decided to get de-

Table 6-4. Lifetime Prevalence of Major Depressive Episodes by Age Adapted from Robins et al., 1984.

	18–24 yrs Born c. 1960 $n = 1,397$	25–44 yrs c. 1945 $n = 3,722$	45–64 yrs c. 1925 $n = 2,351$	Over 65 c. 1910 $n = 1,654$
New Haven	7.5%	10.4%	4.2%	1.8%
Baltimore	4.1	7.5	4.2	1.4
St. Louis	4.5	8.0	5.2	0.8

Source: Robins, L. N., et al. (1984). Lifetime prevalence of specific psychiatric disorders in three sites. *Archives of General Psychiatry* 41:949–958. © 1984 by the American Medical Association. Adapted by permission of the publisher.

finitive statistics on the frequency of different disorders in America (Robins et al., 1984). Toward this end, three centers (New Haven, Baltimore, and St. Louis) were designated, and 10,000 adults, representatively sampled, received standard diagnostic interviews between 1978 and 1981. The study is a gold mine for students of psychopathology, and here we concentrate on one aspect of it: lifetime prevalence of a major depressive disorder with age.

The lifetime prevalence of a disorder is the percentage of a population that has had the disorder at least once in their lifetime. Because this is a cumulative statistic, if the disorder has the same risk across historical time, older people will have a higher lifetime prevalence than younger people, simply because they have had more years in which to develop it. The occurrence of a major depressive disorder was ascertained by asking subjects whether symptoms of depression had occurred at any time of life and to what extent. Table 6–4 shows the lifetime prevalence of different age groups across the three sites.

These data are remarkable. They suggest that if you were born around 1910, you had only a 1.3% chance of having a major depressive episode, even though you have had at least a seventy-year opportunity to get it. In contrast, if you were born after 1960, you already had a 5.3% chance, even though you have only had a twenty-year opportunity. These are whopping differences, suggesting a roughly tenfold increase in risk for depression across two generations.

Birth Cohort Study. Relatives of individuals with major depressive disorders are themselves at heightened risk for depression, probably for genetic reasons. Do the same cohort (decade of birth) trends hold with relatives at risk? To ask this question, 2,289 relatives of 523 people with affective disorders were given the structured diagnostic interview probing for their lifetime prevalence of a major depressive disorder (Klerman et al., 1985).

Again, the effects of historical time are enormous—about one order of magnitude. Consider, for example, women born in 1950 versus women born before 1910. By age thirty, about 65% of the women born in 1950 had experienced a depressive episode, whereas fewer than 5% of the 1910 cohort had experienced one by the time they were thirty. At almost all corresponding points, a more recent year of birth confers more and earlier risk for a major depressive disorder. Overall, we can once again estimate a risk increase of roughly tenfold across two generations.

The Old Order Amish.   At the same time that these two studies were being conducted, the rate of depression among the Amish living in Lancaster County, Pennsylvania, was also being assessed (Egeland & Hostetter, 1983). A parallel diagnostic interview was used. The Amish are an ultrastrict Protestant sect. No electricity is permitted in their homes, horses and buggies are used for transportation, alcoholism and crime are virtually unknown among them, and their pacifism is absolute. They are a closed population, descended entirely from thirty eighteenth-century progenitors. Because they view mental illness as one of the worst ailments affecting humankind, they have cooperated openly with a thorough epidemiological study of depression and suicide in their midst.

For the five-year period from 1976 to 1980, 41 active cases of major depressive disorder were found; this is a five-year prevalence of about 0.5 percent (there are 8,186 adult Amish). If we compare this rate with the parallel figures from the ECA studies, we can roughly estimate that the Amish have about one-fifth to one-tenth the risk for unipolar depression as their neighboring Americans from modern cultures.

A Possible Explanation

Let us assume that the prevalence of normal depression has actually remained constant in this century. Let us also assume, however, that people in the past handled their depressions differently than we do now. Specifically, the low mood and pessimism of normal depression may have been taken less seriously in the past, regarded as less important and more inevitable.

"Accentuate the positive, eliminate the negative"; "When you feel blue, do something for someone you love"; "Life isn't a bed of roses"; and *"Arbeit macht das Leben Suess"* (i.e., "Work sweetens life") were popular guidelines for dealing with low mood in the first half of this century. They are also strategies that minimize one's awareness and reporting of negative feelings. More profoundly, they may prevent normal depression from escalating into unipolar disorder.

In contrast, a culture like our own that takes seriously individuality, control, and hedonism may pay the price of increased depression. Indeed, we do more than just take personal control seriously; we sanction it and glorify it. But suppose depression is in part a disorder of personal control. Suppose depression results from finding oneself helpless and then feeling hopeless. We would predict an epidemic of depression to be raging, and it is.

Modernity has raised our goals and expectations that we can achieve them ("all problems have a solution") beyond any fit with reality. It has increased the sheer number of helplessness experiences, of failures. To the extent that we have more opportunities and choices, we have a greater chance of failing. Finally, to the extent that modernity supports and sanctions internal, stable, and global explanations of why we fail, it enhances a depressive explanatory style. Because we as a people take individual control seriously, it follows that when an individual fails, self-blame—about stable and global faults—is a plausible explanation.

Remember our discussion of the Amish. They are an agrarian society, with limited individual goals and limited personal choice. "Control" lies with their society and their God. With more modest individual goals comes a much greater chance of achieving them. And if they do fail, they may have an explanatory structure that does not place all of the blame on the individual. Failure is seen in terms of unstable and specific causes (an afterlife and God's plan).

Let us further contrast our modern society with the Kaluli (Schieffelin, 1990). They are a depression-free New Guinea culture, in which failure and loss always demand and usually get retribution or restitution. The individual is not often helpless, but when he is, he is *not* equipped with an explanatory structure that makes his present helplessness stable and global, transforming it into hopelessness.

CONTROVERSIES

Within the arena of helplessness and depression, we think there are three main controversies. First, what is the mechanism by which explanatory style puts people at risk for depression? Second, who is in better touch with reality, depressed or nondepressed people? Third, is normal depression continuous or discontinuous with unipolar depressive disorder?

Mechanism of Explanatory Style

The evidence suggests that a depressive explanatory style puts people at risk for later depression. Is this because explanatory style causes later depression, or does it merely correlate with some other process that is the causal factor? If it is causal, does it play a minor or major role? This is not just an academic question. If some other process, like depressive memories, triggers depression and is merely associated with depressive causal thinking, therapy should focus on that process rather than on explanatory style.

In our theory, explanatory style is far upstream in the chain that causes depressive symptoms. We claim that the person's expectation that bad events are uncontrollable is the immediate cause of his depression. The expectation, in turn, is influenced by the reality of the bad events and the explanation he makes. Explanatory style merely influences his particular explanation. But usually, only single links of this theory have been tested (e.g., the link between style and depression), and only studies like Metalsky et al.'s (1987) have tested two or more steps at the same time. Even in this study, explanatory style accounted for only a small part of the variance in depression, as is the case in other longitudinal studies of depression. Other variables seem to be at work here. What other psychological processes are likely to put one at risk for depression? How do they interact with the person's explanatory style?

One contributing factor may be *expectational style*. In the same way that a person may have a characteristic way of explaining bad events, he may also have a characteristic way of expecting bad events to occur. Usually, these two processes are closely related; if you believe you failed an exam because you are stupid, your expectations about future academic failures will be stable and global. But causes and consequences do not always have the same characteristics.

For example, if you are crippled by a drunk driver in a freak accident, the cause is unstable and specific. The consequences, a lifetime in a wheelchair, however, are stable and global. This event is apt to be depressing, no matter how circumscribed its cause. With this in mind, Nolen-Hoeksema, Skinner, and Seligman (1984) devised an Expectational Style Questionnaire (ESQ), which asked people to generate the consequences of the events in the ASQ and to rate them along the stable and global dimensions (internality of consequences does not make much sense). We found a .50 correlation between explanatory style and expectational style, and roughly the same correlation of each with depression. At this point, we do not know what unique contribution each of these variables makes to depression, but it is possible that expectational style triggers depression and explanatory style merely correlates with it.

Hull and Mendolia (1991) have started to explore these possibilities using techniques of causal modeling. In two studies with college students, they found that explanatory style predicted depressive symptoms through an effect on expectations. This is consistent with the reformulation. However, these researchers also found that explanatory style had a direct influence on depressive symptoms, one that did not depend on the hypothesized intermediary of expectations.

Abramson, Metalsky, and Alloy (1989) have also taken a close look at the possibility that expectations of future bad events are critical in producing depression. In what they describe as a revision of the attributional model of helplessness (a re-reformulation, as it were), they propose that hopelessness is the proximal cause of depression. *Hopelessness* entails an expectation of helplessness (response-outcome independence) coupled with the belief that bad events will occur frequently in the future. By their hopelessness account, a belief in helplessness per se need not lead to depression so long as the individual does not expect bad events to occur. For example, an individual may believe that she cannot control the consequences of a nuclear war or a terrorist attack, but she does not find uncontrollability disconcerting so long as she does not expect these events to occur.

The hopelessness theory is persuasive, yet as we write, it is still untested. It may pose overly fine conceptual distinctions that will prove difficult—even impossible—to tease out in actual research. Along these same lines, the helplessness model, in both its original and reformulated versions, can be criticized for never testing all the hypothesized processes at once. This may be due to the difficulty inherent in doing so, given the current status of research techniques. The "re-reformulation" of Abramson et al. (1989) may suffer from a similar fate, even more so. For the time being at least, we are not yet ready to jettison the reformulation in its favor, though we will watch the research it generates with interest.

Another process that might trigger depression, from which explanatory style conceivably follows, is perception of negativity. Explanatory style begins its work only after a bad event is perceived and appraised as negative. But depression may entail a level of information processing much lower than explanations, expectations, and memory, so that events are judged or appraised more negatively. Similarly, depressed people may be accessing their negative memories more easily (Bower, 1981). Either of these processes— more negative appraisals or more negative memories—would tend to produce a more depressive explanatory style.

What is called for is an explicit spelling out and operationalization of these constructs and a longitudinal study of explanatory style, expectational style, hopelessness, appraisal of negativity, and access to negative memories as they uniquely influence an individual's risk for later depression.

Related to this problem is the role of life events. The reformulated helplessness theory purports to be a "diathesis-stress" model in which depressive explanatory style is the diathesis and uncontrollable bad life events the stress. But the evidence is much stronger for the diathesis than for the stress. So, for example, in the Nolen-Hoeksema et al. (1986) study of children and in the Firth and Brewin (1982) study of patients, explanatory style predicted depression, but life events did not. We suspect that this is a technical problem rather than a conceptual one: the usual measures of major events (death, divorce) may be less important than the daily hassles (Kanner, Coyne, Schaefer, & Lazarus, 1981). But there may be an interesting conceptual twist to the problem: the undertoad.

In *The World According to Garp*, Garp's son is told by his parents to watch out for the undertow (Irving, 1978). He mishears this as the name of a dangerous monster, the undertoad, which he eventually imagines to be lurking under the swimming pool drain. Similarly, depressive thinking is tied up with imagined or exaggerated events as well as real ones. Depressives see clouds around silver linings and imagine undertoads to be lurking everywhere. A rupture in the swimming pool liner can throw a depressive into the same tailspin as a rupture in his marriage. The precipitating life events in depression may often be undertoads, not easily measured, rather than objective hassles or major life events. And it is in the realm of the undertoad that psychodynamic thinking may legitimately contribute to theorizing about depression. Why does a rupture in the swimming pool liner so profoundly threaten some people's sense of well-being and not others'?

Dykema, Bergbower, and Peterson (1992) have recently documented the role of the undertoad in depression. In a longitudinal study, we found that pessimistic explanatory style led to subsequent depressive symptoms through its effect on the numbers of hassles a person experienced in ongoing life. Also included in this study were measures of major life events, and these did *not* influence depressive symptoms, alone or in an interaction with explanatory style. Said another way, those with a pessimistic explanatory style see the world as more troubling than do their more optimistic counterparts, and this perception may lead to depression.

Who Distorts Reality?

Maybe the depressive is right about reality, and it is nondepressed people who distort reality, but in a benign, self-serving direction. Many of you reading this chapter probably believe that there is no purpose in the universe beyond the one you create for yourself. Why, then, are you of such good cheer? Could it be that remaining nondepressed requires active illusions that defend against the knowledge that ultimately we all fail and that the universe is indifferent to us?

This is a second arena of controversy. On the one hand, clinicians such as Beck (1967) see depressives as distorting reality in a self-destructive way. On the other hand, experimenters led by Lauren Alloy and Lyn Abramson have gathered quite a bit of evidence implying that it is nondepressives who distort reality, although in a self-serving way. Beck's view is more intuitive. Depressed people often see undertoads—they imagine that the rupture in the pool liner means they are incompetent wives, that they are just a breath away from becoming homeless. This clinical view is also bolstered by a clinical wish: the desire, in treating depression, to be both the agent of truth and the harbinger of happiness.

There are five areas in which distortion has been assessed as a function of depression: judgments of control, expectancies for success, judgments of skill, memory, and explanatory style. We do not have the space to give an exhaustive review of these data, but we can lean heavily on Alloy and Abramson's (1988) review of this literature to take a quick look at the thrust of what is known in each of these areas.

Judgments of Control. In a now classic experiment, Alloy and Abramson (1979) had students with or without depressive symptoms press a button and then judge how much control they had over a light that was then turned on. These researchers varied the amount of actual control from nearly complete to none. All the subjects were accurate when there was some control. When there was no control, the depressed students remained accurate. The nondepressed students became highly inaccurate, reporting substantial control when there was none. Alloy and Abramson (1979) concluded that depressed subjects were sadder but wiser and that nondepressed subjects distorted reality in a self-serving direction.

The illusion of control seems to result from how nondepressed people organize the information they receive, not from the distorted reception of information. Nondepressed people accurately perceive that probabilities of the light going on given that they did or did not press the button, but they organize the information into an inflated judgment of control. They discount their failures to control in a way that depressives do not ("that didn't count—I wasn't ready"). Further, the phenomenon is specific to ego involvement. When depressives judge others' control, they succumb to the illusion and inflate how much control they see other people as having (Martin, Abramson, & Alloy, 1984).

This basic finding has been replicated a number of times (e.g., Tennen & Sharp, 1983; Vazquez, 1987, experiments 1 and 2). But it has not always been found. Vazquez (1987, experiment 4) reported that when negative statements ("my problems are in general unsolvable") rather than a light are the noncontingent outcome, depressed subjects believe they have control, whereas nondepressed subjects detect the noncontingency. Conversely, when the statements are positive, depressed subjects detect the noncontingency and nondepressed subjects show the usual illusion of control.

Overall, the weight of the evidence suggests that nondepressed subjects typically show the illusion of control, whereas depressed subjects estimate control accurately. But under some boundary conditions, at least, the depressed subjects distort what is really going on, and the nondepressed are accurate.

Expectancies for Success.   Golin, Terrell, and Johnson (1977) had depressed and nondepressed people roll dice and estimate the probability of success. A win was defined as a roll of 2, 3, 4, 9, 10, 11, or 12, resulting in an objective win probability of 44 percent. Depressives were accurate, and nondepressed individuals overestimated how well they would do.

Similarly, Alloy and Ahrens (1987) asked students to forecast their academic success. Again, depressed students were accurate, and nondepressed students inflated their chances of success. Numerous demonstrations exist of the optimism of nondepressed individuals, and this phenomenon is so widespread that it has even earned its own name—*positive illusions* (Taylor, 1989). What is interesting to us about nondepressive optimism is the fact that its counterpart is not necessarily depressive pessimism but rather depressive realism.

Judgments of Skill. Some years ago, *Newsweek* reported that 80 percent of American men think they are in the top half of social skills. They must have been nondepressed, if the results of Lewinsohn, Mischel, Chaplain, and Barton (1980) are valid. These investigators asked depressed and nondepressed patients to participate in a panel discussion and later had the patients judge how skilled their performance was. As judged by a panel of observers, depressed patients had fewer social skills than nondepressed patients. Most important, depressed patients judged their skill accurately, while nondepressed patients overestimated their skill (see also Roth & Rehm, 1980; Siegel & Alloy, 1990; Strack & Coyne, 1983).

Memories. There are several studies in which depressed and nondepressed subjects were asked to remember good and bad events that have happened to them (e.g., Teasdale & Russell, 1983). In general, depressed subjects recall more bad events and fewer good events than nondepressed subjects, who show the reverse pattern. But who is more accurate? That is, when the real number of good and bad events is known, who distorts the past, depressives or nondepressives?

There are conflicting data on this, but in general, depressives seem to recall fewer good events and to be accurate about bad events, whereas nondepressives do just the opposite (see Buchwald, 1977; DeMonbreun & Craighead, 1977; Dennard & Hokanson, 1986; Nelson & Craighead, 1977; Wener & Rehm, 1975).

Explanatory Style. "Failure is an orphan, and success has a thousand fathers." We find this to be true of nondepressives; for depressives, however, both success and failure have a single father.

One pattern has consistently emerged in all of our studies of explanatory style: lopsidedness among nondepressives and evenhandedness among depressives. To explain this, we focus on good versus bad events: a depressive's explanatory style is roughly the same for good and bad events; that is, to the extent that a depressive is a bit above average on internality, stability, and globality for bad events, he is also a bit above average on internality, stability, and globality for good events. Nondepressives are lopsided: bad events tend to be external, unstable, and specific, but good events are internal, stable, and global. And the more nondepressed, the more lopsided. The difference score between composite positive and composite negative on the ASQ indexes lopsidedness. The higher the difference, the more lopsided.

Alloy (1982b) reviewed the data from eleven samples of depressed and nondepressed children, students, and patients. She found that in almost every case, nondepressed people showed a greater lopsidedness than depressed people, who tended to hover around zero, indicating no bias at all.

This means that a nondepressed person tends to see a success as caused by him, as abiding, and as enhancing all that he does; whereas a failure is seen as someone else's fault, as going away quickly, and as local. A depressed person, in contrast, sees his successes and failures as caused in the same way. Put another way, nondepressed people see themselves as specially favored in the universe, whereas depressed people see the universe as indifferent to them.

The research on lopsidedness suggests as well that we should be quite careful in saying that depressives favor internal, stable, and global causes for bad events and external, unstable, and specific causes for good events. This is true when it is understood that these conclusions hold *relative to* nondepressives, and indeed, this is the way our research program has always been carried out. They are not true in the absolute sense.

Overall, in five areas—judgment of control, expectancies for success, judgment of skill, memory, and explanatory style—self-erving nondepressive distortion and depressive accuracy emerge, although the data in memory are less clear-cut than in the other areas. We believe that future research should be directed to two central questions about this controversy.

First, are there depressive distortions when very severe depression is involved? The great majority of these studies have contrasted mild or moderate depression with its absence, and the clinical anecdotes about depressive distortion are about very severe depressives. We look forward to a grand study of the five kinds of distortions along the whole range of affect from mania to severe depression.

Second, is depressive realism a risk factor or a mere correlate of depression? All of the studies are cross-sectional, so we cannot tell if the realists tend to become depressed and those with benign il-

lusions tend to remain invulnerable. A longitudinal study of individuals who are not depressed at the outset but who have all five
kinds of depressive realism will answer this causal question.

The results of such an investigation are critical in evaluating how
well learned helplessness captures the phenomenon of depression.
We have argued that the parallels between learned helplessness and
depression are close and numerous, but the phenomenon of depressive realism—if it remains viable—is an important disanalogy.
Remember that helplessness (and we assume depression) is thought
to be tied up with the perception of response-outcome independence. This presumably is a veridical perception. But the research
we just reviewed suggests that people come very reluctantly to this
perception if they are not depressed in the first place. Does this
mean that the learned helplessness model of depression applies only
to those who are already depressed?

Continuity-Discontinuity

Theorists and researchers frequently assert that mild depression and
severe depression are different entities, that we cannot generalize
from the one phenomenon to the other. This discontinuity view
stems directly from the medical model of depression. According to
this view, depression severe enough to require therapy or hospitalization is a disorder. It is an illness, the process of which differs in
kind and not just degree from the normal depression with which
most of us are familiar. But the more we examine this claim, the
more wrong it seems. We believe that depression is continuous,
that the mild versus severe distinction is merely quantitative, and
that this debate has no grounding in good theory or research. The
debate is a guild issue, not an intellectual one.

Let's start by considering different ways of phrasing the discontinuity position. None is compelling upon close examination. So, by
one possible meaning, individuals experiencing mild depression are
distinct from those experiencing severe depression, like collies are
distinct from dachshunds, pennies from nickels, and dwarfs from
short people. The claim of discontinuity implies that there is a sharp
break at the severe tail of the distribution of one or more depressive
manifestations. For example, dwarfism is different in kind from
shortness because at the extreme tail of the height distribution is a
bump, and that bump contains people with features that differ from
other very short people, such as limbs out of proportion to their
trunk. Midgets, on the other hand, seem to differ only in degree

from short people, because (absent the dwarfs) there is no bump at the short tail of the height distribution, and those in the tail have no features different in kind from their neighbors who are up the distribution. Is unipolar depressive "disorder" like dwarfs or like midgets?

Depression is diagnosed by the number and severity of various symptoms. Discontinuity seems to require that symptoms like insomnia, self-blame, weight loss, and so on be distributed bimodally among the population of depressives (and among the population as a whole). There is no evidence that this is the case. In fact, in most of our studies of depression, we routinely correlate some variable (like explanatory style) with severity of depression. We find, of course, that people at the severe end differ from people with no depression, and this group difference is compatible with both the continuity and the discontinuity position. But more important, we always find a linear relationship between the variable and severity of depression; the more depressed, the more of it the person has. In all studies we know of in which the investigators bothered to look at individuals with no, mild, moderate, and severe depressive symptoms, evidence for continuity has emerged. Those studies that claim to support discontinuity simply fail to use individuals from across the entire range of depressive symptoms.

Consider the medical search for strong diagnostic tests of depression. There are medical procedures that attempt to identify depression by exposing individuals suspected of being depressed to some sort of biological challenge. The hope is that their physiological response to the challenge will unambiguously separate them into two groups: depressed and nondepressed. So, after much initial hoopla, the dexamethasone suppression test was branded a failure as a strong diagnostic procedure for depression once the comparison groups began to include people with moderate versions of depression (Nierenberg & Feinstein, 1988). Researchers are currently touting one's response to thyroid-releasing hormone (Loosen, 1988); we suspect it will have the same fate.

The discontinuity view also requires those susceptible to mild depression be unlikely to experience severe depression and vice versa. We know of no evidence that this is the case. It seems just the opposite. Mild depression is the breeding ground for severe depression, and a history of severe depression is a risk factor for mild depression.

A second possible meaning of the discontinuity view is that mild depression is characterized by one symptom or class of symptoms, whereas severe depression is characterized by a second symptom or class of symptoms. Thus, some suggest that mild depression is a cognitive disorder, marked by pessimism and demoralization, whereas severe depression is a somatic disorder, marked by physical and appetitive disturbances. Another way to say this is that mild depression does *not* involve somatic symptoms and severe depression does *not* involve cognitive symptoms, or—more plausibly—that cognitive symptoms outweigh somatic symptoms in cases of mild depression and the opposite is true in cases of severe depression. Again, there is no evidence for this.

A third possible discontinuity view is that mild depression and severe depression have different causes, even though their symptoms fall along the same continuum. Mild depression is a reaction to life's setbacks, and severe depression results from biochemical anomalies that are perhaps genetically transmitted. However, again we find no evidence that this is the case. Indeed, available findings suggest that mild and unipolar depressive disorder have the same risk factors: early loss, experience with uncontrollable events, pessimistic expectations, depression in the family, and so on. Furthermore, genetic risk also does not discriminate between a continuity and discontinuity position. There are indeed studies that show genetic risk for unipolar depression. For example, identical twins have significantly higher concordance for depression than do fraternal twins (Allen, 1976). Evidence for heritability is *not* evidence for discontinuity, however, unless a single gene causes depression, and this is clearly not the case. A continuity view of these data assumes, for example, that the more genetic material of a given kind present, the greater the severity of depression. A discontinuity view assumes that if the genetic material is present at all, depression must occur; if absent, depression does not ensue.

A fourth possible discontinuity view holds that mild depression admits to psychological cure, whereas severe depression requires drugs. In other words, the mild versus severe distinction makes sense in terms of therapy, even if not in terms of symptoms or causes. Consider a person who falls down the stairs and cracks a bone in her leg. The fracture can vary along a continuum from slight to severe, as can the fall from one step to many steps. But in cases of "mild" breaks, the person merely rests, whereas in cases of "severe" breaks, a cast is needed to bring about recovery. Once again, though, there is no evidence that treatments for depression are differentially effective for mild versus severe forms of the problem.

As we examine the different renditions of the discontinuity position, we find no support for any of them. The assumption of continuity wins by default. The question remains, though, as to why some theorists and researchers continue to believe so strongly in the distinction.

We speculate that three related reasons are involved. First, psychopathologists show a bias toward studying phenomena with diagnostic labels (Persons, 1986). Mild depression does not warrant a DSM-III-R or Research Diagnostic Criteria (RDC) or Schedule for Affective Disorders and Schizophrenia (SADS) diagnosis, and so they assume that it must be quite different from severe depression, which of course does earn itself a diagnosis.

Second, psychopathologists who work from a psychodynamic or biological perspective tend to reify problems in living (Szasz, 1961). Because severe depression is more stable and general in its manifestation, it is easier to believe that something must be lurking behind it that is not present in the more transient and circumscribed mild depression.

Third, psychopathologists tend to study problems that bring about psychiatric treatment. Certainly being a patient versus not being a patient, or being hospitalized versus not, is related to severity of depression. And patienthood or hospitalization sets into motion all sorts of social and psychological processes that further distinguish groups of people. But these are secondary to depression. Becoming a patient indicates not only being more severe on a symptom continuum but also being willing to pay money for therapy or to bear the ensuing stigma. Becoming a patient may reflect the details of one's health insurance plan. None of these is a distinction in kind. Perhaps the mild versus severe distinction makes most sense when cast in economic or sociological terms! Regardless, we should not let any of these biases—toward labels, toward reification, toward hospitalization—make the quantitative distinction among depressives into anything more than it really is.

Ultimately, as touched upon earlier, we think that the force behind the belief in discontinuity comes from guild issues. The belief that unipolar depressive disorder is discontinuous from ordinary depression has serious real-world implications. It suggests that depression should be treated by medical rather than nonmedical personnel. It suggests that the mode of treatment should be biological rather than psychological. It suggests that researchers interested in understanding and alleviating depression should choose patients for study rather than students, or factory workers, or housewives. It suggests that the proper setting for research should be the hospital or clinic, not the classroom or shopping center. If there is no evidence for the discontinuity position, these suggestions make little sense.

We do not recommend that theorists and researchers stop paying attention to the severity continuum. Indeed, we recommend that they *start* doing so. Researchers within the helplessness tradition are among the few who investigate the same sorts of questions with samples differing in severity of depression. Only by studying individuals whose depressive symptoms vary in frequency, diversity, intensity, duration, and intractability can we get a full understanding of the process and alleviation of depression.

WHAT WE KNOW

Here is what we believe is known:

1. The naturally occurring symptoms of unipolar depression are reasonably well matched with the symptoms of learned helplessness in animals and humans.
2. Depressed people make internal, stable, and global explanations of bad events and tend to make external, unstable, and specific explanations of good events.
3. This depressive explanatory style is probably a risk factor for later depression.
4. Cognitive therapy provides significant relief from unipolar depression, and it improves explanatory style at the same time.

Taken together, these stamp the learned helplessness model as a useful account of depression. While the processes that are involved in depression are doubtlessly more numerous than those specified by any given model, certainly the learned helplessness approach taps some of the critical factors (cf. Akiskal & McKinney, 1973, 1975). Noteworthy is that the learned helplessness approach to depression has always been theoretically driven, unlike many other explanations of depression, which have developed from unsystematic observation and clinical trial and error.

WHAT WE DON'T KNOW

We already have discussed several controversial areas—mechanism, distortion, and continuity—that are topics of ongoing conflict of theory and data. We have outlined the research that should settle these controversies. But there are still two areas that have yet to be the subject of conflicting data and intense theoretical debate: the basis of sex differences in depression and the prevention of depression.

Susan Nolen-Hoeksema (1987, 1990) has comprehensively reviewed the mass of studies on sex and depression. These studies convincingly point to roughly a twofold risk for females. But we still don't know the cause of this sex difference.

Let us consider just the methodologically strong studies—those that use standardized assessment procedures, large sample sizes, and diagnostic systems that separate out unipolar and bipolar depression. These studies divide into treated cases (people who are undergoing therapy) and community samples, in which the researchers go door-to-door. In seven of the eight studies of treated cases in the United States, females were significantly more likely to be depressed than males, with a mean ratio of 2:1. In the ten studies of treated cases outside the United States, nine showed more females than males with depression, with a mean ratio of 2.3:1.

Treated cases may not reveal underlying sex differences in depression, because women might be more likely to seek out treatment than men. To get around this problem, a large number of community studies have been conducted, and we earlier referred to the most comprehensive one (the ECA study). Most major community studies show a preponderance of females over males, with a mean ratio a bit under 2:1. Nolen-Hoeksema's review makes it clear that this is not an artifact but a genuine difference in the experience of depression.

Overall, the preponderance of depression among women is clearly established. Why this is so is much less clear. There are several hypotheses, not incompatible, that follow from our own theorizing (Nolen-Hoeksema, 1987). One is that the inferior status of women and their early socialization lead them to be dependent and passive and to expect that they will be helpless to control important events in their lives (Radloff, 1975). Another is that women have learned a more depressive explanatory style than have men (Dweck & Gilliard, 1975). A final possibility is that women are more state oriented than men and so are inclined to worry about and explain bad life events (foremost among them, depression itself), whereas men are inclined to more action and less thought. State orientation about depression (particularly if there is depressive explanatory style) will amplify depression, whereas action orientation may dampen depressive mood and bring about the resolution of one's problems.

The data are simply not in on which, if any, of these hypotheses is true. What we first need is a cross-sectional study of male-female differences in perceived uncontrollability, explanatory style, and state orientation. Ultimately, a longitudinal study of the development of these three cognitions in relation to depression should be important. We suspect that the transition to puberty is critical here. Rutter (1986) reported that before puberty there is more depressive disorder among boys, but after puberty a dramatic shift occurs and girls have more depressive disorder. Could it be that perceived helplessness, explanatory style, and state orientation somehow flip-flop between the sexes at puberty?

Once depression has set in, cognitive therapy and a variety of other antihelplessness techniques can relieve it. But people who seek therapy are only a fraction of the people who suffer severe depression. In the United States, about one in ten young people will have a major depressive episode at some point in his or her life. Another one in ten will have a minor depressive episode. A quarter of a million will commit suicide in the next decade. Fifteen percent will become alcohol or drug dependent in their lifetime, with some large fraction of these resulting from depression (Robins et al., 1984). Can some, or even much of this, be prevented?

Depressive explanatory style and an impoverished repertoire for coping with helplessness put one at risk for depression. Cognitive therapy and a variety of behavioral therapies (e.g., assertiveness training, social skills training) improve explanatory style and increase one's coping repertoire. We believe that the techniques of cognitive and behavioral therapy that relieve depression can be taught preventatively. Moreover, these techniques can be taught to groups in the classroom setting. And the crucial time to do this is at the onset of puberty, when the risk for depressive disorder increases manyfold.

We propose the following study. One large group of sixth graders would receive weekly classroom experience in "Personal Control Training": recognizing automatic thoughts, marshaling evidence against them, training in reattribution, searching for alternative explanations, challenging depressogenic assumptions, and so on. Another group would receive a similar amount of sex education or some other useful but nonspecific (vis-à-vis personal control) technique. A third group would receive nothing. These individuals would then be followed through the teenage years, with depressive symptoms, rate of depressive disorder, suicide attempts, substance abuse, and school performance tracked. We predict a lowered rate of depressive problems in the group given preventative personal control training. The most dramatic public health event of our lifetime was certainly the Salk vaccine. Polio was all but eliminated as a health threat by the universal immunization of young people. We speculate that the epidemic of depression afoot today could be markedly reduced by immunization, systematically carried out in the schools, against depression.

7

Learned Helplessness
and Social Problems

There are two stories about learned helplessness in people. The first one has to do with the attempts in the experimental laboratory to produce a phenomenon akin to that observed in dogs following uncontrollable shocks. The second one has to do with the extrapolations of the helplessness phenomenon to explain all manner of failures of human adaptation. There are some striking differences between these stories. As we described in Chapter 4, basic helplessness research has been controversial. In contrast, the applications for the most part have been enthusiastically accepted. But here's an even more interesting wrinkle: the most thoroughly worked through application of learned helplessness has been to depression, and this is precisely the most controversial. In Chapter 6, we touched on some of the reasons for this controversy.

In the present chapter we survey the applications of learned helplessness to social problems other than depression. These applications are numerous and diverse, ranging from the evening news to the tribulations of Saint Paul. We approach these applications with caution, to balance the uncritical use of helplessness concepts by some theorists. We discuss how best to evaluate the application of learned helplessness to particular instances of maladaptive behavior and then survey the most popular areas of application and evaluate them empirically by the criteria we propose.

We end up criticizing some applications of learned helplessness as overly metaphorical. On very flimsy evidence, theorists may argue that learned helplessness is at work. At the same time, we are sympathetic to people's need to explain passivity. Perhaps more so than the excesses of activity (like lust, gluttony, greed, and most other deadly sins), which are readily attributed to passions, the excesses of inactivity are puzzling.

According to popular expression, among the most vexing things we can do are those that involve passivity:

- Sitting there and taking it
- Not lifting a finger in our own defense
- Not thinking before acting
- Giving up
- Not making an effort
- Not sticking at it
- Not caring what happens to us

Psychologists of all stripes have thus tried to explain passivity (Curtis, 1989). Psychoanalysts weave a web of complex ideas like dependency or masochism or the death instinct, proposing that people act passively because they are driven to do so and somehow derive satisfaction from the bad outcomes that follow. In similar fashion, strict behaviorists propose that passivity follows explicit reward for inactivity and/or punishment for activity (Chapter 2).

We're not smart enough to see how the psychoanalytic claims could be tested. The behaviorist account can be tested, but sometimes it is found wanting. Passivity may occur in situations in which the prevailing rewards and punishments should encourage activity. How then do we explain passivity? Here is where learned helplessness as an explanation becomes attractive. Like instrumental explanations, learned helplessness starts with environmental events. But unlike them, it explains why passivity can take on a life of its own. So we recognize the power of applying the helplessness model to social problems. At the same time, we also recognize that the various applications show a range of fit. We are critical because the danger in treating all applications of learned helplessness as equally compelling is to risk the credibility of the model for which it works best.

CRITERIA FOR LEARNED HELPLESSNESS

As the term "learned helplessness" has come to be used, there are three criteria by which the phenomenon is recognized (Chapter 1). First, learned helplessness is present when a group or person or animal displays *inappropriate passivity*: failing through lack of mental or behavioral action to meet the demands of a situation in which effective coping is possible. Second, learned helplessness follows in the wake of *uncontrollable events.* Bad events per se do not cause learned helplessness. Trauma may, of course, produce unfortunate reactions, including passivity, but trauma-induced helplessness is not of the "learned" variety. Third, learned helplessness is mediated by particular *cognitions* acquired during exposure to uncontrollable events and inappropriately generalized to new situations. The exact nature of these cognitions is unclear.

These criteria can be used to judge the degree to which a particular social problem represents learned helplessness. What would the ideal instance of such a social problem as learned helplessness look like? First, the person (or group) would act in an inappropriately passive way. This qualification is critical. Someone may be passive in all sorts of situations for all sorts of reasons, but "learned helplessness" is reserved for passivity in situations in which activity indeed brings about the desired results. We imagine that a great deal of passivity in this world is instrumental, following reward for passivity and/or punishment for activity. What results is a lack of motion, but this inactivity is appropriate given the prevailing contingencies.

Second, the person would have experienced a history of uncontrollable events. As noted, the learned helplessness model accords importance to the uncontrollability of events, not to their other traumatizing properties. In the experimental laboratory, uncontrollability versus controllability can be teased apart from the physical properties of shock with a yoking procedure. In the real world, this is not so simple to accomplish. Nevertheless, it is important that the researcher attempt to show that uncontrollability matters.

The attributional reformulation makes this task easier by emphasizing that objective uncontrollability is not debilitating in the absence of perceived uncontrollability. Only if the person believes events to be uncontrollable does helplessness follow in their wake. What this means in the context of the present discussion is that researchers should ascertain whether "helpless" individuals perceive the events of their life as uncontrollable. The more they perceive them to be beyond their control, the more helplessly they should behave.

If all subjects experience the same general event, individual differences in beliefs should predict variation in subsequent impairment. This is the strategy followed in a study of depressive reactions to the breakup of a romance (Peterson, Rosenbaum, & Conn,

1985). All subjects experienced the same event (breakup), but they differed in terms of the control they perceived. These perceptions predicted the degree of upset they experienced: the less control, the greater the depressive symptoms.

Third, if someone's self-defeating actions are to be well described as learned helplessness, then her passivity would be mediated by her beliefs about helplessness. Learned helplessness is importantly a cognitive phenomenon, although the exact form that the cognitive representations take is unclear.

One reason that the attributional reformulation has caught on is that people can readily tell researchers about their causal beliefs (cf. Nisbett & Wilson, 1977). As noted earlier, we have focused on causal attributions to the relative exclusion of expectations. In retrospect, we regret this decision because expectations—by our theory— indeed are relevant. It stemmed in part from our sense that stated expectations are overly influenced by the disorder they are being used to predict (Dohrenwend, Dohrenwend, Dodson, & Shrout, 1984). Explanatory style, in contrast, appears more stable, over months and even years (Peterson & Seligman, 1987). Manipulations of mood do not affect a person's explanatory style (Mukherji, Abramson, & Martin, 1982), and neither do attempts at positive self-presentation (Schulman, Seligman, & Amsterdam, 1987).

The best way to demonstrate the applicability of learned helplessness is longitudinally, because helplessness theory—in both its original and reformulated versions—is a theory of process. It is only when events unfold over time as predicted by the theory that we can be most confident that learned helplessness is present. Unfortunately, longitudinal investigations are rare. Much more common are cross-sectional studies that look to see if measures of the different constructs covary at the same point in time. Contemporaneous correlations, such as that between causal explanations and passivity, are consistent with helplessness predictions, but they are obviously weak support because other possibilities exist (Peterson & Seligman, 1984).

An excellent example of learned helplessness is one in which all three criteria of helplessness are present. A poor example is one in which only a single criterion (or none at all) has been shown. We believe this view is useful in evaluating applications of learned helplessness because it allows us to classify particular behaviors as midway between excellent and poor examples. We end up concluding that many applications of learned helplessness are middling ones, neither excellent nor poor, demonstrating some of the criteria for learned helplessness but not all. So these applications should not be fully accepted, and they should not be fully dismissed. The ubiquitous recommendation that "more research is needed" of course follows, but at least the explicit criteria for recognizing learned helplessness provide a direction for this future research to take.

SURVEY OF APPLICATIONS

We discuss here a range of behaviors that on the surface look self-defeating and that theorists have hypothesized to be examples of learned helplessness. We evaluate each application empirically in terms of the criteria for learned helplessness. We cover these topics in order from very bad examples to excellent ones. A summary table follows in which we note our judgment of each application with respect to each criterion.

In talking about applications to social problems, we necessarily stray into political matters. Let us comment on the political implications of the learned helplessness model. It proves difficult to pigeonhole as conservative or liberal. Elements of both seem to be present. On the one hand, learned helplessness provides a liberal view of human nature in that helplessness is ultimately attributed to the environment. Change the environment, and preclude helplessness altogether. Further, the passivity of helpless people is not viewed as motivated but as a "rational" response granted certain beliefs about how the world works. Again, an environmental intervention can thwart helplessness.

On the other hand, learned helplessness has a conservative flavor to it as well. In calling someone helpless, for instance, we say, "Yes, things used to elude this person's control, which is why she is helpless, but outcomes can now be influenced, if only she attempted to do so." This analysis is reasonable only if outcomes at the present time really can be controlled. Cognitive interventions are sensible only if one's problems reside in how the world is seen. If the world remains kaleidoscopic, saying that a person who lives there is showing learned helplessness is to make a grievous error.

Very Bad Examples

The very worst examples of learned helplessness rarely make it into the research literature. However, we refer you to two (humorous) articles in the *Worm Runner's Digest*, one applying learned helplessness to dead pigeons (Gamzu, 1974) and the other applying it to pet rocks (Brewster & Wilson, 1976). These end up being instructive, because they show how a theorist can go wrong by assuming that any instance of inactivity necessarily implicates learned helplessness (Maier, 1974).

Without any malice, let us also use as a very bad example a book chapter we once read (the reference is elusive) that attributed the woes of the Philippines to the frequent monsoons that buffet the islands. According to this argument, the monsoons induced learned helplessness in the residents. We are hardly experts on the Philippines, but we know enough to brand this a weak argument, because *none* of the criteria for learned helplessness is documented.

Although we know that the Philippines over the years have suffered a fair share of turmoil, is passivity the best way to describe these problems? (The Aquino revolution, with its grass-roots support, hardly strikes us as evidence of passivity.) And even if passivity is a good description, is it inappropriate passivity? Did the Philippine citizens act passively even though they lived in a responsive world, or was their passivity strategic, a means of avoiding trouble in a dangerous political climate?

Similarly, is it the uncontrollability of the monsoons that creates passivity (if passivity indeed exists), or is it the physical damage that these create? Although it is impossible to perform an experiment in which controllable and uncontrollable monsoons are yoked, it is possible to study different parts of the islands where monsoons are equally uncontrollable but not equally destructive. If learned helplessness is operative, then passivity should occur regardless of damage. Better still, people could be interviewed concerning their perceptions of the uncontrollability of the monsoons. Those who perceive less control should act more passively. Regardless, no data bearing on these possibilities were cited, and we conclude that this is a very bad example.

Poor Examples

Here we include applications of learned helplessness ideas that not only fail to demonstrate all of the relevant criteria but further seem to contradict what is meant by learned helplessness. In other words, enough research has already been conducted to allow the conclusion that these are probably *not* examples of learned helplessness. That these are sometimes identified as examples points to a misunderstanding of the helplessness model.

Alcoholism. Granted the toll that alcohol abuse takes on one's well-being, it is remarkable that people continue to drink as much as they do. To date, alcoholism has eluded conceptualization and treatment (Vaillant, 1983). We're not surprised that the learned helplessness model has been invoked as a possible explanation for alcohol abuse (e.g., Griffith, 1986). We're also not surprised that it falls quite short of a satisfactory account.

Let's start with why learned helplessness has beckoned theorists. Themes of loss of control run through descriptions of alcohol abuse. One common definition of alcoholism points to binge drinking as a critical feature: the inability to control one's alcohol consumption once drinking begins. Alcoholics themselves describe their plight as helpless, and depression frequently accompanies alcoholism (O'Leary, Donovan, Cysewski, & Chaney, 1977). Not surprisingly, so too does a pessimistic explanatory style (Dowd, Lawson, & Petosa, 1986).

The very first statement in the Twelve Steps of Alcoholics Anonymous calls on alcoholics to admit that they are "powerless over alcohol," that their lives "have become unmanageable." On the face of it, this statement seems to proclaim helplessness, but another perspective on this assertion sees it as a way of boosting self-esteem and maintaining abstinence (Beckman, 1980).

And what about the passivity of the alcohol abuser? Surely the person tossing down beers is not inactive in the sense that a dog crouching in a shuttlebox is inactive. If we are to characterize alcoholism as passivity, we must regard inactivity as referring to someone's failure to do anything other than take the path of least resistance (i.e., drinking). This interpretation has its counterpart in the animal literature, which finds that helplessness is not apparent on simple, well-learned tasks (Maier, Albin, & Testa, 1973). Perhaps alcoholism reflects learned helplessness not because the abuser is helpless in the face of alcohol but because he is helpless in the face of all other tasks in his life.

Does drinking occur in the face of uncontrollable events? Noel and Lisman (1980) report a relevant experiment. They recruited female undergraduates and gave them either solvable or unsolvable problems to work, followed by the opportunity to drink beer and ginger ale under the guise of a taste test. Subjects given unsolvable problems indeed were more likely to drink beer as opposed to ginger ale. Interestingly, they drank at the same rate as subjects given solvable problems, but they continued for a longer time, resulting in greater consumption.

However, in light of other data collected, Noel and Lisman (1980) did not interpret these findings as showing that learned helplessness is a mechanism in alcohol abuse. Rather, they argue that uncontrollability produces frustration and stress, which the alcohol in turn reduces. By this view, alcoholism is instrumental behavior, at least in a very narrow sense. A more recent study by Finn and Pihl (1987) is consistent with this analysis, finding that men with a family history of alcoholism showed greater cardiovascular reactivity to uncontrollable shock than men without this history, as well as a greater reduction in reactivity following alcohol consumption. Further, Volpicelli (1987) sketched a physiological interpretation of increased drinking in the aftermath of uncontrollability: alcohol maintains the high level of endorphins produced by one's exposure to uncontrollable events (Chapter 3).

In sum, alcohol abuse is at best a poor example of learned helplessness. Helpless cognitions are present, but none of the other criteria has been well documented. Indeed, the passivity of alcoholics seems to reflect instrumental considerations more than generalized expectations of response-outcome independence, and the addictive and damaging properties of alcohol must be taken into further account in explaining behavioral deficits on the part of alcoholics. Finally, conclusive proof that alcoholics experience more uncontrollable events than do nonalcoholics does not exist (Vaillant, 1983). Perhaps a more promising line of inquiry is Flannery's (1986) suggestion that it is the *children* of alcoholics who really are helpless, the victims of the uncontrollable, aversive environment that their parents create for them.

Bodily Control.   Several researchers have investigated the role of learned helplessness in biofeedback. First, let us provide you with some background on biofeedback. Research shows that certain bodily processes, of which we are not typically aware, accompany desirable psychological states. For instance, particular patterns of brain waves go along with states of relaxation. Perhaps if we can bring these bodily processes under our control, then we can bring the desirable psychological states under our control as well.

Biofeedback provides a set of techniques for accomplishing this goal. Appropriate meters and gadgets are connected to the body, where they record the targeted bodily process—like brain waves, pulse, temperature, and so on. The measured level of the process of concern is represented visually or audibly, literally "fed back" to the subject to provide him with an index of his progress toward the goal of bodily control. Biofeedback thus extends the psychology of learning, from behaviors to physiological processes. Presumably, a person can control his body through trial-and-error learning, so long as the relevant information (feedback) is provided. Biofeedback is very much in a preliminary stage, and early hopes and claims about it have been revised. For instance, at one time researchers envisioned people being able to learn to produce curative reactions in response to illness and injury.

At present, our hopes are more modest. Nevertheless, biofeedback continues to attract the attention of researchers, including those who propose that learned helplessness can interfere with the acquisition of skill in self-regulation (Carlson, 1982). The problem is that studies fail to bear out this analysis. In separate investigations, Carlson and Feld (1981) and Traub and May (1983) found that experience with uncontrollable events *facilitated* later performance at a biofeedback relaxation task.

As we saw in Chapter 4, reactance effects are occasionally produced in learned helplessness experiments, although it is difficult to predict just when they will occur. Perhaps subjects in these biofeedback experiments showed enhanced performance because the task was sufficiently important to them and they hadn't been given sufficient experience with uncontrollability. A more intriguing possibility, one advanced by Traub and May (1983), is that passivity was indeed induced by the uncontrollable events and that it facilitates biofeedback performance. Note that in the above description of biofeedback there was no specification of just how one controls one's bodily responses. This apparently eludes words. Rather, subjects are exhorted to "let go" and not try. Learned helplessness guarantees the appropriate detachment.

If this possibility is borne out by further research, it will provide a striking counterexample to the truism that learned helplessness produces bad outcomes. Perhaps it sheds some light on the ongoing controversy about what helpless people are thinking (Chapter 4). The answer may be nothing, and this may end up being beneficial under some circumstances. At any rate, this argument entails several levels of speculation unencumbered by any evidence. We certainly can conclude that the role of learned helplessness in *failures* of bodily control has not been shown.

Child Abusers. Several theorists have argued that one of the factors involved in why parents abuse their child is learned helplessness (on the part of the parents), engendered by their inability to control the child's crying. Just on the face of it, this seems implausible.

Although uncontrollable crying is an antecedent of abuse (Parkin, 1975), abuse itself is hardly maladaptive passivity: maladaptive—yes; passivity—no. Indeed, in a narrow sense, child abuse is instrumental, because a child sufficiently brutalized will stop crying.

Helpless animals are less likely to make aggressive responses, just as they are less likely to make any responses (Seligman, 1975). But if uncontrollable crying produces helplessness, as shown in laboratory studies (e.g., Donovan, 1981; Donovan & Leavitt, 1985; Donovan, Leavitt, & Walsh, 1990; Kevill & Kirkland, 1979), then this should be expressed in neglect of the child, not in active abuse.

Learned helplessness applications have been popular in a number of areas because they are optimistic. To say that someone has learned to be helpless is to avoid blaming the person for the misfortunes he or she experiences. It is also to provide a ready target for intervention. When we argue against interpreting some phenomenon as learned helplessness, as we do in the present case of child abuse, we hope it is clear that we are not suggesting that we invoke instead masochism or similar convolutions as an explanation. We are merely saying that learned helplessness does not work well in this case. Indeed, we suspect that the most plausible alternative in cases in which learned helplessness fares poorly as an explanation of self-defeating actions is even more mundane: locally prevailing rewards and punishments. These also provide a ready target for intervention.

Middling Examples

Next we survey examples that conclusively demonstrate one criterion of learned helplessness—usually the presence of "helpless" cognitions—but not the others. It might be that further research will show these instances to be well explained by the helplessness model, but perhaps not. At present, we conclude in each case that the argument has only been partially made.

Child Abuse Victims. Although learned helplessness is not relevant to why parents abuse their children, it might still explain negative reactions on the part of the children who are abused. Abused children have been described as withdrawn, depressed, passive, and demoralized (e.g., German, Habenicht, & Futcher, 1990; Green, 1978; Martin & Beezley, 1977). Certainly, a history of abuse involves a history of uncontrollable bad events (Kelley, 1986). Is learned helplessness at work?

Slade, Steward, Morrison, and Abramowitz (1984) investigated whether learned helplessness explained the psychological functioning of abused children by taking a close look at key helplessness constructs in samples of abused and nonabused children. So, if the passivity observed on the part of abused children reflects learned helplessness, we would expect to find that these children show less persistence at tasks, make inadequate use of contingency information, and explain success and failure in pessimistic ways.

Children between the ages of eight and twelve were studied with standard laboratory tasks and questionnaires. For the most part, there were no differences between the abused and nonabused subjects. The one difference that did emerge was contrary to helplessness predictions: abused children were *less* likely to blame themselves for failure than nonabused children. This finding no doubt reflects the reality of child abuse: the victim is not responsible for the bad events that happen. But what this finding further implies is that these reactions to child abuse may be poorly explained by learned helplessness. It might make more sense to look at the passivity of abused children in other terms.

Childhood Autism. Among the defining features of childhood autism is the child's profound social estrangement. He makes few attempts to become involved with others. Although current thinking about autism suspects a biological cause for the disorder, there is no reason to think that psychological processes don't get involved as well to exacerbate the basic biological problem. Perhaps learned helplessness is at the root of the motivational deficits frequently seen among autistic children (Meline, 1985).

Koegel and Mentis (1985) argue for this interpretation, proposing that autistic children perform poorly at learning tasks not because they lack the ability to learn but because they lack the motivation. Because they have difficulties, their early attempts at some task may not gain reward. People working with an autistic child might become frustrated and reinforce them haphazardly, creating an unusual (noncontingent) reward system (Koegel & Egel, 1979). What results is a failure on the part of the child to initiate any responses. Koegel, O'Dell, and Dunlap (1988) supported this line of reasoning by showing that the speech of autistic children improves more when *attempts* are reinforced than sounds per se. In other words, a motivational intervention is more successful than a skill intervention.

Other research shows that the motivation of autistic children can indeed be enhanced by prompting, successful task completion, and more frequent reward (e.g., Dunlap, 1984). These studies show that autistic children can learn more than some believe, and so their problem is not solely a biological defect. Nevertheless, these studies do not argue strongly for the involvement of learned helplessness. Koegel and Mentis (1985) stress the debilitating effect of frequent failure, but they do not appreciate the need to disentangle uncontrollability from failure. Learned helplessness is not simply a reaction to the trauma of bad events. We must conclude that the case here has not been well made.

Domestic Violence.   Not all couples marry and live happily ever after. Physical violence occurs in 15 percent of all marriages, or more (e.g., Kalmuss & Straus, 1982). The question, of course, arises as to why women remain with husbands who beat them (Gelles, 1976). Contrary to what one might expect, the frequency or severity of beating is *not* related strongly to whether a wife leaves an abusive husband (Pageglow, 1981). Theorists have thus searched for other reasons. There is support for two factors that make sense: psychological commitment to the marriage and economic dependence (e.g., Strube & Barbour, 1983). But other theorists have suggested that learned helplessness may be involved as well (e.g., Peterson & Seligman, 1983).

How good is such an application? On the face of it, the decision to stay in an abusive relationship looks like maladaptive passivity. Victims of domestic violence reportedly feel unable to control the beatings they receive and further believe that societal agents like police and social workers are unhelpful (Gayford, 1975; Martin, 1976). According to some studies, these women have poor problem-solving skills (e.g., Launius & Lindquist, 1988). However, we must remember that the decision to stay may reflect purely instrumental considerations. If a woman cannot afford to leave a marriage, then she stays—not because she is helpless, but because that is her only alternative.

Follingstad (1980) reported a case study of a woman that ostensibly conforms to the helplessness model. She describes someone who is weak and ineffectual. However, Follingstad (1980, p. 295) betrays some confusion about learned helplessness by arguing that "battered women . . . find a passive style a sensible one and frequently their only perceived alternative." In other words, she attributes passivity to a mechanism other than learned helplessness. Further, "the consequence for ineffectual change attempts by battered women is typically increased abuse" (p. 295). Follingstad (1980) concludes that the passivity observed in victims of domestic violence is a result of the abuse rather than an antecedent. This is no doubt a reasonable conclusion, but we believe that her case study poorly exemplifies learned helplessness.

Walker (1977–1978, 1979, 1983; Walker & Browne, 1985) has made more extensive use of the learned helplessness model to explain the passivity of abused women. She argues that traditional socialization imparts to women a belief in their own helplessness. Further, she finds that a large proportion of abused wives were abused as children, which satisfies—among these subjects at least—the requirement that uncontrollable events precede helpless behavior.

But we think matters are again misunderstood by this theorist. "The message they received was that in order to be successful and popular with boys, it was necessary to give their power away" (Walker, 1977–1978, p. 529). Such socialization produces helplessness, to be sure, but this is not learned helplessness as we conceive it here. And Walker (1983, p. 47) continues to write about something different from helplessness when she concludes that "the battered woman's terror was appropriate and her fears that separation would make the violence worse were accurate."

In sum, we think the passivity observed among victims of domestic violence is a middling example of learned helplessness. Passivity is present, but it may well be instrumental. Cognitions of helplessness are present, as is a history of uncontrollability. But there may also be a history of explicit reinforcement for passivity. Taken together, these results do not constitute the best possible support for concluding that these women show learned helplessness.

Evening News. We saw in Chapter 4 that helplessness can be acquired vicariously: by watching the induction of learned helplessness in others. One might think that numerous applications of learned helplessness ideas would take off from this possibility, but we know of only one, and it predated the original demonstration of vicarious helplessness. In a fascinating article, Levine (1977) conducted a content analysis of television newscasts during the 1970s. Five-minute news segments on NBC and CBS were coded according to the degree of helplessness evident:

4 = central figure completely unable to affect outcomes
3 = central figure mostly unable to affect outcomes
2 = central figure somewhat able to control outcomes

1 = central figure able to affect outcomes but did not do so
0 = irrelevant; or central figure completely affects outcomes

For instance, catastrophes like airplane crashes and earthquakes were assigned a score of 4, whereas athletic victories due to skilled performances were scored 0.

Results showed that 14 percent of news segments were given the highest helplessness scores, followed by 19 percent in the second highest category. No consistent differences between the two networks were found, although Levine (1977) observed that the "same" story as covered on the two networks frequently received different scores, suggesting that the helplessness modeled on television news does not reside solely in the news event itself but in the way it is covered.

For our purposes, Levine's (1977) study is more of a demonstration than an investigation of learned helplessness. We can only conclude that uncontrollable bad events impinge on television viewers every night. Unknown is the effect of these events and whether the 1970s were a particularly helpless era or not. We wish that newscasts from the 1960s had been compared with those from the 1970s. And now that we are through the 1980s and into the 1990s, we wish that contemporary newscasts could be included in these comparisons as well. If Americans are indeed becoming more depressed (Chapter 6), does this map into differences in helpless newscasts? Was President Reagan involved in more efficacious stories than President Carter? What does a Nixon versus Kennedy comparison show?

Institutionalization.   Learned helplessness research originated in animal learning, but it finds an interesting parallel in the sociological literature. Similarities between helplessness (at an individual level) and alienation (at an institutional level) certainly exist. In both cases, events are seen as independent of the person's actions; estrangement is represented in cognitive terms; and passivity ensues. Not surprisingly, then, researchers have used the learned helplessness phenomenon to explain why some institutions more than others produce listlessness, apathy, and poor morale (Aasen, 1987; Sahoo & Tripathy, 1990).

Thoreson and Eagleston (1983) argue that our typical educational system leads to unnecessary stress among children and adolescents by posing for them tasks that they lack the resources to meet. They use the example of athletics. Schools emphasize not aerobic exercises that can benefit all students (like jogging, swimming, or bicycling) but competitive sports that can be mastered only by the physically elite (like football, basketball, and baseball). What results from this emphasis is helplessness, a lack of activity on the part of the typical student, which recurs later in life as a failure to master other demands, such as the need for exercise to maintain health and combat stress.

Along these lines, Winefield and Fay (1982) reported an interesting study of students in traditional high schools versus those from a school with an "open" format. (Note: Rosen, 1977, showed that open format schools enhance a student's sense of control over academic outcomes.) In a standard learned helplessness experiment, students were exposed to either solvable or unsolvable problems and then tested on a second (controllable) task. Following solvable problems, students from neither school had difficulty. But students from the traditional school were impaired following unsolvable problems, whereas students from the open school were not.

Martinko and Gardner (1982) argue that learned helplessness can explain maladaptivity in work organizations—for example, low productivity, low quality, absenteeism, turnover, passivity, withdrawal, and dissatisfaction. Perceptions of uncontrollability are likely when organizations are centralized bureaucracies with formal rules (e.g., Aiken & Hage, 1966; Blauner, 1964). And workers often regard salaries and benefits as unrelated to performance (e.g., Kerr, 1975; Lawler, 1966).

Yet another example of how learned helplessness may operate within an institution is presented by Malcomson (1980), who argues that hospitals may produce apathy and listlessness among nurses by ignoring their attempts to make policy recommendations. Although formal data are not presented, she recounts personal experiences of uncontrollable events, passivity, and helpless cognitions. However, Malcomson (1980) shows the by-now familiar misunderstanding of learned helplessness when she states that the helplessness per se is reinforced. She quotes a head nurse's recommendation: "You will learn that nothing you do or say makes any difference here *or you will be one of the ones who will only last six months*" (p. 252, emphasis added by us).

Still on the subject of hospitals, Taylor ((1979) proposes that they produce helplessness in patients by conceiving them not as active agents but as broken machines. Patients do not have their actions responded to in a contingent fashion. Raps, Peterson, Jonas, and Seligman (1982) supported this argument by showing that patients in a general medical hospital became more depressed and exhibited greater problem-solving deficits as their length of hospitalization increased, even as their physical conditions improved.

The problem with most of these analyses is threefold. First, they do not explicitly look at whether outcomes are uncontrollable. The case can be made, perhaps more persuasively, that institutions contingently punish active responding (Baltes, 1983; Goffman, 1961). Certainly, this produces helplessness but not of the learned variety. Second, in very few cases does a researcher show that the putative helplessness generalizes from one situation to another, which is the real test of a helplessness explanation (Peterson, Zaccaro, & Daly, 1986). Third, these studies do not make a distinction between collective helplessness and individual helplessness. In sum, we think the case of institutionalization as learned helplessness has not been well made (Lennerlof, 1988).

Loneliness and Shyness. Interpersonal problems like loneliness and shyness seem good candidates as examples of learned helplessness. They are marked by passivity and associated with depression, anxiety, and negative cognitions about the self. Several researchers, most notably Anderson (e.g., Anderson & Arnoult, 1985a, 1985b; Anderson, Horowitz, & French, 1983), have linked explanatory style to these problems (Girodo, Dotzenroth, & Stein, 1981; Goetz & Dweck, 1980; Revenson, 1981; Snodgrass, 1987). People estranged from others are likely to offer internal, stable, and global explanations for bad events.

This work is preliminary, but there are some clues about the exact nature between explanatory style and social difficulties. First, Alden (1984) looked at the relationship between causal explanations and assertiveness. As the helplessness reformulation would predict, assertive people offered optimistic explanations for both success and failure, whereas unassertive people were more pessimistic. Perhaps explanatory style determines someone's characteristic social assertiveness or unassertiveness; this in turn influences her social adjustment.

Second, Gotlib and Beatty (1985) showed that subjects reacted more negatively to an individual who explained bad events in terms of character (internal, stable, and global explanation) than one who explained bad events in terms of behavior (internal, unstable, and specific). In other words, pessimistic explanatory style is a turnoff (see Weary, Jordan, & Hill, 1985). The helplessness reformulation focuses on the intrapersonal events set off by causal explanations, but this study suggests attention to interpersonal processes as well. Needless to say, the individual who elicits bad feelings and rejection from others is apt to be lonely or shy or both.

Are such interpersonal problems examples of learned helplessness? Research to date does not allow us to answer this question fully. Although passivity is implicated, it is not clear that it is always maladaptive. Perhaps social withdrawal represents someone's attempt to harness undue anxiety. And the causes of shyness and loneliness are murky. No one has shown that a history of uncontrollable events is an antecedent. Thus, these social problems represent, at best, middling examples of learned helplessness. Future research may well change this conclusion.

Good Examples

A good example of a social problem with regard to the learned helplessness model is one in which more than one criterion has been demonstrated, yet not all. We survey several such examples here. Again, further research may well show that these instances are indeed excellent examples.

Aging. Recent work in gerontology increasingly reminds us that aging is as much psychological as physical. Several theorists have proposed that some of the disabilities and deficiencies associated with old age reflect learned helplessness (Rodin, 1986; Schulz, 1980). By now we know what to look for in evaluating this claim: maladaptive passivity, a history of uncontrollable events, and cognitions about helplessness.

Do older people experience lack of control? In an obvious sense, yes. As one ages, one almost of necessity experiences an increasing number of uncontrollable events: loss of friends and family members to death, loss of one's job, loss of income, and so on. But in a less obvious sense, we can answer yes again. Consider the widespread stereotypes held about the elderly, even among professionals:

> the need for more bedside nursing, memory loss, physical problems . . . limited interests . . . poor physical condition . . . not important to their families . . . negative personality traits . . . mental and physical deterioration . . . conservative, insecure, lonely, meddlesome, and pessimistic. (Solomon, 1982, p. 283)

When translated into practice, these stereotypes mean that health care professionals respond not to the needs of an older person (i.e., contingent on the person's behavior) but instead to the stereotype. This is the appropriate antecedent for learned helplessness.

On the other hand, arguing against this possibility is the suggestion that health care professionals do not treat the elderly in a non-contingent fashion but rather in a systematic way that reinforces their passivity (Solomon, 1982). As we have seen, this is not what learned helplessness means.

Thomae (1981) described a study of 174 men and women whose age averaged seventy-five. They completed a measure of the degree to which they saw the events in their life as beyond their control. Responses to this measure predicted life satisfaction as well as how forthrightly these people responded to stressful events in their lives. These results were mostly independent of objective measures of resources available to the subject, like income, which argues for the importance of cognitions in producing deficits in old age.

In studies with similar procedures, Langer and Rodin (1976) and Schulz (1976) found that an intervention that enhanced the sense of control among the institutionalized elderly led to improved physical and psychological health. Other studies similarly show that control-enhancing interventions can improve task performance among the elderly (e.g., Kennelly, Hayslip, & Richardson, 1985).

How does aging fare as an example of learned helplessness? We think it qualifies as good but not excellent. Passivity may be present, but it may be instrumental (cf. Voelkl, 1986). Cognitions of helplessness are present among those who show the greatest debilitation. Finally, a history of uncontrollable events may precede helplessness by the elderly, but this has not been clearly shown.

Athletic Performance.   Yogi Berra reportedly said about baseball that 50 percent of this game is 90 percent mental. Inspired by this adage, Seligman and Peterson (1986) wondered if learned helplessness was involved in athletic failure. We used the CAVE procedure to assess explanations for bad events by professional basketball players. Our hypothesis was that some players were prone to helplessness following a bad event (a loss), which means they would play quite poorly under these circumstances. For an entire season, we read the local sports stories in the hometown papers of the teams in the Atlantic Division of the National Basketball Association (Boston Celtics, New Jersey Nets, New York Knicks, Philadelphia 76ers, and Washington Bullets). All of the causal explanations for bad events made by a team's players or coach were extracted and rated for internality, stability, and globality. Then, composite scores were formed reflecting the style of an entire team. Did these scores predict how well these basketball teams responded following a lost game?

We looked at how the teams played during the *following* season. Because teams differ markedly in their ability, we could not look simply at won-lost records. Rather, we made use of "point spreads" originating in Las Vegas. (For our nonbetting readers: a point spread is used by bookies to equate two teams so that equal numbers of bets are made on both teams. Boston may be favored over New Jersey by eight and one-half points, for instance, which means that someone betting on the Celtics is betting that they will win by nine points or more; someone betting on the Nets is betting that they will lose by no more than eight points.) The point spread reflects the home court advantage, slumping or streaking, injuries, and so on—all of the factors that might obscure a relationship between explanatory style and performance. On the average, point spreads work extremely well in equating teams.

Teams with an optimistic explanatory style beat the point spread following a loss more frequently than teams with a pessimistic style. This finding does not occur when we look at performance against the spread following a victory, which is consistent with a diathesis-stress conception. We more or less replicated this result for three consecutive seasons (starting in 1982). However, trades and career-ending injuries then increasingly plagued the Atlantic Division, and our results. We reluctantly conclude that the role of learned helplessness in athletic performance has yet to be definitively documented.

Nevertheless, the design of this research shows the right way to apply learned helplessness to a social problem. We assessed passivity (i.e., losses against the spread), history of uncontrollability (i.e., loss or victory in the preceding game), and mediating cognitions (i.e., causal explanations for bad events). Research with professional athletes via sports page quotes is a long shot (no pun intended), because the relatively small number of teams and athletes works against showing any but the most robust relationships. Further, we ignored the distinction between personal versus collective helplessness (but see Zaccaro, Peterson, & Walker, 1987, for a discussion of individual versus group attributions by athletes).

More promising are three studies with larger groups of athletes. In the first study, we looked at how explanatory style influenced a baseball player's ability to hit in pressure situations; results so far suggest that such an influence does exist (Rettew, Reivich, Peterson, Seligman, & Seligman, 1990). In the second study, the focus is on whether explanatory style predicts how well a wrestler comes back after finding himself behind in the first or second period (of three in a match). And in the third study, we are looking at the explanatory style of tennis players as a predictor of their tournament performance. Like wrestlers, these athletes show great variation in their ability to come from behind. Some are like Jimmy Connors, unaffected by early setbacks, and some are like Ivan Lendl, good players only when ahead. Does this difference reflect learned helplessness?

Chronic Pain. Skevington (1983) wondered if chronic pain would produce learned helplessness among sufferers (see also Chapman & Brena, 1982; Love, 1988; Seltzer & Seltzer, 1986). This is a different strategy than the one typically followed by those applying learned helplessness ideas. Usually, investigators start with some instance of maladaptive behavior and work backward to see if the antecedents of learned helplessness are present. Instead, Skevington (1983) started with chronic pain—unquestionably an uncontrollable bad event—and looked ahead to see if this produced passivity. And if so, did cognitions of helplessness mediate this effect?

A questionnaire measuring depressive symptoms was used to index passivity, and patients with chronic pain indeed reported more symptoms than healthy comparison subjects. A multidimensional locus-of-control scale was also completed, along with a questionnaire measuring self-blame for bad life events. Pain patients who endorsed a chance locus of control were most likely to be depressed, but self-blame had no relationship to depression.

Skevington (1983) suggested that her results show that chronic pain produces universal helplessness and that her findings are fully consistent with helplessness theory. We disagree. Although the majority of her pain patients did not blame themselves for bad events (as would be expected if they were experiencing universal helplessness), there nonetheless was some variation in self-blame, which was not correlated with variance in depressive symptoms (as required by the reformulation). So we conclude that chronic pain is a good example of learned helplessness, showing most of the criteria but not all (Feldman, 1986).

Mental Retardation. Another phenomenon approached from the perspective of learned helplessness is the passivity observed among mentally retarded and learning-disabled individuals (e.g., Ayres, Cooley, & Dunn, 1990; Canino, 1981; DeVellis & McCauley, 1979; Lowenthal, 1986; Stamatelos & Mott, 1983; Wilgosh, 1984). DeVellis (1977) argued that the passivity, submissiveness, and learning difficulty often seen among the institutionalized retarded are produced not by retardation but by the institution itself (see also Floor & Rosen, 1975). He points to three sources of noncontingency: (1) the behavior of the staff, which attends not to the needs of individuals but to matters of convenience (as by always placing a nonambulatory person near the bathroom); (2) the behavior of the individual's peers, which may be unresponsive to what he does; and (3) seizures and other physical conditions that are imposed on the person.

Research by Weisz (1979; Raber & Weisz, 1981) in particular implicates helplessness among the retarded. He starts with the observation that retarded individuals experience accumulated failure as they age (cf. Cromwell, 1963; Zigler & Balla, 1976), more so than nonretarded individuals. This hypothesis was confirmed by observing the feedback teachers give to retarded individuals. Compared with the nonretarded, retarded students are given more negative feedback, relatively and absolutely. Further, the negative feedback is more apt to be intellectually relevant.

This type of experience, as it accumulates, implies that the retarded will be susceptible to helplessness, a finding confirmed in subsequent research by Weisz, which finds that retarded students are disrupted by failure particularly as they get older. This interaction is important, because it shows that as experience with uncontrollability (in everyday life) accumulates, so too does the propensity to be helpless in the face of failure.

One problem here is the failure of Raber and Weisz (1981) to find that retarded children are prone to make attributions in terms of ability. Indeed, relative to the nonretarded, they are more likely to attribute failure to lack of effort as opposed to lack of ability. Perhaps effort is differently construed here, but on the face of it, this fails to support the argument that learned helplessness is involved in mental retardation. In sum, we again see a middling example of learned helplessness in this phenomenon. Two of the criteria are present (passivity and uncontrollability), but the third (cognition) has not been convincingly demonstrated.

Another problem in interpreting the passivity of the retarded as learned helplessness is the finding by Gargiulo and O'Sullivan (1986) that measures of perseverance, response initiation, attributions, and teacher perceptions of helplessness did not covary as expected among a sample of forty-four mildly retarded children. If learned helplessness is really operative, these different measures should be associated with one another.

Sales. Seligman and Schulman (1986) extended learned helplessness to the domain of work. Some jobs can be highly frustrating. Disappointments and setbacks may be inevitable at certain work sites, and so it becomes important to ask what determines a worker's response to these failures. Who keeps on working for a solution? And who gives up? The practical importance of these questions is obvious: witness the great concern with worker motivation shown by industrial-organizational psychologists (e.g., Dunnette, 1976).

According to the helplessness reformulation, workers who make internal, stable, and global explanations for bad events should curl up and give up following setbacks. In marked contrast, those who make external, unstable, and specific explanations keep trying to solve whatever problem stymied them. So Seligman and Schulman (1986) tested these possibilities among life insurance salespeople. As you might imagine, selling insurance policies is a vocation fraught with frustrations. Only a small percentage of potential customers approached by a salesperson ever buy a policy.

Does explanatory style predict success at this frustrating career? Explanatory style indeed predicted not only which salespeople stayed on the job and which quit but also how many policies were sold by those who stayed. These findings are certainly intriguing. Do they show that learned helplessness is operative in poor sales performance? Not exactly, because only one criterion of learned helplessness (cognitions) is clearly shown. Further research is needed to show that poor sales are preceded by uncontrollable events and that they are due to inappropriate passivity on the part of the salesperson (as opposed to poor social skills or poor contacts).

Saint Paul. One of the most interesting applications of learned helplessness we have encountered is by McMinn and McMinn (1983), who interpret the New Testament writings of Paul in view of the model. We are hardly theologians, so we limit our comments here to whether the criteria of helplessness are sensibly applied. We think they are. How about a history of uncontrollability? Here is Paul on the human condition:

> . . . a base mind and . . . improper conduct . . . filled with all manner
> of wickedness, evil, covetousness, malice. Full of envy, murder, strife,

deceit, malignity, they are gossips, slanderers, haters of God, insolent, haughty, boastful, inventors of evil, disobedient to parents, foolish, faithless, heartless, ruth'ess. (Romans 1:28–31)

Further, Paul sees people as powerless to change their nature or that of others: "I can will what is right, but I cannot do it" (Romans 7:18). Besides uncontrollable bad events, cognitions of helplessness abound as well in the writings of Paul. Paul wanted very much to be good, but he could not achieve his aim.

McMinn and McMinn (1983) correctly predict, on the grounds of the helplessness model, that Paul should have been despondent and passive. Surprisingly, though, there is no evidence in Romans that Paul was anything other than active and optimistic. What explains this apparent failure of learned helplessness? We are tempted to blame a small sample size, but the attributional reformulation supplies a good answer, according to McMinn and McMinn (1983). Paul explains the badness of the human condition in external and unstable terms. Rather than experiencing helplessness, Paul instead experiences peace (Philippians 4:7) and joy (Galatians 5:22).

We conclude that McMinn and McMinn (1983) do a good job of applying helplessness theory to the writings of Paul. We hesitate to conclude further that Paul himself is a good example of a person rescued from learned helplessness by an optimistic explanatory style, but we find it intriguing that the constructs we investigate in the United States during the late twentieth century cohere as well as they do in material written so long ago and so far away. (See Reynierse, 1975, for a similar analysis of Job from the perspective of learned helplessness.)

Unemployment.   Several theorists have suggested that learned helplessness can be induced when one loses a job. The resulting passivity and demoralization only make it more difficult for the unemployed person to find a new position, and so a vicious circle is entered. What is the support for this analysis? Baum, Fleming, and Reddy (1986) showed that as the length of someone's involuntary unemployment increased, the person was increasingly disrupted by uncontrollability at a laboratory problem-solving task. Further, with increasing unemployment, subjects tended to think less of their ability to meet the demands of difficult tasks.

These findings converge with some of the results of studies reported by Feather (1982; Feather & Barber, 1983; Feather & Davenport, 1981). In these studies, depressive affect among the unemployed is predicted by an internal, stable, and global explanatory style. However, contrary to the helplessness model, Feather also finds that the more depressed individuals in his sample reported greater efforts to find a new job than did the less depressed individuals.

None of these studies fully assessed the material impact of unemployment on the various subjects, which means that the general category of "unemployed" might well be extremely heterogeneous. Until further work is done that allows the researcher to hold constant the importance of unemployment to different subjects, we cannot say that unemployment is an excellent example of learned helplessness (see Abbott, 1984).

Excellent Examples

Finally, let us describe several social problems that are explained quite well by the learned helplessness model. We certainly do not conclude that learned helplessness constructs are the only ones that need to be brought to bear on these. But the case has been made in each instance for at least some involvement of inappropriate passivity, a history of uncontrollability, and "helpless" cognitions.

Depression. We devoted Chapter 6 to depression, but we mention it again in this context. We think researchers have most conclusively shown the relevance of helplessness ideas to depression, and as such, it is an instructive example—a standard against which other lines of inquiry can be measured.

How does depression satisfy the criteria for learned helplessness? First, depression involves maladaptive passivity; this is part of its very definition (American Psychiatric Association, 1987). Depression also follows bad events, particularly those that people judge to be uncontrollable (e.g., Thoits, 1983). And depression is mediated by cognitions of helplessness, hopelessness, and pessimism (e.g., Beck, 1967). Explanatory style is a consistent correlate of depressive symptoms (e.g., Sweeney, Anderson, & Bailey, 1986) and a demonstrable risk factor (e.g., Peterson & Seligman, 1984).

As we have noted, there has been criticism of the use of learned helplessness to explain depression. By the view advanced here, this criticism is often misdirected, reflecting a misunderstanding of what it means to claim that learned helplessness helps to explain depression (or any failure of adaptation, for that matter). To propose that helplessness is a model of depression is not to suggest that it *is* depression. Models and the phenomena they explain exist at different levels of abstraction, and so equivalence can never occur and hence should not be expected.

In judging the goodness of a model (vis-à-vis some phenomenon), one must ascertain whether the essential features of the model capture something about the phenomenon. The learned helplessness model has three essential features, and all are clearly present in the case of depression. Insofar as these features tell us something about the symptoms, etiology, and therapy for depression (Peterson & Seligman, 1985), we believe they speak meaningfully to the disorder.

Someone wishing to criticize learned helplessness as a model of depression must argue that one or more of the critera for learned helplessness are not present and/or not relevant in depression. Arieti and Bemporad (1978) take this route by proposing that the ostensible passivity of depressives is instrumental. That is, depressed people act in a "helpless" way in order to manipulate others. Research of which we are aware in no way bears out this argument (see Coates & Wortman, 1980, for a review of the reactions that depressives elicit from others), but at least this is an appropriate sort of criticism.

Other criticisms are simply irrelevant because they do not address the adequacy of the model. To dismiss learned helplessness as inapplicable to depression because research in support of it uses college students, for instance, is no kind of argument at all. The point is not whether helpless college students resemble depressives in all ways, but whether they share essential features. These ideas help with the task at hand: recognizing excellent examples of learned helplessness. Once the rules for evaluation are made clear, we can avoid arguments. This lesson can be gleaned from the often pointless controversy that has surrounded learned helplessness and depression (Peterson, 1985).

Academic Achievement. Next to depression, the best-known application of learned helplessness is to school achievement.[1] At least two reasons for this popularity come to mind. First, more so than many domains of life, school represents a situation in which there are right and wrong answers and in which one's efforts indeed matter. Thus, school is a particularly close approximation to the laboratory setting in which learned helplessness was first described. It should allow a straightforward generalization of helplessness ideas.

Second, with the attributional reformulation, helplessness research converges with the investigations by Weiner (1972, 1974, 1979, 1986) of the attributional determinants of performance. Weiner began his work in the achievement motivation tradition, to which he gave a cognitive twist, just as helplessness researchers began in the animal learning tradition, to which they gave the same twist. It is interesting how both lines of work agree on the importance of attributions.

Dweck (1975; Dweck & Reppucci, 1973) was the first to apply helplessness ideas to academic achievement. In her research, she starts with children designated as "helpless" versus "mastery-oriented" by virtue of their responses to a questionnaire asking about the reasons for academic success and failure. Helpless children are those who attribute failure to their lack of ability. When working at problems, they employ ineffective strategies, report negative feelings, expect to do poorly, and ruminate about irrelevant matters (e.g., Diener & Dweck, 1978). When these children encounter failure, they fall apart; prior success has little effect on them (Dweck & Reppucci, 1973).

Dweck (1975) reports that attribution retraining—in which students who attribute failure to a lack of ability are taught to attribute it instead to a lack of effort—indeed improves their reactions to failure. Because this is a cognitive intervention, its success strengthens further the argument that school failures exemplify learned helplessness. Other cognitive interventions effective against school failure have been discussed by Brustein (1978), Cecil and Medway (1986), Craske (1985, 1988), Sowa and Burks (1983), and Wilson and Linville (1982, 1985), among others.

Another analysis of school failure in learned helplessness terms comes from Butkowsky and Willows (1980), who focus on poor readers. In support of their hypothesis that reading difficulties entail learned helplessness, they showed that fifth grade boys with reading problems expect little future success at reading tasks, explain their failures with internal and stable causes, and fail to persist at reading.

Fincham, Hokoda, and Sanders (1989) followed elementary school children for a two-year period, asking their teachers at both points in time to rate the helplessness displayed by the children. "Helplessness" proved stable. And ratings of helplessness at Time One predicted poor performance at objective achievement tests at Time Two.

Still other studies show a link between helplessness constructs and academic outcomes for college students. At the beginning of a school year, Kamen and Seligman (1986) administered the ASQ to two groups of students at the University of Pennsylvania: freshmen and upperclassmen. We also obtained SAT scores of these students as an estimate of their ability. Did explanatory style predict the grades of the students at the end of the year, even when their ability was held constant? Results for the upperclassmen were straightforward and suggest that learned helplessness is involved in school failure. Habitual explanations of bad events in terms of internal, stable, and global causes predicted poor academic performance, even when SAT scores were held constant.

But among freshmen, explanatory style predicted grades only among the less able of the sample. One interpretation of this latter finding is that freshmen students at Penn simply did not encounter enough bad events for their explanatory style to make any difference. Class size in introductory courses tends to be larger than that in upper-level courses, and as a result multiple-choice examinations are used to assign grades. The high-SAT freshmen studied by Kamen and Seligman (1986) may well have breezed through these objective examinations. Because they rarely encountered failure, the manner in which they explained it was irrelevant. In contrast, the low-SAT freshmen no doubt stubbed their toes during their first year at college. Those who made upbeat explanations for the bad events they encountered kept trying to excel, while those who made pessimistic ones gave up.

A similar study among freshmen students was conducted at Virginia Tech, yielding clearer results (Peterson & Barrett, 1987). As judged by their SAT scores, these students were much more "ordinary" than the freshmen studied by Kamen and Seligman (1986). Explanatory style for bad events indeed predicted poor grades for these freshmen during their first year at college, above and beyond the effect of SAT scores. Also determined was the number of times each of the students in the sample sought out academic advising during the year. As to be expected if they were helpless, students who explained bad events with internal, stable, and global causes tended *not* to go to an adviser. In turn, not going to an adviser was associated with poor grades.

The research, then, seems to satisfy pretty well two criteria of learned helplessness: passivity and cognition. What about the third criterion? Kennelly and Mount's (1985) study provides pertinent evidence. These researchers studied eighty-six students in the sixth grade. They devised and administered a measure called the Teacher Contingency Scale that asked students for their perceptions of the degree to which their teachers delivered rewards and punishments in a contingent versus noncontingent fashion. They also measured the students' beliefs about the causes of success and failure, their actual academic performance (grades), and whether or not their teacher saw them as helpless.

Students' perceptions of punishment noncontingency did not relate to the other variables, but their perceptions of reward noncontingency were strongly correlated with helplessness on the part of the students. Further, children who thought that academic outcomes were beyond their control were rated by their teachers as helpless. All these variables in turn predicted actual academic performance.

From a learned helplessness perspective, the piece that doesn't fit is why only the perceived noncontingency of rewards related to the other variables. Other studies find the opposite pattern: that perceived noncontingency of punishments (but not rewards) predicts poor academic performance (e.g., Kennelly & Kinley, 1975; Yates, Kennelly, & Cox, 1975). Perhaps matters differ from classroom to classroom. Regardless, these studies considered together suggest a good fit between learned helplessness and passivity as evidenced in the classroom.

A study reported by Johnson (1981) further implicates the criteria of learned helplessness in school failure. She compared three groups of male students, all between nine and twelve years of age. One group consisted of average students. The second group was composed of chronically failing students. The third group was a group of students who had been chronic failers but were enrolled in remedial classes. All subjects completed an attribution questionnaire, a self-concept measure, and an experimental task that indexed their persistence.

In this study, all three criteria of learned helplessness were assessed—history of bad events, cognition, and passivity. Consistent with the argument that chronic failure in school involves learned helplessness, all these variables covaried, along with low self-esteem. All achieved their lowest values among the chronic failers. Finally, remedial instruction showed some signs of alleviating helplessness.

Asian Americans.   Sue (1977) takes issue with the common stereotype that Asian Americans are the "model minority" in the United States. Discrimination indeed exists, and many Americans of Asian ancestry have a less than ideal existence. He suggests that learned helplessness can clarify aspects of the Asian American experience. How well does his analysis fare?

Let us start with the criterion of passivity. This is the most difficult to document, suggests Sue (1977), because the traditional Asian culture deemphasizes individual assertiveness. One can point to instances of passivity on the part of Asian Americans, such as a failure to mobilize against discrimination, but it is not clear what these reflect: cultural values or learned helplessness (Nicassio, 1985).

It is easier to argue for helpless cognitions on the part of Asian Americans. Sue (1977) reviews research showing that when compared with other (mostly white) Americans, Asian Americans report less autonomy and greater anxiety, nervousness, loneliness, alienation, and rejection. Indeed, Sue (1977) argues that these cognitions are becoming more prevalent as Asian Americans increasingly move into the larger American culture, where they are met with less than full acceptance.

It is also easier to argue for a history of uncontrollable events experienced by many Asian Americans. Early Asian immigrants to the United States were denied the right to vote or testify in court. Extensive legislation explicitly denied them the rights enjoyed by others. The United States government interned over 100,000 citizens of Japanese ancestry during World War II. Even today, Asian Americans are treated in accordance with their race, not their actions. This criterion of learned helplessness is clearly present.

Sue's (1977) analysis is sophisticated, anticipating the refinements of the reformulated model. He observes that helplessness can be domain-specific and that Asian Americans have tended to stay in those situations and circumstances in which control is possible. We judge the case that learned helplessness is involved in the experience of Asian Americans to be well made. Put another way, this is an excellent example of what we mean by learned helplessness.

Black Americans. If Asian Americans experience learned helplessness, can the same be said of Black Americans? Several theorists have explored the possibility. Seligman (1975) hypothesizes that the poverty and discrimination that are the plight of so many Black Americans are devastating not simply because they are deprived of material goods but also because they are deprived of psychological assets. Poverty and discrimination mean uncontrollability, and uncontrollability means passivity and defeatism: in short, learned helplessness (see also Fernando, 1984; Powell, 1990).

Here is Kenneth Clark (1964) on the helplessness inherent in the Harlem ghetto:

> The Harlem ghetto is the institutionalization of powerlessness. Harlem is made up of the socially engendered ferment, resentment, stagnation, and potentially explosive reactions to powerlessness and continued abuses. The powerless individual and community reflect this fact by increasing dependency and by difficulty in mobilizing even the latent power to counter the most flagrant abuses. Immobility, stagnation, apathy, indifference, and defeatism are among the more obvious consequences of personal and community impotence. (p.80)

At the same time, we must not look past the reality of continued discrimination to interpret all instances of passivity by Black Americans as evidence of learned helplessness. In some cases, people don't try because they perceive correctly that their efforts will not win rewards. In other cases, people don't try because they have been punished for active attempts to control outcomes. Learned helplessness is present in neither case.

As with Asian Americans, it is difficult to say whether the passivity of Black Americans is always inappropriate. However, two lines of evidence suggest that passivity on the part of Black Americans sometimes reflects this criterion of learned helplessness. First, Smith and Seligman (1978) conducted a laboratory helplessness experiment with black and white children, finding that blacks were more disrupted in their problem solving following uncontrollable events than were whites. Weisz (1981) reported a similar finding. So these studies show that Black Americans may fail to persevere in situations in which perseverance indeed wins out. Second, research during the ghetto riots of the 1960s showed that the Black Americans most likely to be militant (i.e., active) were those who felt the least helpless about matters. In particular, militants "have very strong beliefs in their ability to control events in their own lives and to shape their own future" (Forward & Williams, 1970, p. 88).

The other criteria of learned helplessness are easier to document. The fact that Black Americans have experienced uncontrollable events is obvious. Let's focus on just one type of uncontrollable event: unemployment. The highest rates of joblessness in our country occur among young Black Americans, with estimates ranging to 50 percent (e.g., Freeman & Wise, 1982). Various reasons for this high rate of joblessness no doubt exist, but the fact of unemployment translates itself into cognitions concerning helplessness. Bowman (1984) interviewed young Black Americans without jobs, finding that fully 23 percent expressed little hope about eventually finding work. And the most hopeless individuals were those who blamed their own lack of ability for their plight: an internal, stable, and global cause.

We conclude, therefore, that learned helplessness can profitably be applied to Black Americans. Although it is critical that one not overlook actual barriers to achievement at school and at work for these individuals, at least some of the passivity shown by Black Americans reflects the operation of learned helplessness (Spencer, Kim, & Marshall, 1987).

Burnout. Burnout is the emotional and physical exhaustion some-times befalling those who provide social services (e.g., Edelwich & Brodsky, 1980; Freudenberger & Richelson, 1980). It appears to be determined chiefly by direct client contact of an intense nature, when immediate needs exceed resources to meet them. The symptoms of burnout overlap considerably with those of depression, except that in most cases, burnout is work related. So burnout is an eight-hour per day depression, and its context-specific nature suggests that learned helplessness might indeed be operating.

Greer and Wethered (1984) concur with this suggestion, and they survey studies of burnout that implicate all three criteria of learned helplessness. Thus, burnout involves maladaptive passivity. Those experiencing work-related exhaustion are rigid and do not seek so-lutions to their problems (e.g., Pines, Aronson, & Kafry, 1981). And burnout is preceded by uncontrollable events, particularly lack of client progress (e.g., Sarata, 1974). Finally, it is accompanied by cognitions of helplessness (e.g., Cherniss, 1980) and a pessimistic explanatory style (e.g., McMullen & Krantz, 1988). Burnout there-fore is an excellent example of learned helplessness.

Crowding. The deleterious effects of crowding have been well doc-umented (e.g., Altman, 1975). Although the physical trauma of crowded conditions of course plays a role in people's reactions to them, so too do perceptions of control. To the degree that crowding diminishes someone's sense that he or she can control outcomes, crowding is experienced as aversive (e.g., Cohen & Sherrod, 1978; Fleming, Baum, & Weiss, 1987; Rodin, Solomon, & Metcalf, 1978). Is learned helplessness the mechanism behind such experiences?

A series of studies by Baum (e.g., Baum, Aiello, & Calesnick, 1978; Baum & Gatchel, 1981; Baum & Valins, 1977) suggest that re-actions to crowding are an excellent example of learned helplessness (Kuykendall & Keating, 1984). The subjects of these investigations were college dormitory residents, who lived under conditions of more versus less crowding. All three criteria of learned helplessness are demonstrated. Students living in crowded conditions show lack of persistence at experimental tasks as well as social withdrawal, report little control over events in their life, and show diminished expectations of future control.

Several further aspects of this line of research are notable. First, the immediate (and short-term) reaction to crowding is an attempt to regain control. In other words, the reactance effect described by Wortman and Brehm (1975) occurs. After chronic crowding, though, passivity follows. Second, interventions that reduce the negative effects of crowding are possible (e.g., Baum & Davis, 1980). The crucial events that cannot be controlled in crowded situations usually involve other people. The constant coming and going of others produces learned helplessness. If dormitories are designed to minimize uncontrollable traffic, therefore, the harmful effects of crowding can be minimized.

Epilepsy.   One way to apply learned helplessness is to start with an uncontrollable bad event and see if it produces maladaptive passivity. This approach was used to investigate the effects of chronic pain. A study similar in spirit investigated epilepsy. Epileptics have been described as passive, noncompetitive, underachieving, inattentive, isolated, and depressed (e.g., Hermann, 1977). Although the physiological basis for epilepsy might have some direct effect on these behaviors, so too might psychological reactions to the seizures. Indeed, epilepsy looks like a reasonable place to find learned helplessness. DeVellis, DeVellis, Wallston, and Wallston (1980) pursued this line of thinking by surveying 289 individuals with epilepsy, asking about the perceived predictability/controllability of seizures, as well as their frequency and severity. As measures of helplessness, subjects completed a depression questionnaire and a locus-of-control measure.

Compared with the general population, people with epilepsy were more depressed and perceived less control over events in their lives. Further, they were depressed to the degree that their seizures were seen as outside their control. This latter correlation held even when the severity of seizures was taken into account (see also Rosenbaum & Palmon, 1984). The results of this research clearly document all three criteria of learned helplessness, qualifying this application as an excellent example.

Noise. One of the most straightforward applications of the learned helplessness model to a social problem concerns noise. We saw in Chapter 4 that uncontrollable bursts of noise are a standard way of inducing learned helplessness in the laboratory, so we should not be surprised that there is ready generalization. In an impressive series of studies, Glass and Singer (1972) showed that uncontrollable noise interfered with problem solving, whereas the identical noise when interpreted as controllable had no such effect.

Cohen, Evans, Krantz, and Stokols (1980) and Cohen, Evans, Krantz, Stokols, and Kelly (1981) extended these laboratory studies by studying the performance of school children whose classrooms were or were not under the flight paths of airplanes. Children bombarded by uncontrollable noise performed more poorly at school than those without this history. In sum, we find the social problem of noise pollution another excellent example of learned helplessness.

WHAT WE KNOW

We have reviewed several dozen phenomena that theorists have suggested as examples of learned helplessness. By our analysis, which involved checking each against a prototypic case of learned helplessness (i.e., maladaptive passivity, history of uncontrollable events, and cognitions of helplessness), several applications fare quite well (see Table 7-1). Most applications prove to be decent but not outstanding examples of learned helplessness. A handful of them appear to be poor ones.

We can conclude that learned helplessness seems to play a role in various social problems. Even in those cases in which it is not an outstanding example, the helplessness model directs our attention away from inner "pathology" and onto more mundane constructs like situational contingencies and cognitions. These provide a readier target for intervention. Interestingly, the role of cognition is better documented here than in the basic work (Chapter 4). At the same time, learned helplessness is not as ubiquitous as some have believed. Examples of its application to social problems show a range of fit.

WHAT WE DON'T KNOW

To date, most applications of learned helplessness to social problems have been noncritical demonstrations. Future research apply-

Table 7-1. Applications of Learned Helplessness

| Social Problem | Criteria of Learned Helplessness | | |
	Inappropriate Passivity	History of Uncontrollability	Mediating Cognitions
Poor Examples			
Alcoholism	Not present	Not shown	Shown
Bodily control	Not present	Not shown	Not shown
Child abusers	Not present	Shown	Not shown
Middling Examples			
Child abuse victims	Not shown	Shown	Not shown
Childhood autism	Somewhat shown	Not shown	Not shown
Domestic violence	Not shown	Not shown	Shown
Evening news	—	Shown	—
Institutionalization	Not shown	Not shown	Shown
Loneliness and shyness	Not shown	Not shown	Shown
Good Examples			
Aging	Not shown	Shown	Shown
Athletic performance	Somewhat shown	Somewhat shown	Somewhat shown
Chronic pain	Shown	Shown	Not shown
Mental retardation	Shown	Shown	Not shown
Sales	Somewhat shown	Not shown	Shown
Saint Paul	—	Shown	Shown
Unemployment	Contradictory	Somewhat shown	Shown
Excellent Examples			
Depression	Shown	Shown	Shown
Academic achievement	Shown	Shown	Shown
Asian Americans	Somewhat shown	Shown	Shown
Black Americans	Shown	Shown	Shown
Burnout	Shown	Shown	Shown
Crowding	Shown	Shown	Shown
Epilepsy	Shown	Shown	Shown
Noise	Shown	Shown	Shown

ing learned helplessness ideas should make an explicit attempt to document the three criteria of learned helplessness. We have been somewhat dismayed in our review of the present literature to discover that not all investigators have a good grasp of what learned helplessness means. The present chapter illustrated repeatedly what is meant by learned helplessness (and what is not), so we hope that future applications will at least be considering the appropriate criteria.

We recommend longitudinal studies as a more stringent way of applying the helplessness model. We suggest that researchers measure several failures of adaptation at the same time, not just a single disturbance. And if learned helplessness is to be of practical importance in designing interventions, helplessness explanations must be pitted against alternatives in a critical way, so that we can understand just how large a role the mechanisms proposed by helplessness theory actually play in particular social problems.

Several issues deserve greater attention in future research. First, applications to date have not always been careful to show that cognition matters above and beyond trauma. The yoking procedure standard in experimental studies is difficult if not impossible to implement in field studies with human subjects, but researchers have often been guilty of not even attempting a reasonable facsimile. Why? Perhaps because it is so "obvious" that people's beliefs can produce difficulties for them. However, trauma can also produce passivity. One theme running through our critique of helplessness applications is the importance of ruling out trauma as a confound before learned helplessness is used as an explanation.

Second, applications to date have tended to fall into two groups: those based on the original helplessness model (Chapter 2) and those based on its reformulation (Chapter 4). The difference is in terms of what researchers look at in arguing that learned helplessness is present. If they are interested in the original model, they stress uncontrollable events as antecedents of observed passivity. If they are interested in the reformulation, they stress cognitions (i.e., causal explanations). However, as we emphasized in Chapter 5, the reformulation is a diathesis-stress model, which means that both cognitions *and* events matter. The reformulation did not replace the original model so much as elaborate it. Applied researchers have not sufficiently recognized this.

Third, as we emphasized in Chapter 4, there still exist unsettled controversies about the basic helplessness phenomenon in people. What is the implication of these issues for the application of helplessness constructs? Not that helplessness fails to exist: deficits can be reliably produced by uncontrollable events. Not that cognitions are unimportant: as a property of the relationship between the person and the world, "uncontrollability" must have a cognitive representation.

Rather, researchers have yet to grasp exactly what the helpless person is thinking and how this produces difficulties for him. The criticisms and questions concerning the laboratory phenomenon have to do with the nature of the cognitions that link uncontrollable events and observed deficits. The attributional reformulation took one step toward a more complex view of the helpless person's cognitions, but we suspect that further steps need to be taken. We know that perceptions, expectations, and explanations are relevant, but what else? The applications of helplessness ideas, even those we have deemed excellent ones, need to be regarded more tentatively than they usually are, because our understanding of the basic helplessness phenomenon is still evolving.

Fourth, although the bulk of the work in the helplessness tradition concerns itself with individual helplessness, these ideas can be extended as well to groups. Peterson and Stunkard (1989) have sketched the beginning of a theory of collective control versus collective helplessness. Collective control is envisioned as a norm—or shared belief—about the way that a group works, what it is that the group can and cannot accomplish by what actions. Note the strict parallel with individual expectations in learned helplessness (Chapter 2).

By further analogy, perhaps a diminished sense of collective control produces low morale, lack of perseverance in the face of failure, little tolerance of interruption and turnover, and poor physical health. For instance, groups within a bureaucracy may experience collective helplessness when group members see no connection between what they do and the eventual products of their activity. In such circumstances, workers may become listless or may begin to define their own—more proximal—goals and ignore those of the organization.

Collective control and helplessness are no doubt more complicated than their analogues at the individual level. Members of a group may not have uniform beliefs about what the group can and cannot do. Members of some groups manifest differences of opinion, and groups fall along the continuum of agreement versus disagreement among its members regarding the group's helplessness or efficacy.

Another reason why collective helplessness is more complicated than individual helplessness is that groups are composed of individual people with beliefs not only about the group's ability to achieve goals but also their own ability to help the group. Collective and individual helplessness mutually influence each other. People may rely on the adequacy of their groups to judge their own helplessness. And people probably judge the potency of their group by the individual competence of its members and leaders. This may be why the success of a sports team is so important to its fans. At the same time, research by Simkin, Lederer, and Seligman (1983) showed that individual helplessness need not generalize to group performance and that collective helplessness need not generalize to individual performance (Chapter 4).

Some of the applications we surveyed concerned themselves with learned helplessness in the context of groups and organizations. None of these cleanly made the distinction between individual and collective helplessness. We believe that helplessness exists at both levels, and the relationship between the two may well vary from group to group. Here is an obvious area in which further work, both conceptual and empirical, is needed (Munton & Antaki, 1988).

In sum, if learned helplessness indeed applies to diverse failures of human adaptation, the model is embarrassingly rich and leads us to the unlikely prediction that people with a history of uncontrollable events who arrive at helpless cognitions end up at risk for everything passive under the sun. Although social problems do occur in clusters, the clustering is probably not as tight as this prediction suggests. Further, when social problems do co-occur, it may well be the result of one problem exacerbating another, as opposed to learned helplessness being at the root of all of them individually.

What's the issue? Theorists have not grappled with *why* uncontrollable events and helpless cognitions produce depression in one group of people, academic failure in a second, cancer in a third, and listless work performance in a fourth. As we suggested in Chapter 5, maybe the solution is to stop referring to learned helplessness as a *model* and start to call it a *mechanism*. This is more than a cosmetic distinction. Models presumably exhaust the relevant features of some phenomenon, whereas mechanisms are simply important ingredients. As a mechanism, learned helplessness must then be combined with other factors.

NOTES

1. See Peterson (1990, 1992a) for more extended discussions.

8

Learned Helplessness and Physical Health

Although many believe that psychological states have something to do with health and illness, actually showing the influence of psychology on physical well-being proves difficult. The best-known arguments in favor of such influence are striking case studies, such as Norman Cousins's (1981) well-chronicled fight against illness through the mustering of his positive emotions. We find these stories of great interest, but at the same time, we are forced to take a skeptical view. Such examples prove very little other than the fact that the course of people's physical health can vary drastically.

They certainly do not demonstrate conclusively that psychological factors have anything to do with good or bad health. They do not identify which psychological factors might be critical. They do not allow us to generalize to other people. We can be happy for Norman Cousins that he survived his life-threatening illness to lead a long and satisfying life, but we don't know what else to say about his story.

Perhaps the real value of such striking examples is that they legitimize closer scrutiny of the link between psychological states and physical well-being. Researchers have recently been taking these closer looks, and findings imply that learned helplessness may play a role. In the present chapter, we describe some of the relevant studies.

Parts of this chapter are based on Peterson and Bossio (1991).

SOME GROUND RULES

What does it mean to say that learned helplessness is involved in poor health? It does not mean that helplessness is a model of illness, which was the working assumption in our research looking at depression (Chapter 6). Rather, we hypothesize that helplessness is a potential *mechanism* for poor health. And it is just one of many. If nothing else is clear about illness, it is obvious that poor health is subject to many influences. We face two tasks, therefore, in asking about learned helplessness and poor health. First, is there a link between helplessness constructs and poor health? And second, if a link can be established, how do we move from being helpless to being in poor health? Our attempts to answer these two questions are ongoing; the pieces of the puzzle are so far consistent, but many are still missing.

Health and illness may seem easy for a researcher to ascertain. But the closer health and illness are examined, the fuzzier the two become. There are many possible criteria for physical illness:

- Someone complaining of feeling ill
- The presence of particular symptoms like swollen glands
- The diagnosis of particular illnesses by examining physicians
- The corroboration of diagnoses by blood tests, urine tests, X rays, and the like
- Bodily responses like immune functioning that show how the body responds to siege
- How long someone lives
- Whether one is alive or dead

Researchers have to settle on a way to measure health status, knowing that no particular operationalization is foolproof. The various criteria of illness do not perfectly agree. There are people who "feel" fine but have critical illnesses; there are people who "feel" poorly but show great vigor. There are diseases without symptoms, symptoms without diseases. One of the best-established epidemiological findings is that morbidity (illness) and mortality (death) do not line up once we take into account people's gender. Females have more illnesses than men, but they also live longer (Verbrugge, 1989).

Our research into learned helplessness and physical health has deliberately measured health in a variety of ways and then looked for convergence across these different studies. We have thereby gained generality. At the same time, we have not stayed long enough with a given research paradigm to rule out all possible confounds there. The research program as a whole is preliminary. Any given study is more flawed than we would like. Until we actually rule out alternative interpretations in each case, all we can say is that our findings do show an intriguing convergence.

RISK FACTORS FOR ILLNESS

What does it mean to ask whether learned helplessness puts one at risk for poor health? Remember that "learned helplessness" encompasses three different components: passivity, uncontrollability, and cognition. So this question should be rephrased to ask about the contributions of these constructs—individually and in combination—to poor health. To date, we have looked most frequently at how cognition, specifically one's explanatory style, pertains to physical well-being.

Passivity

Nonetheless, we believe that passivity produces poor health, more so now than ever before in history. The health professions have gone through three major eras in their attempt to combat illness (Taylor, Denham, & Ureda, 1982). The first era was strictly reactive in nature. Once someone became ill, she received treatment. The second era is a more recent arrival on the historical scene and was an attempt to prevent people from getting ill in the first place by modifying their physical environment, reducing the likelihood that they would become infected by germs. Swamps containing mosquitoes that carried malaria were drained. Trash heaps that housed rats that carried fleas that carried the bubonic plague were removed. Surgeons washed their hands before and after operations.

Both of these eras have been important, and strategies from them are obviously still deployed today. But we are now entering a third era of combating illness that differs dramatically from its predecessors. At this point, it is estimated that most people die from illnesses that have something to do with their life-style. Smoking, drinking, poor nutrition, and not exercising contribute to an incredible number and variety of maladies. So the third era of combating illness tries to induce the individual to get rid of his or her unhealthy habits for good.

This differs from the other eras because no longer is the individual allowed to stand around on the sidelines while physicians fight germs and public health workers alter the physical environment. The third era—which we can call the era of health promotion—requires that the individual act differently. To this end, programs have been undertaken—over television, in schools, at work, and even within whole communities and nations—that try to encourage people to act in healthy ways. Passivity in the face of these exhortations is obviously not healthy.

More controversial are the hypothesized links between uncontrollability and cognitions on the one hand and physical health on the other. We have conducted research that addresses both these links. Animal studies have looked at how experience with uncontrollable events changes the physiology of an organism, including ways that make it more susceptible to illness. And people studies have looked at the correlation between pessimistic explanatory style and poor health.

Uncontrollability

Studies with both animals and people show that experience with uncontrollable aversive events may lead to poor health and early death. We review the studies with people here, postponing until later in the chapter our discussion of the studies using animals. Upon close examination, the animal studies prove quite different from the human studies. We also should note that in a number of cases, researchers have not shown that uncontrollability per se is the critical risk factor. We know that stress is often not healthy, and we know that one of the determinants of stress is lack of control, but it is another thing to say that uncontrollability is *the* reason that stress takes a toll on health.

Survey research shows that stressful life events undercut one's health. Stress has been linked to illness in a number of well-controlled studies (Rabkin & Struening, 1976). For instance, investigators Thomas Holmes and Richard Rahe (1967) created the Social Readjustment Rating Scale to gauge the *quantity* of stress a person has been experiencing. In responding to this questionnaire, a research subject indicates which of forty-three major life events occurred in the past year. The more the event in question disrupts her ongoing life and requires some sort of readjustment, the higher the "life change unit" score associated with the event. As the total score on this scale increases, the more likely she is to fall ill.

It is not just major life events that create stress for us. Kanner, Coyne, Schaefer, and Lazarus (1981) created a measure that parallels the Social Readjustment Rating Scale, except that it asks about hassles: small but annoying events in the course of daily life like losing the car keys, being interrupted at dinner, making a mistake while balancing the checkbook, and having to take care of a pet. As hassles accumulate, so does stress, chipping away at one's physical well-being. In their sheer numbers, hassles may be even more stressful than major life events (Weinberger, Hiner, & Tierney, 1987).

Once the stress-illness link was established, researchers began to take a look at its nature, and they found that psychological factors were critical to this link. Specifically, an event becomes stressful and likely to lead to illness to the degree that one thinks about it in a particular way. The more that one regards events as unpredictable and uncontrollable, the more stressful they are. When one is in conflict about events, this can cause stress. And when one blames oneself for bad events but feels powerless to change them, they too are particularly stressful.

In some cases, these beliefs reflect the reality of the situation, but in other cases, someone's beliefs go beyond the facts of the matter and create unnecessary stress for the person. One way to describe the thrust of these findings is to say that a pessimistic view of life events makes them more stressful and thus more likely to produce illness. Conversely, an upbeat way of thinking may buffer one against the health-threatening effects of stress.

The problem with this work is that it is not experimental, and confounds threaten the conclusion that it is the life event per se that increases one's risk of poor health. Further, a stressful life event is not simply uncontrollable but also traumatic. As we took pains to note in Chapter 7, unless sheer physical trauma can be ruled out, it is impossible to conclude that uncontrollability is the critical factor.

Cognition

We turn next to a series of studies with people that look at the association between explanatory style and poor health. Here we have the best evidence linking some of the cognitions that characterize learned helplessness to one's physical well-being.

A Thirty-Five-Year Longitudinal Study. The Harvard Study of Adult Development is an ongoing longitudinal investigation initiated in 1937 by Clark Heath and Arlie Bock at the Harvard University Health Sciences and now directed by George E. Vaillant of Dartmouth Medical School. It represents a unique source of data about human growth and development across the life span. The Harvard Study has allowed researchers to make important statements about coping (Vaillant, 1977) and alcoholism (Vaillant, 1983). It has also allowed us to carry out a study of explanatory style and its relationship to health (Peterson, Seligman, & Vaillant, 1988).

The study began with physically healthy, mentally healthy, and successful members of the Harvard classes of 1942 through 1944. Potential research subjects were first screened on the basis of academic success (40 percent of the entire student body was excluded), then on the basis of physical and psychological health (another 30 percent was excluded), and finally on the basis of nominations by college deans of the most independent and accomplished individuals. In all, 268 young men were included in the study.

Each subject, while an undergraduate, took an extensive physical examination and completed a battery of personality and intelligence tests. After graduation, the subjects completed annual questionnaires about their employment, family, health, and so on. Periodic physical examinations of each subject were conducted by his own doctor. Ten men withdrew from the study during college, and two more men withdrew after graduation.

The Harvard Study of Adult Development is a very special investigation because it satisfies most of the criteria for an ideal study of how psychological states might influence our physical health. It is longitudinal; it has a large number of research participants; it has low attrition; it has good measures of physical health—namely, physician examinations buttressed with medical tests.

The study also makes it possible for us to ascertain the characteristic explanatory style of the research participants when they were young. Among the many measures completed by subjects was a questionnaire they responded to in 1946 that was open-ended and asked about difficult wartime experiences:

> What difficult personal situations did you encounter (we want details), were they in combat or not, or did they occur in relations with superiors or men under you? Were these battles you had to fight within yourself? How successful or unsuccessful in your own opinion were you in these situations? How were they related to your work or health? What physical or mental symptoms did you experience at such times?

This question is an invitation to be mindful, and research participants certainly were. Their answers to this question were more essays than brief statements.

Our interest centered on 99 of the men, chosen randomly from the larger group. We read through the 1946 essays to find causal explanations of bad events. After locating them, we wrote them verbatim on index cards. For the 99 men, we found a total of 1,102 bad events and causal explanations—an average of 11.1 per research subject.

Four research assistants then rated each extracted causal attribution according to its internality (versus externality), stability (versus instability), and globality (versus specificity). We then combined the ratings by averaging across the judges, across the three rating dimensions, and finally across the different events explained by a particular research subject. What resulted was a set of 99 scores, one per subject, that placed each someplace along the dimension ranging from extremely optimistic explanatory style to extremely pessimistic explanatory style.

Along the way to assigning an explanatory-style score to each research subject, we lingered long enough to calculate whether a given individual explained events in a consistent fashion. Remember our earlier cautions that sometimes the reality of events dictates how they are explained, thus precluding someone's habitual view of things from affecting particular explanations (Chapter 5). This might mean that our scores reflected the particular wartime events encountered by a subject (reality) and not the way he habitually thought about such events (explanatory style). Our check on consistency allayed this fear about the validity of our procedure. Research subjects indeed explained disparate events in the same way.

We have detailed how someone's explanatory style was ascertained. Now let us turn to the assessment of our research subject's physical health. At eight times in a research subject's life—at ages 25 (approximately when the open-ended questionnaire we just described was completed), 30, 35, 40, 45, 50, 55, and 60—his personal physician completed a thorough physical exam and forwarded the results to a research internist at the Harvard Study. This individual—obviously unaware of the research subject's explanatory style because this was not to be ascertained until years later—then rated each subject in light of the exam results in the following way:

1 = good health, normal
2 = multiple minor complaints, mild back trouble, prostatitis, gout, kidney stones, single joint problems, chronic ear problems

3 = probably irreversible chronic illness without disability; illness that will not fully remit and will probably progress—like treated hypertension, emphysema with cor pulmonale, diabetes

4 = probably irreversible chronic illness with disability—for example, myocardial infarction with angina, disabling back trouble, hypertension *and* extreme obesity, diabetes *and* severe arthritis, multiple sclerosis

5 = deceased

From age 50 on, the research internist also had available blood and urine tests, an electrocardiogram, and a chest X ray for most of the research subjects (see Vaillant, 1977).

One more measure was available for each subject. In 1945, a global rating was made by an examining psychiatrist who attempted to predict the individual's likelihood of encountering emotional difficulties in the future. This is important to know about each subject because we would want to rule out the possibility that an underlying emotional difficulty—depression, for instance—might cause both a pessimistic explanatory style and poor physical health.

Not surprisingly, as subjects became older, their health on the whole worsened. However, what also happened was that the *range* of scores increased. In other words, there was an ever greater difference between the most and least healthy. This trend in and of itself is hardly unexpected, because all subjects started out as extremely healthy. Remember the stringent selection criteria. But what is interesting is that even for extremely healthy young men, some became quite sickly as they aged. Of the 99 men we studied, 13 died before age 60. Our appetite was whetted for discovering what might make the difference between those with a good outcome and those without. Would explanatory style be relevant?

Overall, men who used optimistic explanations for bad events at age 25 were healthier later in life than men who offered pessimistic explanations. This correlation held even when their initial physical and emotional soundness were taken into account. Thus, an optimistic explanatory style early in life is associated with good health later in life.

We regard this study as an important demonstration of the link between psychological states and physical well-being. Let us be more specific about the findings. We looked at the relationship between explanatory style and health at each of the eight ages of our subjects. Explanatory style was unrelated to health at ages 30 through

40, but thereafter the relationship emerged. It reached its most robust level at age 45, approximately twenty years after the time that explanatory style was assessed. Thereafter, the relation between explanatory style and health fell off somewhat.

We also looked at how explanatory style (at age 25) was associated with *changes* in a subject's health status from one age to another. This lets us zero in on exactly where an optimistic style starts to have benefits (and a pessimistic style costs). To some degree, pessimistic explanatory style was associated with a worsening of health from ages 35 to 40. But the link became most clear between ages 40 and 45 (partial $r = .42$). Here those with an optimistic explanatory style as youths maintained their health, in contrast to those with a pessimistic explanatory style. These latter individuals showed a marked deterioration.

What did we accomplish in this study? We believe that it is an unambiguous demonstration that a psychological variable—one's explanatory style—is associated with physical health two and three decades later. This association holds up even when possible third variables like initial physical health and initial emotional soundness were controlled.

Explanatory style did not predict immediate health status. This is not surprising because in our sample there was little variation in health to begin with. But by early middle age (35–50), health became more variable, and psychological factors began to play a role. In later middle age (50–60), the relationship between explanatory style and health fell off a bit. We have no good explanation for this right now, but our suspicion is that constitutional factors or lifestyle or both start to dominate the health scene at this time.

Any particular study, no matter how striking its results, falls short of being the final word on a topic. Let us point out a major problem with the study we have just described. Its sample was originally chosen *not* to be representative of the population as a whole. This does not detract from the value of the research as a demonstration. Yes, under some circumstances for some people, psychological states are related to health. But once this demonstration is accepted, questions then arise about its boundary conditions. Is this relationship between explanatory style and health the case for all people in all circumstances? Generalizing from the very special participants in the study is obviously a problem. These were initially healthy, often wealthy, successful men, mostly from the northeast United States.

So our next step was to investigate broadly the link between a person's explanatory style and his or her health. This addresses the problem of limited generality of results from the Harvard Study. Let us next describe other studies that further establish this correlation.

The Common Cold. The next investigation of the relationship between someone's explanatory style and physical health used a different population of research subjects, a different measure of explanatory style, and two different criteria for good versus poor health (Peterson, 1988). Again we asked whether explanatory style is associated with one's physical health.

We addressed this question in a group of 172 college students at Virginia Tech, in Blacksburg, Virginia. The study began during the fall of 1984, what we refer to as Time One. At that time our research subjects completed a version of the Attributional Style Questionnaire. They also completed a measure we dubbed the Illness Scale, a questionnaire that asked them to describe all the illnesses they had experienced during the previous 30 days (Suls & Mullen, 1981). For each illness, the research subjects described the date that the symptoms were first noticed and the date that they were last present. The degree of illness can then be calculated as the number of different days during the month that at least one symptom was present. Scores range from 0 to 30, and the higher the score, the more "ill" we say the individual was. To control for any tendencies to complain by some of our subjects, we also administered to them a measure of depressed mood.

The next time we encountered the subjects—Time Two—was one month later, when they again completed the Illness Scale. Of the original 172 subjects, 170 (99 percent) showed up at Time Two. Note that at Time Two, they were reporting on illnesses and symptoms that had occurred since Time One, when their explanatory style had been ascertained. As in the Harvard Study, our interest was in the relationship between explanatory style at the early point in time and health at the later point.

Finally, we contacted our subjects by letter one year later—Time Three. Enclosing a stamped envelope addressed to us, we asked:

> Would you please indicate in the space below the number of times you have visited a physician since last Thanksgiving for diagnosis and/or treatment of an illness? Do not include routine checkups or visits because of an injury (like a broken leg).

Our rationale for this measure was that the worse someone's health, the more frequently he or she might visit a doctor. Of the original 172 subjects, we heard at Time Three from 146 (86 percent). Again,

Table 8-1. Optimistic and Pessimistic Individuals
(Common Cold Study).

Group	Days Ill in Following Month	Doctor Visits in Following Year
Pessimists (25% of sample)	8.56	3.56
Optimists (25% of sample)	3.70	0.95

Source: Peterson, C., and Bossio, L. M. (1991). *Health and optimism.* New York: Free Press. © 1991 by Christopher Peterson and Lisa M. Bossio. Reprinted by permission of The Free Press, a Division of Macmillan, Inc.

we wanted to see the relationship between explanatory style at Time One and health measured this way at Time Three.

We found the same relationship between explanatory style and health that we obtained in the Harvard Study. Optimistic college students—when compared with their more pessimistic peers—experienced fewer days of illness in the subsequent month and made fewer doctor visits in the subsequent year. These results held even when their initial health status (Illness Scale score at Time One) was taken into account. And these results held even when the depression score, a plausible control for complaining, was taken into account.

The magnitudes of these relationships were somewhat less than those found in the Harvard Study, perhaps because a shorter period of time was involved. We compared the 25 percent of subjects who had the highest scores on the ASQ (the most pessimistic) with the 25 percent of subjects who had the lowest scores (the most optimistic). Table 8-1 shows the average number of days ill for subjects in these groups, as well as the average number of doctor visits. There is more than a two-to-one difference in the first case and more than a three-to-one difference in the second.

Of the subjects describing illnesses at Times One and Two, 95 percent described colds, sore throats, or the flu. The remaining subjects reported illnesses like pneumonia, an ear infection, venereal disease, or mononucleosis. Thus, all of the illnesses were infectious. Although subjects at Time Three were not asked to describe the illnesses that brought them to a physician, some small number of them did so. Every illness was infectious.

These results may tell us something that the Harvard Study did not—the sort of illness to which pessimism might specifically relate. We must be cautious in expecting highly specific relationships between a psychological state and a particular health problem. Still, this finding hints at a possible path between explanatory style and health, one that involves the body's response to infection.

This study is not ideal. As in the Harvard Study of Adult Development, the research subjects did not constitute a cross section of the population. College students on the average are healthier, more intelligent, and more privileged than people in general. The common cold is not in the same league as cancer and heart disease, and perhaps college students—who live in close proximity to one another—are particularly at risk for colds. However, because the results of this study converge with the results of the Harvard Study, we start to have more confidence in the link between explanatory style and good health.

Survival with Cancer. In yet another study of the link between explanatory style and health, Sandra Levy and colleagues at the University of Pittsburgh School of Medicine studied thirty-six middle-aged women with recurrent breast cancer (Levy, Morrow, Bagley, & Lippman, 1988). Their interest was in the factors that predicted how long the women lived following the initial diagnosis of cancer. In particular, they looked at the role played by psychological factors, including explanatory style.

When the subjects initially entered the study, they were given an extensive interview that covered various topics. These interviews were then transcribed, and the CAVE procedure was undertaken to identify, extract, and rate the causal explanations contained therein. The researchers also ascertained other factors thought to affect a woman's survival, like the nature of her cancer. And, of course, physicians proceeded with the appropriate treatments.

Levy and her colleagues followed the subjects for four years. Of the thirty-six women originally participating in this research, twenty-four died during this time; survival time among this group ranged from little more than 100 days to almost 1,300 days (that is, 3.6 years). A number of the factors that the researchers measured in the first place proved to predict the survival time of these women, including explanatory style. As we would expect, the more optimistic a woman's explanations had been during the initial interview, the longer she survived.

Explanatory style was *not* the strongest predictor of survival time; instead, biological factors like the number of initial cancer sites were most critical. Further, the magnitude of the relationship between explanatory style and health (i.e., survival) was modest—more so than the other relationships we have described in this chapter. Levy et al. (1988) exercised appropriate caution and called their results a trend. Finally, the small sample size constrained the number of possible "third variables" that could be taken into account and ruled out.

Even with limitations, these results add to the evidence we have summarized arguing for a link between explanatory style and physical well-being. This particular sample is not the most obvious place to expect that psychological states influence health, because all of the research subjects began the study already ill—indeed, quite ill. Psychological states can influence the *onset* of illness or the *course* of illness, and these are different matters. One influence can occur without the other, and our sense is that when illness has progressed far enough along, psychological factors may well play a decreasing role. All of this ends up meaning that Levy's "trend" is notable.

Heart Attack Recovery.   Gregory Buchanan and Martin Seligman (1989) investigated the influence of explanatory style on recovery from a heart attack. Subjects in their study had been part of the control group of a prior study conducted at Stanford University that was concerned with how to prevent the recurrence of heart attacks. All subjects were men who had suffered a heart attack at least six months prior to their entry into the Stanford study. They were all non- or ex-smokers with no evidence of diabetes.

At the beginning of the study, subjects were given a standardized interview to assess the Type A coronary-prone behavior pattern. This interview was videotaped, which allowed Buchanan and Seligman after the fact to use the CAVE procedure to ascertain their explanatory style. In all, there were 160 men in the control group. They were followed for more than eight years, at which point 60 of these subjects had died from coronary causes, usually a second heart attack.

Buchanan and Seligman matched the deceased subjects with still-living subjects on the basis of their age and PEEL index, a global measure of heart functioning that takes into account the location and extent of damage from previous heart attacks. These two groups of subjects differed as expected on explanatory style. Deceased subjects were more likely than those who still lived to have shown a pessimistic style eight years prior. Here we have some evidence that explanatory style may predispose not just infectious disease but also cardiac problems.

Immune System Competence. The next study we want to describe was conducted by Leslie Kamen-Siegel and colleagues at the University of Pennsylvania (Kamen-Siegel, Rodin, Seligman, & Dwyer, 1991). Major interest centered on the relationship between explanatory style and yet one more indicator of physical well-being: the competence of one's immune system. Like all the criteria of "health" used in our research, this too is less than ideal. There are many indices of immune system competence that can be calculated from a blood sample, and spirited debate occurs among immunologists about their relative merits. Immune competence however calculated bears no one-to-one relationship to health and longevity, although by now we are familiar with a researcher's need to rely on measures that in general are reasonable ones.

Kamen-Siegel and her colleagues conducted interviews with forty-seven mostly healthy adults between the ages of sixty-two and eighty-seven. The interviewers covered such topics as major life events, problems, hassles, and worries. In short, they encouraged the subjects to be mindful, and ample causal explanations were offered. These were scored for explanatory style with the CAVE procedure.

A blood sample was available from each of the subjects, drawn at about the time the CAVE interviews were conducted. The samples were analyzed to yield one measure of immunocompetence: specifically, the ratio between T4 cells and T8 cells. More descriptively, T4 cells are often called helper cells, and T8 cells are often called suppressor cells. These labels reflect the roles that these cells are thought to play in turning on and turning off the body's fight against infection.[1] Thus, a high ratio suggests immunocompetence, because here there are relatively more helper cells and relatively fewer suppressor cells; a low ratio suggests compromised immunity, with relatively fewer helper cells and relatively more suppressor cells.

Optimistic explanatory style was correlated with the T4/T8 ratio—that is, with the competence of one's immune system—to a moderate degree. Although this study used a cross-sectional design, which leaves unclear the direction of the relationship they documented, the researchers did try to rule out some likely third variables. First, an overall estimate of current health status was arrived at by two examining physicians. Someone currently ill of necessity has an immune system under attack, thus giving a misleading T4/T8 ratio. Second, each subject's level of depressed mood was estimated by a questionnaire he or she completed. Research suggests that depression affects immunocompetence, again potentially biasing the T4/T8 ratio (Schleifer, Keller, Siris, Davis, & Stein, 1985). The relationship between explanatory style and immune system competence continued to hold even when these two measures— current health status and depressed mood—were controlled statistically.

Replications. We now want to describe briefly several additional studies that found a link between explanatory style and physical health. The first study asked eighty-three summer school students at the University of Michigan to complete the Attributional Style Questionnaire and to respond to the question "Are you ill right now?" by answering definitely no, maybe, or definitely yes (Peterson, Colvin, & Lin, 1989). Subjects then kept track in a diary of any illnesses they experienced during the next three weeks. Of the eighty-three original subjects, seventy-two (87 percent) returned the diaries to us. We scored their health status as we had scored the Illness Scale in the previous study: the number of different days on which the subject experienced at least one symptom. The more optimistic the individual's explanatory style, the fewer days of illness he or she reported, even when answers to the "Are you ill right now?" question were taken into account statistically. Again, the magnitude of this relationship was moderate (partial $r = .33$), and again, 95 percent of the reported symptoms made it seem like subjects suffered from colds or the flu.

The remaining studies were not longitudinal. We measured both explanatory style and physical health simultaneously. Such designs obviously tell us nothing about the direction of effects. But when combined with the previous studies, this particular investigation broadens the support for our contention that optimistic explanatory style is linked to good health.

Research participants in one of these studies were ninety middle-aged adults who as children had participated in an investigation of the effects of different styles of parental discipline (Sears, Maccoby, & Levin, 1957). Years later, in 1988, these individuals were recontacted for further study (see Peterson & Bossio, 1991). The subjects completed a host of questionnaires and other personality measures.

Relevant to our purposes, they also wrote an essay of about 300 words in response to the following instructions:

Please describe the worst thing that happened to you in the past year. Tell (1) when it occurred, (2) if another person was involved and who it was, (3) the gist of any conversation, and (4) what happened at the end.

The other person can be anyone. The event has to be of major importance to you. Please use at least 800 words in your description.

We used the CAVE procedure with these essays to score each person's explanatory style. As with the Harvard Study, what resulted
was a single score for each research subject reflecting his or her
explanatory style.

Health in this study was assessed with a questionnaire that asked
respondents to report on their current health status. Consistent with
our other studies, those with an optimistic explanatory style were
healthier than those with a pessimistic style. The magnitude of this
relationship was comparable to those found in our other investigations.

Another cross-sectional investigation of explanatory style and
health was conducted by Lin and Peterson (1990). Students at the
University of Michigan completed a version of the Attributional Style
Questionnaire, as well as a questionnaire that asked in several ways
about their physical health:

- In the past twelve months, how many different times were you
  ill?
- In the past twelve months, how many different times did you
  visit a physician for diagnosis and treatment of an illness?
- Are you ill right now?
- On the whole, how would you rate your health compared to
  others your age?

As in our previous studies, we found that a pessimistic explanatory
style was associated with poor health.

Finally, Margie Lachman (1989) administered an explanatory style
measure to a sample of elderly individuals. She also assessed their
physical complaints. One more time, a correlation was established
between a pessimistic explanatory style and poor health.

Lines of Related Research

We have described studies showing that uncontrollable events and
a pessimistic explanatory style are associated with poor physical
health. We have been careful to note that each individual study is
far from definitive. Nonetheless, these particular studies are just
one reason to believe that psychological states can affect our physical well-being. The last decade has seen an explosion of studies

that in general show positive thoughts to be associated with good health. We cannot do full justice to the vastness of this research, but we can at least give you a flavor of several lines of inquiry, which converge with our own.

Let us therefore mention several lines of work that link psychological states—chiefly cognitive styles—to physical well-being. Common themes run through these lines of investigation, connecting their results with the studies that explicitly looked at helplessness constructs.

Psychologists Michael Scheier and Charles Carver have for several years investigated a personality characteristic they dub *dispositional optimism*, particularly as it relates to physical health. Of all the work to be discussed, that of Scheier and Carver bears the closest resemblance to our investigations of explanatory style. They define dispositional optimism as one's general expectation that the future holds good outcomes, and in a series of studies, they have linked optimism to good health and pessimism to poor health (Scheier & Carver, 1985, 1987; Scheier et al., 1989).

Another personality characteristic linked to physical well-being that overlaps considerably with our notion of explanatory style is *hardiness*. Developed by Suzanne Kobasa (1979), hardiness is conceived as an individual difference that spans three entwined dimensions: commitment, control, and challenge. Commitment refers to someone's involvement in personal projects and goals. Someone high on commitment is personally engaged; someone low is merely going through the motions. Control entails a belief that one can control important outcomes and devise solutions to the problems of life. Someone high in control actively confronts her surrounding world; someone low is fatalistic, expecting luck or fate to prevail. Finally, challenge refers to the way that one construes stressful events. These can be looked at as challenges—opportunities for personal growth, or as threats to esteem and security. Studies show that hardiness measured this way predicts which people are less likely to fall ill when they experience stress (e.g., Kobasa, 1979, 1982; Kobasa, Maddi, & Courington, 1981; Kobasa, Maddi, & Kahn, 1982).

Yet another notion related to learned helplessness is Albert Bandura's (1977, 1986) concept of *self-efficacy*, defined as a person's belief that he can perform a particular behavior that will produce a particular outcome. In a number of studies, Bandura demonstrated that this belief in one's own efficacy to perform a particular behavior strongly predicted whether or not it would take place. This belief proves to be a more potent influence on future behavior than an individual's past behavior. There are few generalizations in psychology, but one of the best established is that past behavior leads to future behavior; there is considerable inertia to how we think or feel or act. Self-efficacy is an exception to this generalization and thus worthy of note.

What is the relevance of self-efficacy to health? O'Leary (1985) did an extensive literature review and documented numerous areas of health-relevant behavior under the sway of self-efficacy.

> The evidence taken as a whole is consistent in showing that people's perceptions of their efficacy are related to different forms of health behavior. In the realm of substance abuse, perceived self-regulatory efficacy is a reliable predictor of who will relapse and the circumstances of each person's first slip. Strong percepts of efficacy to manage pain increase pain tolerance . . . [Perceived efficacy with regard to] . . . eating and weight predicts who will succeed in overcoming eating disorders. Recovery from the severe trauma of myocardial infarction is tremendously facilitated by the enhancement of the patients' and their spouses' judgments of their physical and cardiac capabilities. And self-efficacy to affect one's own health increases adherence to medical regimens . . . While specific procedures may differ for different domains, the general strategy of assessing and enhancing self-percepts of efficacy to affect health . . . has substantial general utility. (pp. 448–449)

Stripped of jargon, O'Leary's statement says that people can act in healthy ways to the degree that they believe they can enact the particular behaviors that are pertinent (or refrain from them). Self-efficacy may be one of the critical factors underlying our adherence to diets and other health-promoting activities (Peterson & Stunkard, 1989).

That self-efficacy may have a more direct effect on health is shown by recent studies by Bandura and his colleagues that look at how people's physiological responses to stress are influenced by their levels of self-efficacy with respect to coping responses. The more people believe they can cope with stress, the less the stress taxes their body (Bandura, Taylor, Williams, Mefford, & Barchas, 1985). Related studies suggest that people with enhanced self-efficacy have more robust immune systems (Bandura, 1987).

Common Themes

We have described several lines of research that support the work we discussed earlier linking learned helplessness and poor health. There seems little doubt that psychological states can and do influence one's physical well-being. Let us take a step back from the different lines of work and look for some common themes. Obviously, the influence of the mind on our health is the overarching point. But we also know that people have looked for thousands of years for such an influence; why did these particular lines of inquiry work out as well as they have?

We think the answer to this question is that advocates of the mind's influence on our body finally hit upon just what aspect of "mind" to look at. Here are common emphases in the disparate lines of work:

1. It is people's manifest thoughts and beliefs that pertain most directly to their health. Previous researchers looked mainly at emotions, conflicts, and/or unconscious processes, and the yield was much more modest.
2. It is how someone thinks in particular about setbacks and disappointments that matter. The purpose of thought is to allay doubt (Peirce, 1955), and the current generation of psychological researchers has had the good fortune to focus on people under circumstances in which they are most likely to be thoughtful.
3. It is thoughts about the real world—its events, their causes, and their aftermath—that relate to well-being.
4. It is the sorts of beliefs that lead to action, that are infused with agency and efficacy, that lead to health. Those that result in passivity and demoralization do not.

Not all lines of work that psychologists are pursuing exemplify all of these emphases. Some notions slide more into the emotional/motivational realm and others into a purely ideational one. Some are more responsive to "reality" than are others. Some are more microscopic than others.

Regardless, we find our work on learned helplessness to reside somewhere in the middle of most of these possible contrasts. There is a family resemblance in these lines of work. Learned helplessness is a quite respectable member of the family. Our results, however, are merely descriptive. They do not tell us *how* explanatory style influences physical health. So our current research goal is to map out the pathways between helplessness and physical well-being. We hypothesize no single path but rather several, entailing biological, emotional, behavioral, and interpersonal routes. And we hypothesize that these routes crosscut and influence one another.

MECHANISMS

In this section, we discuss exactly how learned helplessness might affect our health. We talk in detail about the multiplicity of routes that seem to exist. Thus we can specify pathways *inside* the person: biological and emotional processes. We can also specify pathways that exist *outside* the person. This is a somewhat arbitrary way to divide matters, but for the sake of simplicity, we go along with this rough distinction.

In particular, we stress how someone's mundane behaviors can promote or damage his health. We hope thereby to bridge our research on learned helplessness with the enormous literature on health promotion—diets, exercise programs, stress management, and the like (Peterson & Stunkard, 1989). Health promotion has sometimes been pushed upon the public in a mindless way, and we mean this in two senses. First, health promotion has not been based on an overall theory of well-being. Instead, it is phrased in terms of a "more is better" approach in which people ruin their physical and emotional health in order to appear fit (cf. Barsky, 1988). We think that an overarching view of what it means to be healthy might restore some sense to health promotion.

Second, health promotion understandably emphasizes the body, but there is a curious neglect of the mind. Our psychological state is not simply a by-product of our physical state, as health promotion experts often seem to imply. The influence runs in both directions. We want to put the mind into health promotion in a literal way and to argue that the process of bolstering one's well-being must *start* with thoughts and beliefs.

Biological Routes

There are many ways in which the biological changes produced by helplessness can alter the disease process. It is not easy to provide a brief review of these possible influences. As we saw in Chapter 3, the biological concomitants of learned helplessness are complex. Most if not all biological systems are influenced to some degree by uncontrollable stress, and these systems in turn braid together, continually influencing one another. Further, the potential biological mediators of the link between helplessness and illness may well vary with the disease in question.

For example, atherosclerosis is the major cause of heart disease in the United States. High levels of cholesterol contribute to this condition, and for rats, exposure to uncontrollable shock increases the levels of cholesterol that circulate in the blood (Brennan, Job, Watkins, & Maier, 1992). A number of hormones that are released into the blood by uncontrollable shock influence the release of free fatty acids and hence the chemical conversion of cholesterol. So we can specify a rather detailed biological route between helplessness and heart disease. However, neither these hormones nor cholesterol is likely to be important for other diseases, such as those that involve infection. In these cases, an entirely different biological cascade must be specified.

Still, we can point to one biological route that possesses some generality: the immune system. The immune system is made up of organs that make and store immune cells (e.g., the spleen, lymph nodes, bone marrow, and the thymus) as well as the immune cells themselves. These cells are primarily white blood cells that serve various functions in the fight against infectious disease. They recognize molecules foreign to one's body and then destroy or inactivate the foreign molecules that are recognized. The foreign molecules range from external pathogens such as a virus or bacterium to an abnormal internal product such as a tumor. Many different cells are involved in an immune response (e.g., macrophages, helper T cells, cytotoxic T cells, and B cells), and there are various ways in which they combine to mount an attack.

To be successful, the immune response requires the coordination of these different reactions. Signals from the nervous system as well as hormones from the endocrine glands under the control of the nervous system are involved in directing and regulating the sequence of cellular interactions that take place within the immune system. Immune organs such as the spleen and bone marrow are actually innervated by the sympathetic nervous system, and terminals of these sympathetic fibers make actual synaptic "contact" with white blood cells in these organs (for a review, see Felton & Felton, 1991). In addition, the white blood cells have receptors for many neurotransmitters and hormones, notably those secreted by the pituitary and adrenal glands.

The point? The connections necessary for the brain to influence the immune response are certainly present. Moreover, the substances produced by white blood cells during the immune response can in turn gain access to the brain and alter neural functioning. There is bidirectional communication between the nervous and immune systems that makes possible psychological influences on immunity and hence on health and disease.

Many of the neural and endocrine systems that influence immune responding respond to stress, and so it should be no surprise that stress can change how the immune system functions. The relevant literature is large, and easy conclusions do not emerge. The role of stressor controllability in particular is far from clear (Maier & Laudenslager, 1988). Many have wanted to conclude that stress somehow suppresses or interferes with proper immune functioning, thereby promoting disease (e.g., Peterson & Bossio, 1991). This simple statement, no matter how appealing, is not always justified. The effect of stress on immune function depends on the nature of the stressor, the immune measure employed, and a host of other factors.

Stress may reduce, have no effect on, or even enhance some chosen aspect of the immune response. And because the processes responsible for immunity are so complex, a decrease in one particular immune index need not indicate that the integrated immune response has been compromised. Another aspect of the immune response might compensate. It will take much further work to unravel and make sense of the relationships between stress and immune function. In the present context, we can nonetheless offer the positive conclusion that the immune system represents, in principle, a very important biological route between helplessness and physical health.

Granted the complexity involved, it is just as well that we have never wanted to put all of our explanatory eggs in a biological basket. We are not biological reductionists, and we think there is every reason in the world to look for additional routes between helplessness and health.

Emotional Routes

One of the best-established links in the entire psychological literature concerns the association between explanatory style and depression (Chapter 6). Literally hundreds of investigations have reported an association between pessimistic explanations for bad events and increases in one's depressive symptoms—among children, young adults, the middle-aged, and the elderly (Sweeney, Anderson, & Bailey, 1986). By obvious implication, an optimistic explanatory style is associated with positive emotional states, like happiness and joy.

This strong association is important because studies have linked increased depression with increased morbidity and mortality. These relationships hold even when suicide, a common concomitant of severe depression, is taken into account.

Pessimistic explanatory style has been linked not simply to depressive symptoms but also to anxiety disorders, to eating disorders, and to other emotional problems. Perhaps the most conservative thing to say about learned helplessness in general and pessimistic explanatory style in particular is that they lead to a variety of negative emotional states, what psychologists and psychiatrists call dysphoria: simply feeling badly (see Gallagher, 1988). Dysphoria may take the form of depression, or of anxiety, or of guilt, or of anger, or of hostility. The particular mix of these bad feelings probably depends on a host of other factors.

In Chapter 6, we presented arguments that learned helplessness is specific to depression, but there are still reasons to be skeptical. For our purposes in this chapter, the less-than-perfect mapping of helplessness and hopelessness into depression is perfectly alright, because recent evidence suggests that, of the emotional disorders, depression is not *uniquely* linked to poor health either. After reviewing several hundred investigations, Friedman and Booth-Kewley (1987) offer this conclusion: "There is strong evidence of a reliable association between illness and chronic psychological distress. Hence, treatment of medical patients by . . . psychologists seems prudent and worthwhile" (p. 552). Chronic psychological distress includes emotional states like anxiety, anger, hostility, and depression. Research shows these to be associated with illnesses like heart disease, asthma, ulcers, and arthritis, but the association is a general one, not a set of specific links matching particular emotions with particular illnesses. We suggest that pessimism is the underlying factor that cuts across these negative feelings and creates their association with poor health.

Our focus so far in the present section has been on "internal" routes—those inside the person. We looked in particular at biological and emotional routes. We turn next to routes that exist outside people and can be more readily seen. Remember our refrain here. No single route is likely to bear the sole load of linking learned helplessness with health.

Behavioral Routes

The way in which we behave reflects what we are thinking, and so we can expect that one of the most important routes from explanatory style to health lies in our behavior. Individuals with an optimistic explanatory style think and act in different ways than do their pessimistic counterparts. For instance, many studies show that those with a pessimistic style are lousy problem solvers. Just like the helpless animals described earlier in the book, they do not make good use of the evidence presented to them that things are better than they seem. And other studies show that those with an optimistic style persevere when it is reasonable to do so, staying at a task until it is done. In contrast, the pessimistic individual gives up and gives out. These characteristics of the optimistic person help him to achieve good health, whereas the characteristics of the pessimistic person may lead to ill health and even his early death.

Those with a pessimistic view of the causes of events act helplessly, suggesting that one route from pessimism to poor health lies through passivity in their health care. Several studies nicely support this extrapolation.

Healthy Habits.   For instance, Peterson (1988) assessed the explanatory style of 126 college students, along with their reported adherence to habits identified by epidemiologists as associated with good health and a long life (Belloc, 1973; Belloc & Breslow, 1972):

- Eating a balanced diet
- Avoiding salt
- Avoiding fat
- Exercising
- Eating breakfast
- Not smoking
- Not drinking to excess
- Sleeping eight hours a night

Pessimistic subjects were less likely than optimistic subjects to engage in these health-promoting activities.

In learned helplessness terms, the pessimistic individuals are taking the easy way out. This conclusion is buttressed by confidence ratings made by these subjects concerning whether they believed they could change their bad health habits. Those with a pessimistic explanatory style expressed less confidence that they would or could change. This finding is particularly important in light of reports that most people who break their bad health habits try several times before they succeed. For instance, among those who quit smoking, it takes an average of three relapses before the habit is finally broken (Prochaska, Velicer, DiClemente, & Fava, 1988).

Another study making the same point was an investigation by Peterson and Edwards (1992) of how people's explanatory style related to their perception of being at risk for health problems. Although the majority of individuals in their study showed an optimistic bias, perceiving their own risk for a variety of illnesses to be less than average (cf. Weinstein, 1989), people with an optimistic explanatory style were particularly likely to see themselves at low risk. Why? Other ratings by the subjects implied that the link between explanatory style and risk perception was entirely mediated by perceptions of the preventability of the health problems in question. Said another way, individuals with an optimistic explanatory style were optimistic about their health because they believed there were things they could do in order to be healthy.

Responses to Illness.   Another study of explanatory style and health-related behaviors was carried out by Peterson, Colvin, and Lin (1989). Seventy-two young adults in Ann Arbor completed the ASQ at one point in time and then for several weeks kept track of symptoms of illness they experienced as well as what—if anything—they did in order to feel better. Optimistic individuals were *less likely* to fall ill than pessimistic individuals, but when they did become ill, they were *more likely* to take active steps to feel better—resting more, increasing their intake of fluids, and the like.

Let us detail another finding from this investigation. Suppose you were sick during one week and you took active steps to feel better. Did this mean you were less likely to be sick the next week? The answer is no. Doing active things had no demonstrable effect on the course of one's illness. We admit that this finding was at first a bit surprising to us, and a little disappointing. It seems to be inconsistent with the story we have been telling. But then we realized that we were expecting effects of "healthy" habits to take place on a time scale that was implausible.

If it were so simple that resting one week made illness less likely the next week, this would be an obvious relationship that anyone could figure out, whether his or her explanatory style was optimistic or pessimistic. People wouldn't spend so much time mounting health-promotion campaigns if the connection between behavior and good health were direct and immediate, as opposed to subtle and distant. The very nature of these relationships is that they are nonobvious and take years or even decades to unfold. After all, public service announcements do not caution citizens against gargling with lye or sticking their hands in fans. These will have an immediate effect on one's well-being, to say the least!

We know that links exist between behavior and health; epidemiological evidence is unambiguous in documenting the relationships between certain habits and one's long-term health status. For instance, people who smoke live on the average twelve years less than those who do not smoke. So why do people smoke? Because the twelve years come off the far end of life. If everyone who lit up a cigarette suddenly lost the next twelve years, we wouldn't need warnings from the surgeon general on cigarette packages.

The point is that a person's inclination to act on documented links between her behavior and subsequent health must be based on her belief. She must expect with confidence that what she does or does not do today will have effects, for better or for worse, in the distant future. This is exactly what optimistic explanatory style entails, of course, and so our results do make sense. Optimistic people take preventive steps when they are ill, even though the payoffs are not immediate. The benefits of health promotion are not even guaranteed. They are simply generalizations. But the optimistic person goes with what is likely. What other realistic choice is there?

In our next study that looked at the association between explanatory style and health-related behavior, Lin and Peterson (1990) administered the ASQ to ninety-six University of Michigan students, along with a questionnaire describing various active responses to illness (see Table 8-2). Respondents were asked what they usually did when they fell ill in order to feel better. Optimistic individuals were more likely to take active steps—individually and collectively—than were pessimistic individuals.

The same subjects in this study were also asked to describe their most recent bout of illness, as well as their reaction to this episode, using the Ways of Coping questionnaire devised by Lazarus and Folkman (1984). Part of this questionnaire asks a respondent to describe what is "at stake" during a stressful event. There was an association between pessimism and an individual's fear that he or she would be rejected or ridiculed for falling ill. We will return to this finding in the next section when we talk about the interpersonal aspects of explanatory style. For now our point is that the pessimistic individual who falls ill seems to face two problems—her illness and her fear of rejection by others because she is ill.

Also part of the Ways of Coping measure are particular coping attempts that a person may or may not make in a particular situation. We identified a number of responses that seemed to show

Table 8-2. Active Responses to
Illness.

I increase my rest and sleep.
I am more likely to go to bed on time.
I cut back on strenuous exercise.
I decrease my work load.
I visit a doctor or a clinic.
I take over-the-counter medication.
I take prescription medication.
I increase vitamins.
I eat more nutritious food than usual.
I eat less junk food than usual.
I am more likely to eat meals on schedule.
I increase my fluids (juice, soup, and so on).
I get more fresh air than usual.
I get more sunlight than usual.
I use a humidifier.
I use extra covers on my bed.
I increase the temperature in my room.
I put aside any worries I might have.

Source: Lin, E. H., & Peterson, C. (1990). Pessimistic explanatory style and response to illness.
Behaviour Research and Therapy 28:243–249. © 1990
by Pergamon Press Ltd. Adapted by permission
of the publisher.

either a "helpless" reaction to illness or its opposite "active" reaction, like the following:

- I blamed myself (helpless).
- I went along with fate (helpless).
- I felt bad because I couldn't avoid the situation (helpless).
- I realized I brought the problem on myself (helpless).
- I made a plan of action and followed it (active).
- I came up with a couple of different solutions (active).

A composite measure of these responses showed a moderately strong
relationship to a person's explanatory style. Optimistic individuals
were active in their attempts to cope with illness; pessimistic individuals were helpless.

Health Promotion. So we have found in several studies that optimistic explanatory style is reflected in healthy behavior that aims at
either preventing illness in the first place or minimizing its effects
once it occurs. That the actions we take can provide a route be-

tween learned helplessness and our physical well-being is thus quite likely, suggesting a ready target for the health professional who wishes to intervene and help people lead longer and more satisfying lives.

Peterson and Stunkard (1989) recently reviewed the vast literature on health promotion. Despite its promise, we came up with some disappointing conclusions. Health promotion is currently a field without a unifying theory of how to change people's behavior for the better. What it is in effect is a heap of techniques, some of which work some of the time, some of which work other times, and some of which never work—all with no good explanation why. The typical health-promotion message is a mixture of simplistic moral exhortation and complex technical information. ("Is this 'good' cholesterol or 'bad' cholesterol?") Perhaps not surprisingly, some individuals—like minorities and those from the lower class—are notoriously unreached and unmoved by health-promotion messages.

One of the problems with health-promotion programs as they currently exist is that they treat all people the same, neglecting the important social and personality differences that exist among us. In particular, we think that health-promotion programs should pay attention to someone's explanatory style. Those with optimistic versus pessimistic explanatory styles need different messages. The optimistic individual may merely need to be told the right information. The pessimistic individual may need to have her sense of efficacy boosted before such information becomes relevant to her.

Interpersonal Routes

We now consider one final route between explanatory style and health. We have mentioned several times already that other people have something to do with our physical well-being. People with a rich network of supportive individuals to whom they can turn in trouble live longer and healthier lives. They are more robust in the face of stress and hassles in everyday life (Cobb, 1976). The existence of friendships is a good predictor of health and longevity (House, Landis, & Umberson, 1988). Even people with a pet seem to outlive people who do not have a furry friend to keep them company (Friedmann, Katcher, Lynch, & Thomas, 1980). There is something healthy about a good companion, whether with two legs or four.

On the other hand, deficient or ruptured human relationships diminish health and happiness. For example, in the six months fol-

lowing the death of a spouse, the surviving individual is at increased risk for death. People who are lonely do not live as long—
never mind the fact that they may not be coming into contact with
as many germs as people with lots of friends!

It is not our purpose to explain all these effects of other people
on someone's physical health. The influences of social support and
social interaction on health are fully as complex as those of explanatory style, and they probably share many of the same pathways
we have already detailed—biological, emotional, and behavioral.
Rather, let us just take these effects as a given and spend the remainder of this chapter examining the relationship between explanatory style and how we get along with others. The yield of this
examination is the specification of yet another route between the
absence of helplessness and health—one that runs through good
interpersonal relationships.

Craig Anderson and his colleagues have shown in several studies
that pessimistic individuals are lonely and socially estranged (e.g.,
Anderson & Arnoult, 1985a). They administered a version of the
ASQ to research subjects, along with a standard questionnaire measuring loneliness that asks how frequently they experience feelings
like the following:

- There is no one I can turn to.
- I feel left out.
- No one really knows me well.
- My social relationships are superficial.

The link between pessimism and loneliness is as robust as that between pessimism and depression, prompting Anderson to suggest
that these are not altogether separate phenomena. We concur. Optimistic individuals, of course, have more numerous and more satisfying social relationships.

Why are pessimistic people so lonely? A study by Gotlib and Beatty
(1985) gives a clue. They asked research subjects to read about hypothetical individuals who talked about their lives and what was
happening in them. Everything was the same about the vignettes
with the exception of the causal explanations that were tucked into
the narratives. Some of the scenarios depicted people who were
optimistic in their explanations, that is, using external, unstable,
and specific causes. Other scenarios depicted people who explained
events in a pessimistic fashion with internal, stable, and global causes.
Then Gotlib and Beatty asked their subjects how they would re-

spond to these people. They would reject the pessimistic individual yet feel attracted to the optimistic one! Think about how *you* respond to someone who is pessimistic. You may want to cheer him up or give him hope, but his assertions that nothing can be done are daunting, to say the least.

One thing we certainly know about depression and pessimism is that these are contagious states. Depression runs through families. So too does doom and gloom. We have shown, for instance, that pessimistic parents also have pessimistic children (Seligman et al., 1984). Perhaps the subjects in Gotlib and Beatty's study recognize this fact about pessimism, and they take pains to protect themselves from the corrosive presence of a pessimistic acquaintance.

We do not believe that anyone has looked at this matter, but we speculate that people with a pessimistic explanatory style—in addition to whatever other problems they may have—are notably deficient at fending off others who will rain on their already soggy parades. We suspect that they do not actively pursue friends but rather take in whoever walks through the front door. They do not call the shots in their relationships. To the degree that the pessimistic individual ends up with other pessimistic people as friends—and we are pretty sure that this is what happens—we then have yet another one of those vicious circles by now so familiar when we look at pessimism. The relevance to physical well-being is of course obvious. The pessimistic individual does not receive the benefits of "other people." The optimistic individual of course does.

Remember the study we described in Chapter 5, in which college students were asked to think of a particular friend and then to report the frequency with which the friend performed prototypically helpless behaviors (Peterson, 1986). In a followup study, subjects were asked to describe how *they* responded to their friend when he or she acted in these ways. If the friends infrequently acted in a helpless fashion, then they were given help and sympathy. But if the friends frequently acted helplessly, they were treated with anger or ignored or avoided. Who could blame them? Being around listless people has a cost.

These results cohere, showing that pessimistic people are lonely and socially estranged from others because they turn people off, because they act in excessively helpless ways. In the short run, a friend can and does meet the needs and demands of someone who needs assistance. This is rewarding and the very business of friendship. But in the long run, most people do not continue to meet such demands. It must seem to them as if the pessimistic individual is never satisfied—and that is the point. Her friend can himself become pessimistic as he begins to feel "helpless" because of the lack of any connection between what he does and how his friend acts. Or he can pick up and leave. He will take the latter course more often than not, we suppose, leaving the pessimistic person without the buffer against ill health that good relationships can provide.

This cannot be entirely a mystery to the pessimistic individual. Let's return to the finding we earlier described that a pessimistic person who falls ill fears that she will be rejected by others because of her illness. On the face of it, this seems like a groundless fear. By and large, people do not blame each other for falling ill. But perhaps the pessimistic person is like the boy who cried wolf, complaining so frequently that others become indifferent to further requests for aid and support, now legitimate granted the person is ill! Again, we see an example of the pessimistic individual making things worse than they need to be.

HEALTH AND ILLNESS IN ANIMALS VERSUS PEOPLE

Our original intent in this chapter was to integrate the animal research on learned helplessness and health with the human research. At a distance, the findings are certainly parallel. The cognitive, motivational, and emotional consequences of uncontrollability are quite similar for animals and people (Chapters 2 and 4). That these consequences can influence health and illness is clear. Nonetheless, as we looked more closely at the relevant lines of research, trying to bridge them at more than a surface level, we were struck by the disanalogies. With some thought, the discrepancies made sense. Let us share with you our thinking along these lines.

In the typical animal experiment, a research subject is exposed to some stressor or other event and then infected with a pathogen, injected with tumor cells, and so on. The researcher then determines the impact of the stressor on the development of disease. In such studies, exposure to a single session of a stressor such as inescapable shock often promotes illness. Furthermore, the stressor's controllability is important. For example, Sklar and Anisman (1979) gave mice a single session of either escapable, yoked inescapable, or no shock—that is, the triadic design (Chapter 2)—immediately before they injected the mice with tumor cells. In the rats exposed to inescapable shock, the tumor cells grew rapidly, eventually leading to death. Escapable shock had no effect on tumor growth and mortality.

This is just the sort of result that makes the animal and human literatures appear consistent with each other. Why then are we so cautious about drawing parallels? We have two reasons. First, the result just described depends on a host of factors. The stressor has to occur very close in time to the injection of tumor cells (Ben-Eliyahu, Yirma, Liebeskind, Taylor, & Gale, 1991), the general background stress under which the animal is maintained has to be low (Sklar & Anisman, 1980), and so on. Although stress and helplessness seem to have a general impact on health in people, their impact in animals is moderated by numerous special features of the situation.

The second reason we find the animal and human literatures to be different from each other is that repeated or chronic stress among animals most often has either no effect on the development of disease from an administered agent or an actual protective effect. Sklar and Anisman (1979), for example, found that exposing mice to a session of inescapable shock once a day for five to ten days after inoculation with tumor cells did *not* promote tumor growth as a single exposure had. Moreover, other studies have found that chronic exposure to a stressor may retard tumor growth and decrease mortality (see Sklar & Anisman, 1981, for a review). This same result has been reported with respect to other diseases induced in animal experiments. In contrast, the studies with people that we described earlier in this chapter were concerned with chronic stress, not single exposures to discrete stressors; unlike animals, people exposed to chronic stress become less healthy.

We have elsewhere suggested that animals and people show remarkable similarities in their reactions to stressors that vary in controllability, so why the difference here? One critical factor may be that the studies with animals versus people typically proceed quite differently. In the animal experiments, a specific agent is administered that produces a particular disease, and the progress of that disease is tracked. In the human studies, health as a whole is measured by researchers, not a given disease that originates at a single point in time. In the human studies, therefore, the exact timing between stress and pathogen exposure is less critical, because there are so many encounters with so many potential pathogens. There are countless occasions on which the development of disease might be influenced. If the studies with people exposed them to a specific pathogen and a single stressor, the results might well be as situationally specific as those from the animal literature.

Another difference between the animal and human studies of the effects of chronic stress is that the animals are repeatedly exposed to the same stressful event, such as inescapable shock. The possibility of adaptation to this stressor is obviously maximized. This is not the case for the people who participate in studies of chronic stress.

More generally, the mediating links between helplessness and health are probably different in animals versus people. We have already noted that health and illness among people today are determined in part by life-style. People have available to them behavioral choices that can promote health and prevent disease. Personal dispositions such as explanatory style influence these choices and thereby their health. Thus, stress influences health among people in indirect ways that have no counterpart among animals.

Certainly, stress produces hormonal, immunological, and neurochemical changes among people, as among animals, and these changes can affect one's ability to fight off disease. But the power of stress to alter as well someone's health behavior may be an even more important influence, particularly over the long haul.

In animals, stress can influence health only in direct fashion. Rats and mice do not have intentionally chosen life-styles. They do not have knowledge to deploy about healthy versus unhealthy habits. So what we learn from animal experiments about the links between helplessness and physical health is quite different from what we learn from human studies. Learned helplessness ideas have been useful in drawing the attention of researchers to these links in both animals and people, but our conclusion for the time being is that these links are probably not the same.

WHAT WE KNOW

The studies we have described in this chapter are consistent with our hypothesis that learned helplessness is associated with poor health; its absence is associated with good health. Investigations have looked at the three components of learned helplessness—passivity, uncontrollability, and cognition—and found that individually each is linked to physical well-being. These investigations ascertained health status in widely different ways: by physical examinations; by reports of symptoms; by visits to physicians; by survival times following a cancer diagnosis; by recovery following a heart attack; and by T4/T8 ratios reflecting immunocompetence. We conclude, therefore, that learned helplessness is pertinent to health. Our research into this matter includes both animal and human work, convincing us that learned helplessness is a notion of broad applicability.

Just why learned helplessness is involved in health does not admit to such a simple conclusion. Our suspicion is that no single mechanism is entailed. Rather, one can argue for the pertinence of biological, emotional, behavioral, *and* interpersonal routes, with none bearing the sole explanatory burden. Complicating matters further is the possibility that the mix changes from animals to people, from person to person, from illness to illness, and/or across time.

WHAT WE DON'T KNOW

We started the chapter with a caution that this work is still ongoing and much more preliminary than other work on learned helplessness. The role of explanatory style has been investigated much more thoroughly than that of other helplessness constructs, and even here, the relevant data are merely correlational. Not all possible third variables have been controlled. We do not yet know whether explanatory style interacts with stress to predispose illness. More generally, studies to date have not looked simultaneously at the three components of learned helplessness and how they relate to illness. Our prediction would of course be that some interaction among these components should occur, but to date this is untested.

Another shortcoming so far is that most of this work has not been subjected to much critical scrutiny. This is ironic, because we have highlighted conceptual skirmishes throughout the book. In other domains, we could do with less controversy. But in the domain of physical health, we would welcome more. Perhaps our claim that helplessness and pessimism predispose illness is so much an aspect of the current Zeitgeist that everyone accepts it as necessarily true. Perhaps we have done the same. Has learned helplessness come full circle, from a maverick perspective to part of the scientific status quo?

Assuming that learned helplessness becomes a viable account of illness, there is no shortage of unanswered questions. First, does helplessness affect the onset of a person's illness, or the course once it begins, or both? We suspect the answer is both. At the same time, recognize that learned helplessness does not operate in isolation, apart from all the other possible influences on our bodies and our feelings. Someone in the pink of physical health will not court illness by a moment of passivity or an occasional negative thought.

And someone at death's door will not be rescued by feelings of efficacy.

Second, is learned helplessness related to particular types of illness—like cancer or heart disease—or to illness in general? Again, granted the multiplicity of consequences, we suspect that helplessness is a nonspecific risk factor and its absence a generic buffer.

We saw in the studies of college students that colds and the flu seem to be influenced by explanatory style, but this does not mean that other illnesses are not. Similarly, the study by Sandra Levy on survival time of patients with breast cancer shows that the course of cancer is influenced by explanatory style, but again this does not mean that other illnesses are not. In the Harvard Study of Adult Development, illness was explicitly studied in nonspecific terms. If you take a close look at the men in the Harvard Study and the illnesses from which they suffered, you see a variety of maladies. So we suspect a nonspecific link, but we are not entirely sure. There could be one primary problem associated with pessimism, from which the other illnesses stem.

Third, which criteria of poor health are most sensitive to learned helplessness? Probably those that rely on the individual's self-report of symptoms, although there are some subtleties involved in our logic. On the one hand, the individual is in a privileged position to know how he feels. Self-reports in principle can be more sensitive than "objective" medical tests. On the other hand, the individual is also subject to the tendency to distort how he feels, either for better or for worse. Explanatory style might in turn affect these tendencies. Costa and McCrae (1987), for instance, argue that "neurotic" individuals—among whom would be included our dysphoric pessimists—exaggerate their symptoms. Presumably, those with an optimistic explanatory style do not.

In the short run, then, we have reason to distrust self-reported symptoms. But in the long run, we expect them to be valid, because they can become self-fulfilling by setting into operation the processes we have described here. Even if the pessimistic individual isn't quite correct when he first describes his symptoms, he eventually will be!

Several intriguing studies by epidemiologists make a similar point (Kaplan & Camacho, 1983; Mossey & Shapiro, 1982). When people are asked to rate their overall health—excellent, good, fair, or poor—at one point in time, this rating ends up predicting how long they live. Here's the punch line: "perceived" health translates itself into longevity even when every other factor that epidemiologists can think of is held constant statistically: sex, age, so-called objective health status as indexed by chronic diseases and disabilities, health practices, income, education, and so on. When those who considered their health "excellent" were compared with those who considered their health "poor"—and all these other factors were held constant by the researchers—their risk of death within the subsequent decade was about one-third!

Fourth, what about sex differences in the relationship of learned helplessness and illness? Here we tentatively conclude that learned helplessness does not explain the sex differences in morbidity and mortality. Although women are more likely than men to be depressed, and thus more likely to experience the sorts of illness that are made more likely by depression, we do not have any good evidence that the sex difference in depression originates in any tendency for women to be pessimistic and men to be optimistic with regard to explanatory style (see Chapter 6). Our measures almost always yield the same average scores for men and women in our samples.

Fifth, what is the effect on health of someone changing from more to less helpless? We know that explanatory style can be changed through cognitive therapy and that these changes appear stable (Chapter 6). Does the person who has made such changes reap the same health benefits as the person who was efficacious all along? We would think so, granted appropriate time periods. Clearly, psychological influences on health and illness do not take place instantaneously.

We raise these unanswered questions for several reasons. One reason is simply to be honest about the state of our knowledge. These are not trivial matters, and we should not overstate what we know about helplessness and health. We think that the association between thinking "good" and feeling "well" is pretty well established, but no matter how secure this relationship, we need to know a great deal more in order to make sense of it.

NOTES

1. As it turns out, not all T4 cells are helpers, and not all T8 cells are suppressors, which means that the T4/T8 ratio is somewhat equivocal as a measure of immunocompetence. Our earlier point that all measures of health and illness must be regarded with skepticism is again illustrated.

9

Epilogue

We have come to the end of our learned helplessness story, but of course research continues on the many fronts we have described. In this final chapter, we step back and take a look at what we have accomplished in our study of learned helplessness thus far and where we might be headed in the future.

A BRIEF HISTORY OF CHOICES

Learned helplessness was discovered in the animal learning laboratory of Richard Solomon at the University of Pennsylvania in 1964. With their colleagues there, Steven Maier and Martin Seligman were young researchers challenging the scientific status quo. Some thirty years later, their work has become an integral part of psychology. How did this come to pass?

Someone naive to the history of science might assume that the learned helplessness model became popular simply because it was correct. But scientific progress does not work that way. Correct ideas do not inevitably triumph over incorrect ones. All sorts of social factors shape the acceptance or rejection of ideas, and in this case, learned helplessness prospered while other perspectives fell by the wayside. We suggest that it was because some fortunate choices were made, which kept learned helplessness party to what was happening through the 1970s and 1980s, surely a tumultuous time for the whole of psychology.

One good decision was to explain learned helplessness in cognitive terms. As we noted in Chapter 2, learned helplessness theorizing from the very first joined in the battle against S-R conceptions of behavior, siding with the view that thoughts and beliefs—as opposed to peripheral motor movements—were the more sensible way to describe what was going on. Traditional behaviorism put up a fight, but the battle is now over. The "cognitive revolution" has been waged successfully (Gardner, 1985).

Interestingly, with the triumph of cognitive views has come discontent with precisely this perspective, which renders human action too rational, too calm, and too orderly. Learned helplessness may well be able to survive this counterrevolution, which is redirecting psychology's attention to emotion and motivation. After all, learned helplessness is concerned precisely with the motivational and emotional consequences of particular cognitions.

A second good choice was to include human beings as subjects in the research program, in addition to the dogs and rats used when helplessness was first studied. Being able to go back and forth between the animal and the human laboratories is what psychology has wanted to do since animal research became popular at the beginning of the twentieth century, but for the most part, this proved an empty hope. The traditional theories used to explain animal behavior become spectacularly awkward when applied to people. No one—including research subjects—could take the generalization too seriously. Learned helplessness was different because the theoretical emphasis on representations and expectations of control is as plausible for people as for animals.

A third choice we made that has added to the staying power of learned helplessness was the decision to apply the model to significant human problems: depression (Chapter 6), poor achievement (Chapter 7), and illness (Chapter 8). Often the fit has been quite good. But even in those cases in which it has been but approximate, we again have delivered on a promise that psychology has long made, to say something important about the human condition. The fact that our work has pointed to possible solutions for maladaptive behavior is of course all the better.

The cognitive perspective we brought to bear on these problems was exactly what the rest of psychology was doing as well. Witness Beck's cognitive theory of depression, the various attributional interpretations of social problems, and the development of the field of psychoneuroimmunology, all of which were coincidental with our work. What distinguishes learned helplessness from these other cognitive approaches to disparate problems is that it is general, using the same constructs to explain a variety of failures of adaptation. We are able to move readily from one problem to another, using the same explanatory model. The model itself is simple, and our theoretical predictions are always a priori, not after-the-fact summaries of clinical observations.

In earlier chapters, we railed against traditional learning theories, but their spirit still pervades our work on learned helplessness. We have always searched for broadly applicable explanations. We think we have been successful. The earlier behavioristic attempts failed, not because they were general, but because they cast their lot with peripheral rather than central explanations.

A fourth decision we made was to devise simple research procedures—either for laboratory experiments or correlational investigations—and to stay with them until we had mastered them. Some psychology researchers are overly promiscuous in their choice of methods, flitting from one procedure to another. This underestimates the difficulty of conducting even the simplest of studies.

A fifth choice we should emphasize is that at least as far as our own research goes, we have always chosen to look at the glass as half full. We deal in "positive" science, proposing our ideas and seeing how well we can support them. We are, of course, attentive to other theories and anomalous data, but we do not regard complexities as roadblocks. We focus on what we have learned, what is clear, and what is simple, and we keep on working. Too many psychologists become paralyzed at the complexity of behavioral phenomena, to the point where no theory seems to do them justice, no study can be anything but trivial, no conclusion can be anything but wrong. This is the proper stuff for Existentialism 101, we suppose, but it can hardly move us toward a complex, realistic theory of any human behavior.

A sixth choice we made was to use vivid language in explaining the phenomenon of learned helplessness. "Learned helplessness" captures everyone's interest, including our own, more than the descriptive yet dry "failure to escape traumatic shock," which was the title of one of the very first articles describing the phenomenon in animals (Seligman & Maier, 1967). "Explanatory style" is a vivid term for an individual difference in how one offers causal attributions, which distinguishes the notion from any of a number of others with "attributional" labels. Calling explanatory style "optimistic" or "pessimistic" is similarly a vivid choice of terms (Peterson, 1991).

Recently Peterson and Seligman have been writing much more about optimism than about helplessness (e.g., Peterson & Bossio,

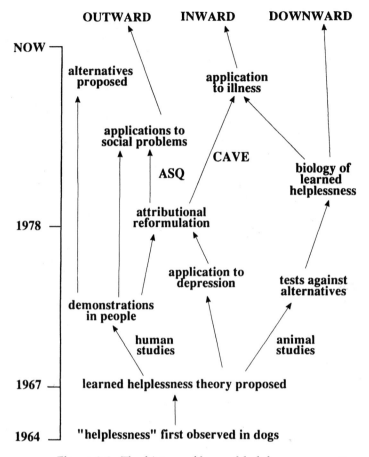

Figure 9-1. The history of learned helplessness.

1991; Seligman, 1990). To some degree, this is nothing new, because we conceptualize these notions as opposites. Everything we have learned about helplessness is something we have learned about optimism, and vice versa. Yet it also puts our work in a fresh context. For twenty-five years we spoke about how notions of control played a role in what went wrong with people. Now we are using the same results to discuss what can go right. That our focus on helplessness occurred during the global malaise of the 1970s and 1980s, whereas our switch to optimism occurred with the more upbeat 1990s, was hardly self-conscious. But it was a good choice.

Figure 9-1 shows the history of learned helplessness. Two things should be emphasized about this depiction. The work has become increasingly diverse as the years have passed, so that it is probably more correct to talk about the *fields* of learned helplessness nowa-days than about a single endeavor. But at the same time, our notion of the basic phenomenon—defined by cognitions, uncontrollability, and deficits—has stayed the same. We have been willing to modify and extend these ideas greatly, but we never wavered in our con-ception of learned helplessness as cognitive.

What about the future of learned helplessness research? Where is it going?

Chris Peterson has taken on the role of a health psychologist, inquiring into the psychological context of health and illness. The research described in Chapter 8 is one example of this new direc-tion, but it also includes asking how people cope with chronic or acute difficulties, in themselves or in their loved ones. The focus here is on causal explanations, perceptions of control, and the like.

Steven Maier has become ever more interested in the psycholog-ical influences on immunology. As described in Chapters 3 and 8, the controllability of stressors has broad effects on the very physi-ology of animals and people. Just why this is so entails a very close look at the biochemistry involved, and Maier is moving in that di-rection. However, it should be stressed that he is not an immunol-ogist. He is still interested in behavior and particularly control, which places his work in a psychological tradition.

Martin Seligman has become interested in social applications of this work, attempting to devise programs that can immunize schoolchildren against the long-term effects of uncontrollability. In particular, he wishes to stem the rising incidence of depression, which is on a precipitous climb among the young (Chapter 6). But these programs may pay additional benefits in boosting achievement at school and work (Chapter 7), and perhaps even adding to chil-dren's physical well-being (Chapter 8). To these ends, he has adapted cognitive therapy techniques to boost one's sense of control and efficacy to classroom exercises and is deploying them in schools in the Philadelphia area.

In Chapter 1, we noted that learned helplessness has proceeded in three general directions: inward, downward, and outward. As we see it, these continue to be the directions of the future growth in the field.

THE IMPORTANCE OF CONTROL

Learned helplessness rode the crest of the cognitive revolution, but it made a unique contribution as well, ushering in a view of control as one of the most important psychological variables. Other theorists had talked about control before, but work on learned helplessness has documented the importance of this variable in the broadest of terms—from biochemical to societal levels.

At the same time, in attempting to explain the consequences of variations in control, we have uncovered an ever-increasing complexity. Every time we try to specify a single mechanism or process by which control or its absence asserts its influence, we discover more and more things going on. The processes we hypothesize are apparently at work, but they are just some of many players on a crowded stage. We saw this in the basic research on learned helplessness in animals (Chapter 2), in the attempt to discover the biological underpinnings of the phenomenon (Chapter 3), in the basic research on learned helplessness in people (Chapter 4), in the attributional reformulation (Chapter 5), and in the various applications of helplessness ideas.

On the one hand, this is frustrating, particularly for self-proclaimed simplophiles. On the other hand, if we take a step back, the multiplicity of control's influences underscores the importance of this psychological process. Control is so crucial that its impact is evident in all possible systems. And why not? What is life if not a struggle against entropy? If ongoing events can be harnessed in useful ways, then we can benefit from our activity. And control is the psychological process by which this harnessing of events and circumstances is registered.

We suspect that notions of evolution can be cast in the language of control as we have been using it—in terms of contingency and noncontingency. Evolution is a struggle to fit one's niche, to know what it affords and what it does not, and to stay vigorous enough to reap these benefits, to survive as an individual and as a species. People, of course, take this struggle one step further, actively manipulating their niche to make it desirable, which is to say, under their control.

Is there a vision of human nature lurking here? We think so. People are highly sensitive to their world, particularly its causal texture. Although our efforts to specify the fine detail of this sensitivity—how it is acquired and represented and used to channel subsequent action—are ongoing, we nonetheless can say with confidence that people strive to appreciate what they can and cannot control. Whatever they learn is registered deeply and profoundly, influencing everything from physiological processes to world politics.

Learned helplessness is of interest precisely in situations where control is possible. Conversely, a blithely efficacious individual in an unresponsive world is just as dysfunctional as the ineffectual person in a controllable situation. Nowhere do we claim that blind perseverance is invariably beneficial. It depends on one's setting, and the learned helplessness vision of human nature therefore leads to an interactional view, one that is currently popular in psychological theorizing.

So perceived control is counterproductive if the person's situation is truly unresponsive. Then "helplessness" becomes a way of conserving energy and a way of coping with that situation. Indeed, as we have noted in passing, there are hints that helpless animals are quicker to catch on to noncontingency, and they pay more attention to external cues (Chapter 2). Along these lines, depressed people are more likely to appraise their lack of control in a realistic fashion (Chapter 6). All of this means that helplessness may be less a deficit than an alternative way of operating, a way of laying low and keeping one's eyes open when the world becomes unresponsive. That helplessness has a time course, in both people and animals, further supports this interpretation. Perhaps if one lays low long enough, the causal texture of the world will change, making it finally safe to begin again and explore the landscape.

Maybe helpless animals or people are well served in the short run by being listless, because they do not further engage their futile worlds. This would only further grind in the lesson of noncontingency. As W. C. Fields supposedly remarked, "If at first you don't succeed, try again. Then quit. There's no sense being stupid about things."

LEARNED HELPLESSNESS AS A MODEL OF SCIENTIFIC DISPUTE AND PROGRESS

Above and beyond our substantive ideas and findings, we regard learned helplessness as an instructive case study of how science progresses. We have referred to the controversies surrounding the theory throughout the book, sometimes with a hint of annoyance, but in point of fact, controversies like these are usually an indication that one is on to something intriguing. If and when the controversy ends, we will assume that we have become boring or redundant or both.

As we have mentioned before, learned helplessness evolved from our stance as simplophiles, and it strikes us as ironic that our simple assumptions have led us to a complex view of behavior. Perhaps the lesson here is that progress in science does not occur when one starts with the position that matters are hopelessly complex— just the contrary.

Besides keeping us on the learned helplessness track, our simple view of matters paid an additional benefit. The complex view at which we have arrived is not an abstract slogan. When we say that control impacts a number of the body's physiological systems, we can enumerate them (Chapter 3). When we say that there are several ways in which uncontrollability produces a cognitive deficit, we can specify them (Chapter 4). When we say that learned helplessness may be involved in a variety of social problems entailing listlessness, we can list what they might be (Chapter 7).

Learned helplessness theory and research are therefore a testimony to the importance of details, of particulars. Some of our critics have charged that we are oblivious to data that do not fit our preconceptions, but this charge seems to be very much at odds with the facts. Learned helplessness has all along been informed by data. There have been several important changes in the way the theory has been conceived, as applied to animals and to people, and in each case, these changes were data driven.

LEARNED HELPLESSNESS AND THE AGE OF PERSONAL CONTROL

As we proposed in Chapter 1, learned helplessness is an important theory for the present because those of us in the Western world seem to be living in an era in which personal control is an overarching issue. We are also wary of the future, because this incredible emphasis on personal control has its costs. We argued that the epidemic of depression among young adults represents a disorder of personal control (Chapter 6). But there may well be less obvious manifestations of this emphasis on personal control, such things as the rise of materialism and cynicism about politics and social institutions. Generally speaking, the incredible selfishness of the American people can be phrased in terms of personal control.

If people's immediate worlds are responsive to them, then they believe they are living the good life. We have become ensconced in technological cocoons, with remote controls for our television sets, our compact disc players, our videotape players. We have cordless telephones, fax machines, and personal computers connected through modems to sources of information around the world. We are not questioning these technological advances. We are suggesting that such devices are seductive, that they promise more than they actually deliver. Rather than allowing us to get to the substance of life in a more efficient way, they have become the substance itself, crowding other matters—murkier and less responsive to be sure—out of the scene.

Our technological world provides a quick fix, the psychological equivalent of junk food. Our research shows why immediately responsive outcomes are so desirable. They are invigorating. They tap something very deep within us, what Robert White (1959) some decades ago called *effectance motivation*. People are motivated to interact in a competent way with their environment. And how else can people judge their competence except by ascertaining the control they have? These technological gadgets are more responsive than anything we have ever seen on this planet. The problem is that the outcomes over which they give us such exquisite control may be trivial.

Many of us have become addicted to technological gadgets because other sources of potential satisfaction are not nearly so responsive. Part of our socialization is to fill each of us with boundless expectations—anyone can be president, or a tennis champion, or a movie star, or a CEO. None of these is an easy role to attain. Indeed, the vast majority of people never come close to these sorts of achievements. No wonder the age of personal control takes such a toll.

We cannot banish the importance of control any more than we can turn back the clock on technology. Control is such an important psychological process that it affects our very brain chemistry (Chapter 3). Its importance will always remain. What we decry is the crowding out of other concerns. Our task as a society is to find better ways of dealing with control, so that we end up with fewer casualties. We should help people satisfy their desire for control in less egocentric ways as well as encourage them to value additional goals.

This would take various forms, we imagine. To begin with, we should endeavor to make the social world as responsive as the world of technology. By this we do not mean simply scheming to get others to be more responsive to our needs. Rather, we must remember that each of us is part of the social world of everyone else, and we should become more responsive to *them:* clearly, directly, and immediately.

Along these lines, we should make our social institutions more responsive. We need to get rid of court cases that drag on for years, laws and social conventions that are flouted, reforms that leave everything exactly as they were, politicians who are indistinguishable from one another except by their one-liners, court decisions that are at odds with what citizens believe, products that do not work, checks that are not in the mail.

More profoundly, we should inculcate an orientation to the common good in our society. We need to make the interdependence of people something that we value. Only when we start to take other people's welfare seriously will they start to do so for us. This seems to be a prerequisite for creating a world that is responsive, one that will encourage efficacy on the part of all. When we stop competing against one another in destructive ways, we all can be satisfied about our accomplishments.

Perhaps at one time such a vision more clearly characterized the United States. Perhaps not. In any case, it does not now. Special interests abound in our society, and their agendas become more narrow every year. Unity has been replaced by diversity. Let us raise the politically unpopular point that increased attention to the differences among our people will not make this society a better one in which to live.

We do not wish to gloss over the past, the fact that racism and sexism have excluded many individuals from the mainstream of our society. But a further split between people today is not a solution to past injustices; bringing them together in a true coalition is. This sounds like a moral argument, but we have arrived at it from our research. Our only assumption is that depression, demoralization, underachievement, and illness are bad. We think the lack of an orientation to the commons—the incredible selfishness that so abounds in our country—is in no small way responsible for these ills.

OPTIMISM INSTITUTES

So much for our sweeping recommendations. How are these to be brought about? Over the years, the United States government has generously funded basic research, including much of our own. We have learned something from this research, and we think it is time to apply what we have learned. We know how to remake society in a way that will benefit the individual and the group. We have seen enough small solutions. We think it is time for some very large solutions.

We call for a reinvigoration of the stagnant community mental health movement. We need more than bumper stickers and pamphlets. Psychology has taught us that information per se does not suffice to change well-established habits. People need the contingencies of the world to change. They need to be taught cognitive and behavioral skills for changing themselves, for thwarting demoralization and listlessness.

Our schools today are called on to do all sorts of things. Why not call on them to educate people in the most basic way possible, to prepare themselves to live in the world as happy, healthy, and productive individuals? Teach them how to persevere, how to maintain hope, how to be realistic on the one hand and visionary on the other. Encourage them to care about others and society as a whole. Reward them for competence and achievement. Acknowledge failure and shortcomings as well. Worry less about the self-esteem of students and more about the skills from which self-esteem will follow as a natural consequence.

At our most utopian, we envision the creation of Optimism Institutes, centers in which basic research on personal control is conducted and then applied, to schools, to work settings, to society itself. Staff these centers with individuals who themselves are optimistic about the possibilities of enlightened change using the lessons of psychological research. Involve citizens in the planning and evaluation of this kind of research and its applications. Make public opinion count. Let society judge whether these ideas are preferable to those that pervade our current age of personal control.

References

Aasen, N. (1987). Interventions to facilitate personal control. *Journal of Gerontological Nursing* 13:20–28.

Abbott, M. W. (1984). Unemployment responses from a community mental health perspective. *Mental Health in Australia* 1:24–31.

Abrams, R. D., and Finesinger, J. E. (1953). Guilt reactions in patients with cancer. *Cancer* 6:474–482.

Abramson, L. Y., Metalsky, G. I., and Alloy, L. B. (1989). Hopelessness depression: A theory-based subtype of depression. *Psychological Review* 96:358–372.

Abramson, L. Y., and Sackeim, H. A. (1977). A paradox in depression: Uncontrollability and self-blame. *Psychological Bulletin* 84:838–851.

Abramson, L. Y., Seligman, M. E. P., and Teasdale, J. D. (1978). Learned helplessness in humans: Critique and reformulation. *Journal of Abnormal Psychology* 87:49–74.

Affleck, G., Allen, D. A., McGrade, B. J., and McQueeney, M. (1982). Maternal causal attributions at hospital discharge of high-risk infants. *American Journal of Mental Deficiency* 86:575–580.

Aiken, M., and Hage, J. (1966). Organizational alienation: A comparative analysis. *American Sociological Review* 31:497–507.

Akil, H., Mayer, D. J., and Liebeskind, J. C. (1976). Antagonism of stimulation-produced analgesia by nalaxone, a narcotic antagonist. *Science* 191:961–962.

Akiskal, H. S., and McKinney, W. T. (1973). Depressive disorders: Toward a unified hypothesis. *Science* 182:20–29.

Akiskal, H. S., and McKinney, W. T. (1975). Overview of recent research in depression. *Archives of General Psychiatry* 32:285–305.

Alden, L. (1984). An attributional analysis of loneliness. *Cognitive Therapy and Research* 8:607–618.

Allen, M. G. (1976). Twin studies of affective illness. *Archives of General Psychiatry* 33:1476–1478.

Alloy, L. B. (1982a). Depression: On the absence of self-serving cognitive biases.

Paper presented at the Ninetieth Annual Meeting of the American Psychological Association, Washington, D.C.

Alloy, L. B. (1982b). The role of perceptions and attributions for response-outcome noncontingency in learned helplessness: A commentary and discussion. *Journal of Personality* 50:443–479.

Alloy, L. B., and Abramson, L. Y. (1979). Judgment of contingency in depressed and nondepressed students: Sadder but wiser? *Journal of Experimental Psychology: General* 108:441–485.

Alloy, L. B., and Abramson, L. Y. (1988). Depressive realism: Four theoretical perspectives. In *Cognitive processes in depression,* ed. L. B. Alloy. New York: Guilford.

Alloy, L. B., and Ahrens, A. H. (1987). Depression and pessimism for the future: Biased use of statistically relevant information in predictions for self versus others. *Journal of Personality and Social Psychology* 52:366–378.

Alloy, L. B., Peterson, C., Abramson, L. Y., and Seligman, M. E. P. (1984). Attributional style and the generality of learned helplessness. *Journal of Personality and Social Psychology* 46:681–687.

Alloy, L. B., and Seligman, M. E. P. (1979). On the cognitive component of learned helplessness and depression. In *The psychology of learning and motivation,* ed. G. H. Bower. Vol. 13. New York: Academic Press.

Altenor, A., Kay, E., and Richter, M. (1977). The generality of learned helplessness in the rat. *Learning and Motivation* 8:54–62.

Altmaier, E. M., and Happ, D. A. (1985). Coping skills training's immunization effects against learned helplessness. *Journal of Social and Clinical Psychology* 3:181–189.

Altman, I. (1975). *The environment and social behavior: Privacy, personal space, territory, and crowding.* Monterey, Calif.: Brooks/Cole.

American Psychiatric Association (1987). *Diagnostic and statistical manual of mental disorders.* 3d ed., rev. Washington, D.C.

Anderson, C. A. (1983). Motivational and performance deficits in interpersonal settings: The effects of attributional style. *Journal of Personality and Social Psychology* 45:1136–1147.

Anderson, C. A., and Arnoult, L. H. (1985a). Attributional models of depression, loneliness, and shyness. In *Attribution: Basic issues and applications,* ed. J. Harvey and G. Weary. New York: Academic Press.

Anderson, C. A., and Arnoult, L. H. (1985b). Attributional style and everyday problems in living: Depression, loneliness, and shyness. *Social Cognition* 3:16–35.

Anderson, C. A., Horowitz, L. M., and French, R. deS. (1983). Attributional style of lonely and depressed people. *Journal of Personality and Social Psychology* 45:127–136.

Anderson, C. A., and Jennings, D. L. (1980). When experiences of failure promote expectations of success: The impact of attributing failure to ineffective strategies. *Journal of Personality* 48:393–407.

Anderson, D. C., Crowell, C. R., Cunningham, C. L., and Lupo, J. V. (1978). Behavior during shock exposure as a determinant of subsequent interference with shuttle box escape-avoidance learning in the rat. *Journal of Experimental Psychology: Animal Behavior Processes* 5:243–257.

Anisman, H. (1975). Time-dependent variations in aversively motivated behaviors: Non-associative effects of cholinergic and catecholaminergic activity. *Psychological Review* 82:359–385.

Anisman, H., deCatanzaro, D., and Remington, G. (1978). Escape performance following exposure to inescapable shock: Deficits in motor response maintenance. *Journal of Experimental Psychology: Animal Behavior Processes* 4:197–218.

Anisman, H., Irwin, J., and Sklar, L. S. (1979). Deficits of escape performance following catecholamine depletion: Implications for behavioral deficits induced by uncontrollable stress. *Psychopharmacology* 64:163–170.

Anisman, H., and Sklar, L. S. (1979). Catecholamine depletion in mice upon reexposure to stress: Mediation of the escape deficits produced by uncontrollable shock. *Journal of Comparative and Physiological Psychology* 93:610–625.

Anisman, H., Suissa, A., and Sklar, L. S. (1980). Escape deficits induced by uncontrollable stress: Antagonism by dopamine and noradrenaline agonists. *Behavioral and Neural Biology* 28:34–47.

Anisman, H., and Waller, T. G. (1973). Effects of inescapable shock on subsequent avoidance performance: Role of response repertoire changes. *Behavioral Biology* 9:331–355.

Anisman, H., and Zacharko, R. M. (1986). Behavioral and neurochemical consequences associated with stressors. In *Stress-induced analgesia*, ed. D. D. Kelley. New York: Wiley.

Antonitis, J. J. (1951). Response-variability in the white rat during conditioning, extinction, and reconditioning. *Journal of Experimental Psychology* 42:273–281.

Arieti, S., and Bemporad, J. (1978). *Severe and mild depression*. New York: Basic Books.

Aston-Jones, G. (1985). Behavioral functions of locus coeruleus derived from cellular attributes. *Physiological Psychology* 13:118–126.

Atlas, G. D., and Peterson, C. (1990). Explanatory style and gambling: How pessimists respond to lost wagers. *Behaviour Research and Therapy* 28:523–529.

Ayres, R., Cooley, E., and Dunn, C. (1990). Self-concept, attribution, and persistence in learning-disabled students. *Journal of School Psychology* 28:153–163.

Baker, A. G. (1976). Learned irrelevance and learned helplessness: Rats learn that stimuli, reinforcers, and responses are uncorrelated. *Journal of Experimental Psychology: Animal Behavior Processes* 2:130–142.

Baltes, M. M. (1983). On the social ecology of dependence and independence in elderly nursing home residents: A replication and extension. *Journal of Gerontology* 38:556–564.

Bandura, A. (1977). Self-efficacy: Toward a unifying theory of behavioral change. *Psychological Review* 84:191–215.

Bandura, A. (1986). *Social foundations of thought and action*. Englewood Cliffs, N.J.: Prentice-Hall.

Bandura, A. (1987). Perceived self-efficacy in the exercise of control over AIDS infection. Paper presented at the National Institute of Mental Health and Drug Abuse Research Conference on Women and AIDS, Bethesda, Md.

Bandura, A., Taylor, C. B., Williams, S. L., Mefford, I. N., and Barchas, J. D.

(1985). Catecholamine secretion as a function of perceived coping self-efficacy. *Journal of Consulting and Clinical Psychology* 53:406–414.

Barber, J. G., and Winefield, A. H. (1986). Learned helplessness as conditioned inattention to the target stimulus. *Journal of Experimental Psychology: General* 115:236–246.

Barber, J. G., and Winefield, A. H. (1987). Three accounts of the learned helplessness effect. *Genetic, Social, and General Psychology Monographs* 113:141–163.

Bard, M., and Dyk, R. B. (1956). The psychodynamic significance of beliefs regarding the cause of serious illness. *Psychoanalytic Review* 43:146–162.

Barsky, A. J. (1988). *Worried sick: Our troubled quest for wellness.* Boston: Little, Brown.

Basbaum, A. I., and Fields, H. L. (1984). Endogenous pain control systems: Brainstem spinal pathways and endorphin circuitry. *Annual Review of Neurosciences* 7:309–339.

Baum, A., Aiello, J. R., and Calesnick, L. E. (1978). Crowding and personal control: Social density and the development of learned helplessness. *Journal of Personality and Social Psychology* 36:1000–1011.

Baum, A., and Davis, G. E. (1980). Reducing the stress of high-density living: An architectural intervention. *Journal of Personality and Social Psychology* 38:471–481.

Baum, A., Fleming, R., and Reddy, D. M. (1986). Unemployment stress: Loss of control, reactance, and learned helplessness. *Social Science and Medicine* 22:509–516.

Baum, A., and Gatchel, R. J. (1981). Cognitive determinants of reaction to uncontrollable events: Development of reactance and learned helplessness. *Journal of Personality and Social Psychology* 40:1078–1089.

Baum, A., and Valins, S. (1977). *Architecture and social behavior: Psychological studies of social density.* Hillsdale, N.J.: Erlbaum.

Beck, A. T. (1967). *Depression: Clinical, experimental, and theoretical aspects.* New York: Hoeber.

Beck, A. T. (1984). Cognition and therapy. *Archives of General Psychiatry* 41:1112–1114.

Beckman, L. J. (1980). An attributional analysis of Alcoholics Anonymous. *Journal of Studies in Alcohol* 41:714–726.

Belloc, N. B. (1973). Relationship of health practices and mortality. *Preventive Medicine* 2:67–81.

Belloc, N. B., and Breslow, L. (1972). Relationship of physical health status and family practices. *Preventive Medicine* 1:409–421.

Ben-Eliyahu, S., Yirma, R., Liebeskind, J. C., Taylor, A. N., and Gale, R. P. (1991). Stress increases metastatic spread of a mammary tumor in rats: Evidence for mediation by the immune system. *Brain, Behavior, and Immunity* 5:193–206.

Berridge, C. W., and Dunn, A. J. (1987). A corticotropin-releasing factor antagonist reverses the stress-induced changes of exploratory behavior in mice. *Hormones and Behavior* 21:393–401.

Bersh, P. J., and Alloy, L. B. (1978). Avoidance based on shock intensity reduction with no change in shock probability. *Journal of the Experimental Analysis of Behavior* 30:293–300.

Biggio, G. (1983). The action of stress, B-carbolines, diazepin, and Ro15-1788 on GABA receptors in the rat brain. In *Benzodiazepine recognition site ligands: Biochemistry and pharmacology*, ed. G. Biggio and E. Costa. Vol. 38. New York: Raven Press.

Blauner, R. (1964). *Alienation and freedom: The factory worker and his industry.* Chicago: University of Chicago Press.

Boakes, R. A. (1977). Performance on learning to associate a stimulus with positive reinforcement. In *Operant-Pavlovian interaction*, ed. H. Davis and H. M. B. Hurwirtz. Hillsdale, N.J.: Erlbaum.

Bolles, R. C. (1967). *Theory of motivation.* New York: Harper & Row.

Bolles, R. C., and Fanselow, M. S. (1980). A perceptual-defensive recuperative model of fear and pain. *Behavioral and Brain Sciences* 3:291–301.

Bower, G. H. (1981). Mood and memory. *American Psychologist* 36:129–148.

Bowman, P. J. (1984). A discouragement-centered approach to studying unemployment among black youth: Hopelessness, attributions, and psychological distress. *International Journal of Mental Health* 13:68–91.

Bracewell, R. J., and Black, A. H. (1974). The effects of restraint and noncontingent preshock on subsequent escape learning in the rat. *Learning and Motivation* 5:53–69.

Brehm, J. W. (1966). *A theory of psychological reactance.* New York: Academic Press.

Brehm, J. W. (1972). *Responses to loss of freedom: A theory of psychological reactance.* Morristown, N.J.: General Learning Press.

Breier, A., Albus, M., Pickar, D., Zahn, T. P., Wolkowitz, O. M., and Paul, S. M. (1987). Controllable and uncontrollable stress in humans: Alterations in mood and neuroendocrine and psychophysiological function. *American Journal of Psychiatry* 144:1419–1425.

Brennan, F. X., Job, R. F. S., Watkins, L. R., and Maier, S. F. (1992). Total plasma cholesterol levels of rats are increased following only three sessions of tailshock. *Life Sciences* 50:945–950.

Brewin, C. R. (1985). Depression and causal attributions: What is their relation? *Psychological Bulletin* 98:297–309.

Brewin, C. R. (1989). Cognitive change processes in psychotherapy. *Psychological Review* 96:379–394.

Brewin, C. R., and Furnham, A. (1986). Attributional versus preattributional variables in self-esteem and depression: A comparison and test of learned helplessness theory. *Journal of Personality and Social Psychology* 50:1013–1020.

Brewin, C. R., and Harris, J. (1985). Induced mood and causal attributions: Further evidence. *Cognitive Therapy and Research* 9:225–229.

Brewin, C. R., and Shapiro, D. A. (1984). Beyond locus of control: Attributions of responsibility for positive and negative outcomes. *British Journal of Psychology* 75:43–49.

Brewin, C. R., and Shapiro, D. A. (1985). Selective impact of reattribution of failure instructions on task performance. *British Journal of Social Psychology* 24:37–46.

Brewster, R. G., and Wilson, M. E. (1976). Learned helplessness in pet rocks *(Roccus pettus)*. *Worm Runner's Digest* 18:111–113.

Britton, D. R., Koob, G. F., Rivier, J., and Vale, W. (1982). Intraventricular corticotropin-releasing factor enhances behavioral effects of novelty. *Life Sciences* 31:363–367.

Britton, K. T., Lee, G., and Koob, G. F. (1988). Corticotropin releasing factor and amphetamine exaggerate partial agonist properties of benzodiazepine antagonist, Ro15-1788, in the conflict test. *Psychopharmacology* 94:306–311.

Brown, G. W., and Harris, T. O. (1978). *Social origins of depression.* New York: Free Press.

Brown, I., and Inouye, D. K. (1978). Learned helplessness through modeling: The role of perceived similarity in competence. *Journal of Personality and Social Psychology* 36:900–908.

Brown, J. D., and Siegel, J. M. (1988). Attributions for negative life events and depression: The role of perceived control. *Journal of Personality and Social Psychology* 54:316–322.

Brown, M. R., and Fisher, L. A. (1985). Corticotropin-releasing factor: Effects on the autonomic nervous system and visceral systems. *Federation Proceedings, Federation of American Society of Experimental Biology* 44:243–248.

Brustein, S. C. (1978). Learned helplessness. *Journal of Instructional Psychology* 5:6–10.

Buchanan, G., and Seligman, M. E. P. (1989). [Explanatory style and heart attack survival.] Unpublished data, University of Pennsylvania.

Buchwald, A. M. (1977). Depressive mood and estimates of reinforcement frequency. *Journal of Abnormal Psychology* 86:443–446.

Bukstel, L. H., and Kilmann, P. R. (1980). Psychological effects of imprisonment on confined individuals. *Psychological Bulletin* 88:469–493.

Bulman, R. J., and Wortman, C. B. (1977). Attributions of blame and coping in the "real world": Severe accident victims react to their lot. *Journal of Personality and Social Psychology* 35:351–363.

Bunney, W. E., and Davis, J. M. (1965). Norepinephrine in depressive reactions. *Archives of General Psychiatry* 13:483–494.

Burns, M. O., and Seligman, M. E. P. (1989). Explanatory style across the life span: Evidence for stability over 52 years. *Journal of Personality and Social Psychology* 56:471–477.

Buss, D. M., and Craik, K. H. (1984). Acts, dispositions, and personality. In *Progress in experimental personality research*, ed. B. A. Maher. Vol. 13. New York: Academic Press.

Butkowsky, I. S., and Willows, D. M. (1980). Cognitive-motivational characteristics of children varying in reading ability: Evidence for learned helplessness in readers. *Journal of Educational Psychology* 72:408–422.

Canino, F. J. (1981). Learned helplessness theory: Implications for research in learning disabilities. *Journal of Special Education* 15:471–484.

Carlson, J. G. (1982). Some concepts of perceived control and their relationship to bodily self-control. *Biofeedback and Self Regulation* 7:341–375.

Carlson, J. G., and Feld, J. L. (1981). Expectancies of reinforcement control in biofeedback and cognitive performance. *Biofeedback and Self Regulation* 6:79–91.

Carver, C. S. (1989). How should multi-faceted personality constructs be tested? Issues illustrated by self-monitoring, attributional style, and hardiness. *Journal of Personality and Social Psychology* 56:577–585.

Castellon, C., and Seligman, M. E. P. (1985). [Explanatory style of patients.] Unpublished data, University of Pennsylvania.

Cecil, M. A., and Medway, F. J. (1986). Attribution retraining with low-achieving and learned helplessness children. *Techniques* 2:173–181.

Cedarbaum, J. M., and Aghajanian, G. K. (1978). Activation of the locus coeruleus by peripheral stimuli: Modulation by a collateral inhibitory mechanism. *Life Sciences* 23:1382–1392.

Chapman, S. L., and Brena, S. F. (1982). Learned helplessness and response to nerve blocks in chronic low back pain patients. *Pain* 14:355–364.

Chappell, P. B., Smith, M. A., Kilts, C. D., Bissette, G., Ritchie, J., Anderson, C., and Nemeroff, C. B. (1986). Alterations in corticotropin-releasing factor-line immunoreactivity in discrete rat brain regions after acute and chronic stress. *Journal of Neuroscience* 6:2908–2916.

Cherniss, C. (1980). *Professional burnout in human service organizations.* New York: Praeger.

Clark, K. B. (1964). *Youth in the ghetto: A study of the consequences of powerlessness and a blueprint for change.* New York: Haryou.

Coates, D., and Wortman, C. B. (1980). Depression maintenance and interpersonal control. In *Advances in environmental psychology: Applications of personal control,* ed. A. Baum and J. E. Singer. Vol. 2. Hillsdale, N.J.: Erlbaum.

Cobb, S. (1976). Social support as a moderator of life stress. *Psychosomatic Medicine* 38:300–314.

Cohen, S., Evans, G. W., Krantz, D. S., and Stokols, D. (1980). Physiological, motivational, and cognitive effects of aircraft noise on children: Moving from the laboratory to the field. *American Psychologist* 35:231–243.

Cohen, S., Evans, G. W., Krantz, D. S., Stokols, D., and Kelly, S. (1981). Aircraft noise and children: Longitudinal and cross-sectional evidence on adaptation to noise and the effectiveness of noise abatement. *Journal of Personality and Social Psychology* 40:331–345.

Cohen, S., and Sherrod, D. (1978). When density matters: Experimental control as a determinant of crowding effects in laboratory and residential settings. *Journal of Population* 1:189–202.

Cole, B. J., and Koob, G. F. (1988). Propranolol antagonizes the enhanced conditioned fear produced by corticotropin releasing factor. *Journal of Pharmacology and Experimental Therapeutics* 247:902–910.

Cole, B. J., and Koob, G. F. (1991). Corticotropin-releasing factor, stress, and animal behavior. In *Stress, neuropeptides, and systemic disease,* ed. J. A. McCubbin, P. G. Kauffman, and C. B. Nermeroff. San Diego: Academic Press.

Cole, C. S., and Coyne, J. C. (1977). Situational-specificity of laboratory-induced learned helplessness. *Journal of Abnormal Psychology* 86:615–623.

Cook, M. L., and Peterson, C. (1986). Depressive irrationality. *Cognitive Therapy and Research* 10:293–298.

Costa, P. T., and McCrae, R. R. (1987). Neuroticism, somatic complaints, and disease: Is the bark worse than the bite? *Journal of Personality* 55:299–316.

Cousins, N. (1981). *The anatomy of an illness.* New York: Norton.

Coyne, J. C., and Gotlib, I. H. (1983). The role of cognition in depression: A critical appraisal. *Psychological Bulletin* 94:472–505.

Craske, M. L. (1985). Improving persistence through observational learning and attribution retraining. *British Journal of Educational Psychology* 55:138–147.

Craske, M. L. (1988). Learned helplessness, self-worth motivation, and attribution retraining for primary school children. *British Journal of Educational Psychology* 58:152–164.

Crawley, J. N., Ninan, P. T., Pickar, D., Chrousos, G. P., Linnoila, M., and Skolnick, P. (1985). Neuropharmacological antagonism of the B-carboline–induced "anxiety" response in Rhesus monkeys. *Journal of Neuroscience* 5:477–485.

Cromwell, R. L. (1963). A social-learning theory approach to mental retardation. In *Handbook of mental deficiency*, ed. N. R. Ellis. New York: McGraw-Hill.

Cronbach, L. J. (1951). Coefficient alpha and the internal structure of tests. *Psychometrika* 16:297–334.

Cronbach, L. J. (1957). The two disciplines of scientific psychology. *American Psychologist* 12:671–684.

Crowell, C. R., and Anderson, D. C. (1981). Influence of duration and number of inescapable shocks on intrashock activity and subsequent interference effects. *Animal Learning and Behavior* 9:28–37.

Cunningham, E. T., and Sawchenko, P. E. (1988). Anatomical specificity of noradrenergic inputs to the paraventricular nuclei of the rat hypothalamus. *Journal of Comparative Neurology* 274:60–76.

Curtis, R. C., ed. (1989). *Self-defeating behaviors: Experimental research, clinical impressions, and practical implications.* New York: Plenum.

Cutrona, C. E. (1983). Causal attributions and perinatal depression. *Journal of Abnormal Psychology* 92:161–172.

Cutrona, C. E., Russell, D., and Jones, R. D. (1985). Cross-situational consistency in causal attributions: Does attributional style exist? *Journal of Personality and Social Psychology* 47:1043–1058.

Darley, J. M., and Latane', B. (1968). Bystander intervention in emergencies: Diffusion of responsibility. *Journal of Personality and Social Psychology* 8:377–383.

Davis, E. R., and Platt, J. R. (1983). Contiguity and contingency in the acquisition and maintenance of an operant. *Learning and Motivation* 14:487–513.

DeBlas, A., and Sangameswaran, L. (1986). Current topics: 1. Demonstration and purification of an endogenous benzodiazepine from the mammalian brain with a monoclonal antibody to benzodiazepines. *Life Sciences* 39:1927–1936.

DeMonbreun, B. G., and Craighead, W. E. (1977). Distortion of perception and recall of positive and neutral feedback in depression. *Cognitive Therapy and Research* 1:311–329.

Dengerink, H. A., and Myers, J. D. (1977). The effects of failure and depression on subsequent aggression. *Journal of Personality and Social Psychology* 35:88–96.

Dennard, D. O., and Hokanson, J. E. (1986). Performance on two cognitive tasks by dysphoric and nondysphoric students. *Cognitive Therapy and Research* 10:377–386.

Desan, P., Silbert, L. H., and Maier, S. F. (1988). Long-term effects of inescapable shock on daily running activity and reversal by desipramine. *Pharmacology, Biochemistry, and Behavior* 30:21–29.

Desiderato, O., and Newman, A. (1971). Conditioned suppression produced in rats by tones paired with escapable or inescapable shock. *Journal of Comparative and Physiological Psychology* 77:427–443.

De Souza, D. E. (1987). Corticotropin-releasing factor receptors in the rat central nervous system: Characterization and regional distribution. *Journal of Neuroscience* 7:88–100.

DeVellis, R. F. (1977). Learned helplessness in institutions. *Mental Retardation* 15:10–13.

DeVellis, R. F., DeVellis, B. M., Wallston, B. S., and Wallston, K. A. (1980). Epilepsy and learned helplessness. *Basic and Applied Social Psychology* 1:241–253.

DeVellis, R. F., and McCauley, C. (1979). Perception of contingency and mental retardation. *Journal of Autism and Developmental Disorders* 9:261–270.

Devins, G. M. (1982). Perceived self-efficacy, outcome expectancies, and negative mood states in end-stage renal disease. *Journal of Abnormal Psychology* 91:241–244.

Diener, C. I., and Dweck, C. S. (1978). An analysis of learned helplessness: Continuous changes in performance, strategy, and achievement cognitions following failure. *Journal of Personality and Social Psychology* 36:451–462.

Dohrenwend, B. S., Dohrenwend, B. P., Dodson, M., and Shrout, P. E. (1984). Symptoms, hassles, social supports, and life events: Problem of confounded measures. *Journal of Abnormal Psychology* 93:222–230.

Donovan, W. L. (1981). Maternal learned helplessness and physiologic response to infant crying. *Journal of Personality and Social Psychology* 40:919–926.

Donovan, W. L., and Leavitt, L. A. (1985). Simulating conditions of learned helplessness: The effects of interventions and attributions. *Child Development* 56:594–603.

Donovan, W. L., Leavitt, L. A., and Walsh, R. O. (1990). Maternal self-efficacy: Illusory control and its effect on susceptibility to learned helplessness. *Child Development* 61:1638–1647.

Dorow, R. (1982). B-carboline monomethylamide causes anxiety in man. *CINP Congress Jerusalem* 13:76.

Dorworth, T. R., and Overmier, J. B. (1977). On learned helplessness: The therapeutic effects of electroconvulsive shocks. *Physiological Psychology* 5:355–358.

Douglas, D., and Anisman, H. (1975). Helplessness or expectation incongruency: Effects of aversive stimulation on subsequent performance. *Journal of Experimental Psychology: Human Perception and Performance* 1:411–417.

Dowd, E. T., Lawson, G. W., and Petosa, R. (1986). Attributional styles of alcoholics. *International Journal of the Addictions* 21:589–593.

Drugan, R. C., and Holmes, P. V. (1991). Central and peripheral benzodiazepine receptors: Involvement in an organism's responses to physical and psychological stress. *Neuroscience and Biobehavioral Reviews* 15:277–298.

Drugan, R. C., McIntyre, T. D., Alpern, H. P., and Maier, S. F. (1985). Coping and seizure susceptibility: Control over shock protects against bicucul-line-induced seizures in rats. *Brain Research* 342:9–17.

Drugan, R. C., Maier, S. F., Skolnick, P., Paul, S. M., and Crawley, J. N. (1985). An anxiogenic benzodiazepine receptor ligand induces learned helplessness. *European Journal of Pharmacology* 113:453–457.

Drugan, R. C., Morrow, A. L., Weizman, R., Weizman, A., Deutsch, S. I., Crawley, J. N., and Paul, S. M. (1989). Stress-induced behavioral depression in the rat is associated with a decrease in GABA receptor-mediated chloride ion flux and brain benzodiazepine receptor occupancy. *Brain Research* 487:45–51.

Drugan, R. C., Moye, T. B., and Maier, S. F. (1982). Opioid and nonopioid forms of stress-induced analgesia: Some environmental determinants and characteristics. *Behavioral and Neural Biology* 35:251–264.

Drugan, R. C., Ryan, S. M., Minor, T. R., and Maier, S. F. (1984). Librium prevents the analgesia and shuttlebox escape deficit typically observed following inescapable shock. *Pharmacology, Biochemistry, and Behavior* 21:749–754.

Dunlap, G. (1984). The influence of task variation and maintenance tasks on the learning and affect of autistic children. *Journal of Experimental Child Psychology* 37:41–64.

Dunn, A. J., and Berridge, C. W. (1987). Corticotropin-releasing factor administration elicits a stress-like activation of cerebral catecholaminergic systems. *Pharmacology, Biochemistry, and Behavior* 27:685–691.

Dunnette, M. D., ed. (1976). *Handbook of industrial and organizational psychology.* Chicago: Rand McNally.

Dweck, C. S. (1975). The role of expectations and attributions in the alleviation of learned helplessness. *Journal of Personality and Social Psychology* 31:674–685.

Dweck, C. S., Davidson, W., Nelson, S., and Enna, B. (1978). Sex differences in learned helplessness: II. The contingencies of evaluative feedback in the classroom. III. An experimental analysis. *Developmental Psychology* 14:268–276.

Dweck, C. S., and Gilliard, D. (1975). Expectancy statements as determinants of reactions to failure: Sex differences in persistence and expectancy change. *Journal of Personality and Social Psychology* 32:1077–1084.

Dweck, C. S., Goetz, T. E., and Strauss, N. (1980). Sex differences in learned helplessness: IV. An experimental and naturalistic study of failure generalization and its mediators. *Journal of Personality and Social Psychology* 38:441–452.

Dweck, C. S., and Licht, B. G. (1980). Learned helplessness and intellectual achievement. In *Human helplessness: Theory and applications,* ed. J. Garber and M. E. P. Seligman. New York: Academic Press.

Dweck, C. S., and Reppucci, N. D. (1973). Learned helplessness and reinforcement responsibility in children. *Journal of Personality and Social Psychology* 25:109–116.

Dyck, D. G., and Breen, L. J. (1978). Learned helplessness, immunization, and importance of task in humans. *Psychological Reports* 43:315–321.

Dykema, J., Bergbower, K., and Peterson, C. (1992). [Explanatory style, life events, hassles, and depressive symptoms.] Unpublished data, University of Michigan.

Eaves, G., and Rush, A. J. (1984). Cognitive patterns in symptomatic and remitted unipolar major depressives. *Journal of Abnormal Psychology* 93:31–40.

Eckelman, J. D., and Dyck, D. G. (1979). Task- and setting-related cues in immunization against learned helplessness. *American Journal of Psychology* 92:653–667.

Edelwich, J., and Brodsky, A. (1980). *Burn-out: Stages of disillusionment in the helping professions.* New York: Human Sciences Press.

Egeland, J. A., and Hostetter, A. M. (1983). Amish study, I: Affective disorders among the Amish, 1976–1980. *American Journal of Psychiatry* 140:56–61.

Elig, T. W., and Frieze, I. H. (1979). Measuring causal attributions for success and failure. *Journal of Personality and Social Psychology* 37:621–634.

Engberg, L. A., Hansen, G., Welker, R. L., and Thomas, D. R. (1973). Acquisition of key pecking via autoshaping as a function of prior experience: "Learned laziness"? *Science* 178:1002–1004.

Engel, G. L., and Schmale, A. H. (1972). Conservation-withdrawal. In *Physiology, emotions, and psychosomatic illness,* ed. A. H. Schmale. Amsterdam: Elsevier.

Epstein, S. (1980). The stability of behavior, II: Implications for psychological research. *American Psychologist* 35:790–806.

Epstein, S. (1983). Aggregation and beyond: Some basic issues on the prediction of behavior. *Journal of Personality* 51:360–392.

Epstein, S. (1984). The stability of behavior across time and situations. In *Personality and the prediction of behavior,* ed. R. A. Zucker, J. Arnoff, and A. I. Rabin. Orlando, Fla.: Academic Press.

Eysenck, M. W. (1982). *Attention and arousal.* Berlin: Springer-Verlag.

Fanselow, M. S. (1986). Conditioned fear-induced opiate analgesia: A competing motivational state theory of stress-analgesia. *Annals of the New York Academy of Sciences* 467:404–454.

Fanselow, M. S., and Bolles, R. C. (1979). Naloxone and shock-elicited freezing in the rat. *Journal of Comparative and Physiological Psychology* 94:736–744.

Fanselow, M. S., and Lester, L. S. (1987). A functional behavioristic approach to aversively motivated behavior: Predatory imminence as a determinant of the topography of defensive behavior. In *Evolution and learning,* ed. R. C. Bolles and M. D. Beecher. Hillsdale, N.J.: Erlbaum.

Feather, N. T. (1961). The relationship of persistence at a task to expectation of success and achievement-related motives. *Journal of Abnormal and Social Psychology* 63:552–561.

Feather, N. T. (1963). Persistence at a difficult task with an alternative task of intermediate difficulty. *Journal of Abnormal and Social Psychology* 66:604–609.

Feather, N. T. (1982). Unemployment and its psychological correlates: A study of depressive symptoms, Protestant ethic values, attributional style, and apathy. *Australian Journal of Psychology* 34:309–323.

Feather, N. T., and Barber, J. G. (1983). Depressive reactions and unemployment. *Journal of Abnormal Psychology* 92:185–195.

Feather, N. T., and Davenport, P. R. (1981). Unemployment and depressive affect: A motivational and attributional analysis. *Journal of Personality and Social Psychology* 41:422–461.

Feldman, H. R. (1986). Self-esteem, types of attributional style, and sensation and distress pain ratings in males. *Journal of Advanced Nursing* 11:75–86.

Felton, S. Y., and Felton, D. L. (1991). Innervation of lymphoid tissue. In *Psychoneuroimmunology*, ed. R. Ader, D. L. Felton, and N. Cohen. San Diego: Academic Press.

Fernando, S. (1984). Racism as a cause of depression. *International Journal of Social Psychiatry* 30:41–49.

Fielstein, E., Klein, M. S., Fischer, M., Hanan, C., Koburger, P., Schneider, M. J., and Leitenberg, H. (1985). Self-esteem and causal attributions for success and failure in children. *Cognitive Therapy and Research* 9:381–398.

File, S. E. (1980). The use of social interaction as a method for detecting anxiolytic activity of chlordiazepoxide-like drugs. *Journal of Neuroscience Methods* 2:219–238.

Fincham, F. D., and Cain, K. M. (1986). Learned helplessness in humans: A developmental analysis. *Developmental Review* 6:301–333.

Fincham, F. D., Hokoda, A., and Sanders, R. (1989). Learned helplessness, test anxiety, and academic achievement: A longitudinal analysis. *Child Development* 60:138–145.

Finn, P. R., and Pihl, R. O. (1987). Men at high risk for alcoholism: The effect of alcohol on cardiovascular response to unavoidable shock. *Journal of Abnormal Psychology* 96:230–236.

Firth, J., and Brewin, C. R. (1982). Attributions and recovery from depression: A preliminary study using cross-lagged correlation analysis. *British Journal of Clinical Psychology* 21:229–230.

Fisher, L. A. (1991). Corticotropin-releasing factor and autonomic-cardiovascular responses to stress. In *Stress, neuropeptides, and systemic disease*, ed. J. A. McCubbin, P. G. Kauffman, and C. B. Nemeroff. San Diego: Academic Press.

Fisher, L. A., Jessen, G., and Brown, M. R. (1983). Corticotropin-releasing factor (CRF): Mechanism to elevate mean arterial pressure and heart rate. *Regulatory Peptides* 5:153–161.

Fiske, S. T., and Taylor, S. E. (1984). *Social cognition*. Reading, Mass: Addison-Wesley.

Flannery, R. B. (1986). The adult children of alcoholics: Are they trauma victims with learned helplessness? *Journal of Social Behavior and Personality* 1:497–504.

Fleming, I., Baum, A., and Weiss, L. (1987). Social density and perceived control as mediators of crowding stress in high-density residential neighborhoods. *Journal of Personality and Social Psychology* 52:899–906.

Fleshner, M., Peterson, P., and Maier, S. F. (1992). The relationship between dominance and learned helplessness. Manuscript, University of Colorado.

Floor, L., and Rosen, M. (1975). Investigating the phenomenon of helplessness in mentally retarded adults. *American Journal of Mental Deficiency* 79:565–572.

Follingstad, D. R. (1980). A reconceptualization of issues in the treatment of abused women: A case study. *Psychotherapy: Theory, Research, and Practice* 17:294–303.

Forsterling, F. (1985). Attribution retraining: A review. *Psychological Bulletin* 98:495–512.

Forward, J. R., and Williams, J. R. (1970). Internal-external control and black militancy. *Journal of Social Issues* 26:75–92.

Fosco, E., and Geer, J. H. (1971). Effects of gaining control over aversive stimuli after differing amounts of no control. *Psychological Reports* 29:1153–1154.

Frankel, A., and Snyder, M. L. (1978). Poor performance following unsolvable problems: Learned helplessness or egotism? *Journal of Personality and Social Psychology* 36:1415–1424.

Freeman, R. B., and Wise, D. A., eds. (1982). *The youth unemployment problem: Its nature, causes, and consequences.* Chicago: University of Chicago Press.

Freud, S. (1905). Humor and its relation to the unconscious. *Standard edition.* Vol. 8. London: Hogarth.

Freud, S. (1917). Mourning and melancholia. *Standard edition.* Vol. 14. London: Hogarth.

Freudenberger, H. J., and Richelson, G. (1980). *Burn-out: The high cost of high achievement.* Garden City, N.Y.: Anchor.

Friedman, H. S., and Booth-Kewley, S. (1987). The "disease-prone personality": A meta-analytic view of the construct. *American Psychologist* 42:539–555.

Friedmann, E., Katcher, A., Lynch, J. J., and Thomas, S. A. (1980). Animal companions and one-year survival of patients after discharge from a coronary care unit. *Public Health Reports* 95:307–312.

Fromm, E. (1941). *Escape from freedom.* New York: Rinehart.

Funder, D. C., and Ozer, D. J. (1983). Behavior as a function of the situation. *Journal of Personality and Social Psychology* 44:107–112.

Gallagher, W. (1988). The DD's: Blues without end. *American Health* (April): 80–88.

Gamzu, E. R. (1974). Learned laziness in dead pigeons. *Worm Runner's Digest* 16:86–87.

Garber, J., Miller, S. M., and Abramson, L. Y. (1980). On the distinction between anxiety and depression: Perceived control, certainty, and probability of goal attainment. In *Human helplessness: Theory and applications,* ed. J. Garber and M. E. P. Seligman. New York: Academic Press.

Gardner, H. (1985). *The mind's new science: A history of the cognitive revolution.* New York: Basic Books.

Gargiulo, R. M., and O'Sullivan, P. S. (1986). Mildly mentally retarded and nonretarded children's learned helplessness. *American Journal of Mental Deficiency* 91:203–206.

Gatchel, R. J., Paulus, P. B., and Maples, C. W. (1975). Learned helplessness and self-reported affect. *Journal of Abnormal Psychology* 84:732–734.

Gatchel, R. J., and Proctor, J. D. (1976). Physiological correlates of learned helplessness in man. *Journal of Abnormal Psychology* 85:27–34.

Gayford, J. J. (1975). Wife battering: A preliminary survey of 100 cases. *British Medical Journal* 1:194–197.

Gelenberg, A. J., and Klerman, G. L. (1978). Maintenance drug therapy in long-term treatment of depression. In *Controversy in psychiatry,* ed. J. P. Brady and H. K. H. Brodie. Philadelphia: Saunders.

Gelles, R. J. (1976). Abused wives: Why do they stay? *Journal of Marriage and the Family* 38:659–668.

German, D., Habenicht, D., and Futcher, W. (1990). Psychological profile of the female adolescent incest victim. *Child Abuse and Neglect* 14:429–438.

Gibbon, J., Berryman, R., and Thompson, R. L. (1974). Contingency spaces and measures in classical and instrumental conditioning. *Journal of the Experimental Analysis of Behavior* 21:585–605.

Gilmor, T. M., and Reid, D. W. (1979). Locus of control and causal attributions for positive and negative outcomes on university examinations. *Journal of Personality and Social Psychology* 13:154–160.

Girodo, M., Dotzenroth, S. E., and Stein, S. J. (1981). Causal attribution bias in shy males: Implications for self-esteem and self-confidence. *Cognitive Therapy and Research* 5:325–338.

Glass, D. C., and Singer, J. E. (1972). *Urban stress: Experiments on noise and social stressors.* New York: Academic Press.

Glazer, H. I., and Weiss, J. M. (1976). Long-term and transitory interference effects. *Journal of Experimental Psychology: Animal Behavior Processes* 2:191–201.

Gleitman, H., and Holmes, P. A. (1967). Retention of incompletely learned CER in rats. *Psychonomic Science* 7:19–20.

Gloor, P. (1978). Inputs and outputs of the amygdala: What the amygdala is trying to tell the rest of the brain. In *Limbic mechanisms: The continuing evolution of the limbic system concept,* ed. K. E. Livingston and O. Hornykiewicz. New York: Plenum.

Glow, P. H., and Winefield, A. H. (1982). Effect of regular noncontingent sensory changes on responding for sensory changes. *Journal of General Psychology* 107:121–137.

Goetz, T. E., and Dweck, C. S. (1980). Learned helplessness in social situations. *Journal of Personality and Social Psychology* 39:246–255.

Goffman, E. (1961). *Asylums.* Garden City, N.Y.: Anchor.

Golin, S., Sweeney, P. D., and Shaeffer, D. E. (1981). The causality of causal attributions in depression: A cross-lagged panel correlational analysis. *Journal of Abnormal Psychology* 90:14–22.

Golin, S., Terrell, F., and Johnson, B. (1977). Depression and the illusion of control. *Journal of Abnormal Psychology* 86:440–442.

Gong-Guy, E., and Hammen, C. (1980). Causal perceptions of stressful life events in depressed and nondepressed clinic outpatients. *Journal of Abnormal Psychology* 89:662–669.

Goodkin, F. (1976). Rats learn the relationship between responding and environmental events: An expansion of the learned helplessness hypothesis. *Learning and Motivation* 7:382–394.

Goodwin, D. W. (1986). *Anxiety.* New York: Oxford University Press.

Gotlib, I. H., and Beatty, M. E. (1985). Negative responses to depression: The role of attributional style. *Cognitive Therapy and Research* 9:91–103.

Grau, J. W., Hyson, R. L., Maier, S. F., Madden, J., and Barchas, J. D. (1981). Long-term stress-induced analgesia and activation of the opiate system. *Science* 213:1409–1411.

Gray, T. S. (1989). Autonomic neuropeptide connections of the amygdala. In *Neuropeptides and stress,* ed. Y. Tache, J. E. Morley, and M. R. Brown. New York: Springer-Verlag.

Green, A. H. (1978). Self-destructive behavior in battered children. *American Journal of Psychiatry* 135:579–582.

Greer, J. G., and Wethered, C. E. (1984). Learned helplessness: A piece of the burnout puzzle. *Exceptional Children* 50:524–530.

Griffith, M. (1977). Effects of noncontingent success and failure on mood and performance. *Journal of Personality* 45:442–457.

Griffith, P. R. (1986). "Learned helplessness" and ego defense mechanisms in alcohol treatment. *Employee Assistance Quarterly* 1:87–92.

Guidotti, A., Forchetti, C. M., Corda, M. G., Konkel, D., Bennett, C. D., and Costa, E. (1983). Isolation, characterization, and purification to homogeneity of an endogenous polypeptide with agonistic action on benzodiazepine receptors. *Proceedings of the National Academy of Sciences* 80:3531–3535.

Guthrie, E. R. (1935). *The psychology of learning.* New York: Harper.

Hammen, C., and deMayo, R. (1982). Cognitive correlates of teacher stress and depressive symptoms: Implications for attributional models of depression. *Journal of Abnormal Psychology* 91:96–101.

Hammond, L. J. (1980). The effect of contingency upon the appetitive conditioning of free-operant behavior. *Journal of the Experimental Analysis of Behavior* 34:297–304.

Hammond, L. J., and Paynter, W. E. (1983). Probabilistic contingency theories of animal conditioning: A critical analysis. *Learning and Motivation* 14:527–550.

Hayes, R. L., Bennett, G. J., Newlon, P. G., and Mayer, D. J. (1978). Behavioral and physiologic studies on non-narcotic analgesia in the rat elicited by certain environmental stimuli. *Brain Research* 155:69–90.

Heider, F. (1958). *The psychology of interpersonal relations.* New York: Wiley.

Hermann, B. P. (1977). Psychological effects of epilepsy: A review. *Catalog of Selected Documents in Psychology* 7(1): 6.

Hineline, P. N. (1970). Negative reinforcement without shock reduction. *Journal of the Experimental Analysis of Behavior* 14:259–268.

Hiroto, D. S. (1974). Locus of control and learned helplessness. *Journal of Experimental Psychology* 102:187–193.

Hiroto, D. S., and Seligman, M. E. P. (1975). Generality of learned helplessness in man. *Journal of Personality and Social Psychology* 31:311–327.

Hirt, M., and Genshaft, J. L. (1981). Immunization and reversibility of cognitive deficits due to learned helplessness. *Personality and Individual Differences* 2:191–196.

Hollon, S. D., Shelton, R. C., and Loosen, P. T. (1991). Cognitive therapy and pharmacotherapy for depression. *Journal of Consulting and Clinical Psychology* 58:88–99.

Holmes, T. H., and Rahe, R. H. (1967). The social readjustment scale. *Journal of Psychosomatic Research* 11:213–218.

House, J. S., Landis, K. R., and Umberson, D. (1988). Social relationships and health. *Science* 241:540–545.

Hughes, J., Smith, T. W., Kosterlitz, H. W., Fothergill, L. A., Morgan, B. A., and Morris, H. R. (1975). Identification of two related pentopepsticks from the brain with potent opioid antagonist activity. *Nature* 258:577–579.

Hull, C. L. (1943). *Principles of behavior.* New York: Appleton.

Hull, J. G., and Mendolia, M. (1991). Modeling the relations of attributional style, expectancies, and depression. *Journal of Personality and Social Psychology* 61:85–97.

Hume, D. (1739/1962). A treatise of human nature. In *On human nature and understanding,* ed. A. Flew. New York: Collier.

Ickes, W., and Layden, M. A. (1978). Attributional styles. In *New directions in attribution research,* ed. J. H. Harvey, W. Ickes, and R. F. Kidd. Vol. 2. Hillsdale, N.J.: Erlbaum.

Irving, J. (1978). *The world according to Garp: A novel.* New York: Dutton.

Iwata, J., LeDoux, J. E., Meeley, M. P., Arneric, S., and Reis, D. J. (1986). Intrinsic neurons in the amygdaloid field projected to by the medial geniculate body mediate emotional responses conditioned to acoustic stimuli. *Brain Research* 383:195–214.

Jackson, M. E., and Tessler, R. C. (1984). Perceived lack of control over life events: Antecedents and consequences in a discharged patient sample. *Social Science Research* 13:287–301.

Jackson, R. L., Alexander, J. H., and Maier, S. F. (1980). Learned helplessness, inactivity, and associative deficits: Effects of inescapable shock on response choice escape learning. *Journal of Experimental Psychology: Animal Behavior Processes* 6:1–20.

Jackson, R. L., Maier, S. F., and Coon, D. J. (1979). Long-term analgesic effects of inescapable shock and learned helplessness. *Science* 206:91–94.

Jackson, R. L., Maier, S. F., and Rapaport, P. M. (1978). Exposure to inescapable shock produces both activity and associative deficits in the rat. *Learning and Motivation* 9:69–98.

Jackson, R. L., and Minor, T. R. (1988). Effects of signaling inescapable shock on subsequent escape learning: Implications for theories of coping and "learned helplessness." *Journal of Experimental Psychology: Animal Behavior Processes* 14:390–400.

Jackson, S. W. (1986). *Melancholia and depression from Hippocratic times to modern times.* New Haven: Yale University Press.

Janoff-Bulman, R. (1989). Assumptive worlds and the stress of traumatic events: Applications of the schema construct. *Social Cognition* 7:113–136.

Joffe, J. M., Rawson, R. A., and Mulick, J. A. (1973). Control of their environment reduces emotionality in rats. *Science* 180:1383–1384.

Johnson, D. S. (1981). Naturally acquired learned helplessness: The relationship of school failure to achievement behavior, attributions, and self-concept. *Journal of Educational Psychology* 73:174–180.

Jones, E. E., and Davis, K. E. (1965). From acts to dispositions: The attribution process in person perception. In *Advances in experimental social psychology,* ed. L. Berkowitz. Vol. 2. New York: Academic Press.

Jones, S. L., Nation, J. R., and Massad, P. (1977). Immunization against learned helplessness in man. *Journal of Abnormal Psychology* 86:75–83.

Kalmuss, D. S., and Straus, M. A. (1982). Wife's marital dependency and wife abuse. *Journal of Marriage and the Family* 44:277–286.

Kamen, L., and Seligman, M. E. P. (1986). Explanatory style predicts college grade point average. Manuscript, University of Pennsylvania.

Kamen-Siegel, L., Rodin, J., Seligman, M. E. P., and Dwyer, J. (1991). Explanatory style and cell-mediated immunity. *Health Psychology* 10:229–235.

Kammer, D. (1983). Depression, attributional style, and failure generalization. *Cognitive Therapy and Research* 7:413–423.

Kanner, A. D., Coyne, J. C., Schaefer, C., and Lazarus, R. S. (1981). Comparison of two modes of stress measurement: Daily hassles and uplifts versus major life events. *Journal of Behavioral Medicine* 4:1–39.

Kaplan, G. A., and Camacho, T. (1983). Perceived health and mortality: A nine-year follow-up of the human population laboratory cohort. *American Journal of Epidemiology* 117:292–304.

Kelley, H. H. (1967). Attribution theory in social psychology. In *Nebraska symposium on motivation*, ed. D. Levine. Vol. 15. Lincoln: University of Nebraska Press.

Kelley, H. H. (1972). *Causal schemata and the attribution process.* Morristown, N.J.: General Learning Press.

Kelley, H. H. (1973). The process of causal attribution. *American Psychologist* 28:107–128.

Kelley, S. J. (1986). Learned helplessness in the sexually abused child. *Issues in Comprehensive Pediatric Nursing* 9:193–207.

Kennelly, K. J., Hayslip, B., and Richardson, S. K. (1985). Depression and helplessness-induced cognitive deficits in the aged. *Experimental Aging Research* 11:169–173.

Kennelly, K. J., and Kinley, S. (1975). Perceived contingency of teacher administered reinforcements and academic performance of boys. *Psychology in the Schools* 12:449–453.

Kennelly, K. J., and Mount, S. A. (1985). Perceived contingency of reinforcements, helplessness, locus of control, and academic performance. *Psychology in the Schools* 22:465–469.

Kerr, S. (1975). On the folly of rewarding A, while hoping for B. *Academy of Management Journal* 18:769–783.

Kevill, F., and Kirkland, J. (1979). Infant crying and learned helplessness. *Journal of Biological Psychology* 21:3–7.

Killeen, P. R. (1978). Superstition: A matter of bias, not detectability. *Science* 199:88–90.

Killeen, P. R. (1981). Learning as causal reference. In *Quantitative analyses of behavior.* Vol. 1, *Discriminative properties of reinforcement schedules*, ed. M. L. Commons and J. A. Nevin. Cambridge, Mass.: Ballinger.

Killeen, P. R., and Smith, J. P. (1984). Perception of contingency in conditioning: Scalar timing, response bias, and erasure of memory by reinforcement. *Journal of Experimental Psychology: Animal Behavior Processes* 10:333–346.

Kilpatrick-Tabak, B., and Roth, S. (1978). An attempt to reverse performance deficits associated with depression and experimentally induced helplessness. *Journal of Abnormal Psychology* 87:141–174.

Klein, D. C., and Seligman, M. E. P. (1976). Reversal of performance deficits in learned helplessness and depression. *Journal of Abnormal Psychology* 85:11–26.

Klerman, G. L., Lavori, P. W., Rice, J., Reich, T., Endicott, J., Andreasen, N. C., Keller, M. B., and Hirschfeld, R. M. (1985). Birth-cohort trends in rates of major depressive disorder among relatives of patients with affective disorder. *Archives of General Psychiatry* 42:689–693.

Kobasa, S. C. (1979). Stressful life events, personality, and health: An inquiry into hardiness. *Journal of Personality and Social Psychology* 37:1–11.

Kobasa, S. C. (1982). Commitment and coping in stress resistance among lawyers. *Journal of Personality and Social Psychology* 42:707–717.

Kobasa, S. C., Maddi, S. R., and Courington, S. (1981). Personality and constitution as mediators in the stress-illness relationship. *Journal of Health and Social Behavior* 22:368–378.

Kobasa, S. C., Maddi, S. R., and Kahn, S. (1982). Hardiness and health: A prospective study. *Journal of Personality and Social Psychology* 42:168–177.

Koegel, R. L., and Egel, A. L. (1979). Motivating autistic children. *Journal of Abnormal Psychology* 88:418–426.

Koegel, R. L., and Mentis, M. (1985). Motivation in childhood autism: Can they or won't they? *Journal of Child Psychology and Psychiatry and Allied Disciplines* 26:185–191.

Koegel, R. L., O'Dell, M., and Dunlap, G. (1988). Producing speech use in nonverbal autistic children by reinforcing attempts. *Journal of Autism and Developmental Disorders* 18:525–538.

Kofta, M., and Sedek, G. (1989). Repeated failure: A source of helplessness or a factor irrelevant to its emergence? *Journal of Experimental Psychology: General* 118:3–12.

Kovacs, M., and Beck, A. T. (1977). An empirical-clinical approach toward a definition of childhood depression. In *Depression in childhood: Diagnosis, treatment, and conceptual models*, ed. J. G. Schulterbrandt and A. Raskin. New York: Raven.

Kuhl, J. (1981). Motivational and functional helplessness: The moderating effect of state versus action orientation. *Journal of Personality and Social Psychology* 40:155–170.

Kuykendall, D., and Keating, J. P. (1984). Crowding and reactions to uncontrollable events. *Population and Environment: Behavioral and Social Issues* 7:246–259.

Lachman, M. E. (1989). When bad things happen to old people: Age differences in attributional style. Manuscript, Brandeis University.

Langer, E. J. (1989). *Mindfulness*. Reading, Mass.: Addison-Wesley.

Langer, E. J., and Rodin, J. (1976). The effects of choice and enhanced personal responsibility for the aged: A field experiment in an institutional setting. *Journal of Personality and Social Psychology* 34:191–198.

Launius, M. H., and Lindquist, C. U. (1988). Learned helplessness, external locus of control, and passivity in battered women. *Journal of Interpersonal Violence* 3:307–318.

Lawler, E. E. (1966). The mythology of management compensation. *California Management Review* 9:11–22.

Lazarus, R. S., and Folkman, S. (1984). *Stress, appraisal, and coping*. New York: Springer.

Lee, R. K. K., and Maier, S. F. (1988). Inescapable shock and attention to internal versus external cues in a water escape discrimination task. *Journal of Experimental Psychology: Animal Behavior Processes* 14:302–311.

Lennerlof, L. (1988). Learned helplessness at work. *International Journal of Health Services* 18:207–222.

Lerner, M. J. (1980). *The belief in a just world*. New York: Plenum.

Levine, G. F. (1977). "Learned helplessness" and the evening news. *Journal of Communication* 27:100–105.

Levine, M. (1971). Hypothesis theory and nonlearning despite ideal S-R reinforcement contingencies. *Psychological Review* 78:130–140.

Levine, M., Rotkin, L., Jankovic, I. N., and Pitchford, L. (1977). Impaired performance by adult humans: Learned helplessness or wrong hypotheses? *Cognitive Therapy and Research* 1:275–285.

Levis, D. J. (1976). Learned helplessness: A reply and alternative S-R interpretation. *Journal of Experimental Psychology: General* 105:47–65.

Levy, S., Morrow, L., Bagley, C., and Lippman, M. (1988). Survival hazards analysis in first recurrent breast cancer patients: 7 year follow-up. *Psychosomatic Medicine* 50:520–528.

Lewinsohn, P. M., Mischel, W., Chaplain, W., and Barton, R. (1980). Social competence and depression: The role of illusory self-perceptions. *Journal of Abnormal Psychology* 89:203–212.

Lin, E. H., and Peterson, C. (1990). Pessimistic explanatory style and response to illness. *Behaviour Research and Therapy* 28:243–248.

Lloyd, C. (1980). Life events and depressive disorder reviewed: I. Events as predisposing factors. II. Events as precipitating factors. *Archives of General Psychiatry* 37:529–548.

Loosen, P. T. (1988). The TRH test in psychiatric disorders. In *Affective disorders*, ed. F. Flach. New York: Norton.

Love, A. W. (1988). Attributional style of depressed low back patients. *Journal of Clinical Psychology* 44:317–321.

Lowenthal, B. (1986). The power of suggestion. *Academic Therapy* 21:537–541.

Luborsky, L. (1964). A psychoanalytic research on momentary forgetting during free association. *Bulletin of the Philadelphia Association for Psychoanalysis* 14:119–137.

Luborsky, L. (1970). New directions in research on neurotic and psychosomatic symptoms. *American Scientist* 58:661–668.

MacCorquodale, K., and Meehl, P. E. (1948). On a distinction between hypothetical constructs and intervening variables. *Psychological Review* 55:95–107.

MacDonald, A. (1946). The effect of adaptation to the unconditioned stimulus upon the formation of conditioned avoidance responses. *Journal of Experimental Psychology* 36:1–12.

McFarland, C., and Ross, M. (1982). Impact of causal attributions on affective reactions to stress and failure. *Journal of Personality and Social Psychology* 43:937–946.

McFerran, J. R., and Breen, L. J. (1979). A bibliography of research on learned helplessness prior to introduction of the reformulated model (1978). *Psychological Reports* 45:311–325.

Mackintosh, N. J. (1975). A theory of attention: Variations in the associability of stimuli with reinforcement. *Psychological Review* 82:276–298.

McMinn, M. R., and McMinn, G. N. (1983). Complete yet inadequate: The role of learned helplessness and self-attribution from the writings of Paul. *Journal of Psychology and Theology* 11:303–310.

McMullen, M. B., and Krantz, M. (1988). Burnout in daycare workers: The effects of learned helplessness and self-esteem. *Child and Youth Care Quarterly* 17:275–280.

Maier, S. F. (1974). Reply to "Learned laziness in dead pigeons" by Gamzu. *Worm Runner's Digest* 16:88.

Maier, S. F. (1986). Stressor controllability and stress-induced analgesia. In *Stress-induced analgesia*, ed. D. D. Kelly. New York: Wiley.

Maier, S. F. (1989a). Determinants of the nature of environmentally-induced hypoalgesia. *Behavioral Neuroscience* 103:131–143.

Maier, S. F. (1989b). Learned helplessness: Event co-variation and cognitive changes. In *Contemporary theories of learning*, ed. S. B. Klein and R. R. Mowrer. Hillsdale, N.J.: Erlbaum.

Maier, S. F. (1990). The role of fear in mediating the shuttle escape learning deficit produced by inescapable shock. *Journal of Experimental Psychology: Animal Behavior Processes* 16:137–150.

Maier, S. F. (1992). The effects of anxiolytics and anxiogenics on choice escape. Manuscript, University of Colorado.

Maier, S. F., Albin, R. W., and Testa, T. J. (1973). Failure to learn to escape in rats previously exposed to inescapable shock depends on nature of escape response. *Journal of Comparative and Physiological Psychology* 85:581–592.

Maier, S. F., Anderson, C., and Lieberman, D. (1972). The influence of control of shock on subsequent shock-elicited aggression. *Journal of Comparative and Physiological Psychology* 81:94–101.

Maier, S. F., and Jackson, R. L. (1979). Learned helplessness: All of us were right (and wrong): Inescapable shock has multiple effects. In *The psychology of learning and motivation*, ed. G. H. Bower. Vol. 13. New York: Academic Press.

Maier, S. F., and Laudenslager, M. L. (1988). Commentary: Inescapable shock, shock controllability, and mitogen stimulated lymphocyte proliferation. *Brain, Behavior, and Immunity* 2:87–91.

Maier, S. F., Ryan, S. M., Barksdale, C. M., and Kalin, N. H. (1988). Stressor uncontrollability and the pituitary-adrenal system. *Behavioral Neuroscience* 100:669–678.

Maier, S. F., and Seligman, M. E. P. (1976). Learned helplessness: Theory and evidence. *Journal of Experimental Psychology: General* 105:3–46.

Maier, S. F., Seligman, M. E. P., and Solomon, R. L. (1969). Pavlovian fear conditioning and learned helplessness: Effects on escape and avoidance behavior of (a) the CS-US contingency, and (b) the independence of the US and voluntary responding. In *Punishment*, ed. B. A. Campbell and R. M. Church. New York: Appleton-Century-Crofts.

Maier, S. F., Sherman, J. E., Lewis, J. W., Terman, G. W., and Liebeskind, J. C. (1983). The opioid/nonopioid nature of stress-induced analgesia and learned helplessness. *Journal of Experimental Psychology: Animal Behavior Processes* 9:80–90.

Maier, S. F., and Testa, T. J. (1975). Failure to learn to escape by rats previously exposed to inescapable shock is partly produced by associative interference. *Journal of Comparative and Physiological Psychology* 88:554–564.

Maier, S. F., and Watkins, L. R. (1991). Conditioned and unconditioned stress-induced analgesia: Stimulus preexposure and stimulus change. Manuscript, University of Colorado.

Major, B., Mueller, P., and Hildebrandt, K. (1985). Attributions, expectations, and coping with abortion. *Journal of Personality and Social Psychology* 48:585–599.

Malcomson, K. (1980). Learned helplessness: A phenomenon observed among the nursing staff of "City Hospital." *Perspectives in Psychiatric Care* 18:252–255.

Margules, D. L. (1979). Beta-endorphin and endoxone: Hormones of the autonomic nervous system for the conservation of expenditure of bodily resources and energy in anticipation of famine or feast. *Neuroscience and Biobehavioral Reviews* 3:155–162.

Marks, I. M. (1977). Personal communication to M. E. P. Seligman.

Martin, D. (1976). *Battered wives*. San Francisco: Glide Publications.

Martin, D. J., Abramson, L. Y., and Alloy, L. B. (1984). The illusion of control for self and others in depressed and nondepressed college students. *Journal of Personality and Social Psychology* 46:125–136.

Martin, H. P., and Beezley, P. (1977). Behavioral observations of abused children. *Developmental Medicine and Child Neurology* 19:373–387.

Martin, P., Soubrie, P., and Simon, P. (1987). The effect of monoamine oxidase inhibitors compared with classical tricyclic antidepressants on learned helplessness paradigm. *Progress in Neuro-Psychopharmacology and Biological Psychiatry* 11:1–7.

Martinko, M. J., and Gardner, W. L. (1982). Learned helplessness: An alternative explanation for performance deficits? *Academy of Management Review* 7:195–204.

Mason, S. T. (1980). Noradrenaline and selective attention: A review of the model and evidence. *Life Sciences* 27:617–631.

Mastrovito, R. C. (1974). Psychogenic pain. *American Journal of Nursing* 74:514–519.

Mayer, D. J., Wolfle, T. L., Akil, H., Carder, B., and Liebeskind, J. C. (1971). Analgesia from electrical stimulation of the brainstem of the rat. *Science* 174:1351–1354.

Meline, T. J. (1985). Research note: Diminished communicative intent and learning theory. *Perceptual and Motor Skills* 61:476–478.

Metalsky, G. I., Abramson, L. Y., Seligman, M. E. P., Semmel, A., and Peterson, C. (1982). Attributional styles and life events in the classroom: Vulnerability and invulnerability to depressive mood reactions. *Journal of Personality and Social Psychology* 43:612–617.

Metalsky, G. I., Halberstadt, L. J., and Abramson, L. Y. (1987). Vulnerability to depressive mood reactions: Toward a more powerful test of the diathesis-stress and causal mediation components of the reformulated theory of depression. *Journal of Personality and Social Psychology* 52:386–393.

Michotte, A. (1963). *The perception of causality*. New York: Basic Books.

Mikulincer, M. (1986). Attributional processes in the learned helplessness paradigm: Behavioral effects of global attributions. *Journal of Personality and Social Psychology* 51:1248–1256.

Mikulincer, M. (1988a). Reactance and helplessness following exposure to unsolvable problems: The effects of attributional style. *Journal of Personality and Social Psychology* 54:679–686.

Mikulincer, M. (1988b). The relation between stable/unstable attribution and learned helplessness. *British Journal of Social Psychology* 27:221–230.

Mikulincer, M., and Caspy, T. (1986). The conceptualization of helplessness: II. Laboratory correlates of the phenomenological definition of helplessness. *Motivation and Emotion* 10:279–294.

Mikulincer, M., Kedem, P., and Zilkha-Segal, H. (1989). Learned helplessness, reactance, and cue utilization. *Journal of Research in Personality* 23:235–247.

Mikulincer, M., and Nizan, B. (1988). Causal attribution, cognitive interference, and the generalization of learned helplessness. *Journal of Personality and Social Psychology* 55:470–478.

Milgram, S. (1963). Behavioral study of obedience. *Journal of Abnormal and Social Psychology* 67:371–378.

Miller, I. W., and Norman, W. H. (1979). Learned helplessness in humans: A review and attribution theory model. *Psychological Bulletin* 86:93–119.

Miller, I. W., and Norman, W. H. (1981). Effects of attributions for success on the alleviation of learned helplessness and depression. *Journal of Abnormal Psychology* 90:113–124.

Miller, W. R., and Seligman, M. E. P. (1975). Depression and learned helplessness in man. *Journal of Abnormal Psychology* 84:228–238.

Mineka, S., Cook, M., and Miller, S. (1984). Fear conditioned with escapable and inescapable shock: The effects of a feedback stimulus. *Journal of Experimental Psychology: Animal Behavior Processes* 10:307–323.

Minor, T. R., Jackson, R. L., and Maier, S. F. (1984). Effects of task irrelevant cues and reinforcement delay on choice escape learning following inescapable shock: Evidence for a deficit in selective attention. *Journal of Experimental Psychology: Animal Behavior Processes* 10:168–181.

Minor, T. R., and LoLordo, V. M. (1984). Escape deficits following inescapable shock: The role of contextual odor. *Journal of Experimental Psychology: Animal Behavior Processes* 10:168–181.

Minor, T. R., Pelleymounter, M. A., and Maier, S. F. (1988). Uncontrollable shock, forebrain NE, and stimulus selection during escape learning. *Psychobiology* 16:135–146.

Minor, T. R., Trauner, M. A., Lee, C. Y., and Dess, N. K. (1990). Modeling signal features of escape response: Effects of cessation conditioning in "learned helplessness" paradigm. *Journal of Experimental Psychology: Animal Behavior Processes* 2:123–136.

Mischel, W. (1968). *Personality and assessment.* New York: Wiley.

Mossey, J. M., and Shapiro, E. (1982). Self-rated health: A predictor of mortality among the elderly. *American Journal of Public Health* 72:800–808.

Mowrer, O. H. (1947). On the dual nature of learning—A re-interpretation of "conditioning" and "problem-solving." *Harvard Educational Review* 17:102–150.

Mowrer, O. H. (1960). *Learning theory and behavior.* New York: Wiley.

Mowrer, O. H., and Viek, P. (1954). An experimental analogue of fear from a sense of helplessness. *Journal of Abnormal and Social Psychology* 43:193–200.

Moye, T. B., Hyson, R. L., Grau, J. W., and Maier, S. F. (1983). Immunization of opioid analgesia: Effects of prior escapable shock on subsequent shock-induced antinociception. *Learning and Motivation* 14:238–251.

Mukherji, B. R., Abramson, L. Y., and Martin, D. J. (1982). Induced depressive mood and attributional patterns. *Cognitive Therapy and Research* 6:15–21.

Munton, A. G., and Antaki, C. (1988). Causal beliefs amongst families in therapy: Attributions at the group level. *British Journal of Clinical Psychology* 27:91–97.

Nelson, R. E., and Craighead, W. E. (1977). Selective recall of positive and negative feedback, self-control behaviors, and depression. *Journal of Abnormal Psychology* 86:379–388.

Newman, H., and Langer, E. J. (1981). A cognitive model of intimate relationship formation, stabilization, and disintegration. *Sex Roles* 7:223–232.

Nicassio, P. M. (1985). The psychosocial adjustment of the Southeast Asian refugee: An overview of empirical findings and theoretical models. *Journal of Cross-Cultural Psychology* 16:153–173.

Niehoff, D. L., and Kuhar, M. J. (1983). Benzodiazepine receptors: Localization in rat amygdala. *Journal of Neuroscience* 3:2091–2097.

Nierenberg, A. A., and Feinstein, A. R. (1988). How to evaluate a diagnostic marker test: Lessons from the rise and fall of the dexamethasone suppression test. *JAMA* 259:1699–1702.

Ninan, P., Insel, T. M., Cohen, R. M., Cook, J. M., Skolnick, P., and Paul, S. M. (1982). Benzodiazepine receptor-mediated experimental "anxiety" in primates. *Science* 218:1332–1334.

Nisbett, R. E., and Wilson, T. D. (1977). Telling more than we can know: Verbal reports on mental processes. *Psychological Review* 84:231–259.

Noel, N. E., and Lisman, S. A. (1980). Alcohol consumption by college women following exposure to unsolvable problems: Learned helplessness or stress induced drinking? *Behaviour Research and Therapy* 18:429–440.

Nolen-Hoeksema, S. (1986). *Developmental studies of explanatory style, and learned helplessness in children.* Ph.D. diss., University of Pennsylvania.

Nolen-Hoeksema, S. (1987). Sex differences in unipolar depression: Theory and evidence. *Psychological Bulletin* 101:259–282.

Nolen-Hoeksema, S. (1990). *Sex differences in depression.* Stanford: Stanford University Press.

Nolen-Hoeksema, S., Girgus, J. S., and Seligman, M. E. P. (1986). Learned helplessness in children: A longitudinal study of depression, achievement, and explanatory style. *Journal of Personality and Social Psychology* 51:435–442.

Nolen-Hoeksema, S., Girgus, J. S., and Seligman, M. E. P. (in press). Predictors and consequences of childhood depressive symptoms: 5-year longitudinal study. *Journal of Abnormal Psychology.*

Nolen-Hoeksema, S., Skinner, E., and Seligman, M. E. P. (1984). [Expectational style.] Unpublished data, University of Pennsylvania.

Norem, J. K., and Cantor, N. (1986). Defensive pessimism: "Harnessing" anxiety as motivation. *Journal of Personality and Social Psychology* 51:1208–1217.

Nussear, V. P., and Lattal, K. A. (1983). Stimulus control of responding by response-reinforcer temporal contiguity. *Learning and Motivation* 14:472–487.

Oakes, W. F., and Curtis, N. (1982). Learned helplessness: Not dependent upon cognitions, attributions, or other such phenomenal experiences. *Journal of Personality* 50:387–408.

O'Hara, M. W., Neunaber, D. J., and Zekoski, E. M. (1984). Prospective study of postpartum depression: Prevalence, course, and predictive factors. *Journal of Abnormal Psychology* 93:158–171.

O'Hara, M. W., Rehm, L. P., and Campbell, S. B. (1982). Predicting depressive symptomatology: Cognitive-behavioral models and postpartum depression. *Journal of Abnormal Psychology* 91:457–461.

O'Leary, A. (1985). Self-efficacy and health. *Behaviour Research and Therapy* 23:437–451.

O'Leary, M. R., Donovan, D. M., Cysewski, B., and Chaney, E. F. (1977). Perceived locus of control, experienced control, and depression: A trait description of the learned helplessness model of depression. *Journal of Clinical Psychology* 33:164–168.

Orbach, I., and Hadas, Z. (1982). The elimination of learned helplessness deficits as a function of induced self-esteem. *Journal of Research in Personality* 16:511–523.

Overmier, J. B., and Leaf, R. C. (1965). Effects of discriminative Pavlovian fear conditioning upon previously or subsequently acquired avoidance responding. *Journal of Comparative and Physiological Psychology* 60:213–218.

Overmier, J. B., Patterson, J., and Wielkiewicz, R. M. (1979). Environmental contingencies as sources of stress in animals. In *Coping and health*, ed. S. Levine and H. Ursin. New York: Plenum.

Overmier, J. B., and Seligman, M. E. P. (1967). Effects of inescapable shock upon subsequent escape and avoidance learning. *Journal of Comparative and Physiological Psychology* 63:23–33.

Pageglow, M. D. (1981). Factors affecting women's decisions to leave violent relationships. *Journal of Family Issues* 2:391–414.

Parkin, J. M. (1975). The incidence and nature of child abuse. *Developmental Medicine and Child Neurology* 17:641–646.

Pasahow, R. J. (1980). The relation between an attributional dimension and learned helplessness. *Journal of Abnormal Psychology* 89:358–367.

Paul, S. M. (1988). Anxiety and depression: A common neurobiological substrate? *Journal of Clinical Psychiatry* 49:13–16.

Paul, S. M., Marangos, P. J., and Skolnick, P. (1981). The benzodiazepine/GABA-chloride ionophore receptor complex: Common site of minor tranquilizer action. *Biological Psychiatry* 16:213–229.

Peele, S. (1989). *The diseasing of America: Addiction treatment out of control.* Lexington, Mass.: Lexington Books.

Peirce, C. S. (1955). *The philosophical writings of Peirce.* Ed. J. Buchler. New York: Dover.

Perkins, C. C., Seymann, R. C., Levis, D. J., and Spencer, H. R. (1966). Factors affecting preference for signal-shock over shock-signal. *Journal of Experimental Psychology* 72:190–196.

Persons, J. B. (1986). The advantages of studying psychological phenomena rather than psychiatric diagnoses. *American Psychologist* 41:1252–1260.

Persons, J. B., and Rao, P. A. (1985). Longitudinal study of cognitions, life events, and depression in psychiatric inpatients. *Journal of Abnormal Psychology* 94:51–63.

Peterson, C. (1976). Learned helplessness and the attribution of randomness. Ph.D. diss., University of Colorado.

Peterson, C. (1978). Learning impairment following insoluble problems: Learned helplessness or altered hypothesis pool? *Journal of Experimental Social Psychology* 14:53–68.

Peterson, C. (1980). Recognition of noncontingency. *Journal of Personality and Social Psychology* 38:727–734.

Peterson, C. (1985). Learned helplessness: Fundamental issues in theory and research. *Journal of Social and Clinical Psychology* 3:248–254.

Peterson, C. (1986). [Explanatory style and helpless behavior]. Unpublished data, University of Michigan.

Peterson, C. (1988). Explanatory style as a risk factor for illness. *Cognitive Therapy and Research* 12:117–130.

Peterson, C. (1990). Explanatory style in the classroom and on the playing field. In *Attribution theory: Applications to achievement, mental health, and interpersonal conflict*, ed. S. Graham and V. S. Folkes. Hillsdale, N.J.: Erlbaum.

Peterson, C. (1991). The meaning and measurement of explanatory style. *Psychological Inquiry* 2:1–10.

Peterson, C. (1992a). Learned helplessness and school problems: A social psychological analysis. In *School psychology: A social psychological perspective*, ed. F. J. Medway and T. P. Cafferty. Hillsdale, N.J.: Erlbaum.

Peterson, C. (1992b). *Personality*. 2d ed. San Diego: Harcourt Brace Jovanovich.

Peterson, C., and Barrett, L. C. (1987). Explanatory style and academic performance among university freshmen. *Journal of Personality and Social Psychology* 53:603–607.

Peterson, C., Bettes, B. A., and Seligman, M. E. P. (1985). Depressive symptoms and unprompted causal attributions: Content analysis. *Behaviour Research and Therapy* 23:379–382.

Peterson, C., and Bossio, L. M. (1989). Learned helplessness. In *Self-defeating behaviors*, ed. R. C. Curtis. New York: Plenum.

Peterson, C., and Bossio, L. M. (1991). *Health and optimism*. New York: Free Press.

Peterson, C., Colvin, D., and Lin, E. H. (1989). Explanatory style and helplessness. Manuscript, University of Michigan.

Peterson, C., and Edwards, M. (1992). Optimistic explanatory style and the perception of health problems. Manuscript, University of Michigan.

Peterson, C., Luborsky, L., and Seligman, M. E. P. (1983). Attributions and depressive mood shifts: A case study using the symptom-context method. *Journal of Abnormal Psychology* 92:96–103.

Peterson, C., Nutter, J., and Seligman, M. E. P. (1982). [Explanatory style of prisoners.] Unpublished data, Virginia Polytechnic Institute and State University.

Peterson, C., Rosenbaum, A. C., and Conn, M. K. (1985). Depressive mood reactions to breaking up: Testing the learned helplessness model of depression. *Journal of Social and Clinical Psychology* 3:161–169.

Peterson, C., Schulman, P., Castellon, C., and Seligman, M. E. P. (1992). The explanatory style scoring manual. In *Handbook of thematic analysis*, ed. C. P. Smith. New York: Cambridge University Press.

Peterson, C., Schwartz, S. M., and Seligman, M. E. P. (1981). Self-blame and depressive symptoms. *Journal of Personality and Social Psychology* 49:337–348.

Peterson, C., and Seligman, M. E. P. (1983). Learned helplessness and victimization. *Journal of Social Issues* 39:103–116.

Peterson, C., and Seligman, M. E. P. (1984). Causal explanations as a risk factor for depression: Theory and evidence. *Psychological Review* 91:347–374.

Peterson, C., and Seligman, M. E. P. (1985). The learned helplessness model of depression: Current status of theory and research. In *Handbook of depression: Treatment, assessment, and research*, ed. E. E. Beckham and W. R. Leber. Homewood, Ill.: Dorsey.

Peterson, C., and Seligman, M. E. P. (1987). Explanatory style and illness. *Journal of Personality* 55:237–265.

Peterson, C., Seligman, M. E. P., and Vaillant, G. E. (1988). Pessimistic explanatory style is a risk factor for physical illness: A thirty-five year longitudinal study. *Journal of Personality and Social Psychology* 55:23–27.

Peterson, C., Semmel, A., von Baeyer, C., Abramson, L. Y., Metalsky, G. I., and Seligman, M. E. P. (1982). The Attributional Style Questionnaire. *Cognitive Therapy and Research* 6:287–299.

Peterson, C., and Stunkard, A. J. (1989). Personal control and health promotion. *Social Science and Medicine* 28:819–828.

Peterson, C., and Stunkard, A. J. (1992). Cognates of personal control: Locus of control, self-efficacy, and explanatory style. *Applied and Preventive Psychology* 1:111–117.

Peterson, C., and Ulrey, L. M. (1991). Can explanatory style be scored from projective protocols? Manuscript, University of Michigan.

Peterson, C., and Villanova, P. (1986). [Dimensions of explanatory style.] Unpublished data, University of Michigan.

Peterson, C., and Villanova, P. (1988). An expanded Attributional Style Questionnaire. *Journal of Abnormal Psychology* 97:87–89.

Peterson, C., Villanova, P., and Raps, C. S. (1985). Depression and attributions: Factors responsible for inconsistent results in the published literature. *Journal of Abnormal Psychology* 94:165–168.

Peterson, C., Zaccaro, S. J., and Daly, D. C. (1986). Learned helplessness and the generality of social loafing. *Cognitive Therapy and Research* 10:563–569.

Petty, F., and Sherman, A. D. (1980). Regional aspects of the prevention of learned helplessness by desipramine. *Life Sciences* 26:1447–1452.

Petty, F., and Sherman, A. D. (1981). GABAergic modulation of learned helplessness. *Pharmacology, Biochemistry, and Behavior* 15:567–570.

Pines, A. M., Aronson, E., and Kafry, D. (1981). *Burnout: From tedium to personal growth.* New York: Free Press.

Pisa, M., and Fibiger, H. C. (1983). Evidence against a role of the rat's dorsal noradrenergic bundle in selective attention and place memory. *Brain Research* 272:319–329.

Pittman, N. L., and Pittman, T. S. (1979). Effects of amount of helplessness training and internal-external locus of control on mood and performance. *Journal of Personality and Social Psychology* 37:39–47.

Pittman, T. S., and Pittman, N. L. (1980). Deprivation of control and the attribution process. *Journal of Personality and Social Psychology* 39:377–389.

Plous, S., and Zimbardo, P. G. (1986). Attributional biases among clinicians: A comparison of psychoanalysts and behavior therapists. *Journal of Consulting and Clinical Psychology* 54:568–570.

Porsolt, R. D., Anton, G., Blavet, N., and Jalfre, M. (1978). Behavioural despair in rats: A new model sensitive to antidepressant treatments. *European Journal of Pharmacology* 47:379–391.

Powell, L. (1990). Factors associated with the underrepresentation of African Americans in mathematics and science. *Journal of Negro Education* 59:292–298.

Prindaville, P., and Stein, N. (1978). Predictability, controllability, and inoculation against learned helplessness. *Behaviour Research and Therapy* 16:263–271.

Prochaska, J. O., Velicer, W. F., DiClemente, C. C., and Fava, J. (1988). Measuring processes of change: Applications to the cessation of smoking. *Journal of Consulting and Clinical Psychology* 56:520–528.

Raber, S. M., and Weisz, J. R. (1981). Teacher feedback to mentally retarded and nonretarded children. *American Journal of Mental Deficiency* 86:148–156.

Rabkin, J. G., and Struening, E. L. (1976). Life events, stress, and illness. *Science* 194:1013–1020.

Rachlin, H. C., and Baum, W. M. (1972). Effects of alternative reinforcement: Does the source matter? *Journal of the Experimental Analysis of Behavior* 18:231–241.

Radloff, L. S. (1975). Sex differences in depression: The effects of occupation and marital status. *Sex Roles* 1:249–265.

Rapaport, P. M., and Maier, S. F. (1978). Inescapable shock and food competition dominance in rats. *Animal Learning and Behavior* 6:160–165.

Raps, C. S., Peterson, C., Jonas, M., and Seligman, M. E. P. (1982). Patient behavior in hospitals: Helplessness, reactance, or both? *Journal of Personality and Social Psychology* 42:1036–1041.

Raps, C. S., Peterson, C., Reinhard, K. E., Abramson, L. Y., and Seligman, M. E. P. (1982). Attributional style among depressed patients. *Journal of Abnormal Psychology* 91:102–108.

Raps, C. S., Reinhard, K. E., and Seligman, M. E. P. (1980). Reversal of cognitive and affective deficits associated with depression and learned helplessness by mood elevation in patients. *Journal of Abnormal Psychology* 89:342–349.

Redmond, D. E. (1987). Studies of the nucleus locus coeruleus in monkeys and hypotheses for neuropsychopharmacology. In *Psychopharmacology: The third generation of progress*, ed. H. Y. Meltzer. New York: Raven.

Rescorla, R. A., and Solomon, R. L. (1967). Two-process learning theory: Relationship between Pavlovian conditioning and instrumental learning. *Psychological Review* 74:151–182.

Rescorla, R. A., and Wagner, A. R. (1972). A theory of Pavlovian conditioning: Variations in the effectiveness of reinforcement and non-reinforcement. In *Classical conditioning II. Current research and theory*, ed. A. H. Black and W. F. Prokasy. New York: Appleton-Century-Crofts.

Rettew, D. C., Reivich, K., Peterson, C., Seligman, D. A., and Seligman, M. E. P. (1990). Professional baseball, basketball, and explanatory style: Predicting performance in the major leagues. Manuscript, University of Pennsylvania.

Revenson, T. A. (1981). Coping with loneliness: The impact of causal attributions. *Personality and Social Psychology Bulletin* 7:565–571.

Reynierse, J. H. (1975). A behavioristic analysis of the book of Job. *Journal of Psychology and Theology* 3:75–81.

Riskind, J. H., Castellon, C., and Beck, A. T. (1989). Spontaneous causal explanations in unipolar depression and generalized anxiety: Content analysis of dysfunctional-thought diaries. *Cognitive Therapy and Research* 13:97–108.

Rivier, C., Rivier, J., and Vale, W. (1982). Inhibition of adrenocorticotrophic hormone secretion in the rat by immunoneutralization of corticotropin-releasing factor. *Science* 218:377–379.

Robins, L. N., Helzer, J. E., Weissman, M. M., Orvaschel, H., Gruenberg, E., Burke, J. D., and Regier, D. A. (1984). Lifetime prevalence of specific psychiatric disorders in three sites. *Archives of General Psychiatry* 41:949–958.

Rodin, J. (1986). Aging and health: Effects of the sense of control. *Science* 233:1271–1276.

Rodin, J., Solomon, S. K., and Metcalf, J. (1978). Role of control in mediating perceptions of density. *Journal of Personality and Social Psychology* 36:988–999.

Rosellini, R. A. (1978). Inescapable shock interferes with the acquisition of a free appetitive operant. *Animal Learning and Behavior* 6:155–159.

Rosellini, R. A., DeCola, J. P., Plonsky, M., Warren, D. A., and Stilman, A. J. (1984). Uncontrollable shock proactively increases sensitivity to response-reinforcer independence in rats. *Journal of Experimental Psychology: Animal Behavior Processes* 10:346–359.

Rosellini, R. A., DeCola, J. P., and Shapiro, N. K. (1982). Cross-motivational effects of inescapable shock are associative in nature. *Journal of Experimental Psychology: Animal Behavior Processes* 8:376–388.

Rosellini, R. A., and Seligman, M. E. P. (1975). Learned helplessness and escape from frustration. *Journal of Experimental Psychology: Animal Behavior Processes* 1:149–158.

Rosen, C. E. (1977). The impact of an open campus program upon high school students' sense of control over their environment. *Psychology in the Schools* 14:216–219.

Rosenbaum, M., and Palmon, N. (1984). Helplessness and resourcefulness in coping with epilepsy. *Journal of Consulting and Clinical Psychology* 52:244–253.

Rosenthal, R., and Rubin, D. B. (1982). A simple, general purpose display of magnitude of experimental effect. *Journal of Educational Psychology* 74:166–169.

Roth, D., and Rehm, L. P. (1980). Relationships among self-monitoring processes, memory, and depression. *Cognitive Therapy and Research* 4:149–157.

Roth, S. (1980). A revised model of learned helplessness in humans. *Journal of Personality* 48:103–133.

Roth, S., and Bootzin, R. R. (1974). The effect of experimentally induced expectancies of external control: An investigation of learned helplessness. *Journal of Personality and Social Psychology* 29:253–264.

Roth, S., and Kubal, L. (1975). Effects of noncontingent reinforcement on tasks of differing importance: Facilitation and learned helplessness. *Journal of Personality and Social Psychology* 32:680–691.

Rothbaum, F., Weisz, J. R., and Snyder, S. S. (1982). Changing the world and changing the self: A two-process model of perceived control. *Journal of Personality and Social Psychology* 42:5–37.

Rothwell, N., and Williams, J. M. G. (1983). Attributional style and life events. *British Journal of Clinical Psychology* 22:139–140.

Rotter, J. B. (1954). *Social learning and clinical psychology*. Englewood Cliffs, N.J.: Prentice-Hall.

Rotter, J. B. (1966). Generalized expectancies for internal versus external control of reinforcement. *Psychological Monographs* 81(1, Whole No. 609).

Rotter, J. B. (1975). Some problems and misconceptions related to the construct of internal versus external reinforcement. *Journal of Consulting and Clinical Psychology* 43:56–67.

Rutter, M. L. (1986). Child psychiatry: The interface between clinical and developmental research. *Psychological Medicine* 16:151–169.

Ryan, S. M., and Maier, S. F. (1988). The estrous cycle and estrogen modulated stress-induced analgesia. *Behavioral Neuroscience* 102:371–380.

Sahoo, F. M., and Tripathy, S. (1990). Learned helplessness in industrial employees: A study of noncontingency, satisfaction, and motivational deficits. *Psychological Studies* 35:79–87.

Sanderson, W. C., Beck, A. T., and Beck, J. (1990). Syndrome comorbidity in patients with depression or dysthymia: Prevalence and temporal relationships. *American Journal of Psychiatry* 147:1025–1028.

Sarata, B. P. V. (1974). Employee satisfactions in agencies serving retarded persons. *American Journal of Mental Deficiency* 79:434–482.

Scheier, M. F., and Carver, C. S. (1985). Optimism, coping, and health: Assessment and implications of generalized outcome expectancies. *Health Psychology* 4:219–247.

Scheier, M. F., and Carver, C. S. (1987). Dispositional optimism and physical well-being: The influence of generalized outcome expectancies on health. *Journal of Personality* 55:169–210.

Scheier, M. F., Matthews, K. A., Owens, J. F., Magovern, G. J., Lefebvre, R. C., Abbott, R. A., and Carver, C. S. (1989). Dispositional optimism and recovery from artery bypass surgery: The beneficial effects on physical and psychological well-being. *Journal of Personality and Social Psychology* 57:1024–1040.

Schieffelin, B. B. (1990). *The give and take of everyday life: Language socialization of Kaluli children*. Cambridge: Cambridge University Press.

Schildkraut, J. J. (1965). The catecholamine hypothesis of affective disorders: A review of supporting evidence. *American Journal of Psychiatry* 122:509–522.

Schleifer, S. J., Keller, S. E., Siris, S. G., Davis, K. L., and Stein, M. (1985). Depression and immunity. *Archives of General Psychiatry* 42:129–133.

Schulman, P., Castellon, C., and Seligman, M. E. P. (1989). Assessing explanatory style: The content analysis of verbatim explanations and the Attributional Style Questionnaire. *Behaviour Research and Therapy* 27:505–512.

Schulman, P., Keith, D., and Seligman, M. E. P. (1991). Is optimism heritable? A study of twins. Manuscript, University of Pennsylvania.

Schulman, P., Seligman, M. E. P., and Amsterdam, D. (1987). The Attributional Style Questionnaire is not transparent. *Behaviour Research and Therapy* 25:391–395.

Schulz, R. (1976). Effects of control and predictability on the physical and psychological well-being of the institutionalized aged. *Journal of Personality and Social Psychology* 33:563–573.

Schulz, R. (1980). Aging and control. In *Human helplessness: Theory and applications*, ed. J. Garber and M. E. P. Seligman. New York: Academic Press.

Schwartz, D. P., Burish, T. G., O'Rourke, D. F., and Holmes, D. S. (1986). Influence of personal and universal failure on the subsequent performance of persons with Type A and Type B behavior patterns. *Journal of Personality and Social Psychology* 51:459–462.

Scott, W. A., Osgood, D. W., and Peterson, C. (1979). *Cognitive structure: Theory and measurement of individual differences.* Washington, D.C.: Winston.

Sears, R. R., Maccoby, E. E., and Levin, H. (1957). *Patterns of child rearing.* Evanston, Ill.: Row, Peterson, & Co.

Sedek, G., and Kofta, M. (1990). When cognitive exertion does not yield cognitive gain: Toward an informational explanation of learned helplessness. *Journal of Personality and Social Psychology* 58:729–743.

Segal, Z. V. (1988). Appraisal of the self-schema construct in cognitive models of depression. *Psychological Bulletin* 103:147–162.

Seligman, M. E. P. (1975). *Helplessness: On depression, development, and death.* San Francisco: Freeman.

Seligman, M. E. P. (1977). Personal communication to I. M. Marks.

Seligman, M. E. P. (1981). A learned helplessness point of view. In *Behavior therapy for depression: Present status and future directions*, ed. L. P. Rehm. New York: Academic Press.

Seligman, M. E. P. (1990). *Learned optimism.* New York: Knopf.

Seligman, M. E. P., Abramson, L. Y., Semmel, A., and von Baeyer, C. (1979). Depressive attributional style. *Journal of Abnormal Psychology* 88:242–247.

Seligman, M. E. P., Castellon, C., Cacciola, J., Schulman, P., Luborsky, L., Ollove, M., and Downing, R. (1988). Explanatory style change during cognitive therapy for unipolar depression. *Journal of Abnormal Psychology* 97:13–18.

Seligman, M. E. P., and Maier, S. F. (1967). Failure to escape traumatic shock. *Journal of Experimental Psychology* 74:1–9.

Seligman, M. E. P., Maier, S. F., and Geer, J. (1968). Alleviation of learned helplessness in the dog. *Journal of Abnormal Psychology* 73:256–262.

Seligman, M. E. P., Maier, S. F., and Solomon, R. L. (1971). Unpredictable and uncontrollable aversive events. In *Aversive conditioning and learning*, ed. F. R. Brush. New York: Academic Press.

Seligman, M. E. P., and Peterson, C. (1986). [Explanatory style of NBA players.] Unpublished data, University of Pennsylvania.

Seligman, M. E. P., Peterson, C., Kaslow, N. J., Tanenbaum, R. J., Alloy, L. B., and Abramson, L. Y. (1984). Attributional style and depressive symptoms among children. *Journal of Abnormal Psychology* 83:235–238.

Seligman, M. E. P., and Schulman, P. (1986). Explanatory style as a predictor of productivity and quitting among life insurance agents. *Journal of Personality and Social Psychology* 50:832–838.

Sellers, R. M., and Peterson, C. (1991). Explanatory style and coping with controllable events by student-athletes. Manuscript, University of Virginia.

Seltzer, S. F., and Seltzer, J. L. (1986). Tactual sensitivity of chronic pain patients to non-painful stimuli. *Pain* 27:291–295.

Selye, H. (1956). *The stress o, life.* New York: McGraw-Hill.

Sherman, A. D., Allers, G. L., Petty, F., and Henn, F. A. (1979). A neuropharmacologically-relevant animal model of depression. *Neuropharmacology* 18:891–893.

Sherman, A. D., and Petty, F. (1980). Neurochemical basis of the action of antidepressants on learned helplessness. *Behavioral and Neural Biology* 30:119–134.

Sherrod, D. R., Moore, B. S., and Underwood, B. (1979). Environmental noise, perceived control, and aggression. *Journal of Social Psychology* 109:245–252.

Short, K. R., and Maier, S. F. (1990). Uncontrollable but not controllable stress produces enduring anxiety in rats despite only transient benzodiazepine receptor involvement. Paper presented at the Society for Neuroscience Meeting, St. Louis, Mo.

Siegel, S. J., and Alloy, L. B. (1990). Interpersonal perceptions and consequences of depressive-significant other relationships: A naturalistic study of college roommates. *Journal of Abnormal Psychology* 99:361–373.

Simkin, D. K., Lederer, J. P., and Seligman, M. E. P. (1983). Learned helplessness in groups. *Behaviour Research and Therapy* 21:613–622.

Skevington, S. M. (1983). Chronic pain and depression: Universal or personal helplessness? *Pain* 15:309–317.

Skinner, B. F. (1938). *The behavior of organisms: An experimental analysis.* New York: Appleton-Century-Crofts.

Skinner, B. F. (1948). "Superstition" in the pigeon. *Journal of Experimental Psychology* 38:168–170.

Sklar, L. S., and Anisman, H. (1979). Stress and coping factors influence tumor growth. *Science* 205:513–515.

Sklar, L. S., and Anisman, H. (1980). Social stress influences tumor growth. *Psychosomatic Medicine* 42:347–365.

Sklar, L. S., and Anisman, H. (1981). Stress and cancer. *Psychological Bulletin* 89:369–406.

Slade, B. B., Steward, M. S., Morrison, T. L., and Abramowitz, S. I. (1984). Locus of control, persistence, and use of contingency information in physically abused children. *Child Abuse and Neglect* 8:447–457.

Smith, R., and Seligman, M. E. P. (1978). Black and lower class children are more susceptible to helplessness induced cognitive deficits following unsolvable problems. Manuscript, University of Pennsylvania.

Smolen, R. C. (1978). Expectancies, mood, and performance of depressed and nondepressed psychiatric inpatients on chance and skill tasks. *Journal of Abnormal Psychology* 87:91–101.

Snodgrass, M. A. (1987). The relationship of differential loneliness, intimacy, and characterological attributional style to duration of loneliness. *Journal of Social Behavior and Personality* 2:173–186.

Snyder, M. L., Smoller, B., Strenta, A., and Frankel, A. (1981). A comparison of egotism, negativity, and learned helplessness as explanations for poor performance after unsolvable problems. *Journal of Personality and Social Psychology* 40:24–30.

Snyder, M. L., Stephan, W. G., and Rosenfield, D. (1978). Attributional egotism. In *New directions in attribution research*, ed. J. H. Harvey, W. Ickes, and R. F. Kidd. Vol. 2. Hillsdale, N.J.: Erlbaum.

Solomon, K. (1982). Social antecedents of learned helplessness in the health care setting. *Gerontologist* 22:282–287.

Soubrie, P., Blas, C., Ferron, A., and Glowinski, J. (1983). Chlordiazepoxide reduces *in vivo* serotonin release in the basal ganglia of encephale isole but not anaesthetized cats: Evidence for a dorsal raphe site of action. *Journal of Pharmacology and Experimental Therapeutics* 226:526–532.

Soubrie, P., Thiebot, M. H., Jobert, A., and Hamon, M. (1981). Serotonergic control of punished behavior: Effects of intra-raphe microinjection of chlordiazepoxide, GABA, and 5-HT on behavioural suppression in rats. *Journal of Physiology* 77:449–460.

Sowa, C. J., and Burks, H. M. (1983). Comparison of cognitive restructuring and contingency-based instructional models for alleviation of learned helplessness. *Journal of Instructional Psychology* 10:186–191.

Spence, K. W. (1956). *Behavior theory and conditioning*. New Haven: Yale University Press.

Spencer, M. B., Kim, S., and Marshall, S. (1987). Double stratification and psychological risk: Adaptational processes and school achievement of black children. *Journal of Negro Education* 56:77–87.

Staddon, J. E. R., and Simmelhag, V. L. (1974). The "superstition" experiment: A reexamination of its implications for the principles of adaptive behavior. *Psychological Review* 78:3–43.

Stamatelos, T., and Mott, D. W. (1983). Learned helplessness in persons with mental retardation: Art as a client-centered treatment modality. *Arts in Psychotherapy* 10:241–249.

Steele, C. M., and Southwick, L. L. (1981). Effects of fear and causal attribution about alcoholism on drinking and related attitudes among heavy and moderate drinkers. *Cognitive Therapy and Research* 5:339–350.

Strack, S., and Coyne, J. C. (1983). Social confirmation of dysphoria: Shared and private reactions. *Journal of Personality and Social Psychology* 44:798–806.

Strube, M. J., and Barbour, L. S. (1983). The decision to leave an abusive relationship: Economic dependence and psychological commitment. *Journal of Marriage and the Family* 45:785–793.

Sue, S. (1977). Psychological theory and implications for Asian Americans. *Personnel and Guidance Journal* 55:381–389.

Suls, J., and Mullen, B. (1981). Life events, perceived control, and illness: The role of uncertainty. *Journal of Human Stress* 7:30–34.

Swanson, L. W., Sawchenko, P. E., Rivier, J., and Vale, W. W. (1983). Organization of ovine corticotropin-releasing factor immunoreactive cells and fibers in the rat brain: An immunohistochemical study. *Neuroendocrinology* 36:165–186.

Sweeney, P. D., Anderson, K., and Bailey, S. (1986). Attributional style in depression: A meta-analytic review. *Journal of Personality and Social Psychology* 50:974–991.

Szasz, T. S. (1961). *The myth of mental illness*. New York: Hoeber.

Taylor, R. B., Denham, J. R., and Ureda, J. W. (1982). *Health promotion: Principles and clinical applications*. Norwalk, Conn.: Appleton-Century-Crofts.

Taylor, S. E. (1979). Hospital patient behavior: Reactance, helplessness, or control? *Journal of Social Issues* 35(1): 156–184.

Taylor, S. E. (1989). *Positive illusions.* New York: Basic Books.

Taylor, S. E., and Fiske, S. T. (1978). Salience, attention, and attribution: Top of the head phenomena. In *Advances in experimental social psychology,* ed. L. Berkowitz. Vol. 11. New York: Academic Press.

Taylor, S. E., Lichtman, R. R., and Wood, J. V. (1984). Attributions, beliefs about control, and adjustment to breast cancer. *Journal of Personality and Social Psychology* 46:489–502.

Teasdale, J. D. (1978). Effects of real and recalled success on learned helplessness and depression. *Journal of Abnormal Psychology* 87:155–164.

Teasdale, J. D. (1983). Negative thinking in depression: Cause, effect, or reciprocal relationship? *Advances in Behaviour Research and Therapy* 5:3–25.

Teasdale, J. D., and Russell, M. L. (1983). Differential effects of induced mood on the recall of positive, negative, and neutral words. *British Journal of Clinical Psychology* 22:163–171.

Tennen, H. (1982). A re-view of cognitive mediators in learned helplessness. *Journal of Personality* 50:526–541.

Tennen, H., Affleck, G., and Gershman, K. (1986). Self-blame among parents of infants with perinatal complications: The role of self-protective motives. *Journal of Personality and Social Psychology* 50:690–696.

Tennen, H., and Herzberger, S. (1986). Attributional Style Questionnaire. In *Test critiques,* ed. D. J. Keyser and R. C. Sweetland. Vol. 4. Kansas City, Kans.: Test Corporation of America.

Tennen, H., and Sharp, J. P. (1983). Control orientation and the illusion of control. *Journal of Personality Assessment* 47:369–374.

Testa, T. J. (1975). Effects of similarity of location and temporal intensity pattern of conditioned and unconditioned stimuli on the acquisition of conditioned suppression in rats. *Journal of Experimental Psychology: Animal Behavior Processes* 1:114–121.

Testa, T. J., Juraska, J. M., and Maier, S. F. (1974). Prior exposure to inescapable electric shocks in rats affects extinction behavior after the successful acquisition of an escape response. *Learning and Motivation* 5:380–392.

Thoits, P. A. (1983). Dimensions of life events that influence psychological distress: An evaluation and synthesis of the literature. In *Psychosocial stress: Trends in theory and research,* ed. H. Kaplan. New York: Academic Press.

Thomae, H. (1981). Expected unchangeability of life stress in old age: A contribution to a cognitive theory of aging. *Human Development* 24:229–239.

Thomas, G. V. (1981). Contiguity, reinforcement rate, and the law of effect. *Quarterly Journal of Experimental Psychology* 33:33–43.

Thoreson, C. E., and Eagleston, J. R. (1983). Chronic stress in children and adolescents. *Theory into Practice* 22:48–56.

Thornton, J. W., and Jacobs, P. D. (1971). Learned helplessness in human subjects. *Journal of Experimental Psychology* 87:367–372.

Thornton, J. W., and Jacobs, P. D. (1972). The facilitating effects of prior inescapable/unavoidable stress on intellectual performance. *Psychonomic Science* 26:185–187.

Thornton, J. W., and Powell, G. D. (1974). Immunization to and alleviation of learned helplessness in man. *American Journal of Psychology* 87:351–367.

Tiggemann, M., and Winefield, A. H. (1987). Predictability and timing of self-report in learned helplessness experiments. *Personality and Social Psychology Bulletin* 13:253–264.

Tomie, A., and Loukas, E. (1983). Correlations between rats' spatial location and intracranial stimulation administration affects rate of acquisition and asymptotic level of time allocation preference in the open field. *Learning and Motivation* 14:471–491.

Traub, G. S., and May, J. G. (1983). Learned helplessness and the facilitation of biofeedback performance. *Biofeedback and Self Regulation* 8:477–485.

Trice, A. D. (1982). Ratings of humor following experience with unsolvable tasks. *Psychological Reports* 51:1148.

Tuffin, K., Hesketh, B., and Podd, J. (1985). Experimentally induced learned helplessness: How far does it generalize? *Social Behavior and Personality* 13:55–62.

Vaillant, G. E. (1977). *Adaptation to life.* Boston: Little, Brown.

Vaillant, G. E. (1983). *The natural history of alcoholism.* Cambridge: Harvard University Press.

Vale, W., Spiess, J., Rivier, C., and Rivier, J. (1981). Characterization of a 41-residue ovine hypothalamic peptide that stimulates secretion of corticotropin and beta-endorphin. *Science* 213:1394–1397.

Valentino, R. J., Foote, S. L., and Aston-Jones, G. (1983). Corticotropin-releasing factor activates noradrenergic neurons of the local coeruleus. *Brain Research* 270:363–367.

Valentino, R. J., and Wehby, R. G. (1988). Corticotropin-releasing factor: Evidence for a neurotransmitter role in the locus coeruleus during hemodynamic stress. *Neuroendocrinology* 48:674–677.

Vazquez, C. V. (1987). Judgment of contingency: Cognitive biases in depressed and nondepressed subjects. *Journal of Personality and Social Psychology* 52:419–431.

Verbrugge, L. M. (1989). Recent, present, and future health of American adults. *Annual Review of Public Health* 10:333–361.

Villanova, P., and Peterson, C. (1991). [Meta-analysis of human helplessness experiments.] Unpublished data, Northern Illinois University.

Voelkl, J. E. (1986). Effects of institutionalization upon residents of extended care facilities. *Activities, Adaptation, and Aging* 8:37–45.

Volpicelli, J. R. (1987). Uncontrollable events and alcohol drinking. *British Journal of Addiction* 82:381–392.

Volpicelli, J. R., Ulm, R. R., Altenor, A., and Seligman, M. E. P. (1983). Learned mastery in the rat. *Learning and Motivation* 14:204–222.

von Wright, G. H. (1974). *Causality and determinism.* New York: Columbia University Press.

Walker, L. E. (1977–1978). Battered women and learned helplessness. *Victimology* 2:525–534.

Walker, L. E. (1979). *The battered woman.* New York: Harper & Row.

Walker, L. E. (1983). The battered woman syndrome study. In *The dark side of families,* ed. D. Finkelhor, R. J. Gelles, G. T. Hotaling, and M. A. Straus. Beverly Hills, Calif.: Sage.

Walker, L. E., and Browne, A. (1985). Gender and victimization by intimates. *Journal of Personality* 53:179–195.

Wasserman, E. A., and Neunaber, D. J. (1986). Reporting and responding to causal relations by college students: The role of temporal contiguity. *Journal of the Experimental Analysis of Behavior* 46:15–35.

Watkins, L. R., Drugan, R., Hyson, R. L., Moye, T. B., Ryan, S. M., Mayer, D. J., and Maier, S. F. (1984). Opiate and non-opiate analgesia induced by inescapable tail shock: Effects of dorsolateral funiculus lesions and decerebration. *Brain Research* 291:325–336.

Watkins, L. R., and Mayer, D. J. (1982). Organization of endogenous opiate and non-opiate pain control systems. *Science* 216:1185–1192.

Watkins, L. R., Wiertelak, E. P., and Maier, S. F. (1992). Delta opiate receptors mediate tailshock-induced analgesia at supraspinal levels. *Brain Research* 582:10–21.

Weary, G., Jordan, J. S., and Hill, M. G. (1985). The attributional norm of internality and depressive sensitivity to social information. *Journal of Personality and Social Psychology* 49:1283–1293.

Weinberger, M., Hiner, S. L., and Tierney, W. M. (1987). In support of hassles as a measure of stress in predicting health outcomes. *Journal of Behavioral Medicine* 10:19–31.

Weiner, B. (1972). *Theories of motivation: From mechanism to cognition.* Chicago: Rand McNally.

Weiner, B. (1974). *Achievement motivation and attribution theory.* Morristown, N.J.: General Learning Press.

Weiner, B. (1979). A theory of motivation for some classroom experiences. *Journal of Educational Psychology* 71:3–25.

Weiner, B. (1985). "Spontaneous" causal thinking. *Psychological Bulletin* 97:74–84.

Weiner, B. (1986). *An attributional theory of motivation and emotion.* New York: Springer-Verlag.

Weinstein, N. D. (1989). Optimistic biases about personal risks. *Science* 246:1232–1233.

Weiss, G., Woodmansee, W., and Maier, S. F. (1992). Long duration changes in adrenergic receptors are produced by inescapable shock. Manuscript, University of Colorado.

Weiss, J. M. (1968). Effects of coping responses on stress. *Journal of Comparative and Physiological Psychology* 65:251–260.

Weiss, J. M., Glazer, H. I., and Pohorecky, L. A. (1976). Coping behavior and neurochemical changes: An alternative explanation for the original "learned helplessness" experiments. In *Animal models in human psychobiology,* ed. G. Serban and A. Kling. New York: Plenum.

Weiss, J. M., and Goodman, P. A. (1985). Neurochemical mechanisms underlying stress-induced depression. In *Stress and coping,* ed. T. Field, P. M. McCabe, and N. Schneiderman. Hillsdale, N.J.: Erlbaum.

Weiss, J. M., Goodman, P. A., Losito, B. G., Corrigan, S., Charry, J. M., and Bailey, W. H. (1981). Behavioral depression produced by an uncontrollable stressor: Relationship to norepinephrine, dopamine, and serotonin levels in various regions of rat brain. *Brain Research Reviews* 3:167–205.

Weiss, J. M., Stone, E. A., and Harrell, N. (1970). Coping behavior and brain norepinephrine level in rats. *Journal of Comparative and Physiological Psychology* 72:153–160.

Weisz, J. R. (1979). Perceived control and learned helplessness among retarded and nonretarded children: A developmental analysis. *Developmental Psychology* 15:311–319.

Weisz, J. R. (1981). Learned helplessness in black and white children identified by their schools as retarded and nonretarded: Performance deterioration in response to failure. *Developmental Psychology* 17:499–508.

Welker, R. L. (1976). Acquisition of a free operant appetitive response in pigeons as a function of prior experience with response-independent food. *Learning and Motivation* 7:394–405.

Wener, A. E., and Rehm, L. P. (1975). Depressive affect: A test of behavioral hypotheses. *Journal of Abnormal Psychology* 84:221–227.

White, R. W. (1959). Motivation reconsidered: The concept of competence. *Psychological Review* 66:297–333.

Whitehouse, W. G., Walker, J., Margules, D. L., and Bersh, P. J. (1983). Opiate antagonists overcome the learned helplessness effect but impair competent escape performance. *Physiology and Behavior* 30:731–734.

Wilgosh, L. (1984). Learned helplessness in normally achieving and learning disabled girls. *Mental Retardation and Learning Disability Bulletin* 12:64–70.

Williams, J. L. (1982). Influence of shock controllability by dominant rats on subsequent attack and defensive behaviors toward colony intruders. *Animal Learning and Behavior* 10:305–313.

Williams, J. L. (1984). Influence of postpartum shock controllability on subsequent maternal behavior in rats. *Animal Learning and Behavior* 12:209–216.

Williams, J. L. (1987). Influence of conspecific stress odors and shock controllability on defensive burying. *Animal Learning and Behavior* 15:333–341.

Williams, J. L., Drugan, R. C., and Maier, S. F. (1984). Exposure to uncontrollable stress alters withdrawal from morphine. *Behavioral Neuroscience* 98:836–846.

Williams, J. L., and Lierle, D. M. (1986). Effects of stress controllability, immunization, and therapy on the subsequent defeat of colony intruders. *Animal Learning and Behavior* 14:305–314.

Williams, J. L., and Maier, S. F. (1977). Transsituational immunization and therapy of learned helplessness in the rat. *Journal of Experimental Psychology: Animal Behavior Processes* 3:240–253.

Williams, J. M. G., and Brewin, C. R. (1984). Cognitive mediators of reactions to a minor life-event: The British driving test. *British Journal of Social Psychology* 23:41–49.

Willner, P. (1985). *Depression: A psychobiological synthesis*. New York: Wiley.

Wilson, T. D., and Linville, P. W. (1982). Improving the academic performance of college freshmen: Attribution therapy revisited. *Journal of Personality and Social Psychology* 42:367–376.

Wilson, T. D., and Linville, P. W. (1985). Improving the performance of college freshmen with attributional techniques. *Journal of Personality and Social Psychology* 49:287–293.

Winefield, A. H., and Fay, P. M. (1982). Effects of an institutional environment on responses to uncontrollable outcomes. *Motivation and Emotion* 6:103–112.

Winefield, A. H., and Jardine, E. (1982). Effects of differences in achievement motivation and amount of exposure on responses to uncontrollable rewards. *Motivation and Emotion* 6:245–257.

Wong, P. T. P., and Weiner, B. (1981). When people ask "why" questions, and the heuristics of attribution search. *Journal of Personality and Social Psychology* 40:649–663.

Wortman, C. B., and Brehm, J. W. (1975). Response to uncontrollable outcomes: An integration of reactance theory and the learned helplessness model. In *Advances in experimental social psychology*, ed. L. Berkowitz. Vol. 8. New York: Academic Press.

Wortman, C. B., and Dintzer, L. (1978). Is an attributional analysis of the learned helplessness phenomenon viable?: A critique of the Abramson-Seligman-Teasdale reformulation. *Journal of Abnormal Psychology* 87:75–80.

Yates, R., Kennelly, K. J., and Cox, S. H. (1975). Perceived contingency of parental reinforcements, parent-child relations, and locus of control. *Psychological Reports* 36:139–146.

Young, L. D., and Allin, J. M. (1986). Persistence of learned helplessness in humans. *Journal of General Psychology* 113:81–88.

Zaccaro, S. J., Peterson, C., and Walker, S. (1987). Self-serving attributions for individual and group performance. *Social Psychology Quarterly* 50:257–263.

Zeiler, M. (1977). Schedules of reinforcement: The controlling variables. In *Handbook of operant behavior*, ed. W. K. Konig and J. E. R. Staddon. Englewood Cliffs, N.J.: Prentice-Hall.

Zigler, E., and Balla, D. (1976). Motivational factors in the performance of the retarded. In *The mentally retarded child and his family: A multidisciplinary handbook*, ed. R. Koch and J. C. Dobson. 2d ed. New York: Bruner/Mazel.

Zuckerman, M., and Lubin, B. (1965). *Manual for the Multiple Affect Adjective Check List*. San Diego: Educational and Industrial Testing Service.

Zullow, H. M. (1984). The interaction of rumination and explanatory style in depression. Master's thesis, University of Pennsylvania.

Zullow, H. M., and Seligman, M. E. P. (1990). Pessimistic rumination predicts defeat of presidential candidates, 1900 to 1984. *Psychological Inquiry* 1:52–61.

Name Index

Aasen, N., 240
Abbott, M. W., 250
Abramowitz, S. I., 237
Abrams, R. D., 173
Abramson, L. Y., 100, 146–50, 153, 155–56, 165, 168, 177–78, 185, 192–94, 197, 199, 203–5, 213–16, 230
Adler, A., 144
Affleck, G., 173
Aghajanian, G. K., 80
Ahrens, A. H., 216
Aiello, J. R., 257
Aiken, M., 241
Akil, H., 82
Akiskal, H. S., 223
Albin, R. W., 233
Alden, L., 242
Alexander, J. H., 48
Allen, D. A., 173
Allen, M. G., 183, 221
Allers, G. L., 68
Allin, J. M., 109
Alloy, L. B., 23, 29, 44, 114, 155, 168, 192, 197, 213, 215–18
Alpern, H. P., 74
Altenor, A., 27–28, 55
Altmaier, E. M., 111
Altman, I., 257
American Psychiatric Association, 188, 250
Amsterdam, D., 157, 230
Anderson, Christine, 188
Anderson, Craig A., 171–72, 242, 292
Anderson, D. C., 45

Anderson, K., 193, 250, 285
Anisman, H., 30, 45, 63–64, 80, 113, 294–95
Antaki, C., 263
Anton, G., 191
Antonitis, J. J., 34–35
Arieti, S., 251
Arneric, S., 91
Arnoult, L. H., 242, 292
Aronson, E., 257
Aston-Jones, G., 66, 90
Atlas, G. D., 180
Ayres, R., 247

Bacon, F., 14
Bagley, C., 275
Bailey, S., 193, 250, 285
Baker, A. G., 46
Balla, D., 247
Baltes, M. M., 242
Bandura, A., 112, 179, 280–81
Barber, J. G., 131, 135, 175, 249
Barbour, L. S., 238
Barchas, J. D., 85, 281
Bard, M., 173
Barksdale, C. M., 78, 84
Barrett, L. C., 180, 253
Barsky, A. J., 283
Barton, R., 217
Basbaum, A. I., 82
Baum, A., 249, 257–58
Baum, W. M., 36
Beatty, M. E., 242, 292–93

Subject Index

357

Date Due